MW01620923

RAV AVIGDOR MILLER

on TEFILLAH

COLLECTED AND ADAPTED BY
RABBI YAAKOV ASTOR

THE JUDAICA PRESS, INC.

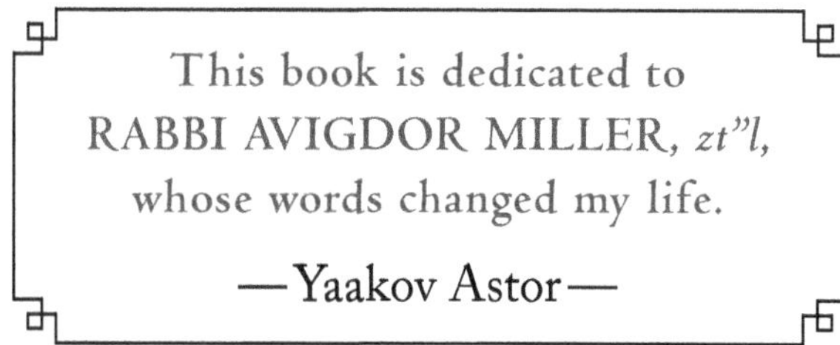

Rav Avigdor Miller on Tefillah

ISBN: 978-1-60763-344-0

Editor: Nachum Shapiro
Proofreader: Diana Drew
Cover design: Justine Elliot
Internal design & layout: Nachum Shapiro
Cover photo: Menachem Adelman

THE JUDAICA PRESS, INC.
Brooklyn, New York
718-972-6200 / 800-972-6201
info@judaicapress.com
www.judaicapress.com

Manufactured in the United States of America

THE FRENKEL EDITION

This *sefer* is dedicated to our beloved father

ר׳ גדליה בן חנוך העניך פרענקל ז״ל

with deep gratitude and appreciation.

A scion of *poskim* for many generations, R' Gedaliah was born in a small town in Poland and raised in a home steeped with Torah, *chessed,* and *chassidus.* From the inferno of Europe, he replanted in America everything that mattered: Torah, *chessed,* and *mitzvos.* His greatest effort was to establish generations that would remain loyal to Torah ideals. He proudly displayed his Yiddishkeit in his home, workplace, and in all his dealings. His word was his bond. Truth was his seal. He led by example, radiating warmth, kindness, faith, and courage. His Shabbos observance, and his adherence to *kashrus* and *halachah,* were unyielding. Our father's legacy is proof that Klal Yisrael, like the Torah, is Eternal. His struggle, hard work, and devotion paved the way for all of us to follow.

This *sefer* is dedicated in honor of our mother

מלכה בת חסיא שתחי׳

A loyal wife and devoted mother to her family, she wisely and lovingly keeps alive and transmits the Torah intact to her children. She teaches by example that wealth means a house loyal to Torah, and *nachas* means children whose lives revolve around Torah and *mitzvos.*

This *sefer* is dedicated to our father

Henry Borger

יחזקאל מרדכי בן אברהם יעקב בורגר ז״ל

Born in the spiritual wasteland of America before World War II, his family clung to the traditions of their Torah-loyal Polish forebears. Despite the Depression and pressure that was insurmountable for many, their observance of Shabbos, *kashrus,* and *halachah* was unyielding. Torah education for his children was of extreme importance to him even when money was tight. His life exemplified the meaning of *kibud av v'eim.* His word was gold, as he was honest in all his business dealings. He was loved by all and he never spoke ill of others. He was a קשה לכעוס ונוח לרצות. His reputation lives on as inscribed on his *matzeivah*:

שלשה כתרים הם: כתר תורה, כתר כהונה, וכתר מלכות.

וכתר שם טוב עולה על גביהן.

ת.נ.צ.ב.ה.

This *sefer* is dedicated to our mother

Resha Borger-Lazar

רחל לאה בת שמואל נפתלי ז״ל

She was the true model of an *eishes chayil*: Dedicated to her family with all her heart, dedicated to *zehirus* in *shmiras halashon,* always judged everyone in a favorable manner (הוי דן את כל האדם לכף זכות), dedicated to Hashem through her *d'veikus* in *tefillah,* and dedicated to *hachzakas haTorah* in every possible way. Her memory shines like a beacon of light that illuminates the lives of our entire family and everyone who knew her.

CONTENTS

***Bareich Aleinu* / ברך עלינו**

"If you study the *siddur*, you'll start seeing that what you thought was a blank wall is really a doorway. If you open the door and step in, you'll be surprised by what's behind it—a whole panorama of wisdom. The *siddur* is a remarkable *sefer*. You can talk about it for years and never finish. There's so much information in the *siddur* that it's like an encyclopedia of every kind of *chachmah*."

—Rav Avigdor Miller, *zt"l*

INTRODUCTION

Several weeks after *Rav Avigdor Miller on Olam Haba* was published, I walked past a *sefarim* store and noticed the book was still prominently displayed on the front shelves. I was pleased but also surprised, since typically a new book enjoys a short career in a store's front display, if it's fortunate to be there at all. Yet there it was. In fact, next to it was the biography, *Rav Avigdor Miller—His Life and His Revolution*, as well as *Rav Avigdor Miller on Emunah and Bitachon*, two books I also had the privilege to work on. Next to them were books by the Simchas Hachaim Foundation, the publishing arm of Yeshiva Gedolah Bais Yisroel, which Rav Avigdor Miller co-founded with his son, Rav Shmuel Miller. All the books had a cover dominated by the beautiful, serene countenance of Rav Miller.

I entered the store incognito, so to speak, and asked the young man behind the desk how the book on Olam Haba was selling. (I must admit I was a little amused when he tried his best to convince me to buy my own book!) Not only was it still selling well, he said, but every Rav Miller book sells well, even long after they come out.

Afterward, I asked myself: *Why? What about Rav Miller's teachings make them popular—arguably even more so since his passing than during his lifetime?*

Rav Miller himself may have answered the question when someone asked him what one could learn from his *rebbi*, Rav Isaac Sher.

> "Rav Isaac Sher was the Slabodka Rosh Yeshiva, the last Rosh Yeshiva of Slabodka in Europe. He was a man of very great intelligence. Everything he said was logical. I admire him no end, and I have very many things to say about him. But right now, I'll say this. We can learn from Rav Isaac Sher the importance of learning and understanding the Torah and the Gemara *al pi seichel hayashar*, in ways that are founded on logic. *Seichel hayashar* is very important. That was his *derech*. It's called learning through *devarim hamiskablim al haleiv*, with ideas that people can grasp and understand. To convince people, to teach people,

> you should talk about *devarim hamiskablim al haleiv*, things that are more convincing. Some people like to say *sisrei Torah*, things that are mysterious, that we don't understand. Nothing wrong with that. There are a lot of mysteries in Torah, too. But if you want to be effective, you should follow the system of saying *devarim hamiskablim al haleiv*—practical things that people understand."

To me, Rav Miller fully absorbed and epitomized his *rebbi*'s approach. He expertly teaches "practical things that people understand."

Beyond that, though, he constantly reiterates the need for us to be proactive. It's not enough to listen and be wowed. He's not speaking to score points with his audience. He wants us to take his words to heart and change for the better.

> "Everything you hear in this place is like good meat (at least I hope so). But even good meat can't be eaten by itself. You must have a little bit of onions. You need a little bit of salt and pepper. You need some condiments. If you buy a piece of meat in a butcher shop and try to eat it straight from the butcher's block, you won't enjoy it much.
>
> "Everything you hear here needs to be explained and applied in practice. You need a great many other things besides these words alone. What you're hearing here are just generalities or generalizations. We're not talking about waving a magic wand and suddenly everything is transformed. You can't expect to hear something once and think you're now ready to face the world.
>
> "You'll have to hear these ideas repeatedly and think into them.... You must get to work changing yourself. Certainly it takes work. Nothing good comes easy. Everything good comes as a result of work! You'll have to go home and practice again and again and again. After years and years, you'll discover that you were rewarded richly for all the effort.... You'll become a more and more perfect *eved Hashem* every day of your life, fulfilling the purpose that you came into this world to achieve."

In summary, to me the secret of Rav Miller's popularity was his ability to translate his vast wisdom into deceptively simple and eminently practical insights for life. And to encourage and inspire us to work on those insights to become better, more perfect people.

Remember Hashem!

Rav Miller's engaging, practical approach to Torah topics is especially appreciated when it comes to *tefillah*. Despite its power to change our lives in the most profound way, many Jews sadly find it a burden, an obligation to get through as quickly and superficially as possible.

"I always tell the story," Rav Miller said, "of how Rav Levi Yitzchak Berditchever once told his *shamash* to walk over to the *bimah,* bang on the table, and make an announcement. So the *shamash* went over and banged. Everybody stopped davening and waited for the *shamash* to make this major announcement, which was so important that the Rebbe told him to interrupt the davening. 'The Rebbe wants everyone to know,' he said, 'that there is a Borei. There is a G-d.' That was the announcement.

"Don't laugh! It's a very important announcement to make in all the synagogues. In the middle of davening, you have to announce that we're davening to Hashem. Because we're too busy davening to think about that. People are davening and they don't think about what they're saying."

We can get so bogged down in the routine of everyday life that we sometimes forget *tefillah* is about the most basic human need—talking to Hashem. That's the first purpose of this book—to help us keep the big picture in mind, to "Remember Hashem!" even as we walk through the beautiful garden of the *siddur*'s details.

Tefillah in Covid Times

I began working on this book before the coronavirus struck the world. Then, suddenly, everything stopped and everyone's life was at risk. We couldn't congregate with others and couldn't go to *minyan*, even on Shabbos. It was as if Hashem was forcing us to turn inward and engage in unprecedented introspection—to think about ourselves, our purpose in life, our families, about who we really are as a people, about the need to pray like never before.

All these heightened emotions found their way into my davening—and this book. It's a union of Rav Miller's teachings and the supercharged emotions coursing through my veins as the coronavirus coursed its way through the world. As of this writing, no one knows the full repercussions and societal changes the virus has introduced, but they've already been tectonic. If nothing else, there's never been more reason to *daven*, to learn how to pray, to become—as David Hamelech said—*tefillah* itself (see "Talking to Hashem" below, p. 35).

As for me, immersing myself in this material not only changed my davening profoundly but often put me on a cloud of *emunah* that carried me through tough times.

List of Lectures

This book is based on numerous lectures Rav Miller left for posterity. Here is a partial list (all of which are available from Simchas Hachaim Publishing):

60—Prayer in Prosperity
63—*Tehillim* 24
86—*Tehillim* 146
108—For What to Pray
215—In David's Footsteps
233—*Tehillim* 122
300—Power of Prayer
305—*Tehillim* 30
457—Shemoneh Esrei 9
523—Shemoneh Esrei 12
550—Is it Good to Sing?
551—*Tehillim* 147
561—Midsummer Teshuvah
591—Shemoneh Esrei 16

595—Shemoneh Esrei 17
668—Shemoneh Esrei 18
864—Seven Objectives of *Tefillah*
908—Shemoneh Esrei 21 (Gathering of Exiles)
965—Shemoneh Esrei 22
E-113—Shemoneh Esrei 24
E-139—Shemoneh Esrei 25

In addition, material for this book was drawn from Rav Miller's lectures on *Sanhedrin, perek Chelek*, and *masechta Brachos*. Of course, his ideas about *tefillah* scattered throughout his *sefarim* also found their way here, especially his *sefer* on *tefillah* itself, *Praise, My Soul.*

As in the earlier books in this series, my methodology has been to combine material from a wide range of Rav Miller's teachings while remaining faithful to his intention, if not always his unique language and delivery style.[1] If, despite my efforts, the content departs in some way from Rav Miller's full intention, I accept full responsibility. That's why I strongly recommend listening to Rav Miller's lectures and reading his *sefarim*, as well.

Like the previous books, this one is presented in question-and-answer format. Many of the questions here are taken word-for-word from the audience in Rav Miller's lectures. Some of those questions have been modified slightly. Other questions were asked by Rav Miller himself as he delivered his lectures. Still others were formulated by the author.

I've incorporated something new in this book—subsections titled, "Practical Advice." For instance, the section about the blessing of *Refa'einu*, about the need to pray for our health, is followed by practical teachings from Rav Miller's lectures about staying healthy. It's not necessarily about the need to pray for health, just how to be healthy. Everything Rav Miller teaches is practical, including broad ideas about *tefillah*, but in the "Practical Advice" sections we get to hear how the

1 See the introduction to *Rav Avigdor Miller on Olam Haba* (Judaica Press) for an example of this methodology.

Rav advised people dealing with everyday challenges.

In addition, we've added a "Summary" section at the end of each of the *brachos* of Shemoneh Esrei, to enable you to solidify the lessons and help focus your thoughts during Shemoneh Esrei.

Acknowledgments

I sometimes ask myself what I would tell a not-yet-observant Jew who asks me about the purpose of life. One answer would be to say "thank You" to Hashem. It sounds simple, but gratitude is not so simple.

To do so, a person must think a lot. As Rav Miller says, he must make a "career" of it—studying Nature,[2] studying history (personal and general),[3] and, of course, studying Torah. But that's our purpose: to appreciate the gift of life to such a degree that we are constantly thanking Hashem—and doing so not robotically but with all our heart, mind, and soul. I therefore begin my acknowledgments with a woefully insufficient "thank You" to the Source of all Sources, to the Being of all Beings, to the Giver of Life. Thank *You*! Better yet, let me quote David Hamelech: "*Tov l'hodos laHashem*" (*Tehillim* 92:2). What is good, what is the good we should all strive for in life? To say thanks to Hashem.[4]

Rav Miller speaks about the need to specify the many things we should thank Hashem for, not just a general thanks. When I discovered Rav Miller's books as a young man, they literally changed my life. The logic of his reasoning and the scope of his knowledge spoke to me in ways little else did. It's a dream come true that I have had the opportunity to disseminate his teachings. Beyond general thanks to Hashem, therefore, let me be specific and thank Him for leading me to the wellspring of Rav Miller's teachings.

---

2 As this book goes to print, Judaica Press is also finishing a new book by the author called *Awaken Your Emunah*, which includes a treasure trove of insights from Rav Miller on the topic of *nifla'os haBorei*, the wonders of creation.

3 Also see the author's books on modern historical events in *The Hidden Hand* series (Judaica Press).

4 See "What should we be thinking when we say *Modim*?" on p. 427.

One way to work on thanking Hashem is by thanking the people He has sent our way and put into our lives. Judaica Press has always done a magnificent job producing my books. This is due to their leadership, starting with the Publisher, Aryeh Mezei, and their Managing Editor, Nachum Shapiro. They consistently put together a great team of editors, proofreaders, and graphic artists. Their professionalism and attention to detail are evident on every page.

I would like to give special thanks to Yeshiva Gedolah Bais Yisroel/Simchas Hachaim Publishing (SimchaPub.com) for making the Rav's lectures available—especially through their magnificent SimchaPod, which is loaded with some 2,000 *shiurim*, including the entire Thursday night lecture series. They advertise it as "life-changing" and, speaking for myself, it truly was and continues to be precisely that.

In addition to the Simchas Hachaim Foundation, the Toras Avigdor organization burst onto the Jewish world several years ago and made a huge impact with their free weekly *parshah* pamphlets, which I read religiously. Many times, their presentation sparked an idea that I incorporated into this book.

My wife has always been and continues to be a true *aishes chayil*. Her *chessed*, encouragement, *mesiras nefesh, hakaras hatov*, and ability to see the good in everyone are among the ingredients that nurture my writer's soul (as well as everything else). Whatever merits accrue from my writings belong to her as well.

Yaakov Astor
Elul 5781

TEFILLAH — PATH TO GREATNESS

Q Does Hashem need our *tefillos*?

Hashem doesn't need our davening—*we* need it! By davening, we accomplish the biggest achievement of life—we gain *da'as Hashem*, True Knowledge of Hashem. The more you talk to Hashem, the more you believe in Him. We were created and put in this world to acquire *da'as Hashem*, and *tefillah* is the great way of achieving that.

When you need something and you turn to the only One Who can help you, it impresses upon your mind most effectively that "*Hashem echad*," that everything comes from Him, and Him alone. That's why our *tefillos* are important—they're important for *us*. Hashem doesn't need our *tefillos*. We need them. We need them to achieve the potential, the perfection, for which we were created.

Q How does *tefillah* help us reach our potential?

The human soul is deep. It's profound and bottomless. It's full of unlimited greatness. Hashem breathed it into us (*Bereishis* 2:7), and anybody who breathes into somebody breathes of himself (*Ramban*, ibid.). But people walk around and never demonstrate it. They don't even know that they have a soul of infinite possibilities.

An American *chaver* of mine, Yehudah Davis, went to Europe and spent Rosh Hashanah with the Chofetz Chaim. When the Chofetz Chaim asked him where he was from, he told him that he had traveled from America to learn in the Mir. "*Amerikaner kumin lernen Torah* (Americans are coming to learn Torah)!" the Chofetz Chaim exclaimed. Then he added, "Your *neshamah* also descended a great distance to come learn Torah—an even greater distance."

We were sent down into this world to draw forth the hidden greatness in our souls and bring it to the surface. How do you bring forth the greatness of your soul? In many ways. The world is full of methods. But let's remember the general rule—we're not in this world to bring *in* things from the outside and put them into us, but to bring *out* from the recesses of our minds, from the depths of our being, the treasures that were there at birth.

The Gemara says that before a child is born, a *malach* teaches him the entire Torah, and as he's about to go out into the world, the *malach* slaps him and he forgets everything (*Niddah* 30b). So what's the purpose of teaching him if he's going to forget it? And the answer is that he doesn't forget. It remains forever within him.

We're unaware of what greatness we have, but it's there subconsciously. Our function in this world is to awaken that greatness within us and to cause it to surface by various means. That's what David Hamelech said, "*Urah, kevodi*—Awake, my glory!" (*Tehillim* 57:9). Everybody has glory within him, but it's asleep. The question is how to stir it, awaken it, and bring it to the surface. And one of the methods of becoming great—of bringing forth the greatness in your *neshamah*—is unfortunately one of the most neglected and ignored methods. That's the method of praying to Hashem.

It's neglected and ignored because we do it all the time. And we're almost total failures in the way we use it. When you pray to Hashem properly, you'll bring forth a greatness that has no end—an awareness of the Borei. It's buried in your *neshamah*. The *emunah* is in us. We don't have to go outside and find *emunah* and put it into our hearts. We're packed with *emunah*. We have an atom bomb of *emunah*, an endless store of spiritual energy. But it's up to us to start letting it come forth. And the way to do so is to cry out to Hashem. When you cry out to Him, when you ask Him, when you pray to Him, it's going to cause the fountains of the heart to swell up and burst forth.

Here's an idealist, a *ba'al teshuvah*, let's say. He came in from the outside, and his heart is full of fire to serve Hashem. And he comes into a place where people have always been observant. He looks up to them. They're his models. But he sees a strange thing. They don't make a big fuss about this business of prayer. If he's not careful and vigilant, after a while he falls into a rut just like them. He also begins wasting this glorious opportunity of *tefillah*. He should disregard those people around him, even though they may be *talmidei chachamim*. They're stuck in the rut of habit.

You only have one life, and the purpose is to bring forth the greatness within you. That's what *tefillah* accomplishes.

Q What system did David Hamelech use to become great?

David Hamelech said to himself, "*Urah, kevodi! Urah, haneivel v'chinor. A'irah shachar!*—Awake, my glory! Awake, O harp and lyre. Let me awaken the morning!" (*Tehillim* 57:9). What does David mean by, "Awake, my glory"? He was cognizant of a certain verse at the beginning of the Chumash, "*Vayipach b'apav nishmas chaim*—Hashem blew into man's nostrils the breath of life" (*Bereishis* 2:7). But didn't Hashem give life to animals and insects, too? Why does it say that He breathed the breath of life only into man?

And the answer is that He breathed a unique greatness into mankind, a greatness that emanated from Himself. It's an infinite greatness, because it comes from an Infinite Being. Everybody possesses the opportunities to make of himself something unlimited. As the Rambam says in *Hilchos Teshuvah* (5:2), "Every man can be a *tzaddik* like Moshe Rabbeinu."

That infinite potential for greatness is called "*kevodi*—my glory." This "glory" is really the *kevod Hashem* within every human being. But it's fast asleep. It's buried deep beneath our subconscious. Therefore, David says, "*Urah, kevodi*—Awake, my glory!"

How do you awake the glory? David bestirred his mind by the strings of the harp. As the melody began to enter his mind, the greatness within him began to well up to meet the harmony of the instrument. Everyone experiences this. When we hear music at a wedding or some other occasion, there's a certain stirring of greatness within us. It's something mysterious. Is it merely that certain vibrations strike our eardrums? Then it's nothing but the irritation of the nerves. What is there about music that makes us begin to see unseen horizons? A certain intuition begins to dawn upon us when we hear music. We call it inspiration. Unfortunately, it gets lost and evaporates because people don't understand. But the purpose of music is to stir the greatness that lies within.

A harp produces meditation, as it says in *Tehillim* (92:4), "*alai higayon b'chinor*—with meditation by the harp." David became great as he walked in the meadows as a shepherd, as he talked to Hashem in his mind. He was studying Nature and thinking about the history of our people, the function of man in the world, and all the aspects of how Hashem demonstrates His presence in the world.

After a while, David felt that these great ideas needed reinforcement, because reason alone isn't enough to make an impression. Unattended, it soon dies out. Therefore, when an idea formed in his mind, he took his harp and began playing a melody. As the melody progressed and his mind began to soar on the wings of the music (that's what music is for), he began experiencing this idea again on a much higher level. It became alive to him. Certain aspects that he hadn't noticed up until then became vivid and stood out boldly in his mind. David did this for a long time, until he reached the level of *ruach hakodesh*.

When David said, "Awake, my glory," it meant, "I have endless greatness. I must stir the harp. I must do certain things that inspire me. I must utilize the situations that bring forth the greatness within me."

There's no end to how much a person can attain in Torah and righteousness, but he has to utilize things that inspire him. Sometimes the harp is a teacher; sometimes it's a good neighbor; sometimes it's a good neighborhood. The Mirrer Yeshiva is a harp. If you live near it, it's inspiring. You see young men from all over America. Sometimes they leave wealthy homes to go there and study Torah. They live in the dormitory, eat in the dining room—not so bad, but at home they had it better. These people are inspiring. Some of them are in revolt against their homes and become very *frum* Jews.

There are many harps in life. We have to listen and find those tunes and utilize the opportunities. Then when we are properly inspired, we'll have to "wake up the morning." It means we'll have to hustle and shake a leg. Whether it's accomplishing in Torah, *derech eretz*, or *emunah*.

Tefillah can make us great if we work on it properly, but we have to show that we really mean what we're asking for. If we pray with our hearts and do the acts that demonstrate that we really mean what we're saying, we can attain true greatness with *tefillah*.

TALKING TO HASHEM

Q What made David Hamelech such a symbol of *tefillah*?

David was a shepherd in his youth. He states that Hashem took him from behind the sheep (*Tehillim* 78:70) and suddenly made him king. [It's a reference to the time when] Shmuel Hanavi came to the house of Yishai with a hornful of oil to anoint one of his sons, but he didn't know which one. Shmuel looked at Yishai's oldest son and thought he must be the one. But Hashem said it wasn't him. "A man looks only with his eyes, but Hashem looks into the heart" (I *Shmuel* 16:7). He's a fine young man, but not the one I want. Then Yishai brought in all his sons, one by one. They were all rejected by Shmuel Hanavi. Shmuel knew that he was sent for a purpose, so he asked Yishai, "You have no more sons?"

"Yes, I have a son, a young son." Yishai didn't think of him as a candidate. "He's somewhere in the fields, lying in the grass with his harp and singing songs."

"Bring him to me," Shmuel said.

The moment David walked in, Hashem said, "Rise and anoint him, for this is the one." Shmuel took out the oil and poured it on David's head. That's what it means, "*Vayikacheni me'acharei hatzon*—Hashem took me from behind the sheep." One moment David was herding the flock, and the next moment he was *Melech Yisrael*—the King, the *Mashiach*, the "anointed one."

There must have been something in David that made him worthy of this. It could be that Hashem foresaw the future, that David would do great things for his people. But there must have been something in the past that had earned him this great honor.

I'm sure David was a very fine young man. He was a *gomel chassadim*; he did favors for everybody. I'm sure he honored his father and his mother. He learned Torah and loved learning Torah. He did everything. But one thing we know that distinguished him was his communion with Hashem—his *Tehillim*. David lay in the fields and spoke to Hashem as long as he could. And when he couldn't speak to Him, he was thinking of Him.

David made a declaration, "*Va'ani tefillah*—I am prayer" (*Tehillim*

109:4). What does "I am *tefillah*" mean? It means, "I'm an *ish tefillah*—I am a man of *tefillah*." It means he spent his entire life, every waking moment, thinking of and talking to Hashem.

He was great in everything. He was great in battle. He was a military hero who conquered all of Eretz Yisrael. David not only conquered the entire Eretz Yisrael, but all the nations around were afraid of him and sent him tribute every year. More than his military prowess, David was a man of great ideas. He is responsible for the institution of the Beis Hamikdash. Before it, [the Mishkan in] Shiloh was a small house without a real roof, covered with old curtains. After Churban Shiloh (I *Shmuel*, Chapter 4), the *Aron Hashem* was in a tent all the time. David said, "Can I allow Hashem's dwelling to be less splendid than the palace of the king?" (II *Shmuel* 7:2). Therefore, he gathered all the materials, and he made all the plans, together with the advice of Gad Hachozeh and Nasan Hanavi. As a result of his efforts, the first and second Beis Hamikdash stood for many centuries. They're both the result of David Hamelech. We're accustomed to the idea of a Beis Hamikdash, but without David Hamelech how would it have ever come about?

He did many great things, yet the central pillar of this man's perfection was, "*Ani tefillah*—I am a man of *tefillah*."

The center of David's personality was *tefillah*. Everything else flowed from it. His *emunah, bitachon, ahavas Hashem, avodah*, and love of the Am Yisrael were all offshoots of that pillar. David became very great because his central theme was *tefillah*. From it, everything else developed.

When David went to battle, he was praying to Hashem. It's a remarkable thing. As he ran into the midst of the battle swinging his ax, he prayed, "Help me, Hashem, that I shouldn't slip" (*Tehillim* 18:37). When a warrior slips and falls, who knows what can happen to him! "*Ki b'cha arutz g'dud uvEilokai adaleig shur*" (*Tehillim* 18:30)—When David saw a wall, he took a running start and jumped over the wall, but only with Hashem's help. As he was jumping over the wall, flying through the air, swinging his battle-axe, he was talking to Hashem,

"Help me, Hashem!" Of course, he was aiming with his battle-axe, too, no question about it, but he was thinking of Hashem at all times. That was the essence of David Hamelech's greatness.

David always asked Hashem to help him when he was in danger. When he was a boy, a lion charged him. He asked Hashem for help, and then he took hold of the lion with his hands, tearing it apart. When he encountered a bear, he broke its feet (I *Shmuel* 17:34–36). David was a very powerful young man. But his true power was his *tefillah*. David prayed to Hashem at every instance in his life. At every occasion, he thanked Hashem.

Do you know what's good in this world? "*Tov l'hodos laHashem*—it's good to give thanks to Hashem" (*Tehillim* 92:2). David did what he said. "*Ulezamer l'shimcha, Elyon*"—the true good in the world is "to sing to Your name, O Most High" (ibid.). When did he do it? All day long. From the moment he got up until he fell asleep at night. "*L'hagid baboker chasdecha*—to relate the kindliness of Hashem in the morning," when he got up, "*ve'emunascha baleylos*—and Your steadfastness in the night" (ibid. 92:3). From morning to night, all day long, David was thanking Hashem.

David was in constant contact with Hashem. There was no time that he wasn't thinking of Hashem. Either he was asking for help or thanking Him. *Tefillah* is divided into two categories. One is making requests of Hashem. We're always asking Hashem for our needs, and it's a very important function, but it's finite. There's only so much we can ask for. The second is *hoda'ah*, to thank Hashem. Thanking Hashem is endless. "*Kol z'man shehaneshamah b'kirbi, modeh ani l'fanecha*—as long as I'm alive, I give thanks to You" (*Birchos Hashachar*). He thanked Hashem every minute. David spent all his days in these two great pursuits.

L'hagid baboker chasdecha—he thanked Hashem in the morning, and he kept it up all day long. That's what made David great. That's why Hashem took him from behind the sheep—because David had spent all his youth preparing for a career of being in constant contact with Hashem.

Tefillah is life. The life of a servant of Hashem is always thinking about Hashem, either in gratitude or in request.

Now, we're not blaming anybody for not attaining this level, but that was David Hamelech's greatness: "*Va'ani tefillah*—I am a man of *tefillah*" (*Tehillim* 109:4).

That's a way to greatness. The more you speak to Hashem in *tefillah*, the more He loves you.

Q Why is the commandment for *tefillah* not explicitly stated in the Torah?

That's a good question. Why is there no open commandment in the Torah for *tefillah*? It's included in "*L'avdo b'chol l'vavchem*—to serve Him with all your heart" (*Devarim* 11:13). But "to serve" Hashem could mean more than one thing. If it's such an important subject like *tefillah*, why shouldn't it be specified? Among the obligations of a Jew, of a servant of Hashem, *tefillah* plays a big part. Why wasn't it included in the Aseres Hadibros or at least in the 613 *mitzvos* openly? It's a good question.

I'll say one answer. *Tefillah* isn't a *mitzvah* you do one time, or ten times. *Tefillah is a way of life.*

What does that mean? It means that you're expected to be in contact with Hashem from when you wake up until you go to sleep, from when you thank Him with *Modeh ani l'fanecha* in the morning to when you say *Hamapil* before you go to sleep at night. You're expected to be in contact with Hashem all day long.

Tefillah comes from the word *pillel*, "to think." *L'hispallel* is the reflexive form, meaning, "to make yourself think." *Tefillah* is thinking. Asking why there's no explicit commandment for *tefillah* is like asking why there isn't a *mitzvah* to think. There are plenty of *mitzvos* to think. There's the *mitzvah* to think about Yetzias Mitzrayim. There's the *mitzvah* of *emunah*. There are *mitzvos* for the mind. *Tefillah* isn't something you do and then you're done. *Tefillah* is a state of existence, a frame of mind—to always be in contact with Hashem.

The *Chovos Halevavos* mentions five purposes of *tefillah*. I will mention only one, which is longing for Hashem, *d'veikus*. Wanting to become one with Hashem.

Tefillah is an opportunity to speak directly to Hashem and say to him the great word, "*Atah*—You." Doesn't that seem presumptuous? How can we even think we have the right to address Hashem, the King of Kings, as "You"? And that He will listen to us? But actually, at that moment, He *is* paying attention and listening to *you*. *Tefillah* is an opportunity for expressing your longing for the World to Come. The more a person spends time in *tefillah*, trying to perfect himself by talking directly to Hashem, the more he is preparing for that great experience when he will have the incomparable joy of basking in the presence of Hashem.

The results of such a career are certainly going to be remarkably great!

PRACTICAL ADVICE

Q Is it disrespectful to talk to Hashem while you're busy doing other things, like taking care of children?

Absolutely not. It's full of respect. Whatever you're doing, talk to Hashem as much as you can. Don't hesitate. Hashem wants your *tefillos*. Of course, if you're able to stop for a moment and talk to Him, you certainly should. But if you're busy all day, then talk to Hashem all day long while you're busy.

Q Wouldn't we have more energy to put into davening if we only had to do it once a day?

And the answer is that we have to put more time and energy into the prayers that we pray three times a day. Even three times a day isn't enough. Because prayers aren't just a function. It's not just a *mitzvah* that you fulfill. It's our life. Just as Torah is our life, davening is also our life. Talking to Hashem is something you should be doing all day long. Therefore, we shouldn't begrudge the time spent in prayers.

You know, old-time Jews, the ones who weren't scholars, used to say *Tehillim* all day long. They didn't waste time. I remember when I was in Europe, there was an old coachman, a wagon driver of the old school. He had a *Tehillim* that he himself had bound in leather, a homemade binding. He kept it on him under his belt. He came into the Slabodka yeshiva wearing his boots, big boots up to his hips because he used to drive in mud. Whenever he had time, he came into the yeshiva, sat in the back, and took out his *Tehillim*. He pulled it out from underneath his belt and got busy saying *Tehillim*. Wagon drivers used to say *Tehillim* all day long as they were driving. And through the night, they said it by memory.

That's a Jew—someone who's always talking to Hashem. That's how David spent his nights, saying praises and singing songs to Hashem. A Jew loves that. It's not a duty—it's his happiness. That's his way of finding Hashem. Therefore, when you pray three times a day, don't consider it excessive. Not at all. If you do it right, it could be your greatest success.

Q **How does one talk to Hashem?**

At first, you have to be a hypocrite. You have to do it superficially. You have to say the words. And that's what we do when we *daven*. "*Karov atah b'fihem v'rachok mikilyoseihem*—You are close in their mouths but far away from their kidneys" (*Yirmiyah* 12:2). That means from their insides. That's what davening is. But from the *navi*'s *mussar* we see, *derech agav*, that you have to start by saying the words. It's only if a person sincerely embarks on a career of learning to *speak* to Hashem that his davening can become meaningful. After a while, when he says, "*Atah*—You," he feels that he's talking to Somebody. When that great day comes, you know you have arrived.

So first do it superficially. Okay, so you're a hypocrite. So what? It's good hypocrisy. You're doing it to train yourself. Little by little, you'll get accustomed to saying the words. After a while, you're going to feel that there's Somebody actually listening. That's what the *Mesillas Yesharim* (7) says—that at first you say it, and after a while the realization enters your mind, because you have an instinct that all human beings have—that Hashem is actually there, and He's listening.

Q **Can I ask Hashem for anything?**

And the answer is yes! There is no limit.

If you're smart, you will ask Him for as many things as you can. Don't pull any punches. Hashem says, "*Harchev picha va'amaleihu*—Open your mouth wide, and I will fill it" (*Tehillim* 81:11). The simple meaning is that Hashem says that the more you ask of Him—the wider you open your mouth—the more you deserve that He should fill it.

Imagine a child who sees ice cream on the table. He opens his mouth wide for his mother to give him some. And she happily shovels it into his mouth. That's our relationship with Hashem. We're like helpless infants. He implores us to open our mouths wide so He can fulfill our desires.

Of course, sometimes a smart mother isn't going to listen to her child. If the child opens his mouth wide for ice cream before the meal, she says, "Wait. First eat the main meal." A wise mother does not fill the child's mouth merely because he opens it.

Hashem is the same way. He hears your prayers. Why hasn't He given you the million dollars you've been asking for? Because He knows it would be the worst thing for you. Your troubles would quickly be multiplied. You'd get unwanted publicity. Money brings all kinds of troubles. It's usually the greatest misfortune to win the lottery. People's lives fall apart.

The *passuk* has two parts—"Open your mouth wide" and "I will fill it." The first part means ask for everything. He will fill it. No question. If you ask, He fills. However, the second part means that *He* will fill it. The emphasis is on Hashem—"*I* will fill it." Hashem doesn't always fill it up the way you want. He fills it up the way *He* wants. When the child opens its mouth wide for ice cream, the mother sometimes shovels in castor oil. The child doesn't like it, but it's for his benefit. That's what he needs. You may open your mouth wide and ask for this or that, but Hashem might do something you don't like. Nevertheless, it's a lifesaver for you.

Sometimes when a man is asking for success in his business, Hashem sees that success in *this* business is not good for him. It brings him into bad company. He has no time to go to shul. Therefore, Hashem sends a gentleman from the criminal underworld to come into his plant at night, light a firebomb, and blow up his business. Suddenly, he's out of business, ruined. But it ends up saving his life. Now he's able to start a new business.

I'm telling you a true story. In his new business, this fellow was able to keep regular hours, which his previous business didn't allow. He told me that his health had been deteriorating because of his first business. Now he kept more normal hours and felt better than he had in years. He went to shul. He even began learning Gemara again—and even began teaching people Gemara! It was truly an amazing thing. And it happened only because his business was firebombed! He opened his mouth wide, and Hashem shoveled in a firebomb!

Don't be ashamed to ask Hashem for things of a material nature. Cry out to Hashem if you want that customer to place a nice order. Cry out to Hashem to heal a toothache. Never be ashamed to ask Hashem—and ask Him for anything you want. Hashem loves when people pray to Him. He loves it. And the more and the louder we pray, the more He loves us. That's a very important idea. A lot of people like to be polite and don't want to burden Hashem too much. They'll remind Him occasionally, but they don't want to be bothersome. So occasionally, quietly, they mention that they want *parnassah*, and good health. No! Open your mouth wide. Constantly.

The Gemara (*Brachos* 50a) says this *passuk* refers to learning Torah. The more you ask, the more you're going to get. Don't hold back. When you ask, don't ask merely to know one *perek*. Ask Hashem for success to know all of Shas. Of course, you must do something about it, too. But keep asking. Open your mouth wide. You'll be surprised how great you'll become eventually. Pray for greatness in *ruchniyus*. Pray for greatness in *emunah*. Pray for greatness in *bitachon*. Pray for greatness in *tefillah*. Open your mouth wide. You'll be surprised.

"Open your mouth wide" means pray as much as you can. Don't pull punches. Ask for all you want.

Don't be stingy with words. Don't limit it to Shemoneh Esrei. Give a donation of *tefillah* during the day for your own benefit. It's even better than health insurance. I'm not against health insurance, by the way. You should have health insurance, too. But say to Hashem, "Ribbono Shel Olam, please help me, please heal me." "*Ki Atah shomei'a tefillas amcha Yisrael b'rachamim*—You listen with compassion to *tefillos*."

Every *eved Hashem* must get into his blood the idea that Hashem is listening, and that he should speak to Hashem constantly.

David Hamelech worked on himself so much, and this way of life became so natural to him, that he said, *Ani tefillah.* Not, "I am *mispallel*." I *am tefillah.* He was a living *tefillah*. That's the way he lived. He lived with Hashem constantly on his mind.

PRAYER IN PROSPERITY

Q When is *tefillah* most beneficial?

It's a *passuk* in *Iyov*. The friends of Iyov (36:19) said to him—"*Haya'aroch shu'acha lo v'tzar?*—Did you arrange your prayers before you were in distress?" Iyov's friends were asking, "Did you pray to Hashem before misfortune came? Had you done so, things would have been different." On this *passuk* the Gemara (*Sanhedrin* 44b) states, "Rabbi Elazar says, 'A man should always pray before trouble [occurs].'" We learn from this how great it is to ask Hashem for something *before* the need arises, before you come into distress.

Another Gemara (*Shabbos* 32a) states something similar—"Always (*L'olam*), a person should pray to Hashem that he not become sick." *L'olam* means *always*. Even when in the best of health, one should pray to Hashem to remain well. That's a piece of very good advice. I should charge admission just for that alone. If I ever told you anything worthwhile, that is it. Pray to Hashem for good health while you still have it.

It's worth repeating. "Always"—even when there's no premonition, even when there's no inkling of misfortune and it seems like you're speeding down the highway of happiness, success, and perfect health for the rest of your days—ask Hashem for good health. Always, always, always. Always means not only during Shemoneh Esrei. Even when you're in your office. Even when you're walking on the street. Afraid somebody might hear you? So walk into a telephone booth, pick up the phone, and make a long-distance call to Hashem: "Hashem, please keep me well!"

The Gemara adds—"If he does become sick, they tell him to bring some proof [a *zechus*, a 'merit'] in order to be freed." Once a man is lying sick in bed, it's much harder for him to get out of it. It's common sense—"An ounce of prevention is worth a pound of cure." It's easier to guard your health than to try to heal yourself after you become sick. No question about it. Don't pick up heavy loads—that's much better than having a hernia operation. It's much better to go to sleep on time and eat on time than to become ill and go to a physician for all kinds of disorders. No question. It's also much cheaper. Much less time is needed for precautions against disaster than for repairing disasters. If you make sure there are no matches within reach of children, if you make sure there's a fire extinguisher in the kitchen, if you make sure that no child is permitted in the kitchen without supervision, it's much cheaper than having to repair the damage.

This is ordinary prudence. Now, however, we're learning something new. Even with Hashem, it makes a very big difference. It's much easier to win with Him *before* trouble comes than after. The Gemara says you should always request [of Hashem] to remain well, because if a person does become sick, he won't get away with mere prayers. They'll say to him, "Bring some proof; show some merit why you should be set free."

Then the Gemara offers a *mashal*. It's like a *sardiot*, which was a Roman "sergeant." It seems that, historically, sergeants always were the same. Once they put the pinch on a man and write his name down in their book, it's much more difficult for him to be released. And it costs much more, too. It's much easier to get him *not* to put your name down in the first place. If you slip him a few dollars, he might act like he didn't see you. But once he writes you down in his book or brings you into the station, it costs more to get out.

The Gemara says that when a man becomes ill, it's like getting arrested. At the least, it's going to cost money. Therefore, it's prudent to pray beforehand not to get a headache. Getting away with a prayer costs a lot less. But once he has the beginning of an illness, Hashem may not listen to his mere *tefillah*. He asks for a *zechus*, a merit. He says, "Tell me why I should free you."

Now suppose a person thought that going to the precinct to bribe the captain was too expensive. Instead, he waits to have his case heard before judges. Well, judges need more than the sergeant and the precinct captain. The Gemara says, "If a man fell ill and became bedridden"—now he doesn't just have a headache; he's already bedridden—then it's like he went before the tribunal, the court. Once there, he has to be prepared to fork over a lot of money.

That's the *mashal.* The sergeant doesn't need as much of a bribe as a precinct captain, and a judge demands even more money. The *nimshal* is—the longer you postpone your efforts in prayer to Hashem, the greater the cost is going to be. That's the system.

Q **How can we improve at davening?**

And the answer is: Hashem gives two motivations. One is adversity and one is prosperity.

Avraham and Sarah waited a long time before they had a child. Sarah was already ninety years old when she had a child. The same thing with Yitzchak and Rivka. For twenty years they had no child. And Yaakov had no children with his favored wife Rochel for a long time. It wasn't an accident. There's a plan. Why did Hashem withhold children from our forefathers? Because, the Gemara says, Hashem desires the prayers of *tzaddikim*" (*Yevamos* 64a). He loves to hear them pray. He has a passion for their prayers.

Our Avos tore their hearts out as they asked for children. Eventually they all had children, but that was just a by-product. That wasn't the purpose. *The purpose was their outcry. The purpose was their prayer.* Through such prayer, they became great in recognition and awareness. When you shout constantly to the Borei, it shows that you recognize the Borei. It shows that you understand He is there. That's the result of working on it for years and years, not just mumbling it politely.

But it's also possible for a person to gain awareness of Hashem in another way. There's another way of becoming great—when Hashem gives you things you didn't expect and you cry out to Him in thanks. Not just a polite, emotionless thank-you. A thank-you with song. Loud, heartfelt song!

Let's say, tomorrow morning, you get up and your joints don't hurt. Do you have a headache? No. A toothache? Not today. When you went to the bathroom, was everything functioning? How do most people react? They don't. What's there to shout about? Just because nothing bad happened?! Just because everything works normally?!

Yes! The way to react is to shout with joy! Shout to Him! *Hallelu es Hashem! Hallelu* means "to shout, to go wild." *Hallelu* means to go *meshuga*. Did you ever hear of a person becoming *meshuga* because he was so happy that things were good with him? Open your mouth and shout at the top of your lungs. Ever tried it? Try it once in a while. It's a good thing. Shout at the top of your lungs to the rooftops and thank Hashem.

Meditating about how much *brachah* you have—with a cool head, in a quiet way—is wonderful, too. But also shout with all your strength—again and again, especially if nobody's around. Now, it doesn't mean that you don't have to learn Torah and do *mitzvos*. But this is one of the very great methods that bring success. Besides learning Torah, shout to Hashem.

You can shout from happiness or *chas v'shalom* from the opposite. Whatever it is—shout! But do your shouting to Hashem. That's what you were put in this world for. The great principle here is that Hashem wants to hear our voices. Whether our voices are in this fashion or in the other fashion, He wants to hear our voices. That's our great function.

Q What would increase the effectiveness of our *tefillos*?

Our prayers to Hashem are especially beloved and acceptable when they're motivated solely by *emunah*. When a man is forced to turn to Hashem, it's also good; it's always good. But there's no comparison to the *tefillah* a man makes when he isn't hard-pressed. Let's provide some examples.

Imagine an expert salesman. He has a glib tongue and an imposing presence, and his merchandise is good. As he waits in the big executive's reception room, he knows his sample case is packed with very good merchandise. He knows his prices are very reasonable. He knows that this executive will be impressed. And if he isn't, the salesman knows that with his persuasive tongue he can convince him of anything. But this man doesn't rely on that. As he's in the waiting room, he spends part of his time praying to Hashem for success. That *tefillah* is a true expression of *emunah.*

When we say (*Tehillim* 145:18), "*Karov Hashem l'chol kor'av*—Hashem is near to all who call out to Him," there is a modifying clause—"*l'chol asher yikra'uhu be'emes*—in truth." Hashem is near to all who call Him *in truth.* Now, who doesn't call Him in truth? When you ask Hashem for wealth, don't you mean it? When you ask Hashem for health, don't you mean it? Who's not calling out in the truth? If so, what does it mean that "Hashem is close to all who call out in truth?"

But "*emes*" means *emunah.* If a person just says words and doesn't think about what he's saying, that certainly isn't calling out "in truth." If a person says *Refa'einu* and he's not thinking what he's saying, it's not in truth. But David Hamelech isn't even talking about such a person. That's beneath his consideration. Such things didn't exist in the ancient times. What he means is that for a prayer to be heard, he has to speak to Hashem with a conviction that only Hashem can grant success, that there's nothing in the world except the *retzon Hashem.* When a farmer calls out in truth and says, "*Bareich aleinu, Hashem Elokeinu,*" what he really means is, "My plowing is meaningless, my planting is worthless, my watering the seeds doesn't accomplish a thing. It's nothing. Only Your blessing will produce the fruits of the earth." If he can muster such a level of *emunah*, then he's calling out in *emes*, and then Hashem is close to him. When this super salesman is sitting in the waiting room and relies only on Hashem and appeals to Him for success—despite the fact that he has good reason to think he could rely on himself—that's called "calling to Hashem in truth."

Q **Why pray to Hashem when we have plenty?**

It states in *Nishmas,* "In a time of famine, You fed us; at a time of satiation [when there was plenty and abundance], You supplied us." So, we understand "in a time of famine You fed us." The populace was expiring from hunger, but we survived. It's a great thing. But what's great about "You supplied us at a time of plenty?" All the stores were bursting with food, crammed with all good things. All the bakeries, meat shops, fish stores, fruit stores, *nosherei* stores—whatever our heart desired—was available. What's so great that Hashem supplies us at a time of plenty?

And the answer is—real greatness is *if we're able to say in a time of plenty* that it's You Who supplies us—You, and only You.

As you walk down King's Highway, lined with stores on both sides with everyone offering his wares, begging you to buy, imagine you were walking down a deserted street. Imagine all the stores were closed, all the windows empty, and there was nothing at all for you to buy. Imagine there was nothing in your home, that your refrigerator was bare, and your cupboards empty—and then pray to Hashem that He should give you your next meal. That's an achievement! That's calling out to Him "in truth." Otherwise, you're not relying on Hashem—you're relying on the butcher and the baker. Therefore, true greatness is when a person enters the kitchen and sees it's stocked with all good things, yet is able to raise his eyes to Hashem and pray for his *parnassah*.

Why beg for bread when you have bread? Because the truth is that you really have nothing.

Why praise Hashem that He is "*malbish arumim*—the One Who clothes your nakedness" when your closet is full? A man looks in his drawer, and it's so full of boxers he doesn't know which one to wear. A woman looks in her closet and has so many shoes that she doesn't know which ones to put on. But that's praying in prosperity. Imagine that now—today—He is clothing you. He's giving you a new suit, a new dress. Even though you used it yesterday, feel the gratitude of a naked man who has just been given a secondhand suit. Use the glorious opportunity of getting dressed in the morning to beg Hashem to give you something to wear. Because it's only Hashem Who is *malbish arumim*. If we had the good sense, every morning we'd pray fervently for our clothing, even though our wardrobe is well-stocked.

True *emunah* is when we free our minds of all physical causes, all physical assurances, and transfer our trust solely to Hashem. That's calling to Hashem *in truth*. That's *emunah*. That's the system that the truly great followed.

I know that's not easy. It may be easy to say, but it's difficult to really believe. That's why it's so prized by Hashem. By the way, even if you don't believe it, say it anyway. Yes, it's easier said than done, but it's easier done when said. Say it, even insincerely. But work on saying it sincerely.

Q **How can I utilize davening to help me feel happy?**

People don't realize how much there is in life to enjoy and be grateful for. The man who prays that Hashem should help him—I should have good health, I should cross the street without any difficulties, I should go for a walk and not bump into rude people or people who want to put their hand into my pocket and take my wallet—is always happy. *Baruch Hashem* when you come home and everything is in order.

The fool goes through life not knowing how many times he was saved from troubles, clueless as to how close he was to danger. Such a man isn't grateful for anything. He thinks he doesn't have a reason to be happy.

This is one of the ways of making life full of *simchah*, of gratitude. Appreciate the fact that you can walk. Here's a man sitting in a wheelchair. When you get past him, say, "*Baruch Hashem*, I can walk!" Ever think of being happy with walking? Yes, a wise man enjoys walking. It's a pleasure. If that man in the wheelchair could experience even a little bit of walking, he'd be in a delirium of happiness. So let's be in a delirium without going through what he has to go through.

Here's another man in the street, taking color pictures with two good cameras—his eyes! What a pleasure it is to look with your eyes. Only we're too foolish to realize what a happiness it is. It's fun to see with your eyes! You see the sun shining, clouds moving, people walking, merchandise in the stores. It's such a happiness to have eyes to see.

Therefore, the man who prays to Hashem when everything is good is a happy man.

Q Does the fact that Hashem denied the Avos and Imahos children to inspire them to daven show that davening that comes from distress is greater?

And the answer is: Avraham and Sarah prayed for children long before they were married. There's no question that they prayed beforehand. They prayed before, during, and after. But since Hashem loves *tzaddikim,* He wanted to elicit from them even more *tefillah.* This great sadness of being childless produced in these *tzaddikim* more and more prayer, which meant more and more *emunah.*

It's like pressing grapes. Pressing a good grape produces an excellent wine. But you want more, so after you press the grapes with your hands, you put it in a machine so every last drop comes out. The second wine isn't as good as the first wine, but we want the second wine, too.

Avraham certainly prayed even without pressure, but Hashem put pressure on him to get him to pray even more fervently. As a result, he became greater and greater. So the quality of prayer that comes from distress is certainly great, but not as great as the prayer that comes before distress.

Q Is davening to Hashem when one is in need more worthy of reward?

Don't we have a principle of *"L'fum tza'ara, agra*—According to the distress, so is the reward" (*Avos* 5:26)? Therefore, when a person suffers some distress and he prays, shouldn't he have more reward?

The answer is—No, because it's more difficult to think of Hashem with a full stomach.

When a rich man looks out of his penthouse window and sees the dome of his savings bank, knowing that under that dome are vaults full of valuables he has put there, it's very hard for him to raise his eyes above the dome and think of something higher than that. The poor man can't even look out of his tenement house window, because it's blocked by other tenement houses. He sees nothing but poverty all around him. He has nothing on which to rely, so it's easier for him to think of Hashem. Therefore, the rich man who prays to Hashem sincerely earns more reward than the poor man.

Q But doesn't Viduy prove that prayer under pressure is the best prayer?

If *Viduy*, a death confession, is so valuable that it can salvage a man's ruined life, doesn't it prove that pressure toward prayer, toward repentance, is valuable despite the fact that it's motivated by urgency?

There's no question that if a man repents when he's healthy and he has a prospect of a long life before him, it's better. "Happy is the man who fears Hashem" (*Tehillim* 112:1), and our Sages explain: "while he's still a man" (*Avodah Zarah* 19a). While you're still young, before you become elderly and infirm, is the best time. "Remember Hashem in the days of your youth" (*Koheles* 12:1). When you're young is the best time. Now, if a man didn't remind himself until his last moments, it's still very valuable, because the end is important. How a person ends his life—how he goes out of this world—is very important.

But there's no question that when you're feeling well and making money—your children still need you, they look up to you, they're all young, they're being supported by you, and everybody around you respects you—is the best time to remember Hashem.

Q In times of prosperity, is there any benefit to recalling our past hardships?

It's a principle that the Gemara teaches us—"We begin our expressions of gratitude with our low state and conclude with our celebrated state" (*Pesachim* 116a). That's why on Pesach we start with "This is the bread of affliction," because when a man is successful, he should always remember the days of his poverty. It's a sickness to forget the past and not to be grateful. Therefore, we begin thanking Hashem by remembering the years of our affliction. We talk about the early time of our history when Yaakov Avinu left his family and traveled alone as a stranger in strange lands. Then we work our way up until we come to, "And now we are in the land that You promised our fathers, and we are enjoying the happiness of living in Eretz Yisrael."

It's a lesson for us. Whenever a person succeeds, he should remember his poor days. That's why, when the Chashmonaim made a feast to celebrate their victories, they used to put poor herbs, *meluchim*, on their table. And they said, "Our forefathers used to eat *meluchim*, poor herbs, when they were building the Beis Hamikdash" (*Kiddushin* 66a). They put the inexpensive herbs on their golden tables because they didn't want to forget their poor origins.

If someday you become a multimillionaire, once in a while bring forth some of the old clothing you left over, as a way of remembering the days when you didn't dress in gold and diamonds. Take out your old worn-out suit as a *zecher* and take a look at it. And that will encourage you in your gratitude to Hashem.

PRAYER IN ADVERSITY

Q What is the benefit of suffering?

We say in the Haggadah, "*Ha lachma anya*—this is the bread of affliction," which our forefathers ate in Mitzrayim. When we say that they ate "bread of affliction," we mean that they ate affliction. And eating affliction, we must understand, is an exceptionally good diet.

The *passuk* says, "Hashem extricates a poor man" (*Iyov* 36:15). The Gemara explains that He saves him "in reward" for his poverty, i.e., *because* of his poverty (*Yevamos* 102b). In reward for affliction, people get success. They get success in *gashmiyus*, in physical ways, and they get success in *ruchniyus*. Whatever it is, suffering is a very great benefit.

Hashem would give us more of it, but He suffers from it. "When a man is in distress, the Shechinah says, '*I'm* in distress'" (*Sanhedrin* 46a). Otherwise, Hashem would give us more of this good thing, for there's nothing that's *mechaper* on a man, purifies him, improves him, and elevates him like suffering.

Q Is there a particular *perek* in Tehillim that teaches us not to take our success and tranquility for granted?

Yes, it's the one we say every morning, *Mizmor shir chanukas habayis l'David* (Chapter 30).

David Hamelech says, "*Ki rega b'apo, chayim birtzono*—His wrath lasts one moment but His will is to give life" (*Tehillim* 30:6). That's a great principle. Even though He's angry at us, it's only for a moment. "*B'erev yalin bechi v'laboker rinah*—at night we go to bed weeping, but in the morning we get up with song."

Next, he explains how all this came about. He goes back to the beginning: "*Va'ani amarti b'shalvi bal emot l'olam*—I said when I was in tranquility that I would never fall" (*Tehillim* 30:7). When a man is successful, when everything is going well, he becomes accustomed to his situation and thinks that it's going to be that way forever. As a result, he forgets Hashem. Peace, success, and well-being cause a man to forget the great truth of the world, that "*birtzoncha he'emadeta l'hareri oz*—Hashem, it was only with Your will that You established my mountain with strength" (ibid. 30:8).

When You saw that everything was going well with me, You decided to do a very great kindness. "*Histarta fanecha, hayisi nivhal*—You concealed Your face, and I became confounded." In that moment, You helped me see that all my security was nothing but imagination. In a flash, my mountain collapsed. You turned Your face away from me, and now I am in the most dire straits.

What did I do? "*Eilecha Hashem ekra, v'el Hashem es'chanan*—I called out to You, Hashem, and I made entreaties to You" (ibid. 30:9). That was the purpose. When Hashem saw that David was secure, feeling that everything from now on was going to be tranquil forever, He concealed His face.

Now, don't think that David forgot about Hashem in the sense we might say about ourselves. But there was a certain cloud over his awareness. When people are secure, they don't feel as much of a need to think about Hashem. Therefore, Hashem conceals His face. At that time, David discovered how helpless he was.

David had conquered all his enemies. His archenemy, Shaul, had died. The Ten Tribes, who had opposed him at the beginning, had finally come over to his side and agreed to become united under him. All the nations around were bringing him tribute. He conquered his enemies on all sides. David was sitting in tranquility on his mountain of strength. That's when Hashem decided to teach a little lesson to His beloved David. He hid His face for a moment.

It's like a mother whose child is skipping around the street, oblivious to her. She doesn't want him to forget she's around, so for a moment she hides. He suddenly looks around and begins calling for her. He suddenly realizes that his whole life, his whole happiness, his whole security, is only because his mother was close at hand.

Similarly, with David. Hashem concealed His face for a moment and suddenly, out of nowhere, from the least plausible place, there sprouted forth one of the greatest troubles David had in his life. It wasn't from a competitor, from Shaul Hamelech. It wasn't from Amon or Moav, the nations who always were hostile and who hated the Jewish people. It was from his own house! His own son, Avshalom, made a rebellion against him, and now David was fleeing to save his life. It came out of nowhere, a bombshell. David's own son, Avshalom! And Avshalom had the best advisors urging him to get rid of his father before he got away.

David fled and took nothing with him. He didn't have any army. He didn't have a retinue. He fled with just a few loyal people. And as he ran, he wept. He didn't weep merely to the skies or to the ground. He was weeping and crying to Hashem. He said, "*Hashem, birtzoncha he'emadeta l'hareri oz*—it was with Your will alone that You established my mountain with strength" (ibid. 30:8). And now I see that I'm nothing without You.

David said to Hashem at that time, "*Ma betza b'dami*—what profit will You gain from killing me?" (ibid. 30:10). If Avshalom and his counselors catch up with me and take off my head, what will You gain, Hashem? "*B'rideti el shachas, hayodcha afar*—if I go down to the grave, will the dust praise You?" (ibid.). A dead David is not going to praise You. "*Hayagid amitecha*—will he relate the truth about You?" (ibid.).

"*Shema, Hashem, v'chaneini; Hashem, heyei ozer li*—Listen, Hashem, and spare me; be a help to me." David didn't say it as briefly as it's said here. He said a lot more. As he was going and weeping, he was crying out these words and a lot more for miles and miles. It wasn't easy going. Shimi ben Gera (the Torah-teacher of David's son Shlomo) came from the town of Bachurim in Binyamin and said, "Get out of here, you bloody murderer! Now you're getting what you deserved!" He picked up dirt and threw it at David's head (II *Shmuel* 16:7–8). It's bad enough he didn't offer him anything to drink. He didn't say, "Do you want something to eat, O King?" No, he gave him dirt. The few loyal people with David wanted to kill Shimi, but David said not to touch him. "Hashem told him to curse me" (II *Shmuel* 16:10). I'm getting what I deserved.

During his entire escape, David was crying out and saying, "Now I see that until now I was not secure. I was nobody. I wasn't victorious.

I wasn't a great king. I wasn't a conqueror. I wasn't wise. I was nothing. It's You, Hashem, Who established my mountain with strength."

What happened in the end? Avshalom went to battle against his father, and as he was riding through the forest, his hair got caught in a low-hanging branch. He was a *nazir* and had beautiful, flowing locks of long hair, for which the people admired him as a holy man. Avshalom was a *talmid chacham*, and he had declared his father a wicked man based on the counsel of the people who engineered the rebellion. Now he was pursuing his father. As he was galloping through the woods with his beautiful hair blowing in the wind behind him, it got caught in the branches and his horse kept running, leaving him hanging. David's general Yoav saw him and attacked. David had given orders not to touch him, but Yoav didn't obey. He riddled Avshalom's body with spears, making a sieve out of him.

After the demise of Avshalom, with the rebellion quashed, David came back to Yerushalayim, more powerful than ever. Yet he said to Hashem, "*You* turned my mourning into dancing for me. *You* took off my sackcloth and girded me with joy" (*Tehillim* 30:12). He didn't take credit. It was all Hashem. He was more aware of and grateful to Hashem than ever. "I'm dedicating everything to You, to sing to You about Your glory and not be quiet. I'm going to thank You forever and ever" (ibid. 30:13). That's the vow he made. And that's why this is printed in the *siddur* at the beginning of our prayers. Whenever Jews—wherever they are and whenever they lived—say this *mizmor* every morning, they're fulfilling David's vow and internalizing the lesson that David learned.

Q **I know a man who's been ill for months. Now his business is failing and he's terribly depressed. Is there hope for him?**

And the answer is that it would have been much better if such a man would have prepared himself in the days when things were going well so that when a crunch came, he'd be able to resist. It says in *Koheles*, "On a good day, be happy" (*Koheles* 7:14). Isn't that superfluous to say? But he means that when things are going well, that's when you should prepare. That's when you should gather for the future all the confidence and happiness you can. That's the best time to understand the ways of Hashem and learn what life is all about. If you do that, you might understand someday that even misfortune is a great benefit.

Let's say this man learned in his younger days that Hashem sometimes sends suffering to make him better. Suffering humbles him, and he cries out to Hashem as a result of his *tzaros*. Crying out to Hashem is a tremendous achievement because you're becoming aware of Hashem. Before, when things were going well, you didn't think about Him. But this man, who took the advice of *Koheles*, learned in his good days all these ideas. It's easier to learn about *tzaros* when you have no *tzaros*. When the *tzaros* come, it's more difficult.

When a man has learned in his youthful days, then when the misfortune comes upon him, he's prepared. First, he understands that it's a preparation. All the *yissurim* are going to be an atonement for his sins. He'll be able to enter the next world purified of his *aveiros* because they were atoned for by his sufferings.

Second, his arrogance—the *ga'avah* that almost everybody suffers—was erased from his mind because a sick man cannot feel arrogant.

Third, all the foolish ambitions, hopes, and desires of human beings—to become rich someday, to have pleasures, and who knows what else—it's all smashed by the waves of misfortunes that come in life. Therefore, he learns that life is not merely about seeking good times. He learns that life is for achievement. And some of the biggest achievements are when he has *tzaros*.

People don't like to hear that, so I'll tell you again what I always say here. Using happiness to become greater and greater is the very best thing. But how many people do that? On the contrary, people are spoiled by happiness. Misfortune is an opportunity to gain, in a short time, that which you couldn't gain before for many years.

Here's a man who's sick, and his business is failing, too. Everything is dropping out from beneath him. He shouldn't think, *chas v'shalom,* that life is not worth living. On the contrary, he should think, "I hope I can live longer, because every day that I'm alive, I'm *mechaper*, I'm atoning. And I'm getting a perfection of *anavah*, of humility. I'm becoming a broken soul." Hashem loves the broken one. "Hashem is close to the broken man, to those who are low of spirit" (*Tehillim* 34:19). "The Shechinah is over the head of a sick man" (*Shabbos* 12b). He's coming closer to Hashem. Isn't that worthwhile?

Suffering itself is a big achievement. It's not so easy to tell that to a man, but if he would listen it would be a blessing for him. He would understand that when he gets the hard knocks of life, the hard knocks really are the blessings of life.

When a man is rich and having good times and getting honor from all sides, those are the worst things that can happen to him—unless he has learned the secrets of using that happiness to sing to Hashem. That's the greatest success. "If you sing to Hashem in this world, you'll sing in the World to Come, too" (*Sanhedrin* 91b). If you learn to be happy and thank Hashem, to be grateful for everything, that's your true success in this world.

You're eating breakfast—ah! Did you ever think about eating breakfast? You have teeth to eat breakfast! Even if you have false teeth, at least you have something to eat breakfast with. And you're eating breakfast! It means you *have* some breakfast to eat!

In Europe, some people were so poor they never ate bread during the week—only on Shabbos. During the week, they only made *Borei pri ha'adamah* or *Shehakol*. Only on Shabbos did they make *Hamotzi lechem min ha'aretz*. To eat bread was a privilege. Wheat bread! Wheat bread was a privilege! When I was in Europe, an old man told me that when he used to ask his mother for another piece of bread, she couldn't give him a second piece. That's how it used to be.

You have enough bread to eat? You have teeth to be able to eat? Did you ever stop and think how grateful you have to be to Hashem? You should sit at the table and sing to Hashem at breakfast. You should thank Him with a full heart—not merely Birkas Hamazon that you say like a tape recorder. No! You're talking to Someone! Say, "I thank

You, Hashem! I'm eating *l'shem Shamayim*! I'm eating to serve You and sing to You." If you can do that, it's the biggest success.

But suppose a man is so sick he can't eat—even then, he's not a failure. He should thank Hashem for his *tzaros*. "A man is obligated to make a blessing over misfortune just as he makes a blessing over good" (*Brachos* 54a). Misfortune is a stroke of good luck. He now becomes somebody beloved by Hashem. Hashem loves those who are suffering. "Hashem will support him on his couch of pain" (*Tehillim* 41:3). Hashem is with him. Why? Because Hashem especially loves people who are not proud. He loves people who are not arrogant. He loves those who are beaten down and feel low. He's with them.

You should use that and feel it's a gift. The more you live in these circumstances, the better you are becoming. Therefore, I say once more to this man—on the contrary, thank Hashem for what He sent upon you. He's making you more perfect than you could have ever become in a time of success and happiness.

Q **Does it pay to complain about your difficulties?**

It depends. If you're going to put an address on it—if you're going to turn to Hashem—it's never wasted. Otherwise, if you bellyache, all you'll accomplish is being a grouch. You're just making the situation worse. If you don't turn to Hashem, it's like dropping an envelope without an address into the mailbox. It's a wasted effort.

Does that mean you have to complain? The truth is that very many times if you try to overlook your issues, it's much easier because the more you talk about it, the more it's going to hurt. That's a big rule in troubles. The more you discuss your troubles, the more you're going to be troubled.

It's easy to find a good excuse to complain—but complaints can make your life miserable. If you must complain, complain to Hashem. When you complain with an address, it's not a waste because you find favor in the eyes of Hashem.

Q Doesn't the Gemara say that if a man has worry in his heart, he should talk it over with others?

The Gemara says, "*Da'agah b'leiv ish, yesichenah l'acheirim*—if a man has some worry in his heart, he should speak it out to others" (*Sanhedrin* 100b). So why did I say that by complaining a person makes things worse?

There's a big difference between complaining and speaking to other people. If you complain to other people, all you're doing is putting a load on that person, too. If you'll tell them, "I had a bad day today. It was dark and rainy and everything I tried didn't work out," all you're doing is making that person also lose heart. You're discouraging him.

But if there's some problem that's pressing on you—not a complaint, not a matter of being dissatisfied—and you discuss the problem with somebody else who is capable, then that person might suggest ways and means that could help you easily solve or dodge that problem. That's what the Gemara means.

Now, the truth is that even if you complain to somebody else, he might be able to turn around your words and change your thoughts so that you'll stop complaining. But "*da'agah b'leiv ish*" doesn't refer to that. It's not talking about complaining. It refers to trying to solve problems.

That's an important point. Many people go around laden with worries that are really nothing. They make mountains out of molehills.

The first way to deal with worry is the way you deal with hiccups. Don't wait. As soon as it begins, control it. If you let it continue, it will be difficult to get rid of. When hiccups begin, you must hold your breath and wait till they pass. Once you let them get a foothold, they're much harder to get rid of. The same with worry. Once it starts and you dwell on it, it finds a toehold in your mind and doesn't let go. Therefore, as soon as possible, knock it out of your mind. The earlier you battle against worry, the more you'll succeed.

That's one way. Another way is by articulating your worry. That doesn't mean you will get rid of it. It depends on who you're speaking to. If you speak to the wrong people, they might make you more worried. But speak to people who are wise, who can give you wise counsel, who can explain to you why there's nothing to worry about. So if you have a worry in your mind, seek out some wise person and talk over your worries with him.

Q **How should we react to turmoil in the world?**

When Haman issued his decree, what did the Jews do? Did they make demonstrations in front of Achashverosh's palace? Did they get together and pass resolutions and send letters? No, they got together and cried out to Hashem.

The purpose of unrest is to come to the realization that we have no security. Jews don't have security in any country. It's a great error to think otherwise. When we fall into such an error, Hashem sends a reminder that the only true security is with Him.

Rabba bar Bar-Chana tells of an experience he had (*Bava Basra* 73b). He was traveling on a ship and they were out at sea many weeks without ever seeing dry land. All of a sudden the lookout cried out, "Land ahead!" Everybody rushed to look. Yes, there was land. It wasn't much, but even a little island was a great blessing. They were so happy. Immediately the captain gave orders to drop anchor, and everybody got off. Everybody rejoiced in the feeling of land under their feet.

After a little while, they decided to build a bonfire. Suddenly, the whole island rumbled. Then it turned over and tossed them into the sea. They discovered that it wasn't an island after all—it was a huge whale! When it felt its back being burned, it turned over and dumped them into the sea. If the boat had been far away, they would have been lost.

This story is a *mashal*. Jews are told that in *galus*, we're never going to have a place where we can rest. Don't deceive yourself; don't keep making that error, generation after generation. There will never be a country where you're going to be secure. When there's civil unrest and trouble, our first reaction must be to cry out to Hashem and remember that He is behind everything. That's the purpose of the trouble—to remember Him and realize that He's in control. He and only He is in control. Our only security is in remembering Hashem. Our only insecurity is forgetting Him.

Q **Was Leah Greater than Rochel? If so, what made her greater?**

Leah understood the greatness of Yaakov Avinu and aspired to be a mother of Beis Yisrael. She knew there would be greatness in her posterity, and she wanted to live up to that destiny as much as she possibly could. But she knew she was his second choice. We hear her anguish in all her prayers. "Maybe this time my husband will join me" (*Bereishis* 29:34). "Hashem has seen my humiliation; maybe now my husband will love me" (ibid. 32). "Hashem has heard that I am unloved" (ibid. 33). My heart aches when I read Leah's words. Again and again, this great woman expressed her heartache to Hashem. She poured out her heart in *tefillah*.

Now, it doesn't mean that Rochel didn't *daven*, but Leah davened even more. And the reason for that is because she suffered more. Because of her suffering, she wept and prayed and strived to be better. It's an important principle you're hearing now. When people have certain challenges, they will try to compensate. That's exactly what Leah did. She didn't sulk and complain about her status in the house. Instead, she made use of it to grow even greater. How she reacted to her suffering is what made her great!

I can't tell you all the details of how she compensated for the awareness that she was the less favored wife. But there's no question that Leah, as a result of her handicap in that house, strove more than Rochel to be an ideal wife and an ideal mother. Of course, she davened with all her heart to find favor in Yaakov's eyes, as well as for children, but she also exerted herself in her behavior, in how she spoke to Yaakov, even in how she fulfilled all her household duties.

I'm sure that both these great women strove to attain perfection in character. That's what all the Avos and Imahos did. Like the Rambam says, they felt that they were standing before Hashem twenty-four hours a day. But Leah was standing before Hashem more than twenty-four hours a day! She went beyond her limits and tried to make up for her encumbrance, and to excel. She strove with all her might to be the very best person she could be.

That's why Hashem rewarded her that she attained a greater perfection than Rochel. Now, this doesn't mean that Rochel wasn't better. Rochel started out being better, and in a certain sense she was always better. That's why she was chosen in the first place. But because Leah wasn't chosen, she struggled mightily to become better and better, and Hashem helped her to become more and more perfect. The fact that Leah made use of her disadvantages was her success.

And what was the end? The end was that Rochel passed away early, and Leah was the one who was buried together with Yaakov Avinu in the Me'aras Hamachpeilah. It's a remarkable end to the story. Leah was the one who lived long enough to be buried together with her husband. I want to tell you a little secret. I think one of the reasons Rochel passed away early was to give Leah her *bakashah*, to give her what she desired so much and worked so hard for—to remain with her husband, to be his main wife. It's not the only reason, but I think it's one of the reasons. I suspect that. When you visit Me'aras Hamachpeilah where the Avos are buried, it's Leah who's buried with Yaakov. Rochel is not there. Of course, she's together with him forever and ever in the next world, but the bodies of Yaakov and Leah are buried together in this world and that's also very important. That means something, too. It's a permanent monument to that great lesson that Hashem wants you to learn—that even though you thought that Rochel was the chosen one (and actually she was), Hashem said, "No. That's why I brought Leah in by trickery, so that she should have the opportunity to become the chosen one!"

As a result of what Leah accomplished, she was rewarded that her sons forever and ever would be the main body of the Am Yisrael. Who are the Jewish people today? We're called "Yehudim." The name carried by the Jewish people today came from Leah's lips—Jew, *Juif*, *Jude*, Yid, Yehudi. All these names come from the name Leah gave to her child, Yehudah, because to a great extent the Am Yisrael is made up of Leah's children. Of course, we give Rochel credit as well; she also contributed to our people. We still have some among us who are from Rochel's children. None of the *shevatim* went lost entirely because Yirmiyah Hanavi brought back some members from every *shevet* (*Megillah* 14b). But it's a minority. Other than a few exceptions, the great masses of the Am Yisrael come from Leah.

It's remarkable that when we look around at the Am Yisrael, now and throughout most of our nation's history, we see the offspring of Leah. Until Mashiach comes and reunites all the *shevatim* in Eretz Yisrael, we will be called after Leah's son Yehudah. We're all called Yehudim because, for the most part, we are not the children of Rochel. Even though we look back to Rochel with the greatest respect, to this day and until the time of Mashiach, Leah is the mother of Beis Yisrael—because of the power of her *tefillos*.

BRACHOS

Q What's the purpose of saying *brachos*?

In *parshas Eikev*, Moshe Rabbeinu declares, "What does Hashem want from you? Only to fear Hashem your G-d, and to walk in all His ways, and to love Him, and to serve Hashem your G-d with all your heart and with all your soul, and to keep all the *mitzvos* of Hashem and to keep all of His laws" (*Devarim* 10:12–13). The *Mesillas Yesharim (Hakdamah)* explains that in this *passuk* we have all the subjects that are necessary for *shleimus amiti*, for "true perfection" in *avodas Hashem*. All of the components of the complete service that is pleasing to Hashem.

There's *yirah*—which means being aware of Hashem, feeling His presence at all times—and "*laleches b'chol d'rachav*—walking in His ways," which means you have to study His ways to know them, and then emulate those ways. But that's only the beginning. Hashem wants us "*l'ahavah oso*—to love Him," which the *Chovos Halevavos* and the Rambam say is the highest of all *madreigos*. And the list goes on: "perfection of your heart in His service," which means not to do it with 10 percent or 50 percent of your mind, but 100 percent! And "to keep all the *mitzvos*," which means you have to learn them all and keep them.

There's a lot in that *passuk*—He's asking a lot of things from you. It's a load of work, a program for a lifetime. The path to perfection isn't easy. Now, one way to gird your loins for this task is to learn Shas. Learning Shas, learning the whole Talmud, will certainly bring you close to Hashem. Only that you have to prepare yourself for a long career of hard work. It entails many difficulties and a great deal of self-denial.

There are other ways, as well, paths that require much heroism and heavy labor. You'll have to learn *Mesillas Yesharim*, *Sha'arei Teshuvah*, and the *Chovos Halevavos* from cover to cover. Many times! Other *sefarim* as well. It will certainly take some heavy lifting to achieve that.

Yet, how does Hashem introduce us to all of these great ideals? With the following words—"What is it that He's asking of you already? Only this ..." And that's hard to understand because we see that what

Hashem wants of you is everything! It's a question that anyone reading the Chumash should ask, and in fact the Gemara (*Megillah* 25a) asks it like this: "Is *yiras Hashem*"—that means the whole program enumerated in the *passuk*—"such a small thing?" If it wasn't easy, if from some angle there wasn't easy access to this greatness, it wouldn't make sense for the Torah to use such words. So, it pays for us to hear what this "easy" path is. Whether it actually is an easy way to come close to Hashem or it's just relatively easier, it's something we need to learn about.

Now, the Gemara's answer there is important and we'll discuss it another time, but for now we'll study the *p'shuto shel mikra*, which makes all of these great accomplishments seem easy.

The Gemara in *Menachos* (43b) says: "Rabbi Meir said, 'Everyone is obligated to make one hundred *brachos* every day.'" And he quotes our *passuk*, "What does *Hashem Elokecha* require of you?" Rabbi Meir says: Don't read the word "*Mah*—What" does He wants of you; rather, read it as "*mei'ah*—one hundred" blessings from you. Instead of *mem hei*, we stick in an *alef* and now it reads "*mei'ah*, a hundred."

Now, it's important to understand that all the *drashos* of Chazal are inherent in the plain meaning. It's not merely a memory aid; it's actually included in the *p'shat* of the *passuk*. So we must understand that this verse, "What does Hashem want from you?" includes the duty of saying one hundred *brachos*. Rabbi Meir used the sharp and witty style of the Sages to make a play on words. Do you know the easy way to come close to Hashem? Instead of saying *Mah*, which literally means "what" but in this context means "easy," say *mei'ah*—"one hundred" *brachos*. That's the key. That's the easy way to come to all those great perfections enumerated in the *passuk*.

Now, whether it means technical *brachos*, or saying your own words, "I thank You, Hashem, for this; I thank You for that," it's all included. One hundred times a day we have to thank Hashem, and that's going to bring you to acquire all of the great qualities. The *hakdamah*, the preface to *yirah* and *ahavah* and all good things in that *passuk*, is to make one hundred *brachos* every day.

You'll say I'm exaggerating—a hundred *brachos* a day is the key to perfection?! Making *brachos* is A, B, C. It's kindergarten talk! But that's what Rabbi Meir is telling us here. He's telling us that the way to come close to Hashem and acquire "all the components of service that are pleasing to Hashem" spelled out in that *passuk* is by means of saying an expression of thanks to Hashem one hundred times every day.

That's the way! If you're looking for the easy way path to perfection, you just heard it here. You can tell your friends about it, too. "*Mah Hashem Elokecha sho'el mei'imach*—What does Hashem want from you?" "*Ki im*—just to say a hundred *brachos* a day."

Now, don't think you can just get up and go home at this point. Don't think you know all about it. No, it's only the beginning of the talk and it needs an explanation. You must act like you never heard the term "*brachos*" before. You'll have to act like you just became *geirim*, and now for the first time in your life you're hearing there's such a thing as *brachos*. Because a *brachah* isn't just mumbling some words, "*Baruch Atah, Hashem*," and you're finished. Even if you're not mumbling—even if you're saying the words slowly, with *peirush hamilos*—even that isn't the *brachah* we're talking about here.

What Rabbi Meir is telling us is that one hundred times a day, *you must enjoy this world and feel gratitude to Hashem.*

After all, what is a *brachah*? It's an expression of gratitude. Otherwise, it's not a *brachah*. It's just words. Of course, you fulfill your obligation *al pi halachah*; you won't make a second one. But just fulfilling the letter of the law is not what the Torah meant, and it's not what Rabbi Meir is talking about. The foundation of everything, of all service to Hashem, is to make *brachos*. And what is the purpose of these blessings? To enjoy the kindliness of Hashem.

The great tragedy of mankind is that we ignore the happiness of life. Hashem especially designed this world for happiness and pleasure. People overlook that; they're ignorant of it. It's such a sadness, such a pity. If I had *koach,* and if people would listen to me, *bli neder*, I would run out in the street and tell people how to enjoy this world all day long. Making *brachos* comes afterwards. First of all, open your eyes and appreciate what you possess.

Q What benefit do we get from saying *brachos*?

I'll tell you a secret now, something I heard from my *rebbi* in Slabodka. In the *Kuzari* (3:13–17), there is a remarkable statement. It says that one of the reasons for our *brachos* is that "it increases your pleasure when you say blessings." You hear that? Eating an apple is a pleasure, but what type of pleasure is it if you don't concentrate on enjoying it? Therefore, the *Kuzari* says that one of the reasons for our *brachos* is to enhance our pleasure. Before you eat the apple, stop and feel gratitude for it. Ah, now you're enjoying it!

But my *rebbi*, *zt"l*, argued on the *Kuzari*. He said it's not "one of the reasons"—it's *the* reason.

Q Why should we be grateful?

That's something many people don't understand at all. People ask me all the time: "What is Hashem giving me?" Last week, a young man was walking on Kings Highway with me and asked, "Why should I be grateful to Hashem?" I took a look at him. He wasn't using crutches. He didn't have braces on his feet. He didn't have a brace to hold his neck up. He seemed to have a full set of teeth—at least, they didn't look like false teeth. He looked to be quite well-nourished, as well, and he didn't seem to have slept last night on a park bench, either. Probably he had bathed that morning, too. And he was clothed. Yet, this *yeshiva man* asked me, "Why should I be grateful to Hashem?" He was serious. He was asking with sincerity.

It's the same as a girl of sixteen who refuses to wash the dishes. "What am I getting out of you?" she says to her parents. The nice ones don't say it, but they still think it. She refuses to even pick up her own stockings in the morning when she runs off. She refuses to bring the garbage down. She doesn't do a thing in the house. She only has one complaint: "What are you doing for me?" That means, besides for giving me free lodging—no rent is charged for the bed she sleeps in—and besides giving me three meals a day and clothing, what else are you doing for me? Besides paying her doctor bills, besides paying for dental care, besides paying her Bais Yaakov tuition. When she washes her face, when she puts on the light in her room, she's using her father's hard-earned money.

You shake your head, "tsk, tsk," when you hear about this inconsiderate girl, but actually she's just a *mashal* for all of us. Most people in this world—I'm talking about even the good ones—think Hashem is not giving them anything. *What am I getting from You?* they're thinking. They won't tell you that. They have some self-esteem. But that's what they're thinking. *What is Hashem doing for me?* I'm afraid that most of us, even though we're polite enough not to say that out loud, are thinking that in our heart.

I once heard from one of my *rebbeim*, Rav Avraham Grodzinski, *zt"l*, something I want to repeat. A Slabodka *yeshiva man* came back to the yeshiva for a visit. When Reb Avraham saw this old *talmid*, he asked, "How are things going?" This man said as follows: "In *ruchniyus, baruch Hashem*! But in *gashmiyus*, not so good; it could be better." That's what the ex-*yeshiva man* told Reb Avraham.

Later, Reb Avraham interpreted that for us. He told us it meant like this: "As far as what I'm doing for Hashem, it's pretty good, can't complain." He's patting himself on the back, "Good job!" His "In *ruchniyus, baruch Hashem*!" means "*Baruch anochi*, Blessed am *I*." That's what it means. But as far as what Hashem is doing for me, He's a little bit behind. "In *gashmiyus*, could be better" means, "What Hashem is doing for me still leaves room for improvement." That's what he means. "Nu, Hashem, when will You produce already?!" Look at this *tzaddik* who's suffering in this world. He's just eating meals every day. He's just sleeping in a bed every night. He's just alive. What are You giving him?

It's no wonder we don't know what a hundred *brachos* are all about. Some think it's a matter of counting. They think it's about the number. Sixteen *Birchos Hashachar*, five more for *Birchos haTorah*, *Asher Yatzar* and *netilas yadayim*, that's twenty-one. Fifty-seven more for three Shemoneh Esreis, that's seventy-eight. I'll *bentch* once—that's another four. And before you know it, you've reached your quota. No, that's not what Rabbi Meir meant!

A hundred *brachos* means that one hundred times every day you have to make yourself aware of the gifts you're enjoying all the time. And if that's the case, we have a lot to talk about because our job now is to discover all these gifts. What *is* Hashem doing for us? That's the great treasure we have to uncover.

But people are asleep. They sleepwalk through life. Unaware of the great treasures they already possess, the great treasures all around. Here is a man standing up to his waist in a stream of good clean water, but as you drive by he begs you, "Please, stop! Please get out of your car and give me a drink." You say to yourself, "This man is crazy as could be! He's standing up to his waist in pure water. Bend over and drink!" People are standing up to their waist in water, but they don't bother to bend down and drink. That's the first thing we have to learn.

Q **Can you give us a practical program to learn to enjoy life?**

Imagine we have an appointment to meet tomorrow morning on the corner of Avenue R and Ocean Parkway. Six o'clock in the morning—that's the best time of the day. We'll walk together on the avenue and we'll study the happiness of life.

Before we meet up, you're going to have to wake up and get out of bed. It won't be much of a walk if you don't wake up. You know that some people won't wake up this morning. I remember once there was a member in my synagogue who went to sleep. In the morning, his wife came and said, "Mordechai! Wake up!" He didn't move. It was all over. This happened to a young man, by the way. Mordechai was a young man. Don't take it for granted! So when tomorrow comes, be enthusiastic in expressing your gratitude.

As soon as you open your eyes, give thanks to Hashem that He allowed you get up in the morning. You should be excited! "*Modeh ani l'fanecha, Melech chai v'kayam, shehechezarta bi nishmasi b'chemlah, rabbah emunasecha!*—I thank You, O King Who lives forever and endures, for returning my life to me with compassion. How great is Your steadfastness!" Thank Hashem for waking you up this morning. When you think about this, it's actually fun to get up in the morning—only nobody thinks about it! It's something you should practice enjoying.

Did you ever go to a *shivah* house and have nothing to talk about? You come in and you walk out. It's still a *mitzvah*, but there's more you can accomplish. What's the first thing to think when you walk out? "*Baruch Hashem*, I'm alive!" You hear the *chiddush*? When you're *menachem avel*, the first thing to think about when you walk out is—"*Baruch Hashem*, I'm alive!"

The thinking person doesn't wait for the *shivah* house, *Rachmana litzlan*. That's how he wakes up every morning! "*Baruch Hashem*, I'm alive!" He just discovered the happy news that he woke up again! It's a *simchah*, a real happiness!

Asher Yatzar

Now that you're reeling in joy from appreciation of what it means to be alive, you go to the bathroom. Ah, the pleasure of going to the bathroom. Don't say, "It's just Nature." For a lot of people, it's not natural. If it goes smoothly for you, enjoy the moment. Don't be afraid to enjoy. Don't be ashamed to enjoy what Hashem is giving you. That's the purpose of all these functions.

I know a very wealthy man who cannot go to the bathroom. He has no kidneys. If he could walk into a bathroom and function like an ordinary person, he'd be delirious with happiness. He told me he remembers the good old days when he could urinate normally. Oh, what a happiness it was then! If he would come here and teach us how to say *Asher Yatzar*, that would be a lesson! You come out and mumble, "*Muh, muh, muh, muh*"?! That's how you say thank you?! If you're happy, you don't just say *Asher Yatzar*. You *sing* it!

Take my word for it. If you put your mind to it, it's a tremendous happiness. The Gemara (*Brachos* 57b) says that going to the bathroom is a taste of Olam Haba. It's such a pleasure! Of course, if you didn't study it, if you don't think about it, there's nothing to sing about. Now, mumbling a *brachah* is better than nothing. You're at least a *frum* Jew if you mumble the *brachah*, but it's a pity. You're losing the great opportunity of achieving all the perfection that *mei'ah brachos* can bring to a person.

Appreciating Small Miracles

Even walking to the bathroom is a *ta'anug*, a pleasure. Think for a moment that Hashem is giving you the blessing that you're able to move your feet. You can move your hips. They swing effortlessly in their sockets. You can move your knees, and your ankles, and your toes, each in its own socket. All these sockets are functioning perfectly! Not to mention the coordination of the muscles. Every muscle that's extended has another muscle pulling it in the opposite direction. You're a trapeze artist when you walk. You balance yourself and move with perfect ease and agility.

As you walk, you should be enjoying those gifts. That feeling should come *before* the *brachah*. First you have to enjoy the marvelous gifts that Hashem is giving you. "*Baruch Atah, Hashem, hameichin mitzadei gaver*—Blessed are You, Hashem, Who prepares the steps of a man." Thank You, Hashem, for this pleasure of being able to walk normally. There are a lot of people who can't. There are some people whose toes cannot function. Everything else is perfect, but if their toes are fused, they won't move in their sockets properly. If the ankle is fused, it won't move. Even if the knee is a tiny bit off-kilter, it can be excruciatingly painful to move it. Such people have very great suffering.

The World Is Made for Me

Now, suppose you are able to walk out of your home, and we meet on Ocean Parkway for our walking club. The sun is coming up now, and we see a beautiful blue sky. Don't miss that opportunity! We have to say, "The sky is a beautiful blue, and Hashem made it that way because He wants us to enjoy it. That's the purpose, and I'm not going to let it go to waste." Now, that's the right attitude. "Hashem is painting a blue sky for me to enjoy." Once you get that attitude, you're looking at the universe with the right perspective.

Don't say, "Well, there are a lot of other people in this world besides me. Did He make the sky blue just for me?" The answer is, yes. That's what the Gemara says (*Brachos* 58a)—"What does a good guest say when he walks into a house and sees a table spread with all good things?" He says, 'Whatever the host labored to do, he did only for me.'" As the good guest walks in and sees cucumbers, egg salad, chopped liver, whiskey, cake, etc., he says about every item he sees, "The host put it there for me."

Now, that doesn't mean he should eat it all up. That's not the intent. What it's telling you is that, as you look at it, you're expected to squeeze all the enjoyment you can from what you see, and feel gratitude. You have to think, "The host put it there for me to enjoy."

Once you know that, you begin to enjoy everything. You open your eyes, and you see all around you glorious, beautiful things. There are beautiful gardens on Ocean Parkway. Some of our neighbors hire gardeners. It costs them a lot of money to tend their gardens. As you pass by, don't think, "Well, what do I get out of it? It's not for me." No, the Gemara says that's what a bad guest says. A bad guest says, "Whatever the host did, he did for himself. He didn't do it for me."

It's for you. Yes, you! "It's all done for me," you should think. Everything is for me. That's how you should walk in this world. That's why man was created at first alone—so that everyone should say, "It's for me" (*Sanhedrin* 37a). The gardens on Ocean Parkway are for me. I enjoy the gardens more than the homeowner who pays thousands of dollars to the gardener. Keep your money in your pocket but put all these things in your head and in your heart, and become happy by looking at them. Look at the gardens. They didn't cost you a penny. The gardener is breaking his back pulling up weeds, and as we pass by we enjoy it no end. The grass is beautiful. The colorful flowers are a pleasure to look at. Ah, ah, ah! How nice it is!

This is the royal road to greatness. Isn't the road to perfection fun? Because while you're doing that, you're becoming happier and happier. You're becoming an *ashir*, a rich man, without spending a penny.

"Who is rich?" It's up here [pointing at his head]. Your wealth is in your mind. And your money remains in your pocket.

Therefore, as we walk out into the world and see the things of the world, we must understand that they're for us. They're all for us. The fact that it's for someone else, too, doesn't detract from that. It's for you. As you walk out and look up and enjoy the blue of the sky, and as you pass by the beautiful gardens, think that noble thought.

These are some practical things you can work on. But even though this is the "easy" path to greatness, it still takes work. It takes practice. Think: Why is the sky such a beautiful sapphire blue? I'll tell you a secret. There's a reason why it's blue. It's for you to enjoy it, because the color blue is soft and sweet on the eyes (*Chovos Halevavos, Sha'ar Habechinah* 5). And you're expected to enjoy it. Isn't that a good thing to practice? See if you can do it tomorrow morning.

Appreciating Gray Skies

Now, let's say our club walks out and this time the sky isn't blue. Instead, it's overcast with gray clouds. Oooh! That's a glorious opportunity! "He who covers the skies with clouds is preparing rain for the earth" (*Tehillim* 147:8). What does that mean? Who cares what He prepares? Is the fact that He prepares rain important?!

Yes! Gray skies are not gray. Cloudy skies mean yellow oranges, pink peaches with rosy cheeks, red apples, purple grapes—they all come from rain! All good things come from rain. David Hamelech looked at the clouds, felt gratitude, and said, "Don't make any mistake about it. He's covering the skies with clouds, and I thank Him for that!"

Therefore, whether the sky is blue or gray, it's an opportunity for happiness. We have to study the sky until it finally creates an impression that causes us joy. If you work on this again and again, and finally a sapphire blue sky makes you happy, you know that you're getting there. There's no *brachah* that you make on the sky, but you have to feel gratitude! You have to say, "Thank You, Hashem, for making me happy by means of Your beautiful sky."

 Opening Our Eyes to the Miracle of Sight

How do you see the sky, anyhow? You can't accomplish that without eyes. Ah, eyes! Ay yay yay, eyes! Ribbono Shel Olam, what would I do without my eyes?!

We must practice enjoying our eyes. You're going to have to learn to be happy that you have eyes. Can we even describe the happiness of seeing? It's impossible to describe that pleasure. You see life, you see movement, you see color, you see your family, you see the world—what a happiness it is!

It takes a long time for these things to penetrate our thick skulls. But if you want to understand that it's a very great happiness, all you have to do is encounter a man with a white stick tapping his way down the street. Tap, tap, tap, tap, tap. Take a good look at him. You think it's an accident that he came across your path? Hashem saw that you're slow in understanding, so He sent this man to teach you a lesson. You see him at the street corner. Someone has to take him by his arm and bring him across. Ay yay yay, what a pity. What a tragedy!

The next time you see a man tapping his way with his stick, don't let that opportunity go by. It's a gift *min haShamayim* for you. You have to thank Hashem that you can see. Hashem has sent that on purpose for you to see and look. "Ooh, I thank You, Hashem—I'm able to see!"

Think—what would that man say if he could suddenly get a pair of eyes like yours? How would he make a *brachah*? Would he mumble, "*Baruch Atah, Hashem . . . pokei'ach ivrim*"? That's how they say it in shul in the morning. Even the best rattle it off! Oh, no! Oh, no! Don't tell me you made that *brachah* this morning and counted it toward your hundred *brachos*! Did you think about what you were saying? Technically, maybe it's a *brachah* and you can count it, but that's not how we enjoy a gift.

A man who appreciates his eyes says thank you like a man drinking the most precious champagne, sipping every word. *Baruch—ah, ah, ah! Atah! Hashem!* Every word is a diamond! The man tapping his way on the street would shell out hundreds of thousands of dollars to a surgeon if he could have working eyes. He'd be eternally grateful to him. He'd call him up every year on the *yahrzeit* of his operation. And Hashem gave them to you for nothing. Hashem isn't sending you bills. He doesn't ask anything from you—except that you should enjoy your eyes. He doesn't want a mumbled *brachah*. That's not what He's asking. He wants you to enjoy the gift. He wants you to be so happy with your eyes that you *feel* like making a *brachah*! Learn to be happy that you can see. That's a big job!

The Happiness of Teeth

As our walking club is walking down the street, don't forget that you have coins in your pocket. Let's say you have a pocket full of quarters, and the change is jingling in your pocket—it feels good. It sounds good. But even if you have nothing in your pocket, you still have everything. You may have no money to jingle, but you have teeth to click. Teeth are better than money!

In the olden days, when somebody grew old and had no teeth, he was finished with life. If he had a nice granddaughter, she'd take an apple, scrape off some mush and give it to her old *zeidy*. But you young fellows, you're rich! You have a mouth full of teeth! Ay yay yay, teeth! What a happiness to have teeth! If you're eating with your own teeth, then you're a lucky fellow—you already have everything.

Even false teeth. You have false teeth? Thank Him! Whether you have false teeth or your own teeth, you have to study them. You have to be rich in the knowledge that you have teeth. A mouth full of teeth is a happiness!

Thanking Hashem for Man-Made Things

Now, the day is almost over, and the sun is going down. All good things have to come to an end, and our walking club has to break up for the night. We all have to go home. Our wives and children are waiting for us, so our laboratory of learning how to enjoy the gifts of Hashem must end now. Tomorrow morning, we can meet again.

But no! It's not over yet. When you walk into the hallway of your home and turn on the switch, you're suddenly bathed in light. Do you thank Him for electric lights? Electric light is a very good thing.

When I was a little boy, we didn't have electric lights — only gas lights! I remember that! The house didn't have electricity. And then electricity came. It was like sunshine in the middle of the night.

How can you live without thanking Hashem for electric lights? Every *motza'ei Shabbos* you say the *brachah*, "*Borei me'orei ha'aish.*" You're thanking Hashem for artificial light. People don't know what that *brachah* is all about. They think it's just a ceremony. No, "*Borei me'orei ha'aish*" means you're thanking Hashem for artificial light. If you spend a little time thinking about how much you benefit from artificial light, you'll love Hashem for that. "I'm thanking You, Hashem, for all forms of artificial light — fire, incandescent, fluorescent, everything."

Besides the light in the house, you have a warm home. Where does the warmth come from? Oil! Petroleum! You have oil in your home! Where does oil come from? Did you ever thank Hashem for oil? What would happen if you didn't have any oil? Imagine a cold house in the wintertime, and there's no oil. You call up and they tell you there's no oil to deliver. What are you going to do? So *baruch Hashem*, there's oil. Hashem is giving us all good things in the home.

And how much happiness a home is! A wife, children, four walls, a roof, plumbing. The pleasures are endless! But it's getting late, and now it's time to put on pajamas and climb into bed. Oh, pajamas! We could talk about the happiness of clothing and pajamas all night. The buttons, the stitching — it's an endless happiness!

Off to Slumberland

And when you fall asleep, that's a miracle, too. Some people can't sleep anymore, *chalilah*. An old man told me, "*Ich hub farloren dem shluff* — I lost my sleep." He meant that he lost his ability to sleep. It's a pity on him. To lose a gift as precious as the sweetness of falling asleep is a tragedy. Sleep is more important than food.

But *you* still have it! Sleep is one of the biggest benefits we enjoy in our lives. It's more important than medicines because during sleep your worn-out nerves become mended. Everything in the body is restored by sleep. That's why, if you're not well, *chalilah*, it's good to sleep all you can. Even in the daytime. Sleep and sleep and sleep.

Sleep is a miracle. Why do you fall asleep? You lie on the pillow and all of a sudden you fall asleep. It's a *neis*. And while you're asleep, all good things are happening. And therefore, when you make the *Hamapil* blessing, you should appreciate that gift because some people unfortunately cannot sleep. It's a tragedy. You put your head down on the pillow—most of you have pillows; you're not sleeping on the ground—and as you fall into dreamland, you're still thanking Hashem. That's the last thought you have as you drift off into your sweet sleep.

At the end of that blessing, we thank Hashem "Who illuminates the world with light." Which means that we are going to sleep with one hope—that Hashem will give us another chance tomorrow. "Hashem, we're going to sleep, and we look like we're dead. We beg You—revive us tomorrow morning and once more let us see the light of day."

You have to be grateful and thank Hashem for sleep. Every night you say *Hamapil*, thanking Hashem for the ability to fall asleep. But do you think about what you're saying? "Thank You, Hashem, for giving me a pillow and a mattress, and for giving me the gift of sleep. I love You, Hashem." In a few hours, we'll be getting up again to say *Modeh Ani* and start thanking Hashem all over again. In a few hours, you'll open your eyes and see the light of day! Oh, what a *simchah*! You should be excited! How great our happiness should be every morning! Another day! You mean to say I get to wake up again?!

The Royal Road to Happiness

Now, if I said this to an ordinary congregation of *b'nei Torah*, they would think it's a waste of time. "I didn't come here to hear such things—it's too simple." To many people, it's just talk. Well, if that's what they want, that's what it's going to remain.

But I'm talking to people now who deserve credit because they came here for a purpose; people who are *mevakshei Hashem*, who are seeking Hashem. And to such idealists we can propose this plan, that we have to use the world to enjoy the *chessed Hashem* and constantly be thanking Hashem.

That's the way for a Jew to live! You can't do it all the time? So at least a hundred times a day you should do it. The more you do it, the more successful you are. But a hundred times is the bare minimum. That means a hundred times a day you have to stop and enjoy the world. You must enjoy it so much that you feel a sincere gratitude to Hashem. Of course, at first it's only artificial. You have to spend time on it. You have to devote time to this work. Plenty of time is needed. Little by little, however, it grows on you.

Once you get into the mode of thanking Hashem for everything, you're going to change your character. You'll start loving Hashem! What is He doing for me? Everything! Once you love Hashem, the rest of the things that Hashem asks of us will follow. You'll walk in His ways, you'll serve Him with all of your heart and soul, and so on.

And you're going to see that this isn't just the road to come close to Hashem, but it's also the royal road to fulfillment and happiness in life. After a while, you become happy with so many things that you actually are a happy person. You'll actually appreciate the gifts. And the happiness will last all your life. Not only all your life here, but in Olam Haba, too. If we'll enjoy this world one hundred times a day and express our gratitude to Hashem each time, that's the royal road to happiness in this world, and to the perfection in *avodas Hashem* that brings you eternal happiness in the World to Come.

PRACTICAL ADVICE

Q How can I improve my *kavanah* for *brachos*?

The *Kuzari* says that when you take an apple in your hand, you're not permitted to rush it into your mouth. You have to stop en route and look at it. Then you say, "*Baruch Atah, Hashem, borei pri ha'eitz.*" But then he says a remarkable thing. One of the purposes of the *brachah* is that you should enjoy it more. The *brachah* causes you to stop and think at least for a second to appreciate that apple.

Saying *brachos* is a career, you know. Every time you eat an apple, you should experience it more intensely. After a while, even before you pop the apple into your mouth and taste it, you'll enjoy it no end. An apple is a marvelous gift. It's a beauty to look at. It's packaged in such a cunning manner. It has sugars and acids mixed in exactly the correct proportions. No chef could outdo what Hashem did when He made that fruit. And it's made especially for your stomach to digest. How did it happen that such an accident grows on a tree, a luscious bundle of food that's fit immediately to eat? It's pre-cooked on the tree. And it's packaged appetizingly with bright colors. When you spend time studying the apple, you eventually become a maven about apples.

Learn how to enjoy a glass of water. Ah, a glass of water! If you study it, if you make a career of it, after a while you'll say *l'chaim* over a glass of water with the biggest *simchah*. You'll say it with more *simchah* than the fellow who runs down to his cellar to pick out something with an old label that says it's 100 proof. It doesn't matter that it's fire water, that it's the worst poison. He pours it out, smacks his lips, and pours it down his throat. It burns the lining of his stomach, but he praises it to the skies. Ah, *geshmak*!

Anybody who has some *seichel*, however, can do much better. He runs to the tap, fills a glassful of clear *mayim chayim*, the elixir of life—not the bottled version you buy in the store—takes a sip, and says, "Ahhh!" It's a thousand times better than the fire water in the basement. When people learn to live that way, the *brachah* is going to help them appreciate what they're getting.

Many people have feelings of regret when they're about to leave this world—they think they missed all the fun. The truth is that they don't begin to realize how much they missed. Here's a man eating cake and drinking wine at a *kiddush*. And he's groaning and complaining to the man sitting next to him. He thinks he understands what the Torah wants of him, but he doesn't understand the first thing! Hashem made this world for us to enjoy.

I'll tell you what my *rebbi* said. It's shocking to *frum* Jews, but what can I do? My *rebbi* was a great man. At the beginning of *Mesillas Yesharim* it says, "*Ha'adam lo nivra elah l'hisaneg al Hashem*—man was created only to enjoy Hashem." But my *rebbi* paused at *l'hisaneg*, as if to say, "*Ha'adam lo nivra elah l'hisaneg*—a man was created only for *ta'anug*," for physical happiness. Where's the catch? There's no catch. You can close the *Mesillas Yesharim* now, the *shmuess* is over.... Only, the *Mesillas Yesharim* goes on and tells us that in addition to the happiness of enjoying *this* world, there's also the purpose of *l'hisaneg AL HASHEM*! Oh, that's even better! "*Ki hi hata'anug ha'amiti*—that's the real pleasure!"

There's pleasure in this world, and Hashem intended to give it to you. He's not trying to deceive you when He gives you a piece of bread. A piece of bread is a *mechayeh*. You chomp down on it with your molars, chew it, swallow it, and enjoy it. Of course, the enjoyment is diminished when you're busy thinking of the chicken and meat to follow. That spoils everything. But imagine someone in a concentration camp. First, their bread wasn't real bread. It was mixed with sawdust and ground potato peels. It had a very tiny percentage of flour in it. But even then, they didn't eat all the bread. They ate some, put the rest away, and nibbled on it little by little during the day. Some people saved it up and put it away; it was more precious to them than anything. But whenever they munched on it, they enjoyed it no end. And don't think it was false imagination. No, their conditions made them aware of what bread really is. Bread is real fun! Bread is happiness!

When I was in Europe, there was a poor old man. He told us that not long ago, before World War I, his family didn't have much bread, and when a child asked for another piece of bread he'd get a scolding. The faces of people in the streets of the small towns were dark with hunger. It wasn't because of persecution. They were extremely poor. In Eastern Europe, everybody was poor. A piece of bread was treasured.

It's a pity today that people have it available and don't enjoy it. Hashem wants you to enjoy it. Besides the nourishment, you can get pleasure from eating bread. Enjoy it! But there's another pleasure—the knowledge of gaining success in thanking Hashem for the bread by making a *brachah*. You're serving Him in return for the bread and eating *l'shem Shamayim* to serve Him more with the energy the bread gives. That knowledge of success is going to end up a greater pleasure, a pleasure that has no end. "*Ha'adam lo nivra elah l'hisaneg*"—but also "*al Hashem*." That's a pleasure even greater than *l'hisaneg* alone.

Q **Aren't we supposed to deny ourselves the pleasures of this world?**

When Hashem made the world, the first thing He told us was that we should know how good the world is. "And Hashem saw everything that He made, and behold it was very good" (*Bereishis* 1:31). Now, if Hashem would have said it was "good"—not "very good," but just "good"—we would understand that it's superlatively good. But if He says it's *tov me'od*, "very good," then you must understand that it's very, very, very, good. When Hashem says *me'od*, it means *me'ooooooooooooooooooooood*! He doesn't give His seal of approval "very good" unless it is very, very, very—and forever we won't stop saying very—good.

The Gemara says that if a person fails to enjoy this world there's going to be an accounting. "A man will someday have to give a reckoning, an accounting before Hashem, on all that his eyes saw, but he refused to eat of it" (*Yerushalmi Kiddushin* 4:12). Whatever your eyes see you should sample, and if you don't you'll be held accountable. Hashem wants us to fully enjoy His world! When you sit down to a plate full of ice cream, you have a right to say, "Ma, give me the pink kind." And you won't be considered a glutton—on the condition that before you take anything you make a big and enthusiastic *brachah*. Then the ice cream is justified.

This whole world is a heaping plate of ice cream. It's full of good things and you're justified [in enjoying it], but you have to make use of it for a purpose. It has a purpose down there, of course—even ice cream gives nourishment to your body. But there's another purpose, a bigger one. Before you eat it and after you eat it, remember Hashem and recognize what He did for you. Not only that He gave you such pleasant-tasting things to eat, but that He even gave it a color, too. Taste and color are signs of the *chasdei Hashem*. Hashem could have made all flowers white, but there are pinks too. And a whole spectrum of colors. It's a very colorful world. *Baruch Hashem* there's pink in this world. The purpose of pink is to be happy.

But don't get any wrongheaded ideas. David Hamelech said, "*Aromimcha*—I am going to make You great" in this world (*Tehillim* 145:1). David's harp was a one-track harp. He wouldn't play on it songs of war, of heroes. His harp wouldn't talk for such things. When his fingers pulled the string of his harp, they wouldn't make sounds in praise of beautiful women, of love, of romance, of bull fights, of hunting, of getting on a horse chasing a poor little fox and other forms of amusement. No! David said, "*Aromimcha*—I'm going to exalt only You." My heart is only for You. Don't give all your emotions to things that aren't paramount in the world. A man who becomes very excited over anything in this world—whether he's excited over success or he's depressed, *chalilah,* over failure—has forgotten Hashem. There's only one thing in this world to be excited about, and that's what David said, "*Aromimcha*—I'll be excited only about You."

But when David said, "I'm going to make You paramount in the world," he didn't mean he was retiring to a cave with an iron door and saying goodbye to the world. By no means. David's heart sang within him in this world but it sang with the song of Hashem. When David saw the beauties of the world, he saw the beauties of the Creator. Therefore, to follow in the footsteps of David our job is to say, "*Aromimcha*—I'm going to elevate You," make You the highest of all things. Nothing in this world matters to me except You. The purpose of this world is to sing to Hashem.

Hashem wants you to enjoy Olam Hazeh, but it's an art you have to learn. You must learn to be happy without luxuries, to appreciate the minimum, to enjoy all the "simple" pleasures of this world, pleasures that are available always. Once you empty your mind of all the manufactured pleasures, you'll find true happiness, true and immense satisfaction, in *avodas Hashem* itself—in a life of Torah, *mitzvos*, *chessed*, raising children. You'll find love of Hashem and you'll sing like David Hamelech. You'll go wild with pleasure.

Q **What if a person is really unhappy? What practical advice can you give him?**

He should appreciate all these gifts Hashem is giving us constantly—all day long and every day. People should be happy constantly. But they're not, of course, and the *Chovos Halevavos* explains why. It's because people began receiving these gifts when they were little children, when they had no sense to appreciate them. Now that they're adults, it's already habituated, so they're not able to appreciate them any longer—without effort, that is. Isn't that a tragedy? All the fun of life is overlooked.

Our Sages tell us, "*Eizehu ashir*—Who is a rich man? *Hasamei'ach b'chelko*—One who is happy with his lot" (*Avos* 4:1). People don't realize that this takes work. It doesn't just happen. But few are willing to take the pains to understand this.

A person thinks he's a failure, he's unfortunate, he's poor. But he has a place to sleep at night. Maybe some furniture also. He doesn't sleep on the floor. And some have clothing, too. Some have a spouse, as well. Some have children. And they're normal children.

Here's a man who married off four daughters, but he's not happy. So when it comes *Hallel*, let him take the *arba minim*, and as he's shaking them, making *nanu'im*, as he's saying the first "*Hodu laHashem ki tov, ki l'olam chasdo*" (*Tehillim* 136:1), he should have in mind that he married off his first daughter. What a happiness!

He should be singing instead of sad. *Ah, I thank You, Hashem. How lucky I am that she got married... and she's still married... and she has children, too!* When he gets to the second *Hodu*, he should have in mind his second son-in-law. The man isn't *meshuga*, and my daughter is still married to him. And they have children, too! That's how a person should say *Hodu*. What *else* should he be thinking about? The *sheva olamos*, the *sheva rekiyim*? No, his sons-in-law. That's what he should be thinking about.

The *Kuzari* teaches that when you make a *brachah*, it helps you appreciate and enjoy what Hashem is giving you. Therefore, say one hundred *brachos* all day, every day—but don't say them without thinking. When you say the *brachah* of "*Hameichin mitzadei gaver*—He establishes the footsteps of a man," think of the person who needs a cane to walk.

Try this exercise. There's a drugstore with a sign outside promoting various products and services. For example, they supply canes to anyone who needs, and there are two kinds: black canes and white canes. White canes are for people who can't see. But if a person needs crutches, they have those, too. If someone needs a walker, they have walkers, too. If someone needs a wheelchair, the drugstore rents them out. If someone needs a stretcher (some people have to be carried around on a bed), they have that as well. They also have commodes. If you ever saw a commode, you'll understand what a great luxury it is not to need one. A commode is a table and a seat with a chamber pot underneath. It's for people who can't go to the toilet. If you have an aide or a loyal spouse, they come from time to time and empty the contents of the chamber pot. All these forms of "happiness" are supplied by the drugstore.

Now, suppose somebody who's not successful in life passes the store. He doesn't have money. His name isn't in the newspapers. But he wants to be happy. He wants to start enjoying life. Let him start from the bottom of the list. First, is he a customer for a commode? No? *Baruch Hashem!* I know a woman who had to use a commode for many years. Her husband served her until the day she died. For many years, she couldn't leave the commode unless he helped her out to put her into bed. Now, suppose somebody offered her the chance to graduate from the commode to a wheelchair. It would be a *yom tov*! They'd call together the entire family and celebrate the miracle. Think how happy she'd be!

Now, imagine that it's you standing in front of that drugstore, and you're graduating from the commode to a wheelchair. You'd sing and dance right there in front of the store. That's what we have to do. Dance a jig! *Baruch Hashem*, we were saved from such a life! Don't forget the person who's in the commode—have pity and say a *tefillah* for them—but if you don't need a commode, it's true happiness in this world.

As you're imagining that, imagine a person graduating from the commode to a wheelchair. Oh, how happy he'd be. He'd be delirious. Now, imagine a person who graduates from a wheelchair to crutches, and then from crutches to a cane. How happy he is! As he plods through the streets slowly with his cane, his heart is singing within him.

Now, imagine graduating from a cane to a person who can walk without help, with his own two feet. Ah, the miracle of walking! Walking is very difficult to learn. A child has to be taught how to walk, to maintain his balance. It's *nisei nissim*. The Borei put into your ears two balances—a balance on one side and a balance on the other. In the inner ear chamber are little stones lying on a bed of microscopic hairs, and as your balance shifts, these little stones shift and tickle the hairs, which set off a reaction. If you're leaning over, it sets off an alarm—*You're falling! Straighten out!* It's a miracle of miracles that you maintain your balance. The ability to walk deserves a very great *hoda'ah*. Every morning you should jump for joy when you say, *Hameichin mitzadei gaver.*

Eizehu ashir—if a man is rich enough to get along without the services of that drugstore, he's a happy man. His entire life is a life of *brachah*. He's *samei'ach b'chelko*.

I know many of you think this is nonsense. People prefer to live a life of darkness, wasting opportunities. A person thinks that happiness in this world isn't possible. So we go back to the *Mesillas Yesharim*. "*Ha'adam lo nivra elah l'hisaneg*—a man was created for the purpose of *ta'anugim*." That's the first step—to appreciate what Hashem gives you, to appreciate the *chasdei Hashem*.

After that, you're ready for the next step. The next step is "*Al Hashem*"[5]—the pleasure of thanking Hashem, of praising Him for all this good He's placed in our midst. David Hamelech tells us, "*Ki tov zamrah Elokeinu, ki na'im*—It's good to sing to our Hashem, it's sweet" (*Tehillim* 147:1). Singing to Hashem is sweet. If you make singing to Hashem an avocation, a career, your whole life is one long experience of sweetness. If you learn what it means to praise Hashem—to really be thankful for all the good He gives you—you're going to be doubly happy. Life is going to be a long career of enjoyment.

When you say in the morning, "*Baruch Atah, Hashem, yotzer hame'oros*—thank You, Hashem, the Creator of the luminaries," you're going to sing it. Unfortunately, people mouth it every day but don't know how good it is. *Yotzer hame'oros* is a very great *brachah*, a great happiness. It's *geshmak*! When you see the sun shining brightly in the middle of the day, it's *simchah*, it's happiness.[6]

Shlomo Hamelech said, "*Umasok ha'or*—how sweet is light, *ki tov la'einayim liros es hashemesh*—how good it is for the eyes to see the sun" (*Koheles* 11:7).[7] Sunlight is a happiness! Here's

---

5 The quote begins "*V'ha'adam lo nivrah elah l'hisaneg*" and ends "*al Hashem.*"

6 See below, the section titled, "*Yotzer Hame'oros.*"

7 From Rav Miller's biography: "At the end of his life, before going upstairs to his home he would stop at the back of the shul after Shacharis and gaze out the window at the sky and sunshine. He was utilizing a teaching of Rabbeinu Yonah that he repeated often. Rabbeinu Yonah (2:9) explains that everyone needs joy to perform *avodas Hashem*, and that elderly people who are about to leave the world and do not have much physical enjoyment need a push. What should they do? They should draw happiness from the

a man standing in front of the travel stores advertising trips to Hawaii or Europe, and he's thinking of the good times far away. This man is an *am ha'aretz*, a blind boor. He doesn't realize that right here in this world, this moment, are opportunities for true happiness—physical happiness. If he would study it properly, his heart would sing. His spirits would soar like an eagle.

Then Shlomo Hamelech says, "*Zechor es y'mei hachoshech*—remember the days of darkness"—he means the days of darkness after a person passes from this world. "*Ki harbeih yiheyu*—for they are many" (ibid. 11:8). Many people are already lying in their graves. We who are alive must appreciate what it means to walk on this earth with open eyes, and to enjoy the splendor of the sunlight.

You know, there will come a time when you won't be alive. Of course, you plan on being here for the next 10,000 years, but sooner or later it will all come to an end, so start learning how to enjoy life—every second of it—now. A time will come when people are going to look back and regret that they didn't enjoy the simplest things in life. When does a person realize it? When he's approaching his last moments. Then he looks back and thinks, "Why was I so stupid? My mind was obsessed with so many superficialities, so many different worries and silly ideas. The mere fact that I could walk down the avenue and see the light of day—cloudy, windy, sunny, any kind of a day—was so much fun."

There's no such thing as an unpleasant day. Every day you should be grateful to Hashem. All the *meisim*, if they could come back for five minutes to this world—even two minutes, one minute—they'd sacrifice a great deal of their happiness. "More precious is one moment of *teshuvah* and *ma'asim tovim* in this world than the entire life of Olam Haba!" (*Avos* 4:15) How

---

sun and its light, as the *passuk* (*Koheles* 11:7) says, 'The light is sweet and it is good for the eyes to see the sun.' Rabbi Miller always said that one must practice experiencing this enjoyment, because it was difficult to start when one was old. Now he was reaping the benefits of his years of practice."

precious life is! Only near the end, when it's too late, do people realize it!

Be happy with life right now. Don't let a minute go by! Every moment that you're breathing, that your heart is beating, that your brain is functioning, is a sweetness. Enjoy the sweetness of life. It's so much fun to be alive! There's no fun on Earth that compares! The greatest fun in this world is the fun of being alive! Isn't that a pity that people spend their days in ignorance of this? Think of all the good times you can have, free of charge. The fact that you exist is the greatest of all kinds of enjoyment. It's a pity that people don't spend enough time thinking about it. It's the most intense pleasure of all.

But unless you're willing to invest a little effort and time, you'll never enjoy life. Once you start thinking these thoughts, you'll be richly rewarded. If you learn how to enjoy life—and enjoying life doesn't mean running around on Caribbean cruises; it means, "Ahh! *Baruch Hashem*, I'm alive!"—you'll be happy always.

Practice up, first thing in the morning! When you open your eyes, the first thing you should feel is an outpouring of gratitude. "I'm alive!" Not everyone wakes up in the morning. It's important to learn to be grateful from the moment we open our eyes. We're one of the lucky ones! When you say *Modeh ani l'fanecha*, feel the sweetness of being alive, first thing in the morning! Everything in this world is made to be sweet, but the sweetness starts with appreciating the fact that you're alive.

By appreciating what Hashem gives us in this world, we'll come to love Hashem, to fear Hashem, to walk in His ways and everything else. To really fulfill the obligation of one hundred *brachos* a day, you have to count your blessings. Not just literally. You have to stop and think. If you say them by rote, it's better than nothing—but not much better. The idea of *mei'ah brachos* is that you have to study what you're getting. Then you'll be *samei'ach b'chelko.*

KAVANAH

Q What does *kavanah* mean?

It means "to aim your mind," to pay attention to what you're praying, which means you have to think about what you're saying.

Q What's the main thing to focus on in davening?

It's very important to understand that even though we serve Hashem by means of our actions, our actions aren't the essence of our *avodas Hashem*. If they were, Hashem could have told us that every Jewish congregation should raise money and place an order for a bunch of robots. We would order a hundred steel robots and seat them in the synagogue. And they would have in their mouths some type of talking machine, a tape player, and then every day at exactly 6:30 in the morning a timer would turn on all the robots, and they'd all start shaking and saying the words of the *siddur*.

Oh, it would be beautiful! It would be the perfect congregation. Nobody would come late, nobody would leave early, and all hundred robots would be shaking in unison. There would be no talking. And no skipping either because it's all recorded, from *Mah Tovu* on the first page of the *siddur* until the end. The steel robots would *daven* perfectly.

Meanwhile, the people would be out doing whatever they want with good consciences, at peace because they know that the service of Hashem is carried out in the very best way. Hashem is being served to perfection! All you need is for a janitor to come in once in a while to oil the robots and see that none have broken down. It would be a perfect *minyan* of *ovdei Hashem*, all serving Hashem with their *ma'asim*.

Don't laugh. If your mind is absent, that's exactly what's taking place. Only, instead of a hundred efficient robots, you have a hundred poorly functioning robots. They're coming late. They're straggling in right before *Barchu*, and some are talking. They're making unnecessary noises besides the noises they're supposed to make on the recording.

The flesh and blood robots are certainly not as good as the steel ones, so why not just order the robots?

The answer is that the service of Hashem is entirely dependent on the mind. Our minds! That's what Hashem wants from us. He says, "I don't want robots. I don't want steel robots, and I don't want flesh and blood robots, either. I want you!" "*Rachmana liba ba'ei*—Hashem wants your thoughts" (*Sanhedrin* 106b). It's your mind that makes you who you are. That's why when you apply for a job and the boss wants to figure out how much to pay you, he doesn't say, "Get on the scale, let me see how much you weigh." Nobody pays employees by weight! He wants to know what kind of mind you have. What's your ability? Therefore, shaking, davening, *mitzvos*, learning Torah, it's all wonderful. But remember, *Rachmana liba ba'ei*—the service of Hashem primarily means serving Him with your mind.

When you come tomorrow morning to the synagogue and bring along your robot and park him in your seat—he's all wound up and you're ready to let him run—it would be a good idea to interrupt him in the middle and take over the controls for a minute and speak to Hashem with your flesh and blood tongue, and your flesh and blood heart, and your flesh and blood brain. Even if it's for just a minute, it's going to be more important than the fifty minutes that the other part of you, the robot part of you, is sitting in the synagogue, shaking and galloping through the davening without you being aware of what's going on.

Q Is it better to say the whole davening every morning or to say part of the davening but with more *kavanah*?

I won't tell you my own opinion. I'll just say what the Tur says. "*Tov me'at tachanunim b'kavanah meiharbos b'lo kavanah*—To *daven* a little bit and think about what you're saying is more valuable than davening a lot without thinking" (*Orach Chaim* 1:4).

It's very important to utilize the opportunity of *tefillah*. The *Chovos Halevavos* says that the purpose of davening is, "*Hamachshavah nimsheches achar hadibur*—that your thoughts eventually follow your words" (*Sha'ar Cheshbon Hanefesh*, *Cheshbon* 9). Once you accustom yourself to saying "*shirei David avdecha*—the songs of David, Your servant" and reliving a little bit of the great emotions that he expressed in his love of Hashem, it awakens in you a response, and you also gain a little bit of that feeling. Therefore, it's very important to spend some time doing that during *P'sukei D'zimrah*.

Shemoneh Esrei, too. Now, you can't say the whole Shemoneh Esrei with *iyun* because it will come time for Minchah and you'll still be standing for Shacharis. However, if every day you concentrate on a little part of Shemoneh Esrei and think into it, you'll be surprised what you'll discover. It's like a gold mine.

People don't realize that the Anshei Knesses Hagedolah who composed the Shemoneh Esrei were *nevi'im* and the greatest *chachamim*. They were able to implant very deep *chachmah* into these words. Therefore, you'd be surprised how much you'll get out of it.

Now, of course, sometimes you might imagine wrong *peirushim*, but the more you think about it, the more you'll see how profound their words are. The purpose of davening, after all, is not merely to say the words, but *l'hispallel*, which means "to make yourself think." *Pillel* means to think. That's the success a person gets from proper *tefillah*. It elevates his mind and brings him to awareness of Hashem and *ahavas Hashem*.

Q Is it better to *daven* a long Shemoneh Esrei even if you will miss Kedushah?

Absolutely! But it depends on what you're thinking. If you're thinking, "I'm davening a long Shemoneh Esrei to make a 'hit' with those around me," then absolutely not. Some people do that, by the way. I see people doing that. But if you're doing it because you want more time to think about what the words mean, then there's no question that it's a very good investment to *daven* with *kavanah*.

Q What's a good preparation to achieve *tefillah b'kavanah*?

The first preparation is to be a *ma'amin.* You must believe in Hashem! Now, people who are in contact with the outside world should know that the outside world poisons the mind. The world today is a world of foolishness. When a person has contact with the outside world, it's difficult to put *emunah* into his mind.

To be a *ma'amin* begins with *emunah p'shutah.* That's a valuable accomplishment. If you learned the *pashtus* of the Chumash, or you heard stories from your parents, these things get into your blood. It's very important to learn what Hashem did for Avraham, for our Avos in Mitzrayim. Little by little, the *emunah* enters your mind. Once you have *emunah* within you, it's easier to talk to Hashem and ask Him to give you what you need.

But there are ways to gain even more *emunah.* The Rambam's *derech* is to see the wonders of Hashem's creation, to see the "*chachmah she'ein lo keitz*—wisdom without end" (*Hilchos Yesodei HaTorah* 2:2). A bottomless complexity of plan-and-purpose. If you are *misbonein*, if you study that, then surely love and a fear of Hashem will come into your mind, the Rambam says. There are other ways, too. Even by learning Gemara, you should know that a certain amount of *emunah* comes in. The fire of the Gemara enters your blood, and many people have become very *frum* Jews just from learning Gemara. The spirit of the Tannaim and Amoraim, all the *chachamim* who put their lives into understanding the *d'var Hashem*, transforms the *talmidim.*

There are many ways to acquire *emunah*, and all of them should be used. Once you're a *ma'amin*, we can start talking about *tefillah b'kavanah,* because now at least you'll know there's Somebody to talk to.

In addition, you must understand what you're saying, not merely the translation of the words. You must spend some time studying these *mishnayos* of the Anshei Knesses Hagedolah. That's really what the Shemoneh Esrei is. It's *mishnayos*, very ancient *mishnayos.* They're very deep. You have to spend time thinking about what each word means. You must spend time understanding the ideas that lie behind each word and every phrase. It's not just the *peirush hamilos*, the translation of the words. It's the concepts that you must make a part of your mindset. When you do that, the Shemoneh Esrei will have more meaning for you.

And not only Shemoneh Esrei. When you say *Ashrei* or other sections from *Tehillim*, or when you say *Kriyas Shema, Az Yashir*, or other selections from the Chumash, it's very important to understand what you're saying. That's number one. Number one is to have a better understanding of the words in the *siddur*. If your understanding is only superficial, your davening will be superficial.

Then, you must train yourself to concentrate. Every time you *daven*, choose one little area where you'll go slow. Dwell on one area for three minutes. No matter how much those around you are rushing through davening, make sure to spend three minutes on one little area, one *brachah*. Let everyone else keep galloping. You stand still and think about that one *brachah* or that one *passuk*. As you're thinking about the ideas, you're learning to concentrate.

It sounds easy, but it won't be in the beginning. If you get busy working on this project, however, you'll be a success. After a while it will become easier and easier to keep your mind focused for longer periods of time.

Q **How can one learn to appreciate the great ideas in the *siddur*?**

How can one appreciate the *siddur*? Look, you can only appreciate something you know. Take my book, *Praise, My Soul*, and every day try to be *mispallel* at least one line according to what's written there. If you find something better, that's also good. You'll find better, too, but I'm just mentioning my own.

You cannot appreciate the *siddur* unless you know what the *siddur* is saying, and people don't know what the *siddur* is saying. Every line is another gem—another important thought we must live with. Even the word "Hashem." What does the word "Hashem" mean? Of course, I'm not going to say that I know—but we do know at least some of what "Hashem" means. You have to study the word "Hashem." First, Hashem means the One Who has existence. We don't have existence. We only imagine that we do. The Rambam says that (*Yesodei HaTorah* 1:1-4). *Hashem Elokim Emes*—only He has true existence. Our existence is an imaginary existence.

Another meaning of the word "Hashem" is that He causes existence. "*Ki Hu amar vayehi*—He causes everything to be" (*Tehillim* 33:9). The world is full of kindliness and Hashem is the "*Mekor hachessed*—the Source of kindliness." The world is full of wisdom and kindliness, and since Hashem is the *M'haveh*—the One Who caused and causes everything to exist—that means Hashem is the Source of all wisdom and kindliness.

There's much more to explain about the words I just told you.[8] I'm only giving you the *roshei perakim*, the chapter headings. Once you start learning what "Hashem" means, the next time you say it, you'll really think about Hashem. You'll have no time to finish davening because you'll be stuck on Hashem. That's how you *should daven*, by the way. You should be stuck on the first word and have no time to finish.

The people who finish in a big hurry are missing out on all the accomplishments of life because in davening lies a very big achievement. But you must study davening to succeed at it. Study *Praise, My Soul* and you'll begin to see what davening is.

Q **What is the benefit of saying the same words every day? I believe it already. Why do I have to keep repeating it?**

The answer is that the repetition makes a tremendous difference in a person's *emunah*. Some people's *emunah* is like a very thin layer of paint. You give a little scrape, and the paint comes off. Some people's *emunah* is thicker than that. Whoever you are, you have to work all your life to grow in *emunah*. We don't repeat these foundations of truth because of a lack of *emunah*. It's not just "belief" that you are trying to

---

8 See *Praise, My Soul* (#15–20, 50–51).

work on. It's more than that. It's called *da'as Hashem*. All your life you must work to become more and more aware of Hashem. When Moshe asked Hashem (*Shemos* 33:18), "*Har'eini na es k'vodecha*—Please show me Your glory," was it because he lacked *emunah*?! No. It was because he wanted to get closer and closer to Hashem.

Therefore, each time we say, "*Ani ma'amin*"—if we say it properly—we're making it clearer and clearer to ourselves. If you say it a thousand times, you're making a much deeper impression than saying it just once, even if you believed it the first time.

That's why it is so important to repeat the same *Kriyas Shema* every day. And the same *tefillos*. Every time you say it, you're ingraining it more and more deeply into your mind. That's why it's so important to repeat the great truths over and over again. Instead of every day saying something new, we repeat it again and again. Spend time impressing upon your *neshamah* the great truths of the Torah. When you repeat an idea over and over again, it becomes part of your personality.

The *Chovos Halevavos* says, "*Hamachshavah nimsheches achar hadibur*—Your mind follows your words" (*Sha'ar Cheshbon Hanefesh, Cheshbon* 9). Do you hear that important *yesod*? Your mind follows your words! Say the right words, and your mind changes. The more you say the same words, the more your mind becomes influenced by these words.

Therefore, we say again and again, "*Shema Yisrael, Hashem Elokeinu, Hashem Echad.*" Of course, you have to know what you're saying. "Hashem" means that He is the One Who is *havayah*—He is the One Who exists. He is the only One Who exists. And He is the One Who causes the world to exist. And He is *Elokeinu*—He is ours. That means that He has chosen us to be His servants. And we must devote our lives to Him. And "*V'ahavta es Hashem Elokecha*—you have to love Hashem" (*Devarim* 6:5).

Each time you say these great truths, you're making it more and more real to yourself. You become more and more convinced. It's precious. It's valuable. Don't think it's a small thing. No, it's a tremendous thing! Each time you repeat the great truths, you're making yourself more and more of an "*ish shalem*—a perfect, complete, whole person."

Q Does a person receive reward in the Afterlife for doing *mitzvos* without intent?

He *doesn't* get reward. There's no reward for things done without intention. Now, there is an opinion that "*ein mitzvos tzrichos kavanah*— *mitzvos* do not need intent" (*Orach Chaim* 60:4). But it's a mistake to think that means there will be *reward.* Let's say someone took the *arba minim* with the intention of throwing them at somebody. He is *yotzei* the *mitzvah* because he did the act of picking up the *arba minim,* and after that he can't make a *brachah* anymore. That's why we pick up the esrog upside down, because otherwise we'd immediately be *yotzei*; we'd be performing the *mitzvah* as soon as we pick it up, before we even make the *brachah*. So we take it upside down to avoid performing the *mitzvah*. Then, after we make the *brachah*, we turn it right side up to do the *mitzvah*.

We do that because we take into account the opinion that considers a *mitzvah* done without *kavanah* as a *mitzvah*. But that's only in Olam Hazeh. It's only in regard to this world. It just means that *beis din* cannot force him to do the *mitzvah* again and that he's not allowed to make another *brachah*. But he will not get reward. Reward is only according to the measure of the intent.

You hear that? So you learned something tonight. Very many people are under the wrong impression. You don't get reward for things you didn't intend to do.

Q Does one get reward for unintentional charity?

If a man loses a dollar and a poor man finds it, there's a statement in *Yerushalmi* in *Pe'ah* (8:9) that he is rewarded for charity. So the question is, "What kind of charity is that?" There's no intent, and I said earlier that without intent there can be no reward.

And the answer is, as the *sefarim* say, that he won't get reward without intent. It's only because we recognize that when a Jew loses a dollar, he's thinking that if he knew that a poor man found it and had use of it, he'd be happy. He would like to have the dollar back, but he's happy that a poor Jew is benefiting from his dollar. Rather than his dollar going down the sewer, he's satisfied that a Jew who is hungry bought some fresh rolls and ate them. So he gets reward for being satisfied with that. But it's not the same reward as if he would have taken the dollar and given it of his own volition.

That's why when a *meshulach* comes to you and asks for a dollar for charity and you give it to him, you get reward. But suppose you go out to the streets looking for a *meshulach* to give him a dollar—you get a much bigger reward for giving away that dollar. Anything that you do of your own volition earns a much bigger reward.

That's why when you give charity, when a man leaves a bequest after his death, it's compared to copper. Copper is a good thing. He gave away copper. It's also something. If he gives it while he's still alive, just before he dies, it's silver. Silver is better than copper. But if he gives it when he's still healthy, then it's gold. That's what the Sages say.[9] The amount of volition involved makes a big difference. When he's dead, he can't take it with him, so he leaves it for charity. That's also good. He could have done much worse—he could have left it to the UJA. Or he could have left it, as many do, for the Homeless Kittens Home. It's not a joke. A true story. So the amount of your volition that goes into it is the amount of reward you get.

Q **Why does the Rav *daven* without making noise or shuckeling?**

I was in Slabodka and I looked at my *rebbeim*. They stood still like trees when they davened. They were "*kulo machshavah*—all thought." Now, I'm not that, but I want to imitate them, at least. And they were *kulo machshavah*.

I told you a story about Rav Yisrael Salanter when he once came to Warsaw to visit the Gerrer Rebbe. When he finished, the Gerrer Rebbe accompanied him down to the street. That was a *chiddush*! All

---

9 *Da'as Zekeinim Miba'alei Hatosfos, Shemos* 25:3.

Warsaw heard that the Gerrer Rebbe had escorted a Litvak to the door. A mob of Gerrer *chassidim* came to see this big *tzaddik* whom their Rebbe gave so much *kavod* to. If the Rebbe did that for him, he must be somebody!

They followed him until he came to a *beis haknesses* to *daven* Minchah. Oh, now we're going to see a performance! We're going to see a *tzaddik* davening! Did you ever see a *tzaddik* davening? I once saw one. He was jumping up and down. Up and down! Jumping up and down with *hislahavus*, with a fire of *ahavas Hashem.*

But Rav Yisrael stood still and didn't move as he davened. The *chassidim* were disappointed. Terribly disappointed! However, there was one person standing nearby, watching him, and as he stared at Rav Yisrael's forehead, he noticed that the veins on his head were pulsating. His mind was working very hard with *avodah sheb'leiv*. That's what *tefillah* is called, "service of the mind." That's how my *rebbi*s davened—with their minds.

Q Why do some people shout during davening, and should we shout as well?

Everybody who prays knows the secret, "*Hachitzoniyus m'oreres es hap'nimiyus*—the outside stirs up the inside" (*Mesillas Yesharim*, Chapter 7). It's hard for a person to move himself inwardly. But by doing outward actions, which suggest to us certain emotions, we respond. That's why it says you should answer "*Y'hei sh'meih rabbah*" with all your strength, *b'chol kocho* (*Shabbos* 119b). Why *b'chol kocho?* The *mefarshim* say because the *kol*, the "loud voice," awakens the sleeping emotions. The voice awakens our inner thoughts.

A man comes to shul in the morning, tired and lazy. He has no enthusiasm. What does he do? Usually nothing. But if he learned from the *Mesillas Yesharim*, he opens his mouth and forces himself to shout, "*Hodu laShem, kir'u bishmo, hodi'u ba'amim alilosav*—Praise Hashem; call out in His name; make His deeds known among the nations!" He doesn't mean it, but he shouts anyway. After a while, his external actions stir up a reaction within him, and he becomes enthusiastic, too. So act like you want to *daven* with *kavanah*, and the result will be that it's going to warm you up and you actually will.

Now, some pious men wish to avoid any appearance of ostentation. They want to show humility. So, in an environment where others sometimes shout superficially, perhaps to attract attention, they use the opposite strategy. Whatever you learn, you have to take with salt—a lot of salt! When we talk about shouting in *tefillah*, it depends on the circumstances. If it's going to arouse within you a desire for showing off, you have to beware. These great men felt that it paid to forgo one advantage for the other.

Q **Are *tefillah* and meditation the same thing?**

Meditation is one thing, and *tefillah* is something else. Don't confuse them. Meditation is wonderful. Meditation is great. No question about it. But meditation doesn't excite your feelings. It's a matter of intellect. Intellect is very important. It's one of the big foundations of greatness. But *tefillah* is something else. *Tefillah* is when you take the results of your meditation and speak directly to Hashem. When you say, "*Atah*," your heart starts pumping because you're talking directly to Hashem. "*Atah*—You, Hashem!"

The philosophers, *l'havdil*, meditated, but they didn't become great. Only the *nevi'im* became great. The *nevi'im* saw visions that brought forth from the depths of their mind such reactions that caused them to become great. The *Kuzari* says that. A *navi* saw in a flash more than all the philosophers did in a lifetime of meditation.

Meditation is a sleepy thing; it's variable. Certainly it should be done, but what *tefillah* does nothing else can accomplish.

Q If whatever Hashem does for us is good, why do we bother asking Him for specific things that we think are good? What intention should we have when asking Him for things?

That's a good question. In other words, we shouldn't say anything in *tefillah* except, "Ribbono Shel Olam, please do what's good for us." We shouldn't specify anything. We shouldn't even say generally, "Give us health," according to this.

I'll strengthen the question with the case of Achav. When he heard bad news prophesied against him, he prayed and was allowed to live. The Gemara says, "It wasn't good for Achav that he was spared" (*Yoma* 87a). Had Achav received the sentence he was given, he would have perished, and it would have been much better for him. Sometimes, it's better for a man to be punished in this world. Otherwise, he continues to amass debits. He does more and more sins, and it ends up being a great misfortune that he lived that long. Therefore, the question remains: Why do we ask Hashem for health? Why do we specify other things that we need or want?

And the answer is as follows: What's the use of being dishonest? If you don't ask for health, does that mean you don't want it? You don't want money? You don't want all forms of happiness? Even if you don't ask for it, you're going to try to get it anyhow! Therefore, a man must say with his mouth what he wants—just that he should add a proviso, "Ribbono Shel Olam, please only do it if it's good for me."

He should ask for what he wants because that's what he sincerely wants. Everybody wants good health. Everybody wants to succeed in business. Therefore, you should ask for it. Otherwise, you're being a hypocrite if you're not saying what you want, and you're going to try to gain those things anyway.

That's one very good reason you should specify what you want in your *tefillos*—so that you shouldn't think you're doing it on your own, so that you should be reminded always that only Hashem is going to give you health, only Hashem is going to give you wealth. That's one reason. There are more, but I won't take up the time now.

Q Should we include in our *tefillos* reasons why Hashem should answer our requests?

Yes. When a person wants to make something out of his life, he has to try to add something to his *tefillah*. For example, when he asks Hashem to give him life, he should include at least one inducement—he'll make use of his life. "Hashem, please give me life. I'll try to make use of my life. I'll try to become a *talmid chacham*. I'll try to teach Torah to other people. I'll try to spread *emunah* among the Jewish nation. I'll try to spread *middos tovos* and *derech eretz* and *ahavas Yisrael*."

"Oh," Hashem says, "that sounds good, very good!"

A businessman should also add inducements. I know two businessmen who are in the business of helping yeshivas. They sit in their offices making money, but they're thinking all the time about how to help yeshivas. That's their main business in life. They say, "Ribbono Shel Olam, please give me success in *parnassah*. Success in supporting yeshivas."

If you want to get married, say, "Ribbono Shel Olam, please give me *nachas*, happiness, *parnassah*." Hashem asks, "What do you want it for?" So you say, "Hashem, I'm going to have children. I'm going to raise them in the *derech haTorah*." A woman can say, "Ribbono Shel Olam, I want to have as many children as I can. I'll bring them up to be *frum*, to have *derech eretz*, and I'll marry them off to *talmidei chachamim*."

"Oh," Hashem says, "if that's the case, it's a big inducement to Me."

That's why you should add an inducement, if possible. Everybody can do that. Say, "Hashem, please let me live longer and I'll try to be a better servant to You. I'll show You that Your investment in me isn't wasted."

Of course, Hashem will listen anyway. If you ask Hashem, "Please let me live to enjoy life," it's also something. Asking alone is already success. But if you ask Him and add the inducement, it's a double-decker success. "Oh," says Hashem, "your asking alone was worthwhile, but now that you're adding the second part, you're surely deserving to get it."

Now you begin to see how easy it is to become great in this world. You don't need heroism. It's not *mesiras nefesh*. What's the difficulty? Just think these thoughts as much as possible. It doesn't cost any money. It doesn't hurt. You can eat your meals and sleep quietly in your bed at night. You can have a nice home, if you want. You can dress well. Just ask Hashem constantly and, if you can, add a postscript that you're asking for the purpose of utilizing your long life and your success to accomplish great things in the service of Hashem. Start a career of talking to Hashem today.

THE DAILY TEFILLOS

KADDISH

What should we be thinking when we say, *"Y'hei sh'meih rabbah . . ."*?

When you come to the *beis haknesses* and hear *Kaddish*, instead of saying "*Y'hei sh'meih rabbah* as a donation—that *others* should bless His name—*you* bless His name. Think of one specific thing. Remember when your tooth was bothering you so much you couldn't even eat for three days, and you thought they would have to drill or maybe take it out altogether? Then, overnight, the pain subsided and the tooth began to function well once again. *Y'HEI SH'MEIH RABBAH M'VORACH!* Thank Hashem for that! You didn't make use of the reminder back then? So do it now!

Remember when you once took a dumb step. You stepped off the curb without looking just as a bus was making a turn? And the bus driver pulled the brakes and cursed you! "I almost hit you! What a crazy dope! Why'd you walk in front of my bus!" And you walked away like a dumbbell, too, not even thinking. Where's the *Y'hei sh'meih rabbah* for that?

Here was a man who had a *din Torah* pending against him. He was afraid. He couldn't sleep—he told me. A whole week his stomach was boiling. A *din Torah* could mean a lot of *tzaros*. At the end, nothing came of it. The other party didn't call him to *beis din*. So what did he do? He forgot all about it. Forgot all about it?! Where's the *Y'hei sh'meih rabbah m'vorach*?!

That's what *Y'hei sh'meih rabbah* is for. Don't wait for the future. Don't think that only in the future, when Mashiach comes, the great name of Hashem will be blessed. No. Don't procrastinate—get started blessing His name right now!

Now, it's a good idea to prepare beforehand. As soon as the *chazzan* starts saying *Yisgadal*, think, "What am I going to thank Hashem for this time?" Think fast. It's better if you think beforehand, before davening, and prepare at least one thing to give thanks for. But if you didn't, then you have to think fast.

Thank Hashem that you have normal children. If you have normal children, thank Hashem for that day and night. Day and night, day and night, day and night, you should be thanking Hashem for normal children. At least by *Y'hei sh'meih rabbah* you should think about it! And not just one *Y'hei sh'meih rabbah* for all your children! One for this child, and another for the next child, and another for the next one. When you finish getting through all your children, you can start again. Every child is a *matanah.* A child is a very big gift. It's a *ta'anug.*

That's what *Kaddish* is for—to praise Hashem for all that He did and does for you. Don't just mumble it. Shout it! Shout, "May His great name be blessed forever and ever!" But don't just shout it. Think about the things you owe Hashem a great debt of gratitude for. Some people yell out these words as loud as they can, but what is it worth if they're not thinking about what it means? How can a person who lives a normal life not be busy all his days thanking Hashem?!

Y'hei sh'meih rabbah is an opportunity—an opportunity that presents itself several times every day. Don't waste it.

Q **What else should we have in mind?**

We have to realize what the *shliach tzibbur* said before this in order to know what that Amein is answering. The *shliach tzibbur* says, "*Yisgadal v'yiskadash sh'meih rabbah*—May His great name be exalted and sanctified." Why does he say that? What's the purpose?

Because that's the reason we are assembled together in shul. We come together to give honor to Hashem, to demonstrate our loyalty and our gratitude to Him. And so, when he says, "*Yisgadal v'yiskadash sh'meih rabbah*—May His great name be exalted and sanctified," so we answer, "*Amein! Y'hei sh'meih rabbah m'vorach*—Let His great name be blessed forever and ever and ever!" It means this: "We agree with you! We wholeheartedly advocate this procedure of coming together and praising Hashem. But we're not satisfied merely with this occasion. "*L'olam ulal'mei al'maya*—We want it to continue forever and ever!" Which means that we want our children and our children's children to follow in our footsteps, that they, too, should congregate in synagogues and in their homes and always praise Hashem forever and ever. That's what we're saying. We're not satisfied merely with now. *L'olam ulal'mei al'maya*—forever and ever. It's a *tefillah*.

But it's not only a *tefillah*, a prayer for the future. It's also a declaration of resolve: "We intend to see this carried out!" So *Y'hei sh'meih rabbah* means that we're going to support yeshivas. We're going to build Bais Yaakov schools in order that His great name should be blessed forever. Bais Yaakov means girls are willing to have babies. Before Bais Yaakov came along, girls didn't want to have any babies. Bais Yaakov means girls who have ten children.

Do you know what they're doing for us? They're saving the Jewish nation! All around us, Jews are destroying themselves. They're committing national suicide. Everybody's going underground and getting lost, but the Bais Yaakov girls started the great movement initiated by Rebbetzin Kaplan in America who brought it over from Europe—an ideal of being a successful mother, an idealistic Jewish mother. They founded these schools, and now girls are having babies.

And they're married to *b'nei Torah*; there are *frum* girls everywhere! Big families! You see them pushing a baby carriage, two inside the carriage and four more holding on to the carriage and walking along with them. That's an inspiration! We should heap blessings on them as they pass by! They deserve all good things in the world, these devoted women. It means a lot of work, but they're working for the future of our people. That's *Y'hei sh'meih rabbah*—she's saying *Y'hei sh'meih rabbah* every minute! You know what it means to have to wash so many diapers! To have to wash so many dishes! It's constant work. So she's saying *Y'hei sh'meih rabbah*.

And the loyal husband who is working all day long to support such a family, sometimes two jobs, he's also saying, *Y'hei sh'meih rabbah*. That's what we mean with *Y'hei sh'meih rabbah*. We want to have generations and generations.

And all those Jews who work for yeshivas, people who are worried about meeting the yeshiva's payrolls, people who come to the Board of Directors meetings and say, "How can we help the yeshiva continue, maybe even expand?" People who have founded yeshivas, idealists who founded Bais Yaakov schools—there's a lot of work involved. All these people are saying *Y'hei sh'meih rabbah.*

When a Jew is training himself for a career of praising Hashem, when a Jew is learning Torah and understanding his obligations to praise Hashem, that's all *Y'hei sh'meih rabbah.* And therefore, every form of service to Hashem is being expressed when we say the words *Y'hei sh'meih rabbah.*

So again, first it's a prayer that this should go on forever—Hashem's name should be blessed forever and ever. Secondly, it is a declaration that this is what we are going to do; we're going to see to it that we carry it out in our lives. And the third is that it's a prophecy. We are foretelling the future. This will continue forever. There will always be a Jewish nation. Even the most important and powerful peoples will eventually go lost, but the nation that says *Y'hei sh'meih rabbah* will continue to say it forever.

So we have three things; I'm repeating them now. The first is, it's a prayer. Secondly, it's a declaration that this is what we're going to do, and thirdly, it's a prophecy that it's going to continue forever.

P'SUKEI D'ZIMRAH

Q How did David Hamelech, the author of *Tehillim*, become so great?

Before his birth he had been prepared for greatness, and he was created from the best materials (*Yoma* 47a). He was of ruddy complexion, had beautiful eyes, was handsome of countenance (I *Shmuel* 16:12), was a gifted musician and poet, possessed an understanding mind, and was a warrior (ibid. 16:18) with the heart of a lion (II *Shmuel* 17:10).

In the many years of solitude in the field where he pastured the flock, he grew great by intellectual exercises of thought and emotion, which brought him close to Hashem. Men who are capable of mental concentration for hours at a time can produce tremendous results of logic and feeling. And following in the footsteps of the great shepherd Moshe, David found all treasures of mind and soul in these long periods of meditation.

We can picture this ruddy and powerfully built boy (he smote a lion and a bear, while guarding his flock), standing in deep thought for hours by some quiet stream (*Tehillim* 23:2) while his flocks rested, and then speaking in song to Hashem with the accompaniment of his harp, which came alive under his inspired fingers. "In the evening and morning and noontime I speak and cry out, and He hears my voice" (ibid. 55:18), a practice followed in all generations, "*Three times a day* he kneeled, as he had been wont to do before" (*Daniel* 6:11). The long solitary hours in meditation on the Torah and in the soul-stirring songs of his harp became his daily program throughout all nights of his lifetime, even in his palace at Yerushalayim (*Tehillim* 57:9, 119:62, *Brachos* 4a). But all this was carried on in secrecy. *His immense mental stature was concealed* even from his own family, to whom he was merely the youngest son, noted only for his songs. (*Behold, A People* #398)

Q What events in David Hamelech's life brought out the greatness of his soul?

The flight into the wilderness, the fear of pursuit and death, and the privations of exile were part of Hashem's plan to prepare David for his historic role as the oracle of the book of *Tehillim*. This book could not have come into existence as a result of a peaceful career. It was indeed founded in the quiet meditations in the meadows when he pastured the flock. But more than meditations were needed to make this book the model of prayer and love of Hashem, to be repeated by countless millions forever after. To create the mighty cry of supplication, the expression of unwavering trust in Hashem, and the outpouring of gratitude, needed the experiences of one trapped by a vengeful enemy and delivered from death by the hand of Hashem.

Every man can find some parallel in David's words to suit his own circumstances and his particular need for expression. But the nation of Israel as an entity is especially identified with the psalms of David. For the prophetic parallel between him and his people is striking. David, the chosen of Hashem, is unjustly accused and persecuted, so that he is forced to flee for his life. Despite everything, he persists in his fervent love of Hashem and his unyielding trust in Him, until finally all his enemies perish and he achieves the highest glory and happiness. So were David's people and achievements the highest glory and happiness. So were David's people to be unjustly accused and persecuted and were forced to flee for their lives or to be exiled. But they would not yield their love of Hashem and His Torah, and their trust that He would finally cause them to be recognized as His chosen ones.

No wonder, then, that these lyrics of entreaty and thanksgiving became the national prayer book and that they have been on the lips of Jews *every day* throughout the thousands of years that have passed. Thus was fulfilled the prophecy of Leah when she bore Yehudah: "Now I shall give praise (*odeh)* to Hashem" (*Bereishis* 29:35). For from Yehudah (meaning "he shall praise") came forth David, who taught the nation how to utter the praise of Hashem. (*Behold, A People* #427)

Q **What was so innovative about what David Hamelech did?**

When David Hamelech came, a new era began in the history of our people, in the world's history. "Who will ascend the mountain of Hashem? He who has clean hands and a pure heart...He shall receive a blessing from Hashem" (*Tehillim* 24:3,5). Who is this man who is going to prove worthy? David is the man. David is a man who came up on a mountain, and he was the one who awakened the world to its duty. It was none other than David who stirred mankind with his great poems, with his inspired teachings. It was none other than David Melech Yisrael who taught the world how to thank Hashem.

David created a wave of thanksgiving that hadn't existed before, and we're still being carried along with that wave to this day. David fulfilled the prophecy that his great ancestress had said. When her son Yehudah was born, she said, "He is going to praise Hashem" (*Bereishis* 29:35). David fulfilled that prophecy when he came on the scene of history.

David was the "*Neki chapayim uvar leivav*—the one who has clean hands and a pure heart." David was the man who "ascended the mountain." He was the one who conceived the great plan of a Beis Hamikdash, from which the message went forth of recognizing and thanking Hashem, of serving Hashem in gratitude.

Q Why did David appear at that particular time in history?

"*Zeh dor dorshav*—This is the generation of those who seek Hashem" (*Tehillim* 24:6). We're so accustomed to saying it that our minds are deadened to it. But it's a big statement. What does it mean? Didn't they seek Hashem before? What's David telling us? Now, pay attention because this is an important fact, and very few people are cognizant of it, even *talmidei chachamim*.

David wasn't an accident. He was a man of destiny. He appeared on the scene just when he was needed. Hashem placed him in that generation for a reason—because it was a generation of "*dorshei Hashem*," those who sought Hashem. How? What happened? Suddenly they became *dorshei Hashem*?

Let me explain. If you recall, when Devorah the prophetess sang her song, she said (*Shoftim* 5:6), "In the days of Shamgar ben Anas people stopped traveling on the roads." They were afraid to go anywhere. Those who dared to travel had to take roundabout routes, side roads and crooked paths. Even the main roads in those days weren't speedways. In the rainy season, they were muddy and almost impassable. You had to cut your way through brambles, through thickets, through forests. In those days, Eretz Yisrael had lions and other wild animals, so it wasn't so pleasant to go through byways. In addition, the enemy was everywhere, and everyone tried to avoid them. That's what Devorah said openly. Therefore, travel stopped. People were confined to their immediate district. As a result, a very important practice fell into disuse—the practice of *aliyah l'regel*, of going up three times a year to Shiloh, to the sanctuary of Shiloh.

Three times a year, every male was required to go up to the Mishkan. "Three times a year, show yourself to the *Adon*, the Master" (*Shemos* 34:23). He's called *Aleph-daled-nun-yud*, in singular. This term for Hashem is almost never used. So why is it used here? The purpose of going up three times a year to be *oleh regel* on *yom tov* to the sanctuary was to show yourself to the "Landlord," to the Master of the land. Your coming declared that the land was not yours, that you were only a tenant. You shouldn't forget that you're only tenants, and He's the real Master of the land. We cannot underestimate the effect this had on the people. When they went up to Shiloh, they took with them so much *emunah*, so much faith and *yiras Hashem*, that it stayed with them the rest of their lives. The purpose was to learn to fear Hashem.

Devorah came with Barak ben Avinoam and conquered the mighty general Sisera. "Then the few were victorious over the mighty. The Am Hashem scored a victory for Me over the mighty warriors" (*Shoftim* 5:13). After the victory, the roads were opened for the first time in a long time. But the old system had fallen into disuse. When a *mitzvah* discontinues due to some reason, the *yetzer hara* tries to keep people from doing it, even though the reason is no longer relevant. As a result, this practice fell into disuse, and a spiritual decay set in. Every community kept to itself. No longer did they all go up to the heart of the nation where the Shechinah dwelt, where the Sanhedrin sat, where the great teachers could influence them. The nation sank into a spiritual regression—until one man came along. This great man was Elkanah, the father of Shmuel Hanavi.

Elkanah started a campaign to revive this *mitzvah*. He traveled throughout the country, awakening the people to the *mitzvah* of *aliyah l'regel*. Each time he went to Shiloh, he took a different route. Each time, he stopped and preached in the towns and villages. He told his fellow Israelites the beauty of this *mitzvah* and said, "Let's fulfill this duty." He got groups to join him. As he passed from town to town, his followers increased. By the time he reached Shiloh, he had a great multitude of enthusiasts following him. They walked on the roads and sang. He did this year after year, until finally there was a great spiritual rebirth.

When Shmuel Hanavi became leader, he took over where his father left off. In those days, a great tragedy happened, a national tragedy. The Philistines went into battle with the Am Yisrael, orchestrated a terrible slaughter, and destroyed the Mishkan of Shiloh, which had stood for 369 years. It was a *churban* Beis Hamikdash. People think the first *churban* was of Shlomo's Beis Hamikdash. That's not true. Shlomo's was the second. The first was the *churban* of Mishkan Shiloh.

Shmuel Hanavi used the years after this catastrophe to pick up where his father left off. He traveled throughout the land, spoke to the people constantly, and worked up their enthusiasm until "the whole house of Yisrael yearned for Hashem" (I *Shmuel* 7:2). For twenty years he was on the move, stirring up the nation and bringing them to a new height. Then David Hamelech came and said, "Now is the time!"—"*Zeh dor darshav*—This is the generation of those who seek Hashem!"

Then the *passuk* adds, "*Mevakshei panecha, Yaakov, selah*—This is the generation of Yaakov, who seek Your face." He calls them the "generation of Yaakov," which means even the plain people, the multitudes, all seek Your face, Hashem. They all yearned after Hashem.

This is a very important episode in our history, which is passed over by most people. It was then that David appeared and used the opportunity to compose his *Tehillim*. From then on, forever, the whole Jewish nation sang David's songs. We are still riding the crest of that great wave, which was set in motion by the spirit of this great man.

Chazal say that this *mizmor* (*Tehillim* 24) that David composed was recited when the Aron was first brought into the Kodesh Hakadashim in the Beis Hamikdash. It is telling us that the world is created for one purpose, which is to praise Hashem. And we needed a great personality to come along just at the right time to make the world aware of this purpose—and that's David. David was the one who decided at that time to erect the Beis Hamikdash. That's why it says, "*Se'u she'arim rasheichem*—Lift up your heads, O gates" (*Tehillim* 24:7,9), which means we needed a tall edifice with high gates in which to praise Hashem. David prepared all the materials for this edifice. He also composed this *mizmor*, and the one recited at the inauguration of the Beis Hamikdash—*Mizmor shir chanukas habayis l'David* (*Tehillim* 30), with which we start *P'sukei D'zimrah*. Therefore, it's really Mikdash David. He didn't build it with his own hands. His son Shlomo did, but David made all the preparations. He was the man who dreamed this great dream, because he understood the purpose of the universe—to praise Hashem. And that purpose is fulfilled by the nation that follows in the footsteps of David.

PRACTICAL ADVICE

In *P'sukei D'zimrah* there are so many selections from *Tehillim*, and the Rav has told us that every word is a gem and an opportunity for perfection of the mind. But can one really concentrate on so many verses and so many different thoughts?

Certainly not. And therefore, you shouldn't even try to say everything. Just to rattle off words and not gain any *da'as*, is worthless. It's not completely worthless, but it's just about worthless.

Instead, take your time. "*Tov me'at tachanunim b'kavanah*

meiharbos b'lo kavanah—Better to *daven* a small amount with concentration, than to *daven* a lot without concentration" (*Orach Chaim* 1:4). Say a little, but think about what you're saying. Study the words and understand what you're saying. That's the real achievement in davening.

Now, of course, if you have a great deal of time, you can start davening three hours before the *tzibbur*, and you'll be able to do justice to a good part of the *P'sukei D'zimrah*. But whatever it is, you should spend time using your head in davening, not just your lips.

Q **The Rav has often been critical of music, but isn't there a certain power in it?**

And the answer is absolutely. Although music per se, music by itself, is nothing, if it's utilized for an ideal it becomes a powerful motor to help you arrive at your destination. Suppose a man has a motor, an excellent motor. It turns over so many revolutions per second and its performance is the smoothest possible—only the motor doesn't have a belt connecting it to the wheels! It accomplishes nothing! The spinning is useless. It's a complete waste of energy.

Music is only important if it's connected to an ideal. When Rav Yisrael Salanter started the study of *mussar*, he introduced the practice of saying it with a *niggun*. He would say, "*Yesod hachassidus v'shoresh ha'avodah hatemimah hu sheyisbareir v'yisameis eitzel ha'adam mah chovaso b'olamo*—The foundation of all piety and the root of the perfect service of Hashem is that one should recognize his duty here in this world" (*Mesillas Yesharim*, Chapter 1). Then he started off singing to himself, "*Mah chovaso b'olamo*—What is my duty in this world? What is my duty in this world?" That's what they did in the old yeshivas at the instigation of Rav Yisrael Salanter. They learned *mussar* with a *niggun*. It was a sad, pensive, meditative *niggun*. That was a way of using music to help the words enter their hearts. "*Mah chovaso b'olamo*?" They said it over and over again, with a tune. It pierced the shell of their hearts, the hard-armored heart, and entered the softness of the heart. They began to think, "Actually, what *is* my duty in this world?"

When music is utilized for *mussar*, for *avodas Hashem,* it's an excellent expedient. Absolutely! That's why, when the *ruach hakodesh* moved David Hamelech, he took out his harp and said, "*Barchi, nafshi, es Hashem*—Bless Hashem, my soul" (*Tehillim* 104:1). The harp helped him ascend on the wings of music to the heights of perfection of the soul.

Q **What's the right way to teach music to children?**

I'll explain. "*Shiru lo, zamru lo*" (*Tehillim* 105:2). What does that mean? *Shiru lo* means to "say poetry to Hashem." Not singing, but poetry. To talk with enthusiasm, to speak in an enthusiastic manner. That's poetry. And then it says, "*zamru lo*—sing with music to Him." Not only to say poetry to Hashem, but to sing with music as well. We see that it's a *mitzvah* to show our happiness and gratitude to Hashem with music.

Now, the first step is to teach our children to be grateful to Hashem. Parents have to teach their children to appreciate all the things that we mentioned here tonight.[10] It's a very big task. But to teach your son how to sing with music before that first step is like telling a person to blow into a horn, but not telling him what to blow. He has no notes. His horn-blowing is nothing. Therefore, the first thing is to train your children in the art of thanking Hashem. Most people play music and don't thank Hashem. They don't think about Hashem. That's why it's a waste of time.

But if you have a *tzaddik*—an *eved Hashem* who learned how to talk about Hashem and how to thank Hashem—and now he wants to express himself with song, that's the "*Shiru lo, zamru lo*" that David was speaking about.

I once went into a certain *shteibel*, and a Rebbe was sitting

10 Lecture E-213, "The First Step on the Path to Greatness."

there, singing. I can never forget it. He was singing "*Ana Avda D'Kudsha Brich Hu.*" It went into my blood and I'll never forget it.[11] That's already something else. A man who has *yiras Shamayim* and singing—putting all of his *yiras Shamayim* into the song—is something else entirely! I was listening to him and it had a tremendous influence on me.

Some people want to play music and sing, but their minds are empty. That's a waste of time. Just to arouse your nerves by the excitement of music without having the noble thoughts to accompany the music is nothing. That's why it's so important to teach our children to sing to Hashem about everything in their lives. *Shiru lo! Lo!* To Him! That's the first step. After they accomplish that—if they are already perfect in the *avodah* of speaking with enthusiasm about Hashem—then you can move onto *zamru lo* and teach your child music, so that he'll be able to sing and thank Hashem with music.

11 From Rav Miller's biography: "At shul dinners, Rabbi Miller made sure that musicians were hired and that there would be spirited dancing. He danced with everyone individually, using the opportunity to add *simchas haTorah* to their lives. He always requested that a favorite *niggun* be played, such as '*V'sein Banu Yetzer Tov*' (Place in our hearts the inclination to do good) or '*Ana Avda D'Kudsha Brich Hu*' (I am a servant of the Holy One, Blessed Is He), which he called 'our national anthem.'"

ASHREI

Q What makes *Ashrei* so important?

The Gemara (*Brachos* 4b) says that if you say *Ashrei* three time every day, you're a *ben Olam Haba*. The Gemara asks, "Why?" What's so important? Of course, it's a marvelous composition of *ruach hakodesh* and very deep wisdom, but what distinguishes it from all the other chapters of *Tehillim*? David said many beautiful things.

The Gemara concludes that it's because of the *passuk*, "*Posei'ach es yadecha umasbia l'chol chai ratzon*—You open Your hand and satiate all the living with their needs" (*Tehillim* 145:16). That's what makes *Ashrei* so important. It's so important that by saying it every day properly, you're becoming a *ben Olam Haba*. You're impressing onto your *neshamah* the idea that Hashem is feeding the whole world.

Now, the question arises why the Gemara quoted specifically that *passuk*. The *passuk* just before it says the same thing, so it seems—"The eyes of all hope to You, and You give them their food in its time." Why not that *passuk*? The answer is that this *passuk* merely tells us that Hashem gives food; He supplies the needs of the living. That's all. But the *passuk* of *Posei'ach es yadecha* tells us something more. "You open up Your hand." Now, Hashem doesn't have a hand. His "hand" means his power, and what does He use his power for? *Chessed*. "*Ki chafetz chessed Hu*—all of Your power is for *chessed*" (*Michah* 7:18). That's what Hashem wants to show us in this world—His kindliness. Nothing interests Him except *chessed*. "He sits on his throne, distributing food to the entire world" (*Pesachim* 118a). That, *kaveyachol*, is His main interest in the world—to feed every creature. And this *chessed* of feeding every living thing is expressed in the words "*Posei'ach es yadecha*."

It's a very great achievement to understand this important principle—that the entire *briyah* is geared to supplying the needs of the living. Rav Saadia Gaon says this is a "food world" (*Emunos V'deyos* 9:6). We must study that.[12] If you study it and know it and really think

---

12 See more on this topic in the *brachah* of *Bareich Aleinu*, p. 283.

about it as you say *Ashrei* three times a day, then you're on the way to becoming a *ben Olam Haba.*

Q **Does living for Olam Haba mean living a depressed life?**

All you sad-faced people—perk up and listen! Instead of being morose, instead of being sad, you have to be happy in this world, and you have to thank Hashem continually for it. There's so much that He's giving us—a veritable smorgasbord! "This world is a lobby before the banquet hall" (*Avos* 4:16). There are so many good things they are serving us in the "lobby" here that we have to continually thank Hashem with the fullest of hearts.

"*Ashrei yoshvei veisecha; od yehalelucha, selah*—Happy are those who sit in Your house; forever they will praise you" (*Tehillim* 84:5). On that *passuk*, Rabbi Yehoshua ben Levi says, "All who busy themselves singing song in this world merit to sing it in the World to Come" (*Sanhedrin* 91b). The emphasis is on *song*. Not prose. When a man says, "Things are good," that's prose. But suppose you get a call from the lottery commission that you just won the jackpot. When you tell your wife, will you speak in prose to her? No. You'll speak in *poetry*! You'll speak in lyric verse! You might even dance!

When you sing your song in this world, don't mumble it. Sing! Sing, "*Baruch Atah, Hashem*" out loud and clearly, slowly cherishing every word. Of course, first you must understand why you're thanking Him. You can't do that unless you appreciate a glass of water. When you take in your hand that glass of crystal-clear liquid—that wonderful elixir of life, a miracle combination of two gases—think about what a miracle it is. Can a person drink gas? Drinking a tank of oxygen and a tank of hydrogen would not do you any good. Yet here you have this wonderful combination of chemicals, and as it goes down your throat it transforms all the organs, tissues, and fluids of your body; it lubricates everything in your body. That's how I drink a glass of water! From now on, say, *Baruch Atah, Hashem, Elokeinu, Melech ha'olam, shehakol nihiyeh bidvaro* with new meaning. When you live that way, all your life you're singing a song of happiness, and you will merit to continue singing it in Olam Haba.

You don't have to be rich to sing this song. In fact, usually the rich don't sing songs of happiness. In the penthouses on Park Avenue, a lot of people have committed suicide. More people commit suicide from Park Avenue penthouses than in Brownsville. Happiness doesn't depend on money. Whatever you have, you must learn to enjoy. You must learn to be happy in this world. You must learn to sing. You must learn to appreciate what Hashem is giving you.

Don't make the great mistake of thinking that this world is only suffering and affliction, saying, "I'll get rewarded in the next world; that's where reward is waiting for me." The man who goes around in this world unhappy is in effect saying this world is nothing; this world is just darkness and bitterness. It's only a place where we're waiting for the real world, the World to Come. That man will never understand his purpose in this world.

Here's a fellow who groans and thinks to himself how afflicted he is, how much suffering he goes through ... as he sits down to a breakfast of eggs, with butter and jam on his bread. He is also afflicting himself with coffee and cream. He is so sad. His plate in this world is so bare. At lunchtime, he goes through the whole torture all over again. Therefore, he's waiting for the next world. There, at least, he'll be paid. There, all his pious deeds, his Torah and his *mitzvos*, will be rewarded.

He's like the fellow who walks into a store, buys a bag full of vegetables and fruits, and puts the money on the table. As he walks away, the storekeeper says, "Come back! It's counterfeit!" Hashem says the same thing. You made *brachos* that were counterfeit. You didn't mean them. While you were consuming so many tons of bread, so many gallons of milk, so many pounds of butter, and so many head of steer, you were thinking that you were getting nothing from Me. So you didn't make a real, heartfelt *brachah*. It was counterfeit! You didn't learn to be grateful. Rav Simcha Zissel, *zt"l*, used to say, "*Olam Hazeh* is an expensive hotel. Everything costs. You have to pay. And the minimum payment is genuine coin—a heartfelt *brachah*.

There's nothing free in this world. This world is expensive."

This world is a great rehearsal, because when we come into the next world, we're going to have something really important to say "thank You" for. However, we won't merit saying and experiencing it if we don't rehearse in this world. Therefore, it's of the utmost importance to rehearse while in this world.

"This world is a lobby before the banquet hall." Hashem gives us good things here, too—a lot of good things. But we must practice saying, "Thank You—*Baruch Atah*." Again and again, "Thank You—*Baruch Atah*," until it gets into our blood, until we recognize Him, until we see Him... until we really feel gratitude.

Part of working hard for the next world is learning how to be happy in this world. You must be happy and grateful for every little thing. When you breathe a lungful of air, you must learn how to be grateful for it. Tonight, you'll put your head on the pillow and be wafted away into slumberland. Appreciate how good it is to fall asleep. In some parts of the world, people don't have pillows or even beds. They sleep on the ground. Do you know how it feels to sleep on the hard ground? Try it. Sleep on the floor tonight. In the middle of the night, you'll get up with aching sides and say, "Rabbi Miller was right." You must be grateful for a pillow. You must be grateful for a bed, for a mattress. You must be grateful for the fact that ten other people aren't sleeping in the room with you, which happens all over the world. You must be grateful for the fact that the room is clean, and the bed is clean. You must be grateful that you're not afraid.

Appreciate the fact that you can fall sleep. How many people go to drugstores to buy pills to help them sleep? And it doesn't even help. They toss all night and get up in the morning sick with headaches from lack of sleep. So when you put your head on the pillow and fall asleep, you're rich! You're a millionaire. You have a Cadillac, a jet that takes you off into the world of slumber—happy, healthy sleep. You must appreciate that.

You must thank Hashem for all the things people take for granted. What kind of thanking is it if you say, "Breakfast is nothing"? If you eat breakfast, it's something. I'm one man who doesn't deprecate Olam Hazeh. I look forward to a meal. Of course, if that's your whole fun in this world, you may come to the next world and say, "What, no steaks?! No mushrooms smothered in *schmaltz*?" So don't say that Rabbi Miller says to run after every pleasure of this world, but you have to eat sometimes. So when you finally eat your *pas b'melach*, bread and salt, and drink your glass of water, learn to appreciate how good it is. When you sink your teeth into a piece of bread, learn to be happy, to enjoy, to feel what a great experience it is to eat. Then, the next time you'll mean it when you say, *Baruch Atah, Hashem ... hamotzi lechem min ha'aretz*! Again, I'm not saying you should pursue expensive items for breakfast, but when you eat breakfast learn to enjoy it to the hilt! Fully! Live deeply, richly, on your piece of bread and salt and water.

Rashi says, "Practice blessing Him in this world, so that you should be accustomed to it in the World to Come" (*Brachos* 63a). In this world, we rehearse for the World to Come. Not only when you say *Ashrei*, not only when you say *Tehillim*, but also when you say *brachos*. Rehearse even in your thoughts. Turn your life into a career of song to Hashem.

This life provides countless opportunities for joy. "He who is of good heart [mind] is at a perpetual banquet" (*Mishlei* 15:15). One who gains insight into the marvels of the apple, the wonder of a glassful of water, the delight of a deep draft of air, the joy of a full night's sleep, the enormous communication apparatus of the senses, the pleasures of walking, the happiness of eyesight, and the countless other joys of living needs no feasts, for he's already enjoying *the best banquet*—the feast of the good mind. The good mind consists of the attitudes gained while living in this world. It's no exaggeration to say that such a man is wealthy beyond *all men.* "Who is wealthy? He who rejoices in his lot" (*Avos* 4:1). He keenly feels the goodness of clouds, rain, wind, snow, sunshine, thunder, lightning, rivers, the moon, the stars, outer space. He enjoys his shoes, clothing, his chair, and the roof over his head. He's happy in his ability to sleep. He rejoices in his teeth, his arms and legs, his stomach, his two kidneys, his healthy bones, his heart, his sane mind, his memory, and his ability to forget what he does not wish to remember. These possessions are nonexistent for those who ignore them. Only one who is happily aware of them truly possesses them. Such a man sings out in gratitude and in praise of the Creator. Of him it's said, "*Ashrei yoshvei veisecha*—Happy are those who sit in Your house," for he "is busy with song in this world" (*Sanhedrin* 91b). And after such a life, the best is yet to come. "*Od yehalelucha, selah*—Still more shall they extol You forever." For this life of joy and singing is but a rehearsal for the everlasting career of happy song.

Q Can you blame a person for not feeling emotionally involved in his davening?

Why should you blame someone for not feeling the words? Feeling is an automatic thing. It's not voluntary. So how can you blame people for not feeling?

And the answer is—they should have worked on it! They should have labored to gain that feeling, because *yiras Shamayim* is the job of a Jew. *Emunah*—that's our purpose in life. A Jew can't say, "Look, I don't feel it. I'm trying, but I don't feel it." That's no excuse. You should have been trying for a long time already, and you should continue trying.

You must slow down; you have to stop and think. You can't fly through davening. You can't allow your davening to become rote. You can't allow your bentching to become rote. What's the purpose of eating? It's not just to gain nourishment. Hashem set up the world so that we need food, but we need food so that we should think of Him and thank Him and realize that He is the Source of everything. When you're eating, you must feel that Hashem is setting your table.

"*Posei'ach es yadecha umasbia l'chol chai ratzon*—You open Your hands and satiate every living thing" (*Tehillim* 145:16). You must feel that He is the One Who opens His hands and feeds you every day. David worked on this every day until he acquired the feeling that he was eating out of Hashem's hands. It was the result of many years' labor.

Every time he took food, he felt that Hashem was opening His hand to feed him. He felt that he was a lamb, and Hashem was his Shepherd (*Tehillim* 24:1), and he was eating out of His hand. When David said *posei'ach es yadecha*, he wasn't just reciting a beautiful phrase. He meant it.

That's what we are expected to strive for—the awareness that when we eat, we experience it as if Hashem is literally opening His hand and feeding us. That's the awareness David achieved. "You open Your hand" and are feeding us. We, too, must feel that Hashem is feeding us. Although your wife is bending over a gas range for hours and hours to make a tasty supper for you—and you certainly must appreciate her and express your thanks with feeling and sincerity—you should never forget that you have to labor in the realization that Hashem is the One Who is stretching out His hand full of these good things, and you're eating out of His hands. That's the feeling that you'll get. *Posei'ach es yadecha umasbia l'chol chai ratzon.*

The farmer, too, must think this way. All the time that he's laboring, he should realize that it's nothing but a formality. He plows the field, sows the seeds, waters it, reaps the grain, threshes it, winnows it, grinds it, bakes it, and then finally, after a long season of toil, there's a piece of bread on his table. He must pick it up and say, "I thank You, Hashem"—*hamotzi lechem min ha'aretz*—"that *You* took this bread out of the earth." He had nothing to do with it. He was only going through certain motions. He has to say that with full sincerity.

That's the test of *bitachon*. All our lives, we must battle in our minds against the effect of our efforts. We have to live our lives going through all the motions of effort while at the same time fostering within ourselves the feeling, the awareness, that Hashem is the Source—and the only source—of all the things that we receive.

That's the purpose of our lives.

Q What does it mean to call out to Hashem "in truth"?

It says in *Ashrei*, "Hashem is close to all who call out to Him *in truth*" (*Tehillim* 145:18). How great it is when a person calls out to Hashem. By calling out to Hashem, He comes close to you. It's not just a *mashal.* The Shechinah comes close to a man who calls out to Him. If you feel that He's the One to Whom you must direct your requests, that's real awareness, real *yiras Hashem.* And then He becomes close to you. But there's a condition: "...to all those who call out to Him in truth." You must call to Him sincerely.

Say a person isn't feeling well and he says in his davening, "*Refa'einu Hashem v'neirafei*—Heal us, Hashem, and we are healed." He certainly wants to get well. The question is: Does he feel that he's speaking to the right address, that Hashem is the One Who can make him well? If he's thinking that the main thing is to go to physicians and that davening to Hashem is a formality, then it's not "*be'emes*—in truth." *Be'emes* means only when he has the *emunah* that Hashem is the "*Rofei cholei amo Yisrael*—the Healer of His people Yisrael." It's the going to a physician that's the formality.

Now, we are required to look for a good physician, and it's a requirement to pay the physician. The Gemara (*Bava Kama* 85a) says you should pay a physician because "a physician who heals for nothing is worth that amount." The example in the Gemara is of a man who wounded his fellow and is obligated to compensate him for several things, including his doctor's bills. If the man says, "I have a friend who's a doctor and he'll heal you for nothing," the wounded man can say, "A physician who heals for nothing is worth nothing." A person must find a good physician and pay. At the same time, he has to know that those are mere formalities. *Bitachon* requires him to understand that Hashem is the One Who heals.

That's what is meant by "all those who call Him in truth." You must call out in truth, with *emunah.* If you don't have *emunah*, you must work on it. It's attainable. Every Jew has within him a store of *emunah*, a deep well of *emunah.* The *emunah* is there. It's instinctive. It's only a question of letting it come out. At first, it's like a deep well that hasn't been used in a long time. You must dip in a bucket and start drawing the water out. After you start drawing the water out, you'll see that the well begins to fill of its own accord. There's a bottomless well of *emunah* in the Jewish heart. I say "Jewish heart," but the truth is it's in the *human* heart.

People don't know that *emunah* is within us. The fact is that it's a bottomless supply. There is no end to how much *emunah* we have within ourselves. Of course, that's only if we start using it. That's why this condition of *be'emes* isn't the result of merely wishing it. Calling out *be'emes* must be the result of continued exertion over time—a long time! After a long time, you'll finally discover that you're calling out *be'emes*.

Now, that doesn't mean you shouldn't call out to Hashem while you're in the process of acquiring the *emes*. No, keep trying and trying. Each time you succeed, try more, not less. Trying less is what most people do. The first time, they have some *kavanah*. Then, they have less and less *kavanah*. Finally, it becomes dulled by habit, and they settle for davening by rote. The mind is hardened and becomes desensitized.[13] It's a tragedy when a person prays by rote. A person must have the attitude that each time he davens, he tries to *daven* better. Each time he says, "Hashem," he tries to think of the Shechinah. Each time he says, "*Atah*—You," he tries to picture what "You" means. "You" means you're talking to Someone.

It's like polishing a mirror. First, you rub off the dirt. Little by little, it becomes clearer, brighter, and more transparent. The *neshamah* is like

---

13 From *Sing, You Righteous* #516: "...Do we not see men whose daily repetition of the prayers makes them more and more hardened and insensitive toward the words which they utter? It would seem that constant repetition actually causes insensitivity. But the answer is that constant repetition of acts of insensitivity certainly increases the insensitivity. The more one prays by rote, the more hardened he becomes to the words and ideas of the prayers; and the longer one continues to view the Universe with unseeing eyes, the less and less he will see as life progresses. 'The Amei Haaretz (ignorami), as they become older, become more and more confused' (*Shabbos* 152a). However, the man who continues to put his mind on his prayers, as the years pass he becomes more and more inspired by them; and he who persists in looking at the phenomena of Creation, and even the very same phenomena, day after day, will come to a deep and full understanding of the great truths for which these phenomena are intended: '*Talmidei chachamim*, as they grow older, increase in the True Knowledge (*Da'as*)' (ibid.)."

a mirror. It reflects the light of Hashem. But it's a mirror encrusted with dirt. You must work at polishing it, little by little. Then it begins to become clear, bright, and transparent, until finally the *emunah* starts shining through. After much labor, he's able to call out *be'emes*.[14]

Therefore, when you call out, it should be with such truth that even Hashem will be satisfied that you really mean what you're saying.

---

14 From *Chovos Halevavos* (*Sha'ar Cheshbon Hanefesh* 5): "Consider as if you were in a place above which is a picture that you are unable to see. ... Take a sheet of metal and polish it until its dullness departs, and rub it for a long time with various polishes. Then raise it up before you so that you see the reflection of that elevated picture which had been concealed from you, and you gaze at it and enjoy its beauty. This delightful picture above you, which you cannot see with your eyes, is the wisdom of the Creator and His power and the splendor of the higher world whose form and nature are concealed from us. The metal plate is the human soul, which can be burnished by means of wisdom and by the Torah. The polish that we apply are the subjects of meditation that I have enumerated. When you continue to think in them, your soul will become clear and your mind will be illuminated, and even the concealed matters will be reflected in your soul, and you will see the true pictures with open eyes, and the gates of perfection will open for you, and the curtain that separates you from the Creator's wisdom will be removed."

AZ YASHIR

Q **What's the main lesson of *Az Yashir*?**

One of the key lessons is *bitachon*. The *Chovos Halevavos* says that if you have something you're enjoying—some success, some happiness—that makes you proud and happy, don't put your trust in it. Don't have any hope that it's going to endure. If it continues every day for years and years, good. But if you make the error of putting your trust in it—saying, "I have a big bank account," and always taking out your bank book and reading it; it's the most interesting thing for you because it gives you a sense of security, that you're fixed for the next 5,000 years—watch out. Because you're not insured. That's one account that's not insured. If you desire to keep something, the *Chovos Halevavos* says, don't put your trust in it.

At *kriyas Yam Suf*, when the sea split and Pharaoh's army was drowned in the waters, the B'nei Yisrael sang, "*Sus v'rachvo ramah vayam*—Horse and rider He threw into the sea" (*Shemos* 15:1). What does that mean? The B'nei Yisrael feared Pharaoh's army, but more than anything else they feared "*sus Pharaoh*" (ibid. 15:19). They feared his cavalry, his horsemen. Pharaoh's horses were specially trained to trample on enemies. When the B'nei Yisrael saw an army coming, mounted on these terrible steeds—the infamous horses of Egypt that were trained to have no pity—they feared for their lives like nothing else. But where should they flee to? In front of them was the sea. They were surrounded by enemies—the sea in front of them and the horses of Pharaoh behind them. There was no place to look but upwards, so they looked toward Hashem and cried out to Him.

What did Hashem do? He caused the horses to leap into the sea with their riders. "*Sus v'rachvo ramah vayam*—He threw them into the sea." As soon as the Egyptian riders saw that the waters were starting to close in, they tried to turn the horses around and go back. But the horses refused. Chazal say the horses kept plunging ahead, deeper and deeper into the waters. In the end, the horses carried all their riders to destruction. And where? Into the sea—the other great fear of the B'nei Yisrael. They had feared the horses behind them and the sea in front of them. What turned out to be our deliverance? The sea and the horses—the very things the B'nei Yisrael feared most!

When they saw that, they learned a lesson—that even the most terrible enemies shouldn't frighten us. They're only a stimulus to cry out to Hashem. When there's peril, *chas v'shalom*, it's not intended to cause us to lose hope. It's a stimulus, a spur, to pray to Hashem, to put our trust in Him.

When the B'nei Yisrael cried out to Hashem, He heard them and said, "Ah, you're crying out to Me? I'll show you that your enemies will cooperate to become your saviors. The very things you feared will save you!"

Think about that tomorrow morning. It's a great lesson. "*Azi v'zimras Kah vayhi li lishu'ah*—My strength and my song are only Hashem, and He became my salvation" (ibid. 15:2).

YOTZER HAM'OROS

Q Why do we talk so much about the *malachim* in the *brachah* of Yotzer Ham'oros?

And the answer is—to be an example for us.

The Mirrer *mashgiach*, Reb Yerucham, *zt"l*, once asked an American boy what the *malachim* are doing. He didn't know, so Reb Yerucham answered for him. "*Tamid mesaprim kevod Kel*—They are always speaking of the glory of Hashem" (the *brachah* of *Yotzer Ham'oros*).

Every morning when we say, "*Baruch Atah, Hashem, yotzer ham'oros*—blessed are You, Hashem, Creator of the luminaries," the Jewish nation acts out a vast drama. We're reenacting a spectacular drama every morning when the sun comes up. It's the drama of the excitement of the *malachim* when they view the phenomenon of light.

How do *we* react? We might be thinking: *What time is it? How long until davening is over? What will I have for breakfast today? How am I going to make money today?*

Well, forget about those things. We were created for the business of recognizing the Creator in this world. And light is the first phenomenon that Hashem said was good. "*Vayar Elokim es ha'or ki tov*—He saw that the light was good" (*Bereishis* 1:4).

Unfortunately, while this is taking place, most people in the audience are fast asleep. They're saying the words, but their minds are elsewhere. When a child sees the phenomena of Nature, he views them without excitement because he has only a young brain that hasn't matured yet. He may think he understands everything. He certainly will not respond with the ecstasy that these phenomena were intended to evoke. But if we put forth the effort to study, and choose to listen to what we're saying, we too can share in the excitement of the *malachim*.

Malachim are very wise creatures, and the *brachah* of *Yotzer Ham'oros* describes their greatness at length. And still, these *malachei elyon* never cease to become excited when they see the light! Light! That's what excites them! They call out *b'raash gadol*! Not the way we say it, mumbling the words quietly. No, they're so excited that they go into ecstasy. They go wild with *simchah* and *hakaras hatov*. They go *meshuga* when they see the light!

Now, some say that the light the *malachim* go wild over is some mysterious influence that pervades the universe. But it's not true; the *malachim* are not talking about *ruach hakodesh* or the Shechinah or some mysterious influence. They're talking about the light of the sun. Physical sunlight. A glowing ball of thermonuclear energy, sending forth its rays with tremendous power—billions of tons of horsepower flowing down to the Earth. Light is a wonder. A miracle. To this day, nobody knows exactly what it is. Is it a substance or a force? It's a huge point of dispute in the science books. It's a mystery. Is it a wave or a particle? They call it a form of energy, but what is energy and how does that energy travel? And it's not just traveling, it's moving at tremendous speed. Light travels at 186,000 miles a second. Not per hour—per *second*! The sunlight that's here now was on the sun 93 million miles away about eight minutes ago! And without it, we couldn't see. Whatever it is, light is a miracle of epic proportions. It's a wonder of wonders.

There's a lot more we could say about light, but the *malachim* go *meshuga* from happiness because of sunlight! They exert their gigantic intellects to the utmost to encompass all that they're able to learn of Hashem's ways—to perceive His greatness both from the work of His hands (Nature) and from His conduct of the world (history). With the furthest limits of their abilities, they arrive at a sublime pinnacle of understanding of Hashem's Perfection, which they express in the word "*Kadosh*—Holy!"

But then they consider and recognize that they have not yet comprehended even a drop in the ocean of their Creator's greatness, and they return to the effort of summoning all their wondrous abilities for a second and greater expression, beginning from where they had left off at the first "*Kadosh!*" All their understanding, together with the new awareness they now gain by additional exertion, are included in the second exclamation, "*Kadosh*!"

Then they perceive that they have as yet said almost nothing, for, "*v'ligdulaso ein cheiker*—there is no searching out His greatness" (*Tehillim* 145:3). So, they resume their efforts and include all their old and new understanding of Hashem in another exclamation: "*Kadosh*!" This continues forever (*Kuzari* IV, 3), and thus these sublime beings labor with their happy function of delving more and more deeply and pursuing the True Knowledge, degree after degree. With each "*Kadosh*," they express a higher level of understanding, and therefore a higher level of excitement. It's this wave after wave of excitement that we're hoping to ride each morning during our own *brachah* of *Yotzer Ham'oros* when we say our "*Kadosh! Kadosh! Kadosh!*"

It's a pity that people say this *brachah* every day entirely unaware of what's taking place. What's taking place is the way the *malachim* greet the sunlight. To wake us up, to make us understand a little of what's taking place, the *malachim* are ushered onto the stage of our *tefillos*, so we can watch how they perform the greeting of the sunlight. They don't look at the sun with equanimity and composure merely because they have seen it so many times. Even though they've seen it longer than any of us have, they spring into action each time anew and say, "*Melo chol ha'aretz kevodo*—Hashem, the One Who created this, is filling the Earth with His glory." What glory are they talking about? The sunlight.

Therefore, when we see light, we should try to emulate the *malachim*. That's why we bring them onto the stage.

Q **What's so important about light?**

Light is good for many things. If not for sunlight, this Earth would be an ice cube. You get free heat. That's certainly good. If not for sunlight, there wouldn't be food. All food requires photosynthesis. Even a piece of chicken. A chicken doesn't need photosynthesis, but a chicken has to eat things that grow via photosynthesis. It's only the sunlight that keeps us going.

It's the sunlight that makes rain. The sun evaporates water from the oceans and raises it up in the form of clouds, and then the clouds travel by the wind and empty their contents on the continent in the form of rain. And that's how things grow.

If not for the sunlight, the waters would remain in the seas and lakes and never rise. The dry land would be sandy deserts and the oceans would always be full and overflowing. It's the sun that's feeding the world. The sun is the energy that makes everything work in this world.

If I'm talking now, it's only because of the sunlight that's in me. If you talk when you come home tonight, it's the sunlight in you that's talking. That's not an exaggeration. Nothing can exist without energy. If you plug a tape recorder into the socket and the tape starts playing, it's not that the tape has the power to play. It's the energy of the electricity that's making it play—and that comes from sunlight. It's not just tape recorders. When our brains are working, it's sunlight.

Ask anybody who knows a little bit about physics. They'll explain that the input of the sun's energy is the foundation of all action, of all growth in this world. If you study the light, you see how wonderfully it operates. If it didn't travel as fast as it does, it wouldn't be efficient. If it didn't conduct images from an object to your eye, you wouldn't see anything. If light didn't hit the chlorophyll cells in plants, there would be no photosynthesis. No starch would be produced. There wouldn't be anything to eat.

When you study the sunlight, you see how it cooperates with the Earth in so many ways that it's a marvel of marvels. It's the result of the most cunning planning that needed an intelligence far beyond anything a human being could muster.

Now, we're not finished studying the blessings of the sun if we merely say that it's life, that it's the cause of all functioning in this world. No, that's not enough. That's only a beginning. Bigger yet is the knowledge that the phenomenon of light makes us aware of the Creator of the lights. That's the greater purpose of the light—to make us aware of *Yotzer Ham'oros*, the Creator of it. The purpose is to give us *da'as*, awareness of Hashem. That's the greatest gift in this world. That's why we do *mitzvos*. *Mitzvos* cause us to be aware of Hashem. Every time you do a *mitzvah*, it has several purposes. But one of the main functions of *mitzvos* is to make us aware that there is a *Metzaveh*, One Who commanded us. *Tzitzis* is to remind you that you're doing what Hashem wants you to do. All *mitzvos* have at their core the purpose to make us more and more aware of Hashem.

When the *malachim*, with their great intellects, perceive the glory of Hashem through the sunlight, they become extremely excited. It's a pity when people receive this great gift but aren't aware of it. It's really the gift of *emunah*, of *yirah*, of awe at the greatness of the One Who made all this. *Malachim* understand how precious this gift is and therefore say, "*Kadosh!*" *Kadosh* means Hashem is perfect. Then they repeat it, over and over again. Each repetition is a new symphony of awareness, a new explosion of excitement.

Then they say, "*Melo chol ha'aretz kevodo*—His glory fills the entire universe." It's not only in one place. If light were available, say, only in China or the mountains of Tibet, we'd tap our way with white canes in darkness and climb that mountain to experience it, to open our eyes and see the light. That light would teach us the most precious knowledge. But it's "*Melo chol ha'aretz kevodo.*" It's not far away from us. It comes to us. In case you're too lazy to lift your head up and look at the sun, it begins to set. It comes down low, right in front of your eyes. At sunset, it's big and red, to be more conspicuous for lazy people. Sunset is a time to take a good look.

That's why the Gemara (*Brachos* 29b) says that that's the best time to *daven* Minchah. "*Yira'ucha im shamesh*—They'll fear You together with the sun" (*Tehillim* 72:5). When they see the sun, they'll fear You. Practically speaking, it's no good to wait until then, because you might miss Minchah, so *daven* earlier. But the original, proper time was "*yira'ucha im shamesh.*" Then the sun looks bigger. It's red and glowing with the *ohr* of glory. It's a testament to the One Who created it.

Now, when the *malachim* have said what they had to say, before they retire from the stage, we repeat their words. Of course, compared to them we're repeating it in a weak voice, but at least we're trying. We can't be the same as *malachim* in our understanding of the greatness of light, but we attempt to, so we say the words after them. Actually, the Gemara says they only say "*kadosh*" after we say "*kadosh,*" but it means that when the time comes for us, they say it, too. And we repeat it during Shacharis so that we should study their model.

Q What does *"Baruch kevod Hashem mim'komo"* mean?

Before *the malachim* leave the stage, they say one more sentence, "*Baruch kevod Hashem mim'komo*—Blessed is the glory of Hashem from His place." What does that mean?

The *malachim* have been trying to impress us with the glory of Hashem. And they made a great performance. If you read the original in the *Nevi'im*, in Yeshayah and Yechezkel, respectively, you'll see that the *malachim* don't merely say these words. They say them "*b'kol ra'ash gadol*—with a very great noise!" We can't shout that loud.

They tried their best to impress us, and before they bow off the stage, they tell us, "Don't make the mistake thinking that you've seen everything, that you know all about the light and the *kevod Hashem*. If you think that what we said is a testament to the true greatness of Hashem, you're in error. It's nothing yet."

Imagine a huge palace full of light, but the windows are shut and people outside are in the dark. There's a keyhole, though, and through that little keyhole bursts forth an intense ray of light. That ray is so powerful it illuminates the entire neighborhood. You deduce that if one ray going through the keyhole is so powerful, how great and vast is the light inside! So, too, if the great light of the sun is only a small hint of what's inside, then how endless is the glory of Hashem that's inside His place!

That's why they say, "*Baruch kevod Hashem mim'komo*—Blessed is the glory of Hashem that we see coming out of His place." We should know that in His place it's infinitely greater than what we see here. We can only imagine what it is if we multiply the light of the sun by trillions—a light that would blind not only men but blast all Nature and turn it into cinders. The light of Hashem is so vast that it's impossible to be calculated even though the *malachim* will sing about it forever and ever. But they haven't even begun, because "*Baruch kevod Hashem mim'komo*—Blessed is the glory of Hashem that comes out of His place." We're only blessing that which comes *out* of His place. What's *in* His place is so vast, we don't even begin to know.

Q **Why did Hashem hide the original light?**

On the first day, when Hashem made the universe, He created a light that didn't come from the sun. It was a glorious light. Then, on the fourth day, Hashem said, "Let there be luminaries!" As soon as the sun began to function, the original light was hidden away. That's a strange procedure. Why did He start with the original light, only to stop it? Why didn't He begin immediately with the sunlight?

Another question: If the light of the first day didn't come from the sun, how could there be day and night? Was it day all the time? If the universe was full of light, how could there be "day and night, one day"? All the *mefarshim* try to answer that. But the answer is simple, because the rotation of the Earth began immediately. The light Hashem created on the first day was shining from a fixed point in the universe. As it shined on the Earth, which was already rotating, there was day and night.

Yet, the first question remains: Why did Hashem first make that light, then remove it and substitute the light of the sun? That's a good question. When we first learned Chumash, we were too young to bother with such questions, but now as adults, it should bother us. However, the Torah itself explains that if we saw a light coming from somewhere in space, without a source, it would be too open a demonstration of the glory of Hashem. Scientists would use telescopes and be unable to discover any physical source. They'd all be forced to conclude that it must come from a Creator. But then the purpose of the world would be frustrated. We're not in this world to be forced to believe, to have *emunah* foisted upon us without using our free will. The purpose of this world is to be tested, to see if we will recognize the truth despite it being hidden. Therefore, Hashem substituted a physical light. Light comes from the sun, one of many stars in the universe.

They say that life is an accident; it's luck. Of course, there's a lot of "luck" involved there. If the sun were a little bigger or closer to us, we'd be burned to a crisp. If it were a little smaller or farther away, we'd be frozen into an ice cube. There's a lot of "lucky" fine-tuning necessary. But people can deceive themselves. That's the principle of free will. So, they deceive themselves that it's an accident. There are lot of stars like the sun, they say. Hashem wanted that. He wanted to give people enough rope to hang themselves, so that He could reward those who don't.

AHAVAH RABBAH

Q If we call Hashem *"Ha'av Harachaman,"* why do we also add *"Hameracheim"*?

Every day in *Ahavah Rabbah* we say, "*Avinu, Ha'av Harachaman*—our Father, the merciful Father." Then we add, "*Hameracheim*—the One Who has mercy." It seems to be repetitious—"The merciful Father, the One Who has mercy." But actually, each term means something different.

Suppose you went out rowing in Coney Island, and you accidentally let go of the oars and they drifted away. Now you're in a little boat on the ocean, buffeted by the waves, drifting farther and farther away from the shore—and getting closer and closer to Ireland! You cry out, "Hashem! You are the *Av Harachaman*—You are my merciful Father! *Racheim aleinu!* Please save me!"

All of a sudden, you hear the whirring of a propeller and there's a Coast Guard helicopter coming down. Ah! What a wonderful sound that is! He comes down from the side of the helicopter and lowers a ladder to you. You seize it and climb up, and you hug him. He says, "Mister! I have to fly this thing! Let me drive." But you hug him anyway. He's your savior!

At that moment you're in great danger because, although you won't forget for a moment that Hashem is merciful, you're also thinking that there are other merciful "*sibos*—causes" in the world. Hashem is the *Av Harachaman*, yes, but you're thinking that it was this Coast Guard man who was the *meracheim*. He's the one who had mercy on you. That's why we add the word *Hameracheim*. Not only is He your merciful Father, but He is also the *Meracheim*. He's the only One Who is *meracheim*. If anybody has mercy on you, it's because he's acting as Hashem's agent. Hashem is doing it.

Of course, you have to be grateful to the Coast Guard man. You have to be grateful to his superiors, who sent him out. But you should always remember that there's a high one above the high one. There's an official over this official. When you start thanking him, he says, "Thank my boss in the Coast Guard Station at Floyd Bennett Field. It was the lieutenant there who sent me out. I was just following orders."

So, you visit the lieutenant in the office to thank him, but he says, "Mister, I'm only doing my job. I take orders from the Coast Guard headquarters."

So, you travel to the headquarters near Washington, D.C., and get into the office in the Pentagon. But they send you to the White House. "The President is my boss." That's what the admiral of the Coast Guard tells you.

So, you go to the President and he says, "Look, my friend, I have nothing to do with this. I'm appointed by the Most High, and He is the One Who saved you." At least I hope he'll say that. But regardless of whether the President is wise enough to say it, that's the truth. And that's what we're supposed to remember at all times. *Hameracheim*—He is the One Who has pity on us. Only Him.

That's why we say, "*Tov l'hodos laHashem*—It is good to give thanks to Hashem, *Ulezamer l'shimcha Elyon*—and to sing to Your name, the Most High." Why is Hashem called "*Elyon*—the Most High"? Because He is the One Who does everything. He's the One in charge of everything.

The moment we forget that, all the *sibos*—all the causes and subordinates—begin to misbehave. The President will forget to give orders. The Pentagon will shirk its duties. The Coast Guard headquarters won't keep tabs on their branches. The lieutenant will be asleep when the time comes. The sergeant who went out in the helicopter to find you will look in the wrong place. And you'll continue on your journey to Ireland.

Of course, sometimes Hashem has other plans for you. Even though you ignore Him, He may bring you home anyway. Then you'll have to face the music a different way, worse than going to Ireland. Sometimes a man is rescued from one thing, only to encounter something worse. When someone forgets that the One Who is doing everything for him is the "*Elyon*," sooner or later it always catches up with him.

Hashem is the One Who comes to our rescue through all the means that He provides in Nature—and sometimes by supernatural means, too. But either way, they are all triggered by the will of the Most High. Hashem is in charge. He's conducting our affairs with wisdom, and there's no greater good fortune than what He's giving to us. We have to study this and be mindful of it at all times. And in proportion to our awareness, so it will turn out.

But listening to me say it isn't enough. It helps, but you also have to say it to yourself. The more you talk about it to yourself, the more Hashem becomes the King in your life. You walk in the street and think, *Hashem Melech—Hashem is King!* He's in complete control. You can say it, too. No harm. Nobody is listening. As you're walking, you can even shout it. There's so much noise from the cars and the trucks and the trains, no one will hear you. Shout "*Hashem Melech!*"

You never tried that once in your life?! I don't mean just on Rosh Hashanah. I'm talking about during the year, on an ordinary Tuesday afternoon. Always tell yourself—you're the most important audience—that Hashem is in charge of the whole universe ... including you.

So, when you're walking on Ocean Parkway and nothing jingles in your pocket—you have no money, no job, no wife, nothing—but you walk and say, "I have Hashem. *Hashem Melech, Hashem malach, Hashem yimloch l'olam va'ed,*" things will start happening to you. Soon the *shadchan* will call you and say, "I have a nice young lady for you."

That's the great principle of *Hashem Melech*—if you make Him your King, that's exactly what He'll turn out to be. If a man puts his trust in Hashem, then suddenly, from the most unexpected source the salvation will come. That's why you must ask Hashem for everything. Constantly! Not only in Shemoneh Esrei. All day long, you should be asking Him for everything—for the things you need, and also to preserve the things you already have. If you're married, say, "Hashem, please keep my wife healthy. Give her long life."

If you're not married yet, say, "Hashem, please send me a good *shidduch*." Ask, ask, and ask. Hashem is the best *shadchan*. All of a sudden, a *shidduch* comes to you from behind your back—not from a *shadchan*. And it's a good *shidduch*! From the best *Shadchan*. It happened to me that way for one of my children. Now, I'm not saying I have *bitachon*, but at least I talk about it. I speak to you about it, and I hear my own words, so a little bit rubs off on me. I wanted a *shidduch* for my daughter, but nobody was answering. Nothing was happening. All of a sudden, a *shidduch* came from an unexpected corner. A beautiful *shidduch*! A *rosh yeshiva* called me up himself and offered me one of his best boys.

And so, we're learning now the secret to the famous subject known as *bitachon*—the *mitzvah* of acquiring a confidence that one's affairs are being properly administered by Hashem. Everyone who hears this immediately thinks that he has it, but we have to realize that it takes a great deal of effort to acquire it. The subject is very big. If you look in the *Chovos Halevavos, Sha'ar Habitachon*, you see how big it is. But it's an obligation we cannot evade. *Bitachon* is one of the great accomplishments that a Jew has to achieve in his lifetime, and the first step is to realize that everything is from Hashem.

Q **Why do we ask for *geulah* in *Ahavah Rabbah*?**

The *brachah* right before *Shema* (*Ahavah Rabbah*) is about the Torah. In it we ask Hashem, "*V'havieinu l'shalom mei'arba kanfos ha'aretz*—Bring us back to Eretz Yisrael." Why here do we stick in a few words about the *geulah* in a *tefillah* where we're talking about the Torah? What's the connection?

The answer is that, as the Rambam says (*Hilchos Melachim* 12:4), we're not asking for Mashiach so we can eat pomegranates, dates, and figs in Eretz Yisrael. We're asking for Mashiach to be able to sit and learn Torah successfully in Eretz Yisrael. To learn Torah doesn't only mean to sit in front of the Gemara. It means to absorb all the great Torah attitudes and ideals. And we want the best environment possible to grow great in. In the meantime, until Mashiach comes, find the best environment possible, and make yourself as great as you can.

Rabbi Yochanan, who lived in Eretz Yisrael, was once told that there were *zekeinim*, old men who lived long, in Bavel. "How could they live long in Bavel," he asked, "when it says, 'If you serve Hashem, you'll live long *al ha'adamah,*' on the land of Eretz Yisrael. So how could they live long in *Bavel*?" They told him that the people there come early to the *beis haknesses* and remain late in the *beis haknesses*. "Oh," he said, "that's what helped them" (*Brachos* 8a). The air of the *beis haknesses* is like Eretz Yisrael. If you are in a *makom Torah*, that's an atmosphere where you'll grow more successfully.

Q **Where in davening does Hashem express His love for us?**

We say in Maariv, "*Ahavas olam beis Yisrael amcha ahavta*—Hashem, You loved Your people with an everlasting love." And right away it explains what this love is: "*Torah umitzvos, chukim umishpatim osanu limadeta*—You taught us the Torah and the commandments, the laws and the statutes." We'll explain this as follows.

Everybody knows that when a *chassan* loves a *kallah*, he gives her *sivlonos*, gifts. He'll buy for his intended a diamond, a bracelet. Now, he's not doing it merely to show off. He gives her gifts to show that he loves her. "You're a diamond to me," he's telling her. That's why she runs right away to the jeweler to ask how much this diamond is worth. She wants to know just how much he loves her!

When Hashem took us out of Mitzrayim and brought us to Har Sinai, He said to us, "I'm going to be your *chassan*. I'll take you to be My *kallah*. And because I love you with an *ahavas olam*, I'm going to give you the very, very great gift of the Torah." The *Torah umitzvos, chukim umishpatim*—that was the wedding gift, the *sivlonos*, to the Am Yisrael.

The *mitzvos*, all the *aseih*s and all the *lavin*, are expressions of great love that Hashem shows us. Not like people think, that it's just obligations and rules and prohibitions. Oh, no—it's jewelry! Every single one is a badge of honor, the medals of a *metzuveh v'oseh*.

You should think about that sometimes when you *daven* Maariv. "*You loved us with an everlasting love... and you gave us all these badges to wear... and we'll be happy with them forever and ever.*" Every *mitzvah* is an ornament for us, and we thank Hashem for each additional one because each one expresses His love for us. *Torah umitzvos, chukim umishpatim*—so many badges, so much honor, so much love.

That's why every Jewish house should have shelves of *sefarim*—shelves and shelves of *sefarim*. It's a way of showing your appreciation for that great gift that Hashem gave us. Whether you have time to learn them all or not, it's still a good thing to display those *sefarim* in your home because that's the pride of our people—it's a demonstration that we are proud of being *metzuveh v'oseh*.

Therefore, when you pass by the *sefarim* shelf, even if you're too busy right then to open a *sefer*, your heart should swell with pride. *Ay yay yay*—precious *sefarim*! Man, woman, boy, or girl—everyone should say that! All the details of our badges of honor are written down there. A Shas on the shelf is a symbol of Hashem's greatest love for us.

Not only Shas. The *sefarim* of the Rishonim are ornaments for us; the *gedolei Acharonim*, too. Here you have the *Shach*, the *Taz*, the *Magen Avraham*. It's precious jewelry from our *Chassan*. Hanging over our necks is the *Chovos Halevavos*, the *Rambam*, the *Rif*, *Emunos V'deyos*... all the great *chibburim*. Hanging from this ear you have the *Ketzos Hachoshen*; the other ear, the *Nesivos*. All kinds of beautiful jewelry—they're all badges of honor that make us the chosen nation.

KRIYAS SHEMA

Q Why do we say Shema before Shemoneh Esrei?

The *passuk* says, "*Kein avarechecha b'chayay, b'shimcha esa kapai*—I will bless You in my life; in Your name, I will raise my hands" (*Tehillim* 63:5), to which the Gemara says: "*Kein avarechecha b'chayay* refers to Shema and *b'shimcha esa kapai* refers to *tefillah*" (*Brachos* 16b).

Brachah comes from the word "*berach*," a knee. A *brachah* means that you feel the need to bend your knee, to bow down and thank Hashem in humility. *Avarechecha* means, "I declare my humility to You." And saying Shema is accepting the *ol malchus Shamayim*, the yoke of the kingdom of Heaven. Therefore, the first thing is to accept the attitude of being humbled before Hashem. In its fullest sense, *avarechecha* means, "In humility I bend my knee to You, in recognition that You are the King."

Once a person does that, he is ready for the next step, which is raising up his hands and beseeching Hashem in *tefillah*. But first you must realize to Whom you are praying. That's Shema. The idea is that for a person to succeed in this world, the most important element is that he must have *emunah* in Hashem, awareness of Hashem. By saying Shema properly, and by saying Shemoneh Esrei after that properly, a person can merit all good things.

Q What should one think about when saying Shema?

The first thing is *kavanah p'shutah*. You have to know the simple translation of the words and think about the words you're saying. But I will give you a good suggestion [to go beyond *kavanah p'shutah*]. Every day you can add in another *peirush*, another layer of "meaning," to that.

Shema Yisrael, Hashem Elokeinu, Hashem Echad—*Echad* means He is "One." What does One mean? If you travel to the North Pole, Hashem is there. If you travel to the South Pole, He is there, too—and everywhere in between, by the way. You can go all the way from the west to the east, and wherever you go you will find Hashem.

If you travel to Tokyo and are all by yourself in a hotel, with a lot of money to spend and a lot of leisure time, know that Hashem is looking at you. You have to behave. If you go all the way to Hungary, someplace in the mountains, and have a lot of money—behave, because Hashem is looking at you. If you're at the North Pole all by yourself—behave, because Hashem is looking at you. If temptations come your way, behave like He is right there—because He is. Think this thought every day. *Mizrach, ma'arav, tzafon, darom, ma'alah, umatah* (East, west, north, south, up, and down)—He is One everywhere.

That is one *kavanah*. Do that for homework one day. The next day, meditate on another *kavanah*—"*Hashem Echad*—Hashem is One." There is only one interest in our lives. We may have a lot of interests, but He should be our sole interest. When I go to work, it's only Hashem that I'm thinking about. When I get married—only for Hashem. When I'm raising children—only for Hashem. When I eat—only for Hashem. Even when I *daven*, I'm davening for Hashem. (It's a good idea, by the way, to think about Hashem when you *daven*.) Therefore, *Hashem Echad* means: In all the things I do in this world, He is the only interest I have.

The next day, add a new *kavanah*, a new layer of meaning. Think of *Hashem Echad* in the following terms. Hashem is in this world—"*Atah Hu ba'Olam Hazeh, v'Atah Hu la'Olam Haba*—It is You in this world and it is You in the next world" (Shacharis). Hashem is in both worlds, this world and the next. Beware and be aware of Him in this world and fulfill His *mitzvos*, because in the next world we will be together with Him, too. You can't take a dive off the Empire State building and think you will escape Him. No. "*Im esak Shamayim, sham Atah*—If I would go up to the Heavens," David said in *Tehillim* (139:8), "there You are. If I would go down to the depths of the sea, there You are."

Another layer of meaning you can have in the word *Echad* is as follows—Hashem, You are the only One Who exists. Nobody else exists in this world. Nothing exists. It's all Hashem's imagination. Hashem imagined the sun and it came into being. If He would withdraw His imagination, there would be no sun. Think about that. When you look at the sun or moon, you're seeing only the *d'var Hashem*, the "word" of Hashem. "*Bidvar Hashem shamayim na'asu*—With the word of Hashem, the heavens were made" (*Tehillim* 33:6). When He said, "*Yehi*—Let there be" (*Bereishis* 1:6), it came to be. That is all you see, the word of Hashem. There are no trees . . . no people . . . no houses . . . nothing. There is only Hashem. He is the only One Who has real existence, as the Rambam says in the beginning of *Hilchos Yesodei HaTorah*. *Hashem Elokim emes*—He is the only true being. *Hu l'vado emes*—he is the only One Who is true. The world is only His imagination.[15] That is another meaning of *Echad*.

In this manner, you can add another *kavanah* every day in the word *Echad*. I gave you a few things to think about. When you finish with them, see me for further homework . . . .

Why do some people say, *"L'sheim yichud Kudsha Brich Hu"* before doing a *mitzvah*?

"*L'sheim yichud*" is a kabbalistic statement; some people say it and some don't. But it's followed by "*Hineni muchan umezuman* . . . ," which is for the purpose of having *kavanah*. Before you do a *mitzvah*, it's important to make sure to prepare yourself so that the *mitzvah* shouldn't go lost. Every day, we say the following prayer, "May He open our hearts in His Torah and put into our hearts love for Him and fear of Him . . . ." Then we finish up, "so we shouldn't labor in vain and toil for nothing" (*Uva L'tzion*).

Most of us davened today a whole davening. But when all is said and done, we should be afraid that maybe it was for nothing, *chas v'shalom*. There's no question that often a great part is thrown out! Isn't that a pity? Suppose that, instead of davening every day, you had a *keviyus* to learn *Mishnah Berurah* in that time. You would be a *lamdan* in *halachah* already! If every day you would learn *mishnayos* or Gemara during that time, you'd be a real *lamdan*. It's a pity when

15 See also: *Sing, You Righteous*, #470–476.

people waste so much time on davening. Therefore, every day we pray, "Ribbono Shel Olam, put into our hearts love of You and fear of You, so that we shouldn't toil in vain, for nothing."

That's why it's important to prepare before you do a *mitzvah*. When you're saying the Shema, keep in mind that you're doing it because of a *mitzvah* of the Torah. Does it take long to think about that? In one second, you can rescue that *mitzvah* from going *larik,* into oblivion. Think, "I'm now about to do the *mitzvah* of declaring *yichud Hashem*"—it takes only a second—and then say Shema.

Next, you come to the *pesukim* of "*V'ahavta.*" The Chofetz Chaim says that while you're saying *V'ahavta*, you might as well do the *mitzvah* and love Hashem (*Mishnah Berurah* 25:14). At least for the time it takes to say one *passuk* you can love Him! Did you ever think about that? At least for one *passuk* love Him. Fulfill the *mitzvah.*[16]

Therefore, it became a *minhag* in a number of cases to say, "*L'sheim yichud Kudsha Brich Hu*" before doing the *mitzvah*, to remind yourself to be *meyacheid* the *leiv,* to focus your thoughts: "I'm doing it for this purpose." A *mitzvah* should be done for the purpose of the *mitzvah.* You should do it because Hashem said to do it. That's how you do a *mitzvah.*

It applies to all *mitzvos*. If you're giving *tzedakah* to a poor person, don't give it because you're bashful, because you can't refuse him. Think in your mind, "Hashem told me, *Posei'ach tiftach*, that I should open my hand (*Devarim* 15:11). And I'm doing it now for that reason."

When you open the door to let somebody in, or you do some other favor, say to yourself, "*V'halachta bidrachav*—And go in His ways" (*Devarim* 28:9). I want to walk in the ways of Hashem, the original *Ba'al Chessed*. "*Mah Hu chanun, af atah chanun*—just as Hashem is merciful, so you be merciful" (*Sifrei* to *Devarim* 11:22).

Even a grocery man standing behind the counter, handing bread to the customer—why shouldn't he think? Does it cost money to

---

16 For practical examples of how to fulfill this *mitzvah*, see *Ohr Avigdor, Mesillas Yesharim*, pp. 57–60.

think? He should think, "*Nosein lechem l'chol basar*—He gives bread to all flesh" (*Tehillim* 136:25). *Hashem is giving bread to the world, and I'm His shliach!* The fact that he's also taking payment doesn't detract from the *mitzvah.*

A mother feeding her children should add that thought, as well. Why is she practicing kindliness to her family? Is it for the same reason an Italian mother in Bensonhurst is cooking and baking for her family? No! A Torah mother is doing it because she's emulating Hashem. She doesn't do it like others. She does it in emulation of the Creator. Just as the Creator makes winds blow, and causes rain to fall, and spreads a table before all mankind, and feeds them, she should feel that she is the hand of Hashem when she brings the food to the table. *Nosein lechem l'chol basar!*

All these things turn everyday acts into acts of *kedushah.* The formula for blessings is, "*Asher kid'shanu b'mitzvosav*—You made us holy with Your *mitzvos.*" Every *mitzvah* confers holiness upon the *neshamah.* The more you think and prepare, the more *kedushah* you are creating.

SHEMONEH ESREI

OVERVIEW

Q Who composed our *tefillos*?

Right after the Tanach was sealed, the Anshei Knesses Hagedolah[17] took over. They were a special body of 120 *chachamim*, who included the last of the *nevi'im*. We know from our historic traditions that they were the ones who fixed the version of the *tefillos*. The Gemara states that they composed the formal texts of our *brachos*, Kiddush, Havdalah, and the Shemoneh Esrei (*Brachos* 33a; *Megillah* 17b; see *Torah Nation*, paragraphs 157–159 and 530).

The *tefillos* they composed are at least as important as a *mishnah*, which were also arranged by the Anshei Knesses Hagedolah. They took the Torah *sheb'al peh*, which had been handed down in various forms, and unified it, giving it one expression. The Mishnah shares the same idiom as the Shemoneh Esrei because it comes from the same source, the Anshei Knesses Hagedolah. And just as every word in the Mishnah has very great content, so too with all the words of the Anshei Knesses Hagedolah.

They did all this at the very beginning of the Second Temple Era. It wasn't a later development. It was accomplished by Ezra and his Beis Din. Among them were Zechariah, Chaggai, Zechariah, and Malachi, the last *nevi'im*. Therefore, every word of our *brachos* and *tefillos* is almost equal to the last of the *kisvei hakodesh*. They're full of the *ruach Hashem*. At the very least, we must understand that they're profound. Their depth is almost endless.

Therefore, when we approach any of their compositions, we must understand that no matter how much we delve into the words, we haven't fulfilled our obligation of understanding them. As much as we think into the *nusach* of Shemoneh Esrei, we will never exhaust

17 "The Men of the Great Assembly." Rav Miller devotes the entire second chapter of his *Torah Nation* to describing the great accomplishments of the Anshei Knesses Hagedolah.

all the ideas the Anshei Knesses Hagedolah intended to convey.

Many people don't appreciate that. They would say so about the Tanach, but they would hesitate when it comes to Shemoneh Esrei. Therefore, it's important to understand that the words composed by the Anshei Knesses Hagedolah are next in importance to the words of the Kesuvim—next to the words of *Tehillim*, *Mishlei*, *Iyov*, and *Daniel*—because they had *nevi'im* among them. Those who weren't *nevi'im* were *chachamim*, and we have a principle that "*chacham adif minavi*"—in some ways, a *chacham* is greater than a *navi* (*Bava Basra* 12a).

So, as we approach these words, we must do so with humility, knowing that we're only scratching the surface.

Q Why study the *siddur*?

It's remarkable how the *siddur* is ignored. But the *tefillos*—whether it's the *tefillos* of David Hamelech or of the Anshei Knesses Hagedolah—are a source of wisdom, real *chachmah*. The whole *siddur* from beginning to end is packed and crammed with wisdom. But you can *daven* all your life and still think the words you're saying are simple. They're not. Every word must be studied.[18] Why is this word used instead of another word?

If you study it, you'll start seeing that what you thought was a blank wall is really a doorway. If you open the door and step in, you'll be surprised by what's behind it—a whole panorama of wisdom. The *siddur* is a remarkable *sefer*. You can talk about it for years and never finish. There's so much information in the *siddur* that it's like an encyclopedia of every kind of *chachmah*.

Therefore, the words of the Shemoneh Esrei are very profound, no matter how simple they seem. That was the genius of the Anshei Knesses Hagedolah. They were capable of transmitting their deepest thoughts in

18 Study Rav Miller's *sefer*, *Praise, My Soul* for his in-depth commentary on the *siddur*.

simple language. We shouldn't be deceived. Therefore, we have to give ourselves time to understand as much as we can about what they say. Take at least a few minutes every day to consider what they're saying.

Magen Avraham

Q **Why does Shemoneh Esrei start with praises?**

"Rabbi Simlai taught, 'One should always set forth praise of Hashem and then pray for his own needs'" (*Brachos* 32a). That's an important principle we follow in a number of places. The first three *brachos* of Shemoneh Esrei are not *bakashos*. We don't make requests of Hashem. We just praise Him. Also, in *Selichos* we say a long piece about the greatness of Hashem, and later we come to, "*Haneshamah lach v'haguf shelach*—The soul is Yours and the body is Yours," in which we ask Hashem for forgiveness.

Some people think the first part, praising Hashem, is superfluous and they want to hurry to get on with business. But the business is really in the first part. It's not merely that we're flattering Hashem beforehand to get Him in a good mood. The purpose of everything is for us to understand the greatness of Hashem. That's what we're here for. That's *yiras Hashem*. That's the number one requirement. The purpose of the world is for us to recognize Hashem's greatness. Meditate and dwell on that subject. Once you do that, you've justified your existence. Then you have a right to ask for whatever you want.

That's why in a number of places, even in one's private *tefillah*, one should first say *shevacho shel Makom*, praise of Hashem. As David Hamelech said, "*Lecha, Hashem, hagedulah v'hagevurah v'hatiferes v'hanetzach v'hahod*—To You, Hashem, belong the greatness and the mightiness and the splendor and the victory and the majesty" (I *Divrei Hayamim* 29:10–13). Only afterward did he ask for what he wanted. First he demonstrated that he was aware of the *gedulas Hashem*.[19]

19 See also *Awake, My Glory*, #807–811 and #890–902.

Q What's the significance of the first *brachah* of Shemoneh Esrei?

The first *brachah* of Shemoneh Esrei is our ticket of admission to Hashem. It's our contract with Him because Hashem has said that the reason He loves us is because of our forefathers. "*Rak ba'avosecha chashak Hashem l'ahavah osam*—Only in your forefathers did Hashem delight, to love them" (*Devarim* 10:15). Our history began with the covenant Hashem made with our forefathers. It's only because of them that we have anything in this life or in the World to Come.

When it states, "All Yisrael have a portion in the world to come" (*Sanhedrin* 90b), it's because of the virtue of our forefathers. To us it's surprising. If somebody did great favors for us, maybe we wouldn't forget for some time. We might be friendly to his son or his grandson, maybe even as far as the fourth generation. But suppose we lived forever—how long would that love continue? Human beings cool off. Cousins sometimes become estranged. Brothers and sisters all grow up together under the same roof, with the same father and mother, but as time goes on, the old love is forgotten or diminishes. Not so with Hashem. Hashem is the "*zocher chasdei Avos*—the One Who remembers the piety of our forefathers." He never forgets. Today is like the first minute. Just as He viewed with love the deeds of our forefathers the first time they did them, He still loves them and loves us because of them. That's why our covenant with Him, and all our prayers, are based on our forefathers. That's our ticket of admission to His presence. That's why He's willing to pay special attention to our prayers.[20]

A man should always appeal to the virtues of his forefathers. He shouldn't say that Hashem should give him this and that because he's such a great *tzaddik*. He should pray in the *zechus* of his forefathers.

---

20 See *A Nation Is Born*, 32:13.

Q Why is *zechus Avos* so important?

After Yaakov Avinu reached Charan, the *passuk* says, "*Vayifga bamakom*—He encountered a place" (*Bereishis* 28:11). The word *Vayifga* is unusual. The Gemara says it means he "prayed" there (*Sanhedrin* 95b). *Pegiyah* means to pray very hard. As the Gemara explains, he prayed with great energy at the place his forefathers prayed, at the future site of the Beis Hamikdash. It was a place where *tefillah* was accepted, where Avraham and Yitzchak had davened.

The Gemara connects this *tefillah* of Yaakov with the later event when he wrestled with the *malach* (*Bereishis* 32:32). It was a supernatural event. While Yaakov was wrestling with the *malach*, every minute was agony, a terrible agony. The *malach* wanted to tear him apart, but Hashem helped him endure. The sun appeared before its time to save Yaakov from further agony. The Gemara ties this abrupt sunrise to the abrupt sunset years earlier when Yaakov prayed at the future site of the Beis Hamikdash. The sun that had set early for him years before now rose early for him, for his sake.

Here's what it means. When somebody is loyal to the faith of his fathers, as it says, "*Elokeinu vElokei Avoseinu*—our G-d and the G-d of our fathers," then *Elokei Avoseinu* steps in to extricate him from his difficulties. That's why we always appeal to Hashem in the name of our Avos. That's why we always start Shemoneh Esrei with "*Elokeinu vElokei Avoseinu*." And that's what it's telling us here. The sun that set for Yaakov back then, when he desired to pray in the place where his fathers prayed, now rose early to rescue him from the agony of his encounter with the *malach*.

This entire story also has an allegorical meaning. Yaakov represents the Jewish people, who yearn to come back to the place where their forefathers prayed, to the *Makom Hamikdash*. A Jew's greatest desire, if his *neshamah* hasn't become numbed with assimilation and false ideas, is to connect to Hashem, to come close to Him. That's why the Gemara (ibid.) says that Yaakov "desired" (*hirheir*) to return to where his forefathers had prayed. When people desire Eretz Yisrael for the right reason—not merely because they're looking for refuge, or a place to live in security and wealth—but to serve Hashem, Hashem makes *kefitzas haderech* for them; he "shortens the path miraculously." Against the natural course of history, they find themselves back. That's what happened in Bavel. In that short period when they were in Bavel, they yearned to return. "On my couch, in the night, I sought Him Whom my soul loved" (*Shir Hashirim* 3:1). So Hashem made *kefitzas haderech* and they came back from Bavel.

When Yaakov prayed, he wasn't praying for himself. Everything he did was for the Am Yisrael. He had only one interest, as the Rambam says about the Avos, "*L'ha'amid umah ovedess Hashem*—to raise a nation that would serve Hashem." So Yaakov came to that place and prayed with all his heart—*Vayifga*—for the future of the Am Yisrael. The sun set early to keep him there, to make him pray more. The longer he was there, the more he prayed. Therefore, when the time came later in his life and he was in peril, the sun rose early to save him, because Yaakov was wrestling then not for himself, but for the future of the Jewish nation. [So when we say, "*Elokeinu vElokei Avoseinu*," we, too, invoke the *zechus Avos* and give a special power to all our prayers.]

Q **Why are our *tefillos* composed in the plural form?**

To identify with Klal Yisrael. We don't say, "*Refa'eini, Hashem*—Heal *me*, Hashem." We say, "*Refa'einu, Hashem*—Heal *us*." And we say, "*Baruch Atah, Hashem, rofei cholei amo Yisrael.*" We *daven* for all the *cholei Yisrael.* All our *tefillos* are like that, in the plural. And it's an important element that must be emphasized. It's a form of identifying with the Am Yisrael. We are together. We're all one. And when you *daven* with a *minyan*, you're identifying with Klal Yisrael even more.

And there's another reason. David Hamelech said, "Remember me, Hashem, in Your favor to Your people, and keep me in mind in the time of Your salvation" (*Tehillim* 106: 4). The Gemara (*Sanhedrin* 93b) says that when a man asks in his own *zechus*, based on his own merit, it's a weak basis on which to request anything, even if he has *zechuyos*. But when a man asks in the merit of being a member of the Jewish people, it's a different story, because collectively we have a very big account with Hashem. "*Zocher chasdei Avos*—Hashem remembers the piety of the forefathers." That's why we're constantly drawing on that account. Our own personal account was overdrawn from the beginning. We didn't have anything. We start on the first day drawing on our forefathers' account, and Hashem tells us, "There's plenty left." That's why all our *tefillos* are in the plural—because we are praying in the *zechus* of the entire Klal Yisrael. This certainly is justified. And the more we do it, the more Hashem will listen to us and favor us.

PRACTICAL ADVICE

Q **Can a parent's *zechus* save a child from Gehinnom?**

The Gemara says, "*B'ra mezakei Abba; Abba lo mezakei b'ra*—a son gives merit to a father, but a father doesn't give merit to a son" (*Sanhedrin* 104a). The deeds of the son are considered, in a sense, the deeds of the father. But not the reverse—the deeds of the father are not the deeds of the son. And the Gemara cites the example of Avraham—"*Ein Avraham matzil es Yishmael*—Avraham could not save Yishmael." Although Yishmael subsequently did *teshuvah*, Avraham couldn't rescue him before he did *teshuvah*.

Now, there are *kashya*s on this. First, there's the question of *zechus Avos*. Second, there's a question, among others, of the case of Avshalom. David interceded for him. The Gemara says that David brought him up from Gehinnom with his *tefillos* (*Sotah* 10b).

We'll start with the second one. If the father is a great man and intercedes for his son in *tefillah*, that could help. *Tefillah* is a special procedure. The *zechus* of the father wouldn't rescue the son, but if the father would pray, yes. But once a father passes into the next world, he can't pray. Praying is only when you're alive. Therefore, when it says Avraham can't save Yishmael, and Yitzchak can't save Eisav, it means *after they pass on*. But if they had seen in their lifetimes that it was necessary to pray for their sons to get Olam Haba, they would have prayed. David was alive when Avshalom perished, so he prayed for him, and with his prayers he brought him out of Gehinnom. Therefore, we say that the *zechus* of the father cannot save his son from not getting Olam Haba, but the *tefillos* of the father, while he's alive and still has *bechirah*, can bring his son into the next world, as David did with Avshalom.

Now, to the question of *zechus Avos*—of Avraham, Yitzchak, and Yaakov. How can their merit help after they passed on from this world? There are two explanations. First, in their lifetime, the Avos prayed for the future of their seed. Therefore, Hashem granted their prayer. He had a *bris* with the Avos where He told them that He'd be with them and with their seed *forever*, a *bris olam*. They accomplished this *bris* in their lifetimes. But if they hadn't prayed for it, their merit alone wouldn't necessarily have helped their descendants.

There's also a second explanation. There's a difference between reward and *zechus*. When we say *zechus Avos*, we also mean the reward. There's a reward. Like it says, "I never saw a *tzaddik* forsaken or his seed begging for bread" (*Tehillim* 37:25). Because of the father, the son might be paid off in this world. But that's only *s'char*, reward; it's only a payoff. It's not considered as if the son had done the *mitzvah*. No. The *mitzvos* of the father are not considered the son's *mitzvos*. It's only because the father did *mitzvos*. As a reward, his son gets paid off.

But the son won't get Olam Haba because his father did *mitzvos*. Olam Haba is a different *cheshbon*. A person has to merit it with his own *mitzvos*. At the same time, if a *son* does *mitzvos*, the father gets *s'char* in Olam Haba, because the son's *mitzvos* are as if the father did the *mitzvos*. The son is considered like a limb of the father, and the son's *mitzvos* go to the father's *zechus*.

Q **If we can't *daven* with concentration, is it better not to *daven* at all?**

No. Everybody should continue to pray that way—only that at least for the first *brachah* they should put in all they have. In the first *brachah*, you should be *moser nefesh*! Put all your *kochos* into it! That *brachah* is *m'akeiv* according to the *din*. It's very important to at least concentrate during the first *brachah* in Shemoneh Esrei. The rest, if a person is ambitious, he can undertake a program. Every day he should try to do a little more, and by the time he's in his sixties or seventies, maybe he'll be trained to keep his mind concentrated on the davening.

It's a great pity when a person prays without any thought. A great opportunity is lost. A big part of life is wasted. First, learn what the words mean. There are deep things in the *siddur*, and they deserve to be studied. By the way, I would like to talk about *tefillah* all the time, but it would be boring for you. I would talk about it for a whole year, an entire year only on the subject of prayer. We could take every word and analyze it. We could study it deeply and it would be worth every minute. But I don't want to bore you.

Tefillah is a career that's available for every Jew. It's a great tragedy that many people waste the opportunity. The truth is that it's one of the greatest failings in Jewish life today. Restoring *tefillah* to its rightful place should be one of our highest aspirations. *Tefillah* is called "*devarim ha'omdim berumo shel olam*—one of the things that stand at the top of the world" (*Brachos* 6b, *Rashi*). It's a pity, a terrible waste, when people fail to take advantage of the opportunity it offers.

SUMMARY

- We begin Shemoneh Esrei by praising Hashem so that we will internalize the greatness of the One to Whom we are praying.
- We start by thinking about our Avos to help us realize that our

privilege to stand before Hashem in prayer is due only to their merit.

- We declare our loyalty to the faith of our forefathers.
- We pray in plural form in recognition that we are calling upon the merit of all Klal Yisrael, not our own merit.
- It is the *bris* that Hashem made with our Avos that confers merit on us, their descendants.
- It is absolutely necessary to have *kavanah* for the entire first *brachah*.

Mechayeih Hameisim

Q How come we never mention Olam Haba in Shemoneh Esrei, yet we mention *Techiyas Hameisim* many times?

The second *brachah* of Shemoneh Esrei mentions some of the many benevolences Hashem bestows upon us, including "causing the wind to blow" (*mashiv haruach*) and "the rain to fall" (*morid hageshem*), both of which are necessary parts of the miraculous chain of events that make life possible. The *brachah* continues that Hashem is "*m'chalkel chayim b'chessed*— He supplies the living with kindliness." He gives us our clothing, our homes, and the means of keeping our homes warm, as well as countless other forms of kindliness. It mentions that Hashem is "*rofei cholim*— He heals the ill." The body comes ready-made with the means of battling all types of illnesses. We are constantly attacked by bacteria, yet the body fights them off and heals itself miraculously. It's a miracle how a cut heals. A tear in clothing will never heal, but a cut on your skin mends itself! Miracle of miracles, nerve endings come together, and cells re-form and create new tissue. The mending of a wound is a spectacular miracle.

But there is one thing that is constantly reiterated in this second *brachah*— the theme of *Mechayeih meisim*, that Hashem will revive the dead. Right before the conclusion of the *brachah*, it says, "*V'ne'eman Atah l'hachayos meisim*— You are trusted to revive the dead," which means the following. When the time comes to say farewell to this life, and your soul is saying goodbye to your poor body, and you see your body being consigned to the dust, it hurts you. As the *neshamah* heads off to Olam Haba, it consoles the body: "My dear friend, we were companions for so many years. We won't be separated forever. We trust that Hashem will one day reunite us." Finally, after the three mentions of reviving the dead, we conclude with a fourth, "*Baruch Atah, Hashem, mechayeih hameisim*—Blessed are You, Hashem, Who revives the dead."

Why is *Techiyas Hameisim* emphasized so much, and why is it mentioned with other kindnesses that Hashem does for us? The answer is—revival of the dead is an all-inclusive benefit. All the things that Hashem does for us can be included in and summed up in this great phenomenon of *Techiyas Hameisim*.

Now, we know that before *Techiyas Hameisim*, there is an interval called Olam Haba (*Olam Haneshamos*). That's the world in which all the *tzaddikim* are right now seated and enjoying a tremendous ecstasy of happiness (*Brachos* 17a). The whole Torah stands on the principle that we live for the World to Come. When Avraham consented to be cast into the furnace of fire rather than bow to idols, he did so with the awareness that after his body was consumed, he would continue to live forever.

In Hebrew, "*mus*, to die," is the same as "*mush*, to move away."[21] *Mush* means merely "to move away." It doesn't mean to stop living. In other words, death is "moving" from one state of existence to another. This is fundamental in the ideology of everyone who accepts the Torah. There's no such thing as religion without Olam Haba. And a great deal must be said about Olam Haba. Our forefathers in all the generations gained entrance to Olam Haba, and that's where they have been and are at this very moment. Yet, as important as Olam Haba is, not one word is mentioned of it in this prayer, the second *brachah* of the Shemoneh

21 For example: "...the pillar of cloud by day, and the pillar of fire by night, did not depart (*lo yamish*) from before the people" (*Shemos* 13:21–22). And "This book of the Torah shall not depart (*lo yamush*) from your mouth, and you shall meditate on it day and night..." (*Yehoshua* 1:8).

Esrei. When we speak of the kindnesses of Hashem, nothing at all is said about this great state of existence that has been going on since the beginning of the world. There, Avraham our father, and others since him and before him — countless generations, billions of men and women who were loyal to Hashem and kept His Torah — are sitting and enjoying the incomprehensible joys of the World to Come. Yet not one word is mentioned about that in this *brachah*. Only *Techiyas Hameisim*, the Revival of the Dead. Therefore, we begin to perceive something new and unique. We learn that everything — this world *and* the World to Come — is merely a preparation for *Techiyas Hameisim*. That is the final happiness, the greatest of the Great Reward.

That's not a simple statement. It's a very puzzling statement, in fact. How can the *Techiyas Hameisim* state of existence promise much more reward and greater happiness than the *tzaddikim* are experiencing right now in Gan Eden? The way we understand Gan Eden, from what has been revealed to us, is that it is the highest form of pleasure anyone could envision. What is left?

Yet now we see that it is only the beginning. It leads up to the great period in which the righteous will resume their existence in this world, which will last forever and ever. Olam Haba will come to an end, because all those who are worthy will then once more revisit this world and remain here forever and ever. Once more, we will be reunited with our body and come back to this world. Once more, we will walk in the streets. Once more, we will be with our wives and our children. Once more, we will have neighbors.

The pleasure of Olam Haba, in the "*Olam Haneshamos* — the World of Souls," will be nothing compared to *Techiyas Hameisim*. Therefore, although we thank Hashem in the second *brachah* of Shemoneh Esrei for everything He does for us in this life, as we should (indeed, thanking Hashem in this world is part of our pursuit of perfection), thanking Him so that He will bring us back to life in the ultimate existence is greater than everything else. That's why we mention *Techiyas Hameisim* and not Olam Haba.

Q What's the meaning of, "Anyone who sings [to Hashem] in this world will merit to sing in the World to Come" (*Sanhedrin* 91b)?

The Gemara brings different opinions about sources for Olam Haba. Rabbi Meir says it's in *Az Yashir* (*Shemos* 15:1). Rabbi Yehoshua ben Levi says it's in *Ashrei*, "Happy are those who sit in Your house; forever they shall praise You still more" (*Tehillim* 84:5). Then he enunciates the great principle—"Anyone who sings in this world will merit to say it in the World to Come" (*Sanhedrin* 91b).

Each one of these *chachamim* concentrated on the *passuk* that he quoted. Rabbi Meir concentrated on *Az Yashir*. Whenever he read it, he reminded himself of *Techiyas Hameisim*. Whenever Rabbi Yehoshua ben Levi came to that verse in *Ashrei*, he sat and meditated on these thoughts, that it was a hint that he and his comrades who sit in the House of Hashem would be rewarded forever and ever. Whenever they reached these verses in Tanach or *tefillah*, they reminded themselves of this cardinal principle of *Techiyas Hameisim*.

We learn from this that we must rehearse in this world for the World to Come. Not only when you say the second *brachah* of Shemoneh Esrei or *Tehillim*, but when you say all *brachos*. And not only when you say *brachos*, but even in your thoughts during the day. If you're walking down the street, sing in your heart to Hashem, in gratitude for what He does for you. Sing at the wonders you see in the world. The more you sing to Hashem in this world, the more you will sing in happiness in the World to Come. Hashem will allow you to continue this career on a much bigger scale in Olam Haba.

The principle, "Anyone who sings in this world will merit to sing in the World to Come," means that if you express gratitude to Hashem by singing to Him in this world—not just mouthing it perfunctorily but really *feeling* gratitude—you will be rewarded to say it in the World to Come. And the reason is that here in this world you're doing it with your *bechirah*, your free will. To the degree that people are happy that they are sitting in the house of Hashem—they appreciate their good fortune so much that they praise Hashem — so will they praise Him in happiness forever in the World to Come.

What was Cleopatra's question to Rabbi Meir about *Techiyas Hameisim* (*Sanhedrin* 90b)?

At *Techiyas Hameisim*, there will be a physical body, but it will be an entirely different kind of body. Just like physical earth and mud can be reconstituted into a beautiful rose petal, so too our physical body will be reconstituted into an entirely different form, not recognizable from the material it sprang from. The *neshamah* will come into the body with all the brilliance that the *neshamah* actually possesses. The true brilliance of the *neshamah* is stifled today. When you look at a person today, all you see is flesh. The *neshamah* doesn't shine through. But in *Techiyas Hameisim*, when the *neshamah* will reenter, it will be like a lantern with a strong bulb inside. The body will be illuminated. It will shine with a brilliance that will make it almost impossible to recognize that it's a physical body.

That's what happened at the beginning. When Adam Harishon was created, the *malachim* wanted to sing songs to him as if he were a deity. They thought he was Hashem. The light of the soul so illuminated his body that the *malachim* couldn't see his flesh. Adam had to inform them that he was only a creation. His flesh was incandescent. It was so illuminated by the *neshamah* that the *malachim* couldn't see it. And that's what's going to happen at *Techiyas Hameisim*.

If that's the case, if it's not going to be an ordinary body, why would it be necessary to cover up the nakedness of the body? That's only for human beings who are subject to low passions. But then it will be a different plane of existence. So maybe we won't need clothing anymore? That was Cleopatra's question.

Rabbi Meir answered: No, there is something more to clothing than just covering up nakedness. And that was a *machlokess* between Adam and Hashem. Initially, after Adam sinned, he and Chavah took fig leaves for themselves to cover up their genitals (*Bereishis* 3:7).

They understood the need for modesty but believed it was enough for them to cover up the minimum. But then Hashem made them "*kasnos or*—leather tunics" (ibid. 3:21). Why did He have to make them tunics if they already had skirts of leaves? The answer is that clothing has two entirely different functions. One is to cover up nakedness. The other is to convey dignity to the wearer. Clothing demonstrates that man stands apart from all the creatures in the world. It shows that man is royalty. A king wears royal garments not merely to cover up his nakedness. He wears royal garments to show that he's the king.[22]

Therefore, Rabbi Meir answered that that's going to be the purpose of clothing in the World to Come, too. Even though people won't need clothing to hide their nakedness because they will be above that, they will still need it as a sign that Hashem has bestowed on them the privilege of being made *b'tzelem Elokim*. Even after *Techiyas Hameisim*, they'll be beautifully robed. Therefore, he told Cleopatra that you can look forward to a career of wearing fine clothing if you will be there at *Techiyas Hameisim*. You will have a glorious wardrobe—to demonstrate the truth that man is the most important creature, other than Hashem.[23]

Q How can we appreciate rain and sincerely praise Hashem for sending it when it makes our day dreary and difficult?

I once told you about a foolish Hebrew poet who wrote a poem about rain coming down. "*Tif tif al chaloseinu k'ish bab'chi m'marmer*—Drip, drip on our windows, like a man weeping." This *shoteh*, this fool, saw drops falling against the windowpane and it reminded him of weeping. When he saw raindrops, he saw tears of unhappiness. He's a *shoteh*, because rain is the greatest happiness.

What do we do? We say, "*Al kol tipah v'tipah modim anachnu lach*—We thank You for every drop" (*Ta'anis* 6b). We thank Hashem

---

22 See *A Nation Is Born*, 28:40.

23 For more on the themes of *Techiyas Hameisim* and the World to Come, read *Rav Avigdor Miller on Olam Haba*.

for every drop of rain because it comes down "*livrachah*—with a blessing." We have to study that, or we'll begin to think like that *shoteh*.

Not only is rainwater itself wondrous, but also the way it falls is marvelous. A huge amount of water accumulates in the clouds. If it fell to the ground as a huge sheet of water, it would smash houses, destroy crops, and drown people. But, wonder of wonders, it falls in small, separate droplets. Isn't that a wonderful thing? At the same time, it falls in a way that's made special-to-order for the vegetation. You're standing in the house as it's raining and happy you're dry, but the trees are enjoying it. They love that it falls gently, drop by drop, pit-pat.

Oh, what a beautiful day it is when it rains. Diamonds are falling from the sky! Better than diamonds—pure water. And the earth needs every life-giving drop. The rain you see falling now means next spring the trees will bloom. Apples will start coming out—pears, peaches, and cherries. All the good things will come because of the rain that falls today. And not only pears and peaches and plums, but babies. Most of a baby is water. Adults, too. We're 70 percent water. When it rains, people are coming down. Ever thought about it that way? We once came down in the rain. When it rains, entire generations are coming down. When you see baby carriages on the street, they are full of rainwater that rained a year or two or three years ago. Ten years later, you'll see buses full of children going back and forth. That's all because of the rain. So when you see rain, don't make the mistake and say it's not a nice day. *Baruch Hashem*, it's a wonderful day![24]

David Hamelech specialized in that. When it was snowing, David Hamelech was ecstatic. "*Hanosein sheleg katzamer*—He lays down snow like wool" (*Tehillim* 147:16). David compared snow to wool. Snow encloses the soil with a coat of insulating air. Air can't easily go through it; air is imprisoned within the snow. The snow protects the earth from becoming frozen and allows the roots, buried inside the earth, to survive and grow next spring. So the snow that falls from

---

24 *Rav Avigdor Miller and the Rainy Day* (Judaica Press) teaches these lessons in a child-friendly way.

the sky serves the same purpose as wool. The wool that grows on the sheep imprisons the air and warms the body.

The Gemara says that snow is even better than rain (*Ta'anis* 3b). When it rains, the rainwater goes down the hill and to the river. But snow lies on the ground a long time and melts gradually. It allows the earth to absorb more of the water. "*M'alei talga l'turei k'chamsha mitrei l'ara*—One snowfall is better for the vegetation on the mountains than five rains," the Gemara says (ibid.). Snow means bread. Snow means cherries and apples. Snow means meat, good times, and children.

It rarely snowed in Eretz Yisrael, but when David saw it, he took the opportunity to contemplate it and praise Hashem. "He scatters frost like ashes, tosses ice particles like bread" (*Tehillim* 147:16–17). When David saw snow scattered all over the ground, it was like icing on a cake. That's how David understood the happiness of snow.

David also enjoyed the wind no end. "He makes the winds His angels" (*Tehillim* 104:4). The winds are like angels, he said. Hashem is sending the wind. "The world can't exist without winds" (*Ta'anis* 3b). If the wind didn't exist, the world wouldn't exist. Winds carry the clouds in the air. Winds freshen the air; they take away stale air and bring fresh air. They change the chemistry in the atmosphere. David contemplated and studied the function of wind and thanked Hashem with a full heart for it.

Every winter, three times a day, we say in our Shemoneh Esrei, "*Mashiv haruach*," thanking Hashem for making the wind blow, but we don't know what we're saying. We have to think about it to appreciate it. When the wind blows, enjoy it. Get excited about what a great benefit it is. *Baruch Hashem*, there are winds!

SUMMARY

- We talk about *Techiyas Hameisim* in the second *brachah* because it is the ultimate fulfillment of our existence.
- We declare our belief in *Techiyas Hameisim* repeatedly because it serves as a merit to help us deserve it when the time comes for Hashem to resurrect the dead.

- We have to think deeply about the great benefit of rain, snow, and wind, so that we'll feel truly grateful to Hashem for His kindness.

Atah Kadosh

Q What's the purpose of the *brachah* of Atah Kadosh?

The third *brachah* in Shemoneh Esrei (*Atah Kadosh*) is unusual. We pray, "Hashem is holy, and His name is holy." Every other *brachah* in Shemoneh Esrei has some kind of prayer or expression of thanks, but *Atah Kadosh* seems to have neither.

The answer is ... we *are* thanking Hashem. Do you know what for? Because He is holy. *Kadosh* means "perfect." Hashem is perfect. All happiness is in Him. All wisdom is in Him. Everything is in Him. People and objects and certain traits and practices are only called "holy" because of their relationship to Hashem.

The heavenly beings, the *Kedoshim* [mentioned in *Atah Kadosh*], are intrinsically holy and cannot choose to increase holiness, but Am Yisrael continues to gain holiness by means of their efforts of free will to overcome obstacles of inertia and error. In reality, the intrinsic holiness of Am Yisrael surpasses that of the angels. "The righteous are greater than the ministering angels" (*Sanhedrin* 93a). The intelligence of the angels surpasses by far that of men in this world, but whatever understanding and praise people gain by their own free will are prized by Hashem immensely more than the splendid understanding and praise of the angels, which is accomplished without the struggle of free will.

That's why awareness of Hashem's holiness is the preface to the prayer for knowledge, for *da'as* (*Megillah* 17b), which follows this one. It opens the door to higher levels of understanding and wisdom. We thank Hashem for revealing His *kedushah* to us, to some extent, so we could have a model to follow in our pursuit of *shleimus*.

PRACTICAL ADVICE

Q How does one make oneself holy?

What's a program for me to become a holy man? Say a lot of *Tehillim*? Finish Shas? Could be. Could be that's also included in the *mitzvah* of "*Kedoshim tihiyu*—Make yourselves holy" (*Vayikra* 19:2). But let's listen to what Chazal have to say on the subject. *Kedoshim tihiyu* means "*Perushim tihiyu*—You should be abstainers" (*Toras Kohanim*). To become a *kadosh*, you have to learn how to say "no" to yourself, to abstain from some of the worldly pleasures readily available to you. And it's not something optional. It's a command. Learn how to separate from this world!

The Gemara (*Ta'anis* 11a) says, "*Kol hayosheiv b'ta'anis*—Anyone who fasts voluntarily" (not a public fast, but an individual who accepts upon himself a voluntary fast) "*nikra kadosh*—is called holy." We learn this from a *nazir*. Because he volunteers to abstain from wine, the Torah puts a crown on his head: "*Ki neizer Elokav al rosho*—A crown of *kedushah* is on his head" (*Bamidbar* 6:7). Just because of his abstinence.

Q What are some examples of *prishus* (abstaining)?

The *Mesillas Yesharim* has a section on this subject of *prishus* (Chapter 13). He brings many examples to prove to the reader that it's a *mitzvah* to train oneself to abstain, to separate from things in this world. He quotes from *Midrash Pesikta* (6:2). Chizkiyah, the king of Yehudah, had a royal table, and even though every kind of delicacy was available to him—he was a king, after all—he ate vegetables. Now, I cannot tell you what he did for protein. He probably wasn't starved for that, either. But if you'd be able to take a peek through the palace window and see King Chizkiyah having lunch, you would see a plate piled high with vegetables and greens. Spinach, cabbage, other similar things. That was his meal.

And Chazal praise Chizkiyah for that. It says about him, "The *tzaddik* eats to satiate himself" (*Mishlei* 13:25). It means he eats for a purpose. Green leafy vegetables are certainly purposeful. Although he had expert chefs who could concoct for him pastries and every kind of delicacy, Chizkiyah never ordered that. Maybe he did for his guests, but he himself avoided any kind of superfluities. He was happy to eat his fill of ordinary green leafy vegetables. That's how this great man, the king of the Jewish nation, lived.[25]

Q Is *prishus* only for great people?

"*Kedoshim tihiyu,*" which means, "*perushim tihiyu*" means that anyone can make himself holy by abstaining. It's an attitude. *Prishus* is an attitude that's highly approved of by the Torah. Of course, it requires training. It requires thought. When yes, when

25 The Gemara (*Sanhedrin* 94b) compares Chizkiyah's vegetable diet to that of Pekach ben Remalyahu, who was leader of the Ten Tribes at that time, and whose table boasted "forty bushels of pigeons" just for dessert. In his lectures on *Perek Chelek*, Rav Miller says how "some people in Yehudah" looked at Pekach ben Remalyahu admiringly. They were in awe of his lavish table at his gatherings — a "*fress* house," as Rav Miller calls it. "They were always busy eating and consuming. He was a man admired by some Judeans. They said, 'There is a leader; a man to admire, not like the Beis David.' They despised Chizkiyah because he was a gentle man, a king who ate vegetables. Not all the people, of course, but some of them. These were people who looked for externalities, for false glories. They said, 'A king who conducts such a poor table is not a real king.'" They disparaged Chizkiyah for engaging in *prishus*.

As the Gemara goes on to explain, the Ten Tribes and all their wealth were about to go lost with the invasion of the Assyrian tyrant Sancheriv, and it would serve as a great object lesson, especially to those Judeans who rejected or disparaged the humble ways of the House of David. As Rav Miller puts it, "Because the people rejected David and wanted leaders of the type of Pekach ben Remalyahu, now the Ten Tribes are going to be flooded with the torrent of Sancheriv."

no. Sometimes *prishus* is forbidden. Let's say, a man's diet is deficient and he's not willing to eat nutritious foods; he's *poreish* from healthy foods. It's forbidden for him to deny himself the pleasures of a normal diet. He should eat all the nutritious foods he needs. *Prishus* from foods he needs to stay healthy is harmful and therefore wrong.

Here's a man who is *poreish* from speaking. That's also good. But what if a man refuses to greet his wife or his friends? What if he won't spend a minute or two to console someone who is suffering melancholy? With a few friendly words, he could cheer that person up. But because of *prishus*—because he doesn't want to violate his principle of keeping silence—he won't do it. It's a sin!

The word *prishus* means to separate oneself from something that is permissible *but not essential.* Even though we strive for abstinence in as many ways as possible, it should be done in ways that don't harm other people and don't harm our health. Yet, there's no doubt that the principle of kosher *prishus* is extremely important and should be an ideal for all of us. Whether you're capable of fulfilling it to a big extent or only a small extent, every Jew should aspire to some measure of abstinence.

Q **What's the motivation to be an "abstainer"?**

We look into the *Mesillas Yesharim* and see that he says that we abstain from superfluous things because we want to be "*misrachek min ha'aveirah*—to keep away from sin." By being far away from even permissible things, we will be protected from encountering forbidden things. Therefore, anything that might lead to something wrong—whether it's harmful or sinful—even though right now this matter does not cause it and the matter itself is perfectly permissible, nevertheless the *parush* abstains from it because of the possible consequences. That's how the *Mesilas Yesharim* understands this quality.

For example, let's say someone eats without control. We're

talking now about a man who eats only the best *hechsheirim*— Lieber's chocolates, Paskez candy, and kosher danishes. But he eats and eats and eats! Once he's used to eating anything his eyes see, it's difficult for him to abstain from forbidden foods. If the doctor tells him that too much sugar is dangerous for him, it will be very difficult for him to abstain. He tries, but each time it's a struggle because the desire for eating has gained mastery over him. When a person, however, abstains from unnecessary things, when he eats only wholesome and essential foods, he learns self-control. He says "no" to himself repeatedly, and by means of that he builds up his "no" muscles. And now, besides being healthy, it also becomes easier for him to say "no" to worse things. If he's ever confronted by something forbidden, he'll say "no" because he's already habituated to deny himself certain things.

You can practice this in various ways. Let's say you ate a good meal and they put a piece of chocolate cake on the table. So you say, "It's enough. I'm satiated. I don't need it." Or maybe you're at a *kiddush* and someone offers you a drink of whisky. "*Nu*? A *l'chaim*?" he says. Say, "Thank you," make a *Shehakol*, drink a drop and say, "*L'chaim*!" If you ask me, the best place for whiskey is on the floor.

Now, I'm not telling you what to do. If you want to sit down tomorrow and eat whatever you want, that's up to you. But if you want to fulfill the words of *Kedoshim tihiyu*, you're going to have to start training yourself to be an abstainer.

Prishus applies to every aspect of life, not only eating. It applies to talking, too. The Vilna Gaon said that the best *prishus* is when you don't talk. He even recommends a *ta'anis dibbur*, to once in a while set aside a day when you won't talk. A fast from talking. However, you don't have to go to such extremes. If a person trains himself to abstain from careless conversation in general, that's already something. And by means of this *prishus* from speaking extraneous words, it becomes easier for him to keep his mouth closed when he falls into company where he might commit many *aveiros* by means of his mouth.

Let's say he's sitting at a wedding where he's sentenced to remain for three hours in one seat, and he happens to be next to a bunch of chatterboxes, feather-headed people who like to talk about everybody. Now, had he been a man who never learned the lesson of *kedoshim tihiyu*, he would fall into the trap. Those three hours could be his undoing. A few hours of *leitzanus, lashon hara*, and *ona'as devarim*, and the rest of his life could be spent atoning for that one occasion. But because he's a *parush*, because he accustomed himself not to open his mouth unless necessity requires it, he sits and makes it his business to pay no attention to what they're saying. Or he finds excuses to go stand in the lobby. Even when he returns and he's sitting at the table, he spends most of his time in dignified solitude.

There's also *prishus* in looking. He doesn't look where it's not necessary. And certainly when he passes a movie theater. He doesn't read the billboards. That saves him from developing the desire to see unnecessary things. What may be a *nisayon* for someone else is nothing for him because he doesn't even see it! He has no urge to enter a movie house or look at television. He's gained control over his eyes. He's not tempted to look in places where his eyes don't belong. He has trained himself to utilize the gift of sight for important things, like making a living, or dealing with people the way Hashem demands.

There's also being a *parush* in spending. Wise people train themselves not to spend money unnecessarily. The signs say, "Come in and save!" But you decide to "stay out" and save more! Until you saw the sign, it never even occurred to you that you need what they want you to buy. If there's no need to buy it, if you can live without it, leave it in the store and keep your money in the bank. People who are in the habit of spending money become slaves to that urge. They buy just because things are displayed in windows. Sometimes that's the beginning of a lot of trouble.

Now, I only mentioned a few examples. There are more branches of *prishus*. If you put some thought into it, you will discern in what areas of your life it pays to be a *parush*. But whatever it may be, the common denominator according to the *Mesillas Yesharim* is that it keeps a man from coming into contact with forbidden situations.

Q Are there motivations for *prishus* other than keeping away from forbidden things?

Like the *Mesillas Yesharim*, the *Chovos Halevavos* also has a large section on *prishus*. It's the same subject, but he approaches it from an entirely different angle. Not that he disagrees with the *Mesillas Yesharim*, but the *Chovos Halevavos* teaches us that there's another compelling reason for learning how to abstain from the superfluities of this world. The *Chovos Halevavos* says that to understand the motivation for *prishus*, we have to first understand that man comes into this world to fill his mind with thoughts of Hashem. The *Chovos Halevavos* explains that our motivation to abstain from this world is to free our minds for higher things, more valuable things.

Suppose you have a storage compartment that you rent for $10,000 a week. Would you put your shoes there? It's too expensive to waste on that. You would store only the most precious furniture there because you cannot waste an inch of that valuable space. You can leave your shoes in the hallway. Shlomo Hamelech tells us, "By means of thoughts, the chambers of your mind will be filled with all precious and pleasing furniture" (*Mishlei* 24:4). Your mind is the most expensive apartment. Every inch is valuable real estate. Therefore, it must be left uncluttered, free of any kind of superfluous furniture, so that you can move in all the necessary things.

We need space in our minds for all the valuable furniture of the Torah. That's what the mind is for. But we don't do it because our minds are cluttered with superfluous things. Suppose you're thinking of some argument you had with someone, or some little hobby that clutters up your mind. It's the law of physics that two objects cannot occupy one space at the same time.

If you want to be someone of a higher nature, when you walk out of this place tonight, spend a minute thinking that the One Who created the universe out of nothing is looking at you. Try that! From here to the corner. It takes a minute. That's a very valuable piece of furniture. When you're walking home from shul in the morning or waiting at the grocery to buy a bottle of milk, instead of filling your mind with cheap furniture, like thoughts about what type of cereal you'll be having for breakfast, begin to move in expensive furniture, like thoughts of the *briyah yeish mei'ayin*, that Hashem created everything *ex nihilo*, out of nothing. Use your imagination. Paint a beautiful picture. It's a pity that people don't realize that this is the kind of furniture that should be occupying their mind. Spend one minute in picturing the creation of the universe. The entire Torah is built on that premise.

Let's say you have in your mind the "beautiful" ideal of an automobile. Your mind is filled with thoughts of tinkering with the engine of your car. Maybe you're obsessed with worrying about the tires or with washing your car. You're thinking that tomorrow morning, if you have time, you'll take the vacuum cleaner and clean all the upholstery. It's car and car and car and more car. Your mind is a car-mind. Instead of filling it with the beautiful furniture of Torah ideals, it's filled with oil changes and carburetors.

That's only one example. People's minds are filled with all types of things that are superfluous. Clothing and money and expensive gadgets. Food and travel and other things, too. But suppose a man has no car or expensive toys. His head is empty. Of course, having an empty head is not desirable, either, but if he's interested in moving things into that empty apartment, he can begin transferring the beautiful furnishings of a royal suite into his head and turn his mind into a royal palace. He moves in a golden bed and golden chairs and golden goblets and other beautiful furniture.

As you train yourself to abstain from the less important things in this world, you gradually add more and more appurtenances to this royal apartment of the mind—pictures of *briyah yeish mei'ayin*, Matan Torah, Yetzias Mitzrayim. The more you value your mind, the more time you'll spend thinking Torah thoughts. But it all begins with a mind that's not cluttered with the superfluous things of this world.

Q If Hashem wants us to enjoy His world, why is it a *mitzvah* to train oneself to abstain from Olam Hazeh?

First, understand what type of pleasures Hashem wants you to enjoy. It states in *Koheles* (11:7), "How sweet is the light; how good it is for the eyes to see the sun." Listen to what Rabbeinu Yonah says (*Sha'arei Teshuvah* 2:9). "If you're an old man and you have no teeth, you might think that you have no pleasure in life any longer." But that can't be, says Rabbeinu Yonah. Hashem already said that this is a very good world. He didn't say it's a good world until you turn seventy. So, what does Rabbeinu Yonah tell us is the pleasure that invigorates and brings joy to the old man? Sunlight! If he learns to enjoy sunlight, he'll never be unhappy again. We have to understand the joy of sunlight. It's a pleasure! How foolish people are when they live their lives without appreciating sunlight.

Now, this is certainly a foreign idea to many people. "That's fun?! Daylight?! Heh, heh, heh. It's so free, so available." But you're learning a big secret now. All the best things in life are free! Only, people don't know how to be happy with them. The *Chovos Halevavos* says that people tend to ignore the *tovos hakolelos*, the "general pleasures" that everybody has. They seek only *tovos meyuchados*, "pleasures that only *they* have." If he has something that nobody else has, then he's happy with it. Only that's a pleasure, he thinks.

But the *Chovos Halevavos* says that he's a fool, because Hashem wants us to enjoy the gifts He's giving to everyone. Does the fact that your neighbor is benefiting from the sunlight make it any less enjoyable?! Hashem is giving and giving and giving. We just have to keep our minds open and study the gifts and enjoy them. You're going to be held accountable for not enjoying them!

Sunlight is just one example of how a *parush*, an abstainer, lives a life of happiness and *kedushah*. Do you know how much fun it is to have two eyes? Two eyes?! Ask a blind man what he would give to get back one eye. One eye?! He'd pay millions. He'd go crazy with happiness.

The pleasure of eating a piece of bread. Ah, ah, ah—eating a piece of bread. As you sink your teeth into the bread and the saliva flows, it's a *ta'anug*! That's one of the greatest pleasures in the world. The pleasure of drinking a glass of water! Water! What a pleasure it is! Ah! A life-giving substance. Learn how to enjoy water. The pleasure of breathing! Take a deep breath. You're drinking a cocktail of gases that gives you vigor, makes your blood red, and invigorates your entire body. Every breath that goes into your body gives you a new burst energy. Breathing is fun!

This kind of kosher *ta'anug* is a *chiyuv*. It's a *mitzvah gedolah* to enjoy life this way. But you'll never be able to fully enjoy these gifts if your mind is cluttered up with luxuries, with superfluous things, with substitute pleasures. You'll never enjoy the gifts of Hashem if you think that fun comes from traveling. It could be that you'll find some fleeting happiness—the trip to Switzerland might tickle your nerves a little bit. But you'll never be a happy person because of that. Only a *parush*, a person who has trained himself to separate from these false pleasures, lives happily—extremely happily—in this world.

When a person has artificial pleasures in his mind, he won't be able to appreciate the pleasure of *avodas Hashem*, of doing *mitzvos*. That might sound strange to some people, but trust me, there's a happiness in doing *mitzvos*. When Rabbi Akiva stood in Shemoneh Esrei, he wept buckets of tears on Shabbos. After he finished, they said to him, "Are you allowed to weep on Shabbos?" Rabbi Akiva answered, "I was weeping out of happiness." He was so happy. He was talking to his Best Friend, the one true Friend he had. It's like a child who comes home after a long absence and talks to his mother and father, pouring out his whole heart to them. He was among strangers for a long time, and now he's back home again talking to the ones he loves, the ones who love him more than anything. Rabbi Akiva opened up his heart to Hashem, and he was so happy, he couldn't restrain the flow of tears.

There's a happiness to *tefillah*! As it says, "I'll make them happy in My place of *tefillah*" (*Yeshayah* 56:7). It means that when you come to talk to Hashem, it's a pleasure. It's *geshmak*! But when someone has accustomed himself to superfluities, he has no appetite for, and no understanding of, these real pleasures of life.

There's happiness in learning Torah, too. Some people have learned how to enjoy learning Torah. A person who has learned how to be *poreish* from the substitute pleasures in this world experiences a tremendous joy sitting in front of a Gemara. That's why it's *assur* to learn Torah on Tisha B'Av. It's fun to understand the *s'vara* of the Gemara, to understand the *terutz* of *Tosfos*. Rava was so happy when he learned Torah, he was so immersed in the love of Torah that he didn't know his hand was bleeding (*Shabbos* 88a). He was unaware of it because he was so happy with the Torah. It was a real love! A joy of Torah!

Only someone who learns how to abstain from this world can understand the ecstasy of doing *mitzvos*, of serving Hashem. When a mother is cooking supper for her family, if she learns to enjoy the *mitzvah*, how happy she is that her children are going to eat what she made for them, that she is fulfilling the *shlichus* of Hashem. She's a messenger of *chessed*. Isn't that a privilege for an intelligent mother? As she stands and dishes out food to this child and that child, she's a *shliach* of Hashem. She's so happy that her children are relishing her meal. That's her delight in life. She's an *oved Hashem* in happiness because she's not thinking about dresses and *sheitel*s.

Get out of your head any thoughts that *prishus* means being unhappy! If you fill your mind with false, manufactured pleasures, you're going to ignore the true pleasures in this world. Hashem wants you to enjoy Olam Hazeh, but it's an art you have to learn. *Prishus* means to be happy without luxuries, to learn to appreciate the minimum, to enjoy all the simple pleasures of this world, the pleasures that are available always. Once you empty your mind of all these manufactured pleasures, you'll find the true happiness, true and immense satisfaction, in *avodas Hashem* itself—in Torah, *mitzvos*, *chessed*, raising children. You'll go wild with pleasure in your love of Hashem.

All these things together add up to *kedushah*. "*Kedoshim tihiyu—perushim tihiyu.*" Be abstainers, and you'll walk through this world all the days of your life with noble thoughts in your mind, serving Hashem in happiness, while enjoying all the pleasures that Hashem is showering down upon you constantly. Therefore, every Jew should aspire to whatever level of *prishus* he's capable of, because the more he achieves, the happier and more *kadosh* he becomes.

SUMMARY

- In this *brachah*, we thank Hashem for His perfection, and for serving as a model for our own efforts to achieve *shleimus.*
- To become more *kadosh*, we have to learn to abstain from physical pleasures to some extent, to say "no" to ourselves and develop our self-control.
- We must distance ourselves from things that are *permissible, but not essential.*
- One motivation for doing this is to distance ourselves from *aveiros.*
- Another motivation is to free up our minds to be used for more elevated purposes.
- However, practicing *prishus* does not mean not enjoying the world. A *parush* can enjoy the world more than anybody, by learning how to recognize Hashem's kindness in the joys of life that most people overlook.

Kedushah

See *Yotzer Ham'oros* on p. 147, above.

Atah Chonein

Q What's the most important thing we should ask for in life?

We see that the first thing we ask for in Shemoneh Esrei is "knowledge," *da'as*. We infer from this that it's the most important of all needs.

Now, we need a lot of things. We need health. We need to be rescued from oppressors. We need *parnassah*. But the first of our requests is the most urgent. We cannot wait. It's the one we need most of all.

Da'as is the most important thing—more important than life, more important than being happy, more important than having peace and good health and *parnassah*. The most important thing in life is to acquire *da'as*.

Da'as/de'ah means "knowledge" or "understanding." It doesn't mean merely to know technical things. The person with *de'ah* perceives clearly with his mind. He understands all the issues that are only abstractions to others. He comprehends them more thoroughly. Someone can say the name of Hashem yet be far away from feeling the presence of Hashem. The person who has *de'ah* has a certain feeling of the imminence of Hashem, of standing before *Hashem*. That's called *de'ah*.

Every day we ask for these three things—*de'ah*, *binah*, and *haskel* (*chachmah, binah*, and *da'as* in *nusach Sephard*). It's important to know what we're asking for. It's possible we don't even understand what they mean. First, let's understand what *de'ah* means.

The Gemara (*Brachos* 33a) tells us, "*Gedolah de'ah!*—How great is *de'ah*!" Right away, we see we're asking for a very important thing. "*Zu kanisa*—If you gain this," if you gain *de'ah*, "*mah chasarta*—what are you lacking?" (*Nedarim* 41a) You're lacking nothing. So we see that we're asking for something that's so important it includes everything.

Now, pay attention because you're going to learn something that will come in handy in almost everything you do.

It's possible for a person to be a millionaire and not know it. If a person has a million dollars but he's totally unaware that he possesses it, he's a pauper. Wealth is not defined by the fact that he legally owns that money. Imagine a bachelor. In his apartment is a rug. He never picks it up except to sweep the dirt under it. Now, say somebody came in and secretly stashed a bag with a million dollars in big denominations as a gift under that rug without the bachelor knowing. Years pass and this bachelor never once lifted the rug. Finally, the day comes when it's all over. He's gone. There's an inquest and they start carting out all the junk in his house. Junk a mile high. Then they start lifting up the rug and see a bag underneath. In it are a thousand thousand-dollar bills. A million dollars total. But this bachelor didn't possess them in his lifetime because he never knew about it. So *de'ah* means knowing what you have.

Mankind lives in darkness and therefore in unhappiness. Now, some people listen to this and nod, *yes, yes, yes*. But I'm talking to them, too. The mere fact that you're not bubbling over with enthusiasm proves that you haven't even begun to acquire *de'ah*. If you would understand what you possess, you'd become so full of joy that your life would be transformed.

De'ah is easy to talk about, but it isn't easy to get. *De'ah* means to know, to really know. "*V'ha'dam yada es Chavah ishto*—Adam knew his wife Chavah" (*Bereishis* 4:1). He already knew her, but *yada* means he "came closer to her." It means he became more familiar with her. *De'ah* means to get familiar with something that you already know, to understand it more clearly. When you understand how fortunate you are, you begin to realize that you are a millionaire. Now, we're just studying the *brachah* of *da'as*, but we must realize that we're blessed not just in this one way, but in tens of thousands of ways.

De'ah includes all happiness. No millionaire can be happy unless he has learned to appreciate what he has. Despite the travel ads, all the travel agencies that sell tickets to fly to other parts of the world, happiness isn't over there. You know where happiness is? It's right here. Happiness is in your head. It's in *de'ah*. When you learn to understand what life really is, what you really possess, you'll pick up that rug and discover that there was a million dollars there all along, in your own home.

There's so much we're missing in life. Everybody is missing out. We're all living in ignorance of everything that was put here for us to have, to understand, and to enjoy. That's why *de'ah* is number one of all the requests. If you have everything but you don't have the one thing that makes everything else worthwhile, what do you have? But if you have *de'ah*, you have everything. That's why we ask for it first.

Now, it's not right for me to end here and leave you hanging. Therefore, I invite you to come and listen to these lectures for the next ten thousand years. That'll be a good *beginning* of the subject of *de'ah*. I'm not exaggerating. Included in *de'ah* are all the great qualities Hashem implanted in us and that we're capable of achieving. It's a whirlwind of happiness, a world of perfection. And it's the life of the World to Come. The perfection of the mind that you acquire in this world lives on with you in the World to Come forever and ever.

Now we begin to understand a little more why we say at the very beginning, "Please, Hashem, bestow upon us *de'ah*, *binah*, *v'haskel*." That's a little introduction to this *brachah*.

Q What's the benefit of knowing details?

Da'as, "knowledge," doesn't mean to know more *details*. It means to know things more *clearly*. And it's a great achievement in life.

All *ma'aminim*, all believers, believe in Olam Haba. They know this world is only a *prozdor*, a vestibule, before the World to Come (*Avos* 4:16). But this piece of information is put away someplace in the attic of their minds. If you'll ask them, they'll be happy to bring it down from upstairs. They'll say, "Yeah, sure, I believe it." But it doesn't affect their daily lives. However, people who have transformed *chachmah* into *de'ah* feel this great principle more keenly. Any idea that's sharp and clear is called *de'ah*. When a person lives in this world with the intention of producing as much as he can, something that helps him in his career in the World to Come, he has *de'ah*. He knows more clearly this great principle.

Everybody who says the Shemoneh Esrei believes in Hashem. Yet our Sages tell us, "When you pray, know before Whom you stand" (*Brachos* 28b; cf. *Avos* 3:1). Don't we know that already? Every little boy and girl knows. But they don't really *know*. To *know* means to gain a clear picture.

The *Mesillas Yesharim* explains that this isn't easy to do. Our senses don't help us. You're standing in front of a wall, saying words, and trying hard to feel the meaning of the words, but your senses don't help you. Still, the *Mesillas Yesharim* tells us, don't be discouraged. Although at first it's not easy, you should keep trying to gain that impression that Hashem is in front of you and listening. If you keep trying, you'll eventually succeed.

At the same time, "A man is led in the direction that he wishes to go" (*Makkos* 10b). He has to *wish*, to *want*, to *desire*. He has to *try* to know before Whom he's standing, to try to gain that awareness. Picture that Hashem is standing right in front of you and listening intently to your words. Sometimes you might not listen carefully to what you're saying, but He is always listening. "*Ki Atah shomei'a tefillas amcha Yisrael b'rachamim*—You listen to the words of Your people Israel with compassion." Hashem is listening to us with a sympathetic ear. We should at least try to do the same; we should at least listen to what *we're* saying to Him.

We have to *desire* that. If we don't, then we have to desire to gain that desire. Most adults are davening the way they did when they were four years old. The way they davened at four is the way they *daven* when they're eighty-four or ninety-four. But the *Mesillas Yesharim* promises us that if you make the attempt, as time goes on you'll acquire *de'ah*, a clarity of feeling that Hashem is actually listening to your words. That's a great success.

Therefore, the Mishnah exhorts us: When you stand up to prayer, please don't waste this glorious opportunity to know before Whom you stand. That achievement is number one in the purposes of *tefillah*— to gain *de'ah*, a feeling that Hashem is right in front of you.

Q How do we develop a sensory awareness of Hashem?

When you say "*Avinu*— our Father," don't just say it as in a dream. I was told by a *rosh yeshiva* in Europe that when old-time Jews said *Avinu Malkeinu*, they spent time on the first two words. We mumble and rush through the words "*Avinu Malkeinu.*" We want to get to the "*sh'lach refuah sheleimah l'cholei amecha*— send a complete healing to the ill of Your people." We want to get to "*kasveinu b'sefer parnassah v'chalkalah*— inscribe us in the book of *parnassah.*" But old-time Jews spent time on the first two words. They said each syllable slowly. *A-vi-nu*— that's the important point. *Mal-kei-nu*— that's the important point. The most important part is to acquire the feeling that He's *Avinu*.

Any time in the Shemoneh Esrei you say the word *Atah*, you should pause and think. And not only in the Shemoneh Esrei. Any time or place that you're talking to Hashem. In Yiddish we say "*Du*, You," not "*Ir*, Him." "*Tatte, Du helpf*— Father, You help." If you're saying "You" in any language, it's a glorious and important opportunity. Think about it— you're saying "You" to Hashem! Now, the best thing would be to spend a long time on *tefillah*, but you have to eat breakfast, and go to work, too. However, once in a while at least, stop and think a little bit about that word *Atah*. Use that opportunity. *Atah* is a powerful word. Of course, when the Shemoneh Esrei speaks about Hashem in the third person, "He," it's an opportunity, too. But we should especially use the opportunity when we're speaking to Him directly, addressing Him as "You."

Whether it's during the *tefillah* we say three times a day, or while saying *Tehillim*, or whenever you come across any expression that is directed to Hashem, it's important to pause and think for a moment. That's how we gain certain attitudes about Hashem. The *siddur* isn't a simple *sefer*. It's a *lomdishe sefer*. We're losing a glorious opportunity if we just say the words without thinking.

One of the great objectives of *tefillah* is to gain a sensory awareness, a *yediah chushis*, a real *emunah* that Hashem hears our words. "Know what's above you, an Eye that sees" (*Avos* 3:1). You have to think about that. Every child knows that Hashem sees everything, but when he's misbehaving he forgets. As adults we're the same way. Always remind yourself that Hashem is looking. As you walk in the street, Hashem is looking. Where? He's looking down at you from the window. Of course, He doesn't need a window to see. "Hashem looks down from the heavens" (*Tehillim* 14:2). He's looking all the time. But we need to use that window to remind ourselves that Hashem is looking.

He's listening, too—"An Ear that hears" (*Avos* 3:1). Hashem hears everything you say, and He doesn't forget. Whatever you say is recorded forever and ever. Picture a tape recorder recording everything you say. Hashem doesn't need a tape recorder, but we should think about tape recorders to gain an awareness that everything we say is heard by Hashem.

When a person lives with even a little sensory awareness, he gradually acquires some of this excellence. That's one of the reasons that *tefillah* is called "*devarim ha'omdim berumo shel olam*—things that stand at the top of the world" (*Brachos* 6b, *Rashi*).

Q **What should we be picturing in our minds when we think about Hashem?**

The Torah has given us a very big *heter*, the "permission" to do something that otherwise we should not do—and that's to picture Hashem in a *gashmiyus* way.

Now, that's absolutely wrong. It's *assur* to believe that Hashem looks like anything we know. How can a man presume to picture that he's standing before a *Melech* or a Father, *Avinu* or *Malkeinu*? How can you presume to do that if it's against the truth? And the Rambam says that if he really thinks so, he's a *min* (heretic). So how could you risk such a thing?

The answer is there's a bigger danger—the danger of not thinking at all. Therefore, to gain that great achievement of feeling that Hashem is listening to you, He gave us certain pictures through His *nevi'im*. They visualized Him in numerous ways—as an "*Ish Milchamah*, a Warrior" (*Shemos* 15:3), as a victorious hero in a chariot with a bloody sword (*Yeshayah* 63:1–3), as a "*Melech yosheiv al kisei ram v'nisa*—a King sitting on a high and exalted throne" (*Yeshayah* 6:1), as "*Avinu*—a loving father." Our business is to use this great gift. If Hashem permitted something that's absolutely not true for the opportunity of gaining an awareness, we should use it.

Q Why did Hashem create us with a higher intelligence?

Why did Hashem give us this great brain that's a lot more capable than, say, a cow's brain? We could function perfectly with a smaller brain. Hashem could have given us a cow's brain. A cow's brain allows it to take care of all its bodily needs. So why did Hashem give us such a big brain?

And the answer is that He gave us a big brain to accomplish big things.

Maybe you'll inscribe Shas on that brain. Everybody can learn Shas. Learn, even without *Tosfos*. Go over it again and again. Why waste *motza'ei Shabbos* sitting home doing nothing? Why waste Sunday night visiting your relatives? Why waste your evenings? Instead, listen to tapes of Gemara. Listen and repeat, listen and repeat. In the course of time, you could inscribe Shas on your mind. It's possible. At least inscribe one *masechta*. At least one *perek*.

If you're a woman, you can inscribe the great lessons of all the *sefarim* on your mind. You can listen to tapes and inscribe deep *emunah* on your mind. There's no end of wisdom that people can inscribe on their minds.

PRACTICAL ADVICE

Q **Which *sefarim* are most important for learning *emunah*?**

I would say that besides for the Torah, which is the *yesod hayesodos,* study the *Chovos Halevavos*—especially the *Sha'ar Habechinah*. Now, not everybody will agree with me. Some people will say it's a waste of time, because they think the *Sha'ar Habechinah* is just a method of proving that there is a Borei, and they don't need that, they say. But that's an error. The *Sha'ar Habechinah* is not made to prove there's a Borei. It's made so that you should learn to feel, to be *margish,* the presence of the Borei.

Moshe Rabbeinu didn't need proofs that Hashem existed! He had spoken to Hashem many times. He knew very well—better than anybody—that Hashem existed. Yet, he said, "Hashem, show me Your Glory." Because it's never enough. You can never see Hashem enough! The desire of our *neshamah* is to come closer and closer to seeing Hashem. In the World to Come, that's the great happiness. *Tzaddikim* look at the Shechinah (*Brachos* 17a). That's their heart's desire.

When people look into the world and on all sides they see evidence of Hashem's greatness—on all sides they witness His *chessed,* His kindliness—they're becoming greater and greater. You want practical advice? Try this. Walk into a fruit store and see the beautiful red apples. Each is a work of art. Your heart melts within you to see such beautiful products—beautiful oranges, beautiful grapes. And you know, each one has seeds inside. They're like coupons. Once you've finished the fruit, there's a coupon inside. If you spit it out it will cause a new plant to grow and give you more fruit. You see the miracles of plan and purpose; you see the hand of Hashem.

There's no question that the *Sha'ar Habechinah,* in my mind, is one of the most important preparations for living a successful life.

However, among other important *sefarim*, I would also suggest *Mesillas Yesharim*. It's a *sefer* written by an Acharon, but the Vilna Gaon said he read through the first eleven *perakim* and that every word is precious. He said that if the *Mesillas Yesharim* were alive, he would walk across Europe to make him his *rebbi*.

Sha'arei Teshuvah of *Rabbeinu Yonah* is also one of the great sources of *avodas Hashem*. The *Rambam Hilchos Dei'os* and *Hilchos Teshuvah*, and part of *Hilchos Yesodei HaTorah* also. It's very easy language to read, but the words of the Rambam are extremely profound.

All these *sefarim* contain a world of knowledge. Now, I'm not saying that these are the only ones. There are other *sefarim* in addition to these. But for people who are ambitious to grow great in *da'as Hashem*, I would recommend that they become familiar with these *sefarim*.

Q **When I thank Hashem for *da'as*, what should I have in mind?**

At its most basic level, *da'as* is sanity. We're asking for sanity. Did you ever think about that? Many people have prayed three times a day for years and never once realized they're asking Hashem to protect their sanity.

If you didn't have *da'as*, you'd be a raging lunatic. Hashem is giving you *da'as*—and giving it to you every minute. It's a gift He's giving you right now. Don't think that because you were born sane, you will always be sane. Nothing is guaranteed. Sanity is a gift. The reason you're not, *chalilah*, in an asylum knocking your head against the wall like a lunatic is because of the *da'as* Hashem is giving you. He's the One making you sane.

The *Chovos Halevavos* explains that it's not enough to thank Hashem for the exceptional gifts He gave you. It's not enough that He made you better than others in some ways. You have to thank Him *first of all* for the *tovos hakolelos*, which means "the general benefits" that you have in common with others.

You must stop and think how lucky you are that you have a nose. That's not a jest. It's very serious. If you never stop to think about it, it won't help that you shake a lot in your *tefillah*. It won't help even if you're a *lamdan*. Being a *lamdan* is adding a second story and a third story. If a person doesn't have the first story, it's a "*migdal haporei'ach ba'avir*—a building floating in the air" (*Sanhedrin* 106b).[26] First you have to thank Hashem that you have the things everybody else has. Once you start thinking into it, there's no end to the *tovos hakolelos.*

Some people have the depraved attitude that they don't feel grateful as long as they have only what everybody else has. It's a well-known sickness. He's only grateful if he is superior to others in some way. If he would have, say, a million dollars or a nice nest egg in the bank, then he'd feel satisfied with life. He doesn't for a moment realize how happy he should be that he has food on the table. Today, even people who are so poor that they need government aid have plenty to eat. Even poor people are on Weight Watchers.

And you have plenty of water to drink, as well. Don't think that's a small thing. In other countries, clean drinking water is a big luxury. You even have toilets inside your homes. In most of

---

26 The Gemara applies the phrase to Doeg and Achitophel, two great Torah scholars during David Hamelech's time. In Rav Miller's commentary to *Perek Chelek*, he explains, "Hashem wants a man's Torah. But Rashi adds: He also wants something else. He wants a man's heart.... 'heart' in *lashon kodesh* means the mind. A man has to develop a Torah personality. If he only acquires abstract Torah knowledge that doesn't become part of his heart, his personality—if he remains unchanged despite his learning—he's a failure.... A *talmid chacham* who studied Torah but didn't change his personality is worse than a failure. He is a loss; he's a pest to the world."

Rav Shimon Schwab (*Devarim* 29:18) explains, "They [Doeg and Achitophel] discussed hundreds of *halachos*, and the Gemara tells us that this included the *halachah* of "a tower that was suspended in the air." And they did not even know that it was talking about them! They were also big towers—big *talmidei chachamim*, suspended in the air and not connected to the ground, and therefore not implementing the principle of *yiras Shamayim* into daily living. Therefore, they could be considered as if hovering in the air."

the world, they don't have toilets in their houses. You have heating in wintertime. When I was a boy, we didn't have heating in every room. If you wanted to warm up, you went to the kitchen, where your mother shoveled coal into a stove. We had a bucket of coal and a little shovel, and someone shoveled coal into the stove to keep the fire going. In the rest of the house, you had to put on an overcoat and a couple pairs of socks.

Today people have food and water and heat and a lot more—yet they're complaining. What's bothering them? Not the fact that they're lacking things. It's the fact that somebody else has more. That's what's burning them up. That's the unhappiness of most of mankind.

Therefore, when we talk about sanity, don't underestimate it. Did you know that 10 percent of the world's population is insane? I'm not talking about people who have idiosyncrasies or eccentricities. I'm talking about plain insanity that interferes with their lives. If you're not one of them, you owe Hashem a very great debt of gratitude. Just because you're part of the 90 percent of the world that's able to function normally doesn't absolve you from your obligation.

The *Chovos Halevavos* in *Sha'ar Cheshbon Hanefesh* says that a person must spend time thinking about all the great things Hashem has bestowed upon us—and one of the first things is intelligence. To help us along, he asks us to imagine a person bereft of intelligence. Here's a man in a fog all day with a blank stare; he doesn't function at all. Then a specialist comes along, opens up his skull, and inserts a functioning brain. How much would he owe this man! How great would his gratitude be toward this benefactor! He could spend all his days thanking him and it wouldn't be sufficient.

Certainly, then, we should thank our Creator, Whose benefits include giving us a mind capable of functioning properly. If you want to serve Hashem at even a minimum level, you must spend some time thinking about the gift of a mind. We're not now talking about genius, about brilliance. We're talking about the gift of basic intelligence.

I was once called suddenly to visit a *talmid* of a yeshiva who, unfortunately, had lost his mind. I went there after visiting hours and needed a big guard to go with me. But the experience was enlightening. It pays to visit an asylum like that. It helps you appreciate what you have. When you walk out, you realize that you possess something valuable.

Q Why does this *brachah* begin with the declaration of *"Atah chonein"*?

None of the other *brachos* in Shemoneh Esrei begin with a statement, "You give." It doesn't say, "You heal people and therefore heal us." It starts immediately, "Heal us." It doesn't say, "You give *parnassah* and therefore give us a livelihood." It starts immediately, "Give us our livelihood." But this *brachah* begins with a statement "You bestow intelligence upon a man." Why does only this *brachah* begin this way?

The answer is that we mistakenly consider ourselves and our intelligence inalienably connected. We think of them as one. We think we are our intelligence. It doesn't occur to us that, *chas v'shalom*, we could be separated from our intelligence. It doesn't enter our mind that the intelligence is something outside of us, that it's a gift that's been bestowed on us. In fact, you are not your intelligence. We know this to be true because we see people who lose it. The person is one thing and his sanity, his intelligence, is something else. Therefore, when we make this declaration "*Atah chonein*," we are saying, "We realize that something has been given to us." And who is the giver? "*Atah*—You" are the One Who has bestowed it upon us.

That brings us back to the great necessity of thanking Hashem three times a day that you're not in an insane asylum. You're expected to have that in mind at least three times a day. If you do, it's going to change your Shemoneh Esrei.

Q What is a practical way to better appreciate the greatness of the gift of a mind?

Anybody who's not committed to atheism — if he hasn't been hopelessly indoctrinated — if he would take an honest look at this single most startling phenomenon in the universe, he'd be convinced of a Borei. And that's the human brain. There's nothing like it.

One savant ventured a guess that the human brain can store fifteen trillion different bits of information. Not "million." Not "billion." Trillion! I really don't believe it. I think it's an understatement. I believe that the brain learns to store more and more because the endless number of electric circuits in the brain are developed so that each circuit takes over a lot of functions. People who learn more are accustomed to memorizing more. The less you learn, the less you remember and the dumber you are. The more you use your mind, the more agility it acquires and the more facts it's able to register.

Another scientist ventured a statement not about what the brain is able to contain — ideas — but about messages. Every second, the brain is receiving an endless number of messages. Let's say New York City had a central telephone exchange. So this scientist says that the brain is like one thousand New York Metropolitan switchboards. All these messages are coming in constantly, every second, because we have receptive nerves in our fingertips that acknowledge touch, feeling, temperatures. We have these nerve endings all over our body. Your skin is in contact with the fibers of your clothing and is reporting on it. Your underwear, your socks, your shoes, your hat — everything is making an impression, and messages are coming in every second to your brain.

Every second, light is coming in through your eyes and sending messages to your brain. I look at the faces here. I look at the furnishings of this hall. The eye is literally taking thousands of pictures each second. And not only of an individual as a whole.

I see your face, nose, lips, ears. I see the separate hairs in your beard. There are more pictures than I can enumerate. I couldn't enumerate as much as I see in one second. It's all registered and photographed. Every second, photographs and photographs and photographs in great detail continue to come in.

And not only sights but sounds, too. Every second, sounds are coming in—not merely the sound of my voice, or the sounds of your restlessness as you're sitting bored, but sounds from far away, from Coney Island. Even the faintest sounds are registering. The mind is receiving all these messages.

In addition to that, the mind is receiving an endless number of messages from the body itself. Your feet are telling you to take off your shoes. Your side is telling you to stand up; you're tired of sitting. Your mouth is telling you you'd like a drink; your mouth is dry. Your blood is telling you the pH level has to be adjusted because you have too much acid in your blood, and immediately the brain sends a message to the various glands and tells them to adjust.

All over the body, a tremendous activity is taking place from hundreds of thousands of places. All these messages are being sent to the brain. And the brain is sending back messages and signals about what needs to be done. Even when you're asleep, your brain is functioning and employing unconscious methods of controlling the body.

When we spend even a minute thinking about this wonderful apparatus, we realize that it's lunacy to say it resulted from accidents. We have to use the existence of the mind to recognize that there's an "*Atah.*" The brain is the greatest testament in the world of an "*Atah.*"

If Hashem would open the skies, call out to us, and say, "Here I am," it would not be as clear a proof of His presence as the human brain. I say human brain—but I should say even an ant's brain. An ant's brain is miracle of miracles. That's why this *brachah* begins with "*Atah.*" Who else? You are the One Who bestowed *da'as* on man.

The Creator of the brain has to be not only the greatest scientist in the world, but a scientist of infinite wisdom, wisdom that extends far beyond the stars. There's no end to the planning that's necessary to create a tool as magnificent as the human brain.

The mind is vast without end. It's a universe of wisdom. We're not supposed to overlook that. The fact of a brain should be considered a most convincing evidence. If we're not impressed, it's because we haven't spent any time thinking about it. It's like a child who never thought about anything, which is true even of most *frum* Jews. They never thought about the wonders of the mind—that "*Atah chonein*—You, Hashem, are the One Who bestows" a mind, and nobody else could ever think of such a thing.

Q **What can be done about emotional instability?**

There are two kinds of emotional instability. If a person is *pashut meshuga,* if he's crazy, then he needs special treatment. I can't tell you right now what to do about that. But if a person is still sane yet is unstable emotionally, he must take himself in hand and practice happiness. The antidote for every kind of emotional disturbance is happiness. You must learn how to be happy in life! It's so important!

How do you do that? The first thing, the emergency fix, is to start singing. Sing! Not in your heart. Sing aloud. Once you start singing, things will start responding within you. You'll be singing inside of you. Your outward actions will awaken your inside.

Learn how to sing in this world. Learn how to sing about the thousands of things you really *are* enjoying. And once a person gets the attitude of being happy, emotional instability will disappear. Emotional instability is a sign of unhappiness in one form or another. Happiness is the antidote to emotional instability! Unless somebody has gone insane. That's a different story.

Q **How can I overcome depression?**

That depends on a number of circumstances. First, what kind of person is asking that question? The answer may depend on the person's age and health and social circumstances. But if we had to give one general answer, there is no question that to be busy is the very best method to combat depression. There are also mental attitudes that one could learn, but they take time. There are medicines, but that needs a physician. Yet this is one thing that everybody agrees on—if the concerned party becomes busy and has no time to think, that is the very best therapy.

There's a reason for this. The human being is built in a particular way, both physically and mentally. One of the peculiarities of mankind is that *atzlus* and *atzvus*—laziness and sadness—go together. You see that from the Gemara (*Gittin* 67b). "Work is great because it warms (*mechamemes*) the one working." It's a play on words. The *mishnah* says that work brings honor (*mechabedes*) to a person. This statement adds that work is also *mechamemes*, it warms up a person. It means that it gives him enthusiasm.

That's because Hashem created man with a desire to achieve. Now, his true achievements are in *ruchniyus*: achievements of the spirit, the *neshamah*—*ma'asim tovim*, and Torah above all. Torah and *mitzvos*. However, when a person does something that looks like achieving—like bricklaying or sewing, anything that's creative—then that person has a sensation of achieving. Even though he's not fulfilling the prime achievement of life—it's only a shadow or a substitute—to an extent it stills the hunger, the craving of the soul. Therefore, people are happy when they're doing something—even when they're doing things that are in themselves almost valueless. So being busy is most important.

Now, this person will complain, "But how can I do anything? I don't have the spirit to do anything." It's the same as saying, "I'm so weak, I don't feel like pulling myself out of the water when I'm drowning!" Well, you'd better muster energy and start swimming.

Do something before you go down! And the same is true when someone is too weak to do anything. The first thing is — do it. That's going to bring you out of your mental weakness.

There's no such thing as being happy if one is entirely unoccupied. And no one could give you better advice, even if he charges hundreds of dollars an hour.

Q Should one spend time thinking if it's bad for his mental health?

Question — It was said that people need time to think. Isn't it better for people to be busy so they should avoid mental illness?

People should eat and work. But sometimes a man is so ill that he's forbidden to eat, so we give him intravenous nourishment instead. And sometimes he's forbidden to work, too.

Yes, sometimes we tell people, "Don't think"— and that's the best therapy for them. They must keep busy so they won't have time to think. It's like the teeth. Teeth are for chewing food, but when a man uses his teeth to chew up his cheeks and his tongue, he's misusing them. When people use their minds to chew up their own minds, we tell them to get busy making rugs or climbing mountains. Do something to take your mind off your mind. Don't think. But when people are healthy, thinking is a very good prescription. It's a great thing to spend time on Shabbos thinking.

Therefore, it depends for whom. Sometimes you must stop thinking to save yourself. But for most people we say: Think! Of course, you have to think properly. If you think about all kinds of *narishkeiten* and *yetzer hara* things, it certainly won't do any good. But if you think the proper ideas, then you're going to make use of the purpose for which leisure was given.

SUMMARY

- The most important thing to ask Hashem for is *da'as*. It enables us to appreciate all that Hashem does for us.

- *Da'as* is not something you either have or don't have. It means to understand things more and more clearly, and there's no end to that process. We should always desire to acquire more *da'as*, more clarity.
- One of the most important concepts we need to understand is that we're standing before Hashem when we *daven*. Even though it's forbidden to think that Hashem has any physical form, the Torah describes Him with physical expressions to help us internalize the idea that He is real, and that we are standing in His presence.
- Hashem gave us such powerful brains because He wants us to use them to acquire more and more *da'as*.
- We should use our *da'as* to study *mussar sefarim*, which will enable us to perceive Hashem more clearly in our lives. *Da'as* helps us recognize Hashem's endless kindness in the world.
- At its most basic level, *da'as* means sanity, for which we should always thank Hashem. When we contemplate the complexity of the human brain, we should be filled with gratitude to Hashem for the great gift He gives us.

Hashiveinu

Q **What's the first step in *teshuvah*?**

Our first request is asking Hashem to give us understanding—"*Atah chonein la'adam da'as.*" We don't begin "*Hashiveinu Avinu l'Sorasecha*—Bring us back to Your Torah." That's the next *tefillah*. First we say, "Bestow upon us understanding," which means the first step in coming back, in returning to Hashem, is understanding. Good intentions aren't enough. If a man makes a firm resolve to go to a certain place, he first has to discover how to get there. Without that, it's very likely he's headed in the wrong direction. Of course, nobody thinks so. Everybody trusts his own intuition. He thinks he has a homing instinct like a pigeon that knows where to go without being directed. The *Mesillas Yesharim* says in his introduction that if you don't have the training, you won't be able to move in the right direction.

You must be educated in what is right if you want to do what is right.

That's why first we ask for *da'as*, understanding. We've spoken about what that means at length. Now we presume that everybody is fully aware of this great necessity, this prerequisite to gain *da'as*. Of course, even if you heard it, you have to hear it again, but for right now it's enough to know that it's important to have *de'ah*, to work on *de'ah*, to seek *de'ah*, to yearn for *de'ah*, and even to be ready to pay money and make sacrifices to acquire *de'ah*. That's the beginning—to enlighten the mind. That's the first step to do *teshuvah*.

Q Why do we call Hashem "Avinu, our Father"?

The word *avinu* is connected to the word *ahav*, "to love." It's not a *drash*; it's etymology. *Avinu* is also connected to the word *avah*—spelled *aleph, beis, hey*—meaning "to desire." Desire and love are the same word. *Ahav* and *avah* are the same letters transposed. *Avinu* means, "the One to Whom our desire turns." It means we must have a desire to come to Hashem.

We have to understand that our happiness depends on being joined in love to Hashem. Not only our happiness in this world, but our happiness forever. What is the hope that every human soul harbors instinctively? We have an intuition that death isn't the end, and everybody who passes out of this world, even the greatest *rasha*, hopes that something will remain.[27] Sometimes a man thinks he can satisfy that instinct with token gestures, for instance, by building monuments to himself. But everybody wants perpetuity; everybody wants eternity. There's an instinct in mankind not to die. Everybody wants immortality, not just symbolically but in actuality.

The great happiness of joining our Father is like a son who was estranged from his father for many years and wandered around the world among strangers. He never felt he had his own kin, his own flesh and blood, and always yearned to come back to the place where

---

27 For more on this topic, read *Rav Avigdor Miller on Olam Haba.*

he belonged, to his own parents. When we finally go to Olam Haba, we're coming back to our true Father. That's the sensation of happiness that transcends overwhelmingly any kind of pleasure imaginable. It's the greatest joy a person can ever imagine. It's the joy of being connected to Hashem.

That's very far from our minds right now, and from our feelings and emotions. But the truth is that this is the happiness for which we were created. Eventually, we come back to our Source. "*Vayipach b'apav nishmas chayim*—Hashem blew a soul into man" (*Bereishis* 2:7). When the soul returns to its Source, it's the greatest form of reward and pleasure possible. And that's the joy of *Avinu*. The Torah says, "Is He not your Father, the One Who made you?" (*Devarim* 32:6).

When we say, "*Hashiveinu, Avinu*—Bring us back, Our Father," it refers to the emotion of yearning. Like David Hamelech said, "My soul yearns for Hashem like a deer in the wilderness yearns for springs of cool, fresh water" (*Tehillim* 42:2). Even the happiest, most fortunate man in this world feels as if this world is a desert. He's all alone in a barren desert and yearning to come back to the great spring—"*mekor mayim chaim*—the well of living waters," which Hashem alone will provide when we return to Him in *teshuvah*. That's the emotion of *Avinu*.

That's very important for people to understand, whether they have the feeling or not. They must *yearn* to come to Hashem. And if they can't yearn, they must learn how to yearn. We can do it in this world in a certain sense. It's not an emotion that has to be postponed. Even today, there are people of varying degrees of perfection who have attained a love of Hashem, and that's a rewarding experience. It's a form of happiness. Some people are very happy in this attachment to Hashem that they've gained here. But whatever we feel right now, the first step is to learn the necessity of fostering that emotion. That's why we say "Return us, our Father" at the beginning of our *tefillah* for *teshuvah*.

When people want to do *teshuvah*, they may not know which direction to go. They might think they should do more *mitzvos*—excellent, do more *mitzvos*. They might think they should put on a *frum* appearance—excellent, do that, too. But neither of those is the heart of *teshuvah*. The heart of *teshuvah* is to start yearning for Hashem. The essence of *teshuvah* is *wanting* to come back to Him. If people want to be *frum*—they want to live in *frum* neighborhoods, look like *frum* Jews, have a *frum* home—all that is very good. But if in their hearts they haven't yet developed a yearning, a longing to come close to Hashem, they haven't begun the real *teshuvah*.

We're not minimizing any good deeds. We're happy that anybody does anything, and he's certainly fortunate if he does so. Happy is the man who becomes a *shomer Shabbos*. He has saved himself. Happy is the couple who begin keeping *taharas hamishpachah*. Wonderful! Happy is the man who learns how to do all the *mitzvos*. Wonderful! Nevertheless, he has not started on the true road to *teshuvah*.

We shouldn't deceive ourselves. *Teshuvah* means to turn back to Hashem. When a man intends to fulfill the *mitzvah* of *teshuvah*, it's, "*V'shavta ad Hashem Elokecha*—You have to come back to your Hashem" (*Devarim* 30:2). It's not just *Elokim*, but "*Elokecha*—*your* Hashem." *Elokecha* is your individual Hashem. It's talking about someone who is devoted to Hashem personally. "You're my G-O-D." You must learn how to love Hashem at least as much as you love a good friend.

That's an understatement, of course. But suppose there's somebody in the world whom you love very much, for whom you have a strong affection. If you don't have such a person, you should know that you're lacking in one of your limbs, one of your moral or spiritual organs. But if you're capable of loving at least one person to some extent, you should use that as a criterion and say, "How much more so Hashem."

David said, "*Ki avi v'imi azavuni*—for my father and mother abandoned me" (*Tehillim* 27:10). Now, his father didn't forsake him. His mother didn't throw him out in the street. It meant *it was as if* he had no parents. David honored his parents, and certainly they deserved honor. His parents were remarkable people and he revered them exceedingly. But when he was talking to Hashem, it was as if he had no parents.

David concludes, "*VaHashem ya'asfeini*—Hashem has gathered me." Hashem took me off the street. I was a foundling lying in the street. He picked me up out of the dust, washed me off, and raised me. It's all Hashem. Of course, He did it by means of His agents. And his parents were worthy agents. He certainly said "thank you" to the agents. The Gemara says, "Wine belongs to the owner, but say 'thank you' to the one who pours it" (*Bava Kama* 92b). When you go to a *simchah* and the man next to you pours some wine for you, thank him. But know that all the wine in this world belongs to Hashem. We have gratitude to our father and mother, but it's all Hashem. Therefore, David said, "*VaHashem ya'asfeini.*" That's how he learned to feel.

Now, it didn't happen all at once. He worked for years on this emotion until he finally developed the attitude of "*Avinu*—our Father." A world of love lies concealed in the words of this *brachah*. The more a person delves into the words, the more he will eventually get out of it. He'll begin to feel a personal attachment to Hashem, which is one of the prime *mitzvos* of the Torah, "*V'ahavta es Hashem Elokecha*" (*Devarim* 6:5).

Q Why do we mention Torah here in the prayer for *teshuvah*?

We say every morning just before Shemoneh Esrei a special blessing on the Torah, "*Ahavah Rabbah*—the great love." What is this "great love" that Hashem loves us with? The answer is Torah. Hashem expressed His great love by bestowing upon us the greatest gift, the Torah. Some people wish it to be expressed in dollars, in long life, in all forms of joy in this world. It doesn't mean those are ruled out, but the very first and greatest understanding of Hashem's love for us is that He gave us such a gift.

Therefore, we say, "*Hashiveinu, Avinu, l'Sorasecha*—Bring us back, our Father, to Your Torah."

What does "Torah" mean? It doesn't mean merely keeping the Torah. Here it means bring us back to learning "Your Torah," to studying the Torah. The very first request in *teshuvah* isn't to bring us back to fulfill your *mitzvos*, but to the study of Torah. *Mitzvos* are certainly important. *Mitzvos* are paramount in our lives. But our very first request is to learn and know the Torah. That's our expression of love.

Now, Hashem doesn't merely give Torah; He gives everything else, too. He gives us all the things that make life enjoyable, and certainly we're grateful for every one of them. But there's no gift greater in importance than the gift of Torah. And He's given it to us Jews, not to the nations. They also have life. Sometimes they enjoy life, too. But of all the blessings we have been chosen for, the very greatest privilege is Torah, because that's the sign of His special love for us.

You've all heard that from me many times, but the point being emphasized here [in the *brachah* of *Hashiveinu*] is that this idea, this attitude, is the very first step in *teshuvah*. When somebody wants to repent, what's the first step? Number one is to try to gain a true love of Hashem, a personal love. That's a big order but a very important one. The second one, and it's a condition of the first, is Torah.

"Torah" doesn't mean what some people think. It's not to gain prestige, to become important. Now, if people learn Torah *shelo lishmah*, not for its own sake, we're happy with them. As long as Torah is being propagated, we're not going to examine the motives. But we're talking here about *teshuvah*, and *teshuvah* requires approaching the Torah *because we love Hashem*. Like the *tzaddikim* who were so in love with the Torah that it was their highest pleasure in this world. Rav Yitzchak Elchanan, the Kovno Rav, was very busy with *tzarchei tzibbur*, helping Klal Yisrael fight decrees of the Russian government. The *chachamim* and *askanim* came to his home constantly to discuss what to do, and the discussions went on for a long time. Finally Rav Yitzchak Elchanan would say, "Enough Olam Haba. Let's have some Olam Hazeh." And he sat down and began learning.

So, what's a practical, tangible way to love Hashem? Love learning His Torah.

This love can be experienced in many ways. We love to breathe air, to look at the blue sky, to eat, to live normally. There's no question that happiness in this world also depends on *gashmiyus*, on loving Hashem for the physical and material good He gives us. When you realize that the One Who loves you most is giving you this gift, you begin to appreciate your socks, your shoes, your trousers, your underwear, your belt, your necktie, your shirt, your coat, your hat, your eyeglasses, and everything else. When you understand that it's all a gift from your Father and that He intends it for your benefit, there's no question you're happier, that you have greater joy in your physical possessions in this world.

But of all the great benefits that Hashem gave us, the one with which He demonstrated His special regard for us is the knowledge that we're his son. "*Banim atem laHashem Elokeichem*—you are sons to Hashem" (*Devarim* 14:1). The *Tomer Devorah* has an interesting expression: "*Am krovo*"—we're "His relatives." Now, this isn't merely said as a random idea. "*Yei'ameir lahem b'nei Keil chai*—we're called "children of the living G-d" (*Hoshea* 2:1). He's our father, and we're His children.

And of all the signs by which He denotes His fatherhood to us, the greatest is the Torah.

That's the beginning of *teshuvah*. If a man intends to come back to Hashem, let him think of Hashem as a loving Father, and the One Who bestowed upon him the greatest gift—the Torah.

Q Why do we also call Hashem "Malkeinu, our King"?

In *Hashiveinu*, after our request to help us do *teshuvah* by calling out to Hashem as "*Avinu*—our Father," we then say, "*v'karveinu, Malkeinu, la'avodasecha*—bring us close, our King, to Your service." Now we call Him "King." A king is served out of fear, and that sensation of fear is a great benefit. We shouldn't underestimate the benefits that we gain from *yiras Hashem*.

An example: Somebody is advised by his physician to avoid a certain kind of indulgence because it will lead to a certain illness. That already contains the element of fear. But then the physician bolsters it with an illustration. "You know the man in the house next door to you?

He was careless in this matter, and that's why he became ill. That's why he passed away at an early age." That's a tremendous incentive to obey the physician's instructions.

The more fear you put into a certain thing, the more it's going to affect you.

Q **Is it necessary to fear Hashem? Isn't love sufficient?**

Love of Hashem must be balanced with fear of Hashem. "*V'gilu bir'adah*—rejoice in Hashem with trembling" (*Tehillim* 2:11). This isn't a contradiction at all. You can love a king immensely and intensely, and you can also be afraid of him because you know that with one motion he could sentence you to death. We must encourage both emotions. "*Es Hashem Elokecha tira*—Fear Hashem, your G-d (*Devarim* 10:20). To learn to be afraid of Hashem is a positive commandment, and it's reiterated many times.

The Gemara (*Shabbos* 32a) provides an illustration of how to fear Hashem. When you go out in the street, let it be in your eyes as if a Roman sergeant arrested you. That's how you should fear Hashem. When you walk in the street, you should fear Hashem. What could happen? Anything could happen! The street is full of lunatics, dope addicts, *resha'im*. There are drunk drivers who could drive up on the sidewalk. People could drop things from windowsills. All sorts of things could happen—and they do happen. When you walk out into the street, you're in danger. The truth is, at home there are also plenty of dangers, but if you walk out on the street the dangers multiply because now you're among others, among people you don't know. Therefore, when you go out to the street, use the opportunity to fear Hashem.

That doesn't mean you should live your life with apprehension, but you should make use of the opportunities. When Yaakov Avinu saw Eisav coming with four hundred men, the Torah says, "He was very much afraid and distressed" (*Bereishis* 32:8). Where was his *bitachon*? Didn't Yaakov Avinu rely on the promises that Hashem gave him? Didn't Hashem say, "I'll be with you, and I'll bring you back in peace to your father's house" (ibid. 28:15)? Why was he so afraid and distressed when he saw Eisav coming? Did he forget Hashem's promises?

No, Yaakov didn't forget. But it was an opportunity—an opportunity to be afraid of Hashem. He saw danger threatening, so he mustered the natural reaction of fear and transferred it to Hashem. The threatening situation is an opportunity to increase *yiras Hashem.* That's how Yaakov Avinu reacted.

We, too, should use every opportunity to learn to fear Hashem. We shouldn't disdain that. When you see what happened to somebody else, think to yourself, "Why am I different?" Learn how to fear Hashem more. That's one of the steps of *teshuvah.*

Teshuvah isn't a simple matter. Of course, if you can rectify even one thing right now, do it. If your *tefillin* are *passul*, certainly, get kosher *tefillin*. But the fundamentals of *teshuvah* are *Avinu* and *Malkeinu*—that's *ahavah* and *yirah.*

Q **What does "serving Hashem" mean?**

We say, *"V'karveinu, Malkeinu, la'avodasecha*—Bring us close, our King, to Your service." What is *avodah*? What is meant by serving Hashem?

Briefly, *avodah* means to behave like an *eved*. An *eved* means someone who feels humble in the presence of his master. That's how we serve Hashem. Did you ever think of that? Maybe you're thinking of serving Hashem by helping yeshivas—excellent. Or maybe you're thinking about being *mekarev* Jews—excellent. But great ideas like that can sometimes deceive you. All these things are very good, but the main thing is to feel humility. That's the real obligation. Learn how to be an *eved* to Hashem. Learn to do things solely for the purpose of demonstrating your humility before Him.

I know that in this age humility is not stylish. It's very unpopular to talk about humility and being lowly before a ruler. Today it's stylish to glorify rebels. People don't like the idea of being humble before a master. They can stomach loving Hashem a little bit, but not being afraid of Hashem. They want to throw off the yoke. But that's a fundamental error. We are ships floating on the waves of the ocean. Our lives are buffeted by all kinds of circumstances. Nobody is a master of his fate in this world. Don't we see people at the apex of their success suddenly disappear? A famous performer, a successful movie star — the world is at his feet. He makes millions every year. He has whatever his heart desires — and then suddenly he's gone. We must acknowledge our weakness, our smallness, our unimportance in this universe.

Why should we merely be servants and slaves of random and chaotic chance? Why should we be the victims of meaningless tragedy when we can transform our fears — not the fears of a blind, dark Nature, but fear of a wise and understanding King! *Melech* means *nimlach, milka*, one who has counsel. "*Hashem b'chachmah yisad aretz* — Hashem founded the world with wisdom" (*Mishlei* 3:19). He conducts it with great wisdom. Such a *Melech* has no equal. It's a great *simchah* to serve such a ruler. Therefore, nobody should feel that it's beneath his dignity to bow down at the beginning of Shemoneh Esrei. Bow down low. It's not necessary to bow too low, but practice bowing down and making yourself nothing in the presence of your King.

That's what we're doing when we bow down on the ground on Rosh Hashanah or Yom Kippur. We're "ground," we're "earth" before You, we're "nothing" before You, our King. We recognize our Ruler. That's *avodah*. That's what it means to be an *eved*.

Now, to be called an *eved Hashem* is a very great title. Moshe was called *eved Hashem* (*Devarim* 34:5). Yehoshua was called *eved Hashem* (*Yehoshua* 24:29). David Hamelech was called *eved Hashem* (II *Shmuel* 3:18). But not everybody is called that. There were other great men in Tanach whom the *nevi'im* approved of greatly, but they weren't called *eved Hashem*. Still, each of us must aspire to even a fraction of that *madreigah*.

Avodas Hashem means, first of all, to recognize "*Hashem Melech* — Hashem is King." The greatness of Hashem is an endless subject, but that doesn't mean we're excused from studying it. "There's no searching out His greatness" (*Tehillim* 145:3). Yet, "I will speak of Your greatness" (ibid. 145:6). Unfortunately, the subject of studying the greatness of Hashem is largely ignored, even among good Jews. Let's say a person walks into a *shteibel*, gives a knock on the *bimah*, and says we must talk about the greatness of Hashem. They'll think he's crazy. *The greatness of Hashem? Certainly Hashem is great. Why waste time talking about it?*

If that's the case, you don't know His greatness. You must speak constantly on the subject and think constantly about it. It's not so simple. You have to learn how to do it. How to be an *eved Hashem* is one of the most important subjects. It's not enough just to say general words. You must be specific. You have to talk about things that illustrate and make the greatness of Hashem real.

Avodas Hashem doesn't mean doing something to help out Hashem by making the world *frum* and making the world serve Him. No, we're not helping Him. We're just demonstrating that we're subservient to Him in the sense of, "*Mah ashiv laHashem kol tagmulohi alay*—How can I pay back Hashem for all that He bestowed upon me?" (*Tehillim* 116:12). That's called *avodas Hashem*. That's the definition the *Chovos Halevavos* gives of *avodah*. We're not doing a thing for Hashem; we're only showing that we're *avadav*, we're his servants.

Q *V'hachazireinu* — What does that mean, "Bring us back"?

Now we say, "*v'hachazireinu*—and bring us back." Back to what? "*Biseshuvah sheleimah l'fanecha*—in complete repentance before You."

"Bringing back" implies returning to a place we were before. We want to return to a specific situation—we're asking Hashem to return us to our level at Har Sinai, when we accepted the Torah with the utmost love and gratitude.

Just before we came to Har Sinai, we experienced *Kriyas Yam Suf*. We were in grave danger. A wicked and vengeful army was pursuing us. They were armed to the teeth and intended to wreak havoc and have their vengeance. "*Amar oyev erdof*—The enemy said, 'I'll pursue.'"

"*Asig*—I'll overtake." "*Achalek shalal*—I'll take away all that they have. "*Arik charbi*—I'll draw out my sword." "*Torisheimo yadi*—My hand shall take revenge" (*Shemos* 15:9). The enemy was looking forward to taking revenge, to a general slaughter. There was no way to escape the Egyptian army. It was the biggest army in that era. They were pursuing an unarmed people, people who had just been freed from slavery and were helpless.

Suddenly the tables were turned—they were cast into a sea and drowned. The waters covered them. "*Yardu bimtzolos k'mo aven*—They went down like stones" (ibid 15:5). "They sank like lead" (ibid. 15:10). The Am Yisrael went wild. They were delirious with happiness when they saw that. And so, when they came to Har Sinai, their love for Hashem was great. They had an endless, burning fire of *ahavas Hashem* in their breast when He offered them the Torah through Moshe Rabbeinu. They shouted in unison, "*Na'aseh v'nishma*—We will do, and we will listen." "*Amru k'echad*—They shouted it altogether." Not one of them held back.

It was the climax, the greatest point in our history. Never again did we have such a moment. It was so perfect that Hashem said, "*Mi yiten v'hayah l'vavam zeh l'yirah osi... kol hayamim*—Would that their hearts be like this to fear Me forever and ever" (*Devarim* 5:26). As we say in *Shir Hashirim* (1:2), "*Yishakeini mineshikos pihu*—Once more, let Hashem kiss us with the kisses of His mouth." That refers to the great love at Har Sinai, when the entire nation was intoxicated with *ahavas Hashem*. They had reached the highest *madreigah* of love for Hashem.

That's what we're saying when we say: "Bring us back."

Now, in case we can't get back all the way, even one step is worthwhile. One step back toward Har Sinai is already something worth asking for. "*Hachazireinu*—Bring us back," back to You, when we had that meeting with You, when You loved us and we loved You, when we shared that great kiss of *ahavas Hashem* at Matan Torah.

Q **What is *teshuvah sheleimah*?**

Teshuvah sheleimah, "perfect *teshuvah*," means we shouldn't hold back anything. Not only should we stop doing what's wrong and begin doing everything that's right, but we should also do it with the highest degree of *lishmah, chassidus*, and *ahavas Hashem*, with the highest devotion. Everything should be done with full fear and love of Hashem. That's what we request. However, after that we say, "*Baruch Atah, Hashem, harotzeh biseshuvah.*" We don't say *teshuvah sheleimah*. Why?

And the answer is that Hashem is waiting for us to take just one step. Even though people with wisdom are yearning for the fullest expression of *teshuvah*, for a *teshuvah sheleimah*, it's very important to at least do some form of *teshuvah*. I'll explain that briefly.

Teshuvah sheleimah is difficult, but a *miktzas teshuvah*, a partial *teshuvah*, isn't. The more difficult something is, the less responsible we are, and the less the punishment if we don't do it. The easier something is, the greater the punishment for not doing it.

The *mitzvah* of writing a *sefer Torah* costs many thousands of dollars. The *mitzvah* of putting up a *mezuzah* costs much less. For which *mitzvah* does a person get a greater punishment if he neglects it? For most of us, it's not so easy to shell out thousands of dollars. Therefore, even though it might be an obligation on everybody, Hashem is willing to wait. But a *mezuzah* costs a few dollars. Even if there's a question, a *safeik*, if he has to put up a *mezuzah* on a particular doorway, he might as well buy a *mezuzah* and put it up anyway without a *brachah*.

Teshuvah sheleimah is certainly a desire for great people. It's an ambition. Everybody should have that ambition, and we should ask for help to fulfill it. But everybody can do at least a partial *teshuvah*. All around us are little bits of *teshuvah* waiting to be done. In case you can't have proper *kavanah* for the entire davening, at least concentrate for part of the davening. At least the first *brachah* of Shemoneh Esrei. The Gemara says that if you don't have *kavanah* for the first *brachah* of Shemoneh Esrei, you have to repeat Shemoneh Esrei again. We don't do it because we're afraid the second time won't be any better. But you have to have *kavanah*. Some *poskim* say *Modim* also needs proper intention. Some *poskim* say that if a person said *Modim* without *kavanah*, he must repeat Shemoneh Esrei.

When a person is busy all day long, clucking with his tongue and talking *devarim b'teilim*, at least when he comes to the *beis haknesses* he should keep his mouth shut. That's a partial *teshuvah*. In the *beis haknesses*, he clamps his lips together and refuses to open them. Of course, he has to open them for davening. Unfortunately, some people have their lips clamped together when they're davening, too. You sit next to them and you don't hear a word. Don't clamp your lips while you're davening. Open up your mouth wide. But otherwise, keep it shut. And after davening, too.

When you're finished davening, the first thing is "*Lecha dumiyah tehillah*—To You, Hashem, silence is praise" (*Tehillim* 65:2). In Hashem's house, silence is praising Him. So when you finish davening, keep quiet. You can say "good day" to people, but then walk out and keep quiet—unless you want to sit and learn. Otherwise, keep quiet. Clench your teeth together.

Like I always say—a man who smokes twenty cigarettes every Shabbos but takes it upon himself to only smoke nineteen should be praised. He's done a partial *teshuvah*. Now, he has to stop entirely at some point, but putting in effort to reduce it by even one is a partial *teshuvah*.[28]

At the beginning, we say "*Hashiveinu, Avinu*—Bring us back" any kind of way, even a little. Later, we say we want *teshuvah sheleimah*. A person should strive to make the best that he can out of himself and come back with a perfect *teshuvah*, but any kind of *teshuvah* is a success. Just remember not to stop there. Once a man says, "I did *teshuvah* and that's enough," Hashem says, "You retired? Alright, I'll stop giving you your salary. You want to be paid every day? You want *parnassah* every day? You want your heart to pump every day? Then keep making progress in *teshuvah*. That's what life is for."

It's like the boy who said to his father, "Pa, do I have to *bentch* every time I eat?" The father replied, "No, only when you eat."

As long as a person is here, he's here to do *teshuvah*. If he feels that it's time to retire, it's a bad sign.

---

28 The *Yom Tov Drashos* by Yitzchak Goldstein, published by Simchas Hachaim, has a chapter where Rav Miller expounds on this theme—"*Miktzas Teshuvah*" (pp. 202–205).

Q Are there different kinds of *teshuvah*?

There are two kinds of *teshuvah*. To repent for your sins, there are some minimal requirements you must be aware of, certain things that you must do, and then you have fulfilled the *mitzvah* of doing *teshuvah* for that sin. You must have *charatah*, regret for your sins. Then you have to resolve that you won't return to those sins; you must forsake your evil ways. You also have to ask Hashem for *mechilah*, and you have to say *Viduy*. These are not such simple matters, but when you do them properly, you have fulfilled the basic requirements of *teshuvah*.

But there is another *teshuvah*, a more difficult and much higher *teshuvah*. And that is, "Come all the way back to Hashem" (*Hoshea* 14:2). Not just to "do *teshuvah*" but to actually come back to Hashem. That's the real *teshuvah* Hashem wants from you. And that *teshuvah* is endless. The pursuit of *shleimus*, the perfection of trying to get close to Hashem, is a lifelong endeavor. Moshe tried all his life. Although he succeeded enormously, he didn't fully succeed. Nobody can succeed completely. Coming back to Hashem means not merely to stop doing *aveiros*. *Hashem wants you to be perfect*, as perfect as you can be. And that perfection means returning to Him by keeping Him before you all the time. All day long. That's *teshuvah*.

All your life, you must strive for more and more perfection. It's a *chiyuv*, an obligation! Hashem says to us, "Would that their hearts be like this to fear Me forever and ever" (*Devarim* 5:26). Hashem wants from us that same attitude we had at Matan Torah when we heard His voice. It was tremendous! Everyone was overwhelmed by the *d'var Hashem* at Har Sinai. The voice of Hashem! And Hashem said, "I want it to be that way always!" How could it always be that way?! That's a very difficult *avodah*. It's a *teshuvah* that involves coming back to constant awareness of Hashem.

So real *teshuvah*, the *teshuvah sheleimah*, is a very serious undertaking because there's a lot of work to do to achieve that attitude of feeling the presence of Hashem always. But it's an attitude all of us can achieve. It just takes work. All our lives we have to strive to do the best we can by constantly seeking more and more *shleimus,* by coming back to Hashem as much as possible. The more you think about Hashem, the more you are coming back to Him in real *teshuvah.*

PRACTICAL ADVICE

Q What does *teshuvah* mean, practically?

When we talk about repenting or doing *teshuvah*, let's not make an error. We're not talking merely about righting some wrongs that a person did. *Teshuvah* in that sense is too limited. When we talk about *teshuvah*, we talk about, "*v'shuvu el Hashem*—to return to Hashem" (*Hoshea* 14:3). Which means, not merely to repent for things that were done incorrectly. What *teshuvah* really means is to come closer to Hashem and to gain certain qualities, certain attitudes, and certain practices that were never done before in your life. It means to get better. *Teshuvah* actually means to get better.

Q How come I never change, no matter how much I intend to?

Let me tell you something. You *do* change. Don't think you're the same. You're getting worse! As time goes on, "If one does a sin, and repeats it again and again, it becomes permissible in his eyes" (*Yoma* 87a). So if you're not improving, you're actually getting worse.

When you make a *kabbalah bli neder*, you must commit to something specific, at least one specific thing that you're going to work on changing. "If you try to grab too much at one time, you're going to grab nothing at all" (*Yoma* 80a). It's all going to fall out of your hand. To say in general, "I'm going to be good this year," is better than nothing, but not much better. You have to specify something. Say, "This year, no matter how mean my wife is to me, and how much she bothers me and criticizes me and nags me, I won't say anything impolite to her. I'll keep my mouth closed." That's already something specific, something you can grab onto.

Actually, even though it's specific and limited, it's not so small in Hashem's eyes. The *passuk* says, "The world hangs on nothing" (*Iyov* 26:7). Chazal tell us that it means the following, "The world exists only on account of the person who keeps his mouth closed at a time of provocation" (*Chullin* 89a). The *zechus*, the merit, of keeping your mouth closed when people are insulting you is very great. So start with your wife. You can start with somebody else as well. Let's say you have an employer who insults you—keep quiet! You want to keep your job, don't you? So keep your mouth closed. Make a *kabbalah*: "I'm going to keep quiet. I won't answer back." It's a tremendous thing to do that.

You have to commit to something clear-cut. Then you'll be able to carry it out. Don't talk in general. General means nothing at all.

Let's say you want to *daven* with *kavanah*. You can't just say, "This year, I'm going to *daven* with *kavanah*." It's too much to grab onto at once. Make up your mind that you're going to fight for that first *brachah*. Every word in *Magen Avraham*, the first *brachah*, you're going to focus on clearly. And don't let go of it. Hold onto it. Take a little bit at a time and hold onto it very tightly.

Let's say you make a *kabbalah* to learn Torah. So don't say, "I'm going to start learning more seriously this year." It's too broad, too vague. Do it like this—"*Bli neder*, I'm going to learn fifteen minutes every day no matter what." And then do it. Learn every night, fifteen minutes. It's better than nothing. At home, fifteen minutes. No matter what! Take out a *sefer* and learn for fifteen minutes. You want to learn an hour, very good. I'm not stopping you. Or go to a *shiur* every night. That's even better. Every night, no matter what. That's a *kabbalah* that's clear-cut. It's something you can sink your teeth into.

Now, even though there are probably so many more things that you should be doing that you're not doing, still, at least one thing you're doing. Hashem sees that you're headed in the right direction. If you're headed in the right direction, then, "If you're trying to get better, He'll help you go further and further" (*Menachos* 29b). But you have to do at least one thing! And then you'll get *siyata d'Shmaya* to progress more and more.

Q When is the best time for *teshuvah*?

Until recently, Elul was considered the month of *teshuvah*. Elul was the month when the Jewish nation prepared for Rosh Hashanah. Today, they prepare for Rosh Hashanah on Rosh Hashanah evening. They start thinking about *teshuvah* as they go to Maariv of Rosh Hashanah. If a man has some good sense, he says to his wife before he leaves the house, "Forgive me for everything." And she says to him, "Forgive me, too, for everything." By the way, that's a good idea. But wise people do it earlier.

The Alter of Slabodka forsook his beloved yeshiva — Slabodka, where he was the mentor — and went to his old alma mater, so to speak, in Kelm, in the middle of Av. Kelm was the source of the old *ba'alei mussar.* Although he was an old man, he sat there as a disciple for half the month of Av, preparing for Elul, because Av is a glorious month of happiness, well-suited for *teshuvah.* Av is summertime, when everything is operating at its maximum. All of Nature is alive — bugs, birds, bears, and other animals; trees are loaded with foliage, shrubs, flowers, leaves; apples and tomatoes in the gardens are becoming distended with juice and will soon become red. The fruit stands are loaded with local produce. All over, Nature is busy.

The Gemara tells us that the fifteenth day of Av is among the happiest occasions (*Ta'anis* 26b). There's so much happiness that it's important to know how to tap into it. If it's used properly, the *yetzer tov* can flourish in the month of Av, because the highest *teshuvah* is that which is done when the *briyah* is most active, when the cornucopia of Hashem's blessings is shedding happiness upon mankind.

People may not think so because they're accustomed to griping all the time and complaining that it's hot. They talk to each other about the heat and the humidity. But each heat wave causes another growth spurt. The apples are baking on the trees. You don't have to do anything to prepare apples; they're ready to eat by the time you buy them, baked by the summer heat. When your wife is baking a cake, you don't complain, saying, "Look how hot it is." So don't complain about the heat of summer. That's when Hashem is baking apples. And He's baking everything else we enjoy.

Summer is a time for gratitude, because it's also a time when Nature is alive. Therefore, it's the time to do *teshuvah*. That's a new idea, but it's really an old idea. The original Torah concept of repentance—of coming closer to Hashem—was not by means of chastisement, tribulations, or sufferings. In Gan Eden, Hashem could have created fast days for Adam Harishon. He could have created plants with thorns, plants that needed a lot of work before they could be eaten. But instead there were only good times. That's how the world began. That was the original plan—that man would choose to be good due to happiness. The happiness he enjoyed would fill him with overwhelming gratitude to the One Who gave him all that good.

But this plan is still valid, still accessible today. Everybody is happy when he sees that his fields are growing. When the crops begin to ripen, when he sees big sheaves of grain standing in the field, that's the time of *bikkurim*. Everybody's happy in the time of the *assif*, when you gather in your wheat and your barley and your rye and your spelt and your oats, when you take in all the wine you pressed and put it in your wine cellars. Everybody is happy when you take in the olives that you pressed and have plenty left over for all year round. Everybody is happy when you have all good things to eat and your plate is full.

On all sides in the middle of the summer the voices of Nature are crying out. All Nature is speaking—the red roses are speaking, the violets are speaking, the tulips are speaking. Every color of flower is speaking. If you pass a fruit stand and see red watermelons—ah, what a beautiful sight! The red colors are blazing, announcing the sweetness, the wetness, and the coldness. Ah, a delicious meal waiting for you! The best dessert is a slab of watermelon. Forget about the garbage they concoct like ice cream and all kinds of *chazerai*. A slab of watermelon is healthy, as well as beautiful and tasty. It's Hashem's dessert.

On the fruit stands, you see all the testaments of summertime. Walk into a fruit store, stand there for three minutes and look around. Don't buy anything. Go in just to soak in the sights.[29] Let your eyes drink in the glories of Hashem's summer. Then, while you're there, bang yourself on the breast and say, "*Ashamnu, bagadnu, gazalnu.* Ah, Ribbono Shel Olam, look what You're doing for me! I repent. I'm going to keep my mouth closed and watch what I'm saying. I won't waste my evenings anymore. I'm going to *shiurim.* On Shabbos, I'm going to learn in the afternoons instead of sleeping all day. I'm going to give more *tzedakah.* I'm going to keep my mouth closed when I get home and not disturb my wife as she works in the kitchen. I won't talk *lashon hara* about my neighbors. I'm going to be *mekayem mitzvos* with more *zerizus.* I'll *daven* with more *kavanah.*"

You can say all those things as a result of "*v'achalta v'savata,*" eating and being satisfied (*Devarim* 8:10). That's what it's intended for.

I was standing this morning on the curb and waited a moment for the cars to pass. I looked down and saw the pits of wild cherries that had fallen. The cherries were gone but the pits were lying there. Then my eyes fell upon the winged, floating seeds of maple trees. Every seed is a miracle. A seed has in it all the plans for the future tree. The wings are masterpieces of engineering. Take the trouble to pick them up once in a while and throw them into the wind. They revolve. They fly. They have

29 Rav Miller once walked into a fruit store and some *bachurim* recognized him and invited him to check out before them. "No," he said, "I'm just browsing." Some people browse bookstores; Rav Miller browsed fruit stores.

levitation. Some are like helicopters with propellers at both ends!

It's a marvel. All these marvels, *nissim*, and *nifla'os* speak of the glory of Hashem. The *Kuzari* says you don't need the sun and stars to appreciate "*Hashamayim m'saprim*—The heavens declare" (*Tehillim* 19:2). A seed underfoot has as much to say as the stars overhead. Therefore, summertime is when the voice of the *yetzer tov* is speaking most loudly.

Of course, you have to beware because it's also a time for the *yetzer hara*. All the *sheker* of Olam Hazeh can be found in the summer nights—midsummer night's madness. Yes, summer is the best time for the *yetzer tov*, but it's also the best time for the *yetzer hara*. Early in Av is the saddest of days, Tisha B'Av, but it switches to one of the happiest, the fifteenth of Av. We think of Av as a sad month, but the truth is just the opposite. Av is a month when there's so much happiness that it's important to know how to use it—and how to watch out for the dangers of too much *gashmiyus*. In this month, everything is alive—but all the negative instincts are also alive. The *yetzer tov* can flourish in the month of Av, but so can the *yetzer hara*. Oh yes, on summer nights people are busy looking for things to do. The nations, the *mishpechos ha'adamah*, are busy in their cars, driving back and forth, looking for good times. They're busy in the streets, back and forth. But we're sitting here, talking about Hashem and studying His wonders.

That's why summertime precedes the Yom Hadin, precedes Rosh Hashanah. Why wasn't Rosh Hashanah at Pesach time or at Chanukah time? Or in the middle of winter? The cold months are a wonderful time for *teshuvah*. Everybody is indoors. They come into a warm building to hear *drashos*. That's the most feasible time, it seems, for repentance. But Hashem is the architect Who planned this universe, and He made Rosh Hashanah follow the summer—just when you took in your crops. Just when everything is ripe and you've studied the greatness of Hashem. Because that's the very best time to do *teshuvah*. The very best time for *teshuvah* is riding the crest of the *yetzer tov*.

Q Are we really on a lower level than generations past?

Let me explain something to you. In the ancient times—and by ancient, I mean a hundred years ago—when they bentched Rosh Chodesh Elul there was a trembling, a *tziternish.* Yes. As soon as they mentioned Elul, there was a *tziternish.* And that's because in those days, people lived with *emunah.* Today, even though we have very *frum* people, we are saturated with the *apikorsus* of the outside world. So many people—Orthodox Jews, *frum* Jews—are really *apikorsim* just underneath the skin. Our minds are full of the atmosphere that comes in from the street. One must work very hard to fight this influence. You really have to work at it. Once upon a time, a hundred years ago, Jews didn't have any significant contact with the gentiles. They did business with them. They bought and sold. But did they ever read non-Jewish things? Never.

Here, today in America, we're facing a *gezeirah.* Our children in school must read English books. Even if they're not full of *apikorsus,* English books are still non-Jewish books. And the best of them are still a harmful influence. I know what I'm talking about. They get into the heads of our children. And into our heads, as well. That's why we say, "*V'kabtzeinu v'hatzileinu min hagoyim*—Hashem, please gather us together and save us from the nations" (*I Divrei Hayamim* 16:47). We want to be able to come together once again and live the way Jews are supposed to live, without any influence at all from the outside.

Therefore, what's the question?! We're very far away from how they used to approach Elul because we're very far away from *emunah.* Rav Yerucham, the Mashgiach, once said this about eighty years ago. He said, "We cannot even understand the greatness of our great-grandmothers." They had such *yiras Shamayim* that even Rav Yerucham himself couldn't feel it. The outside world had begun to seep in. It was gradual, but it began to make its way in. And that's how the Jewish world began to spoil.

Although today, *baruch Hashem*, there is a big movement for *teshuvah*, we have to also make a very big movement for *teshuvah p'nimis*. To create a pure Torah mind requires work. A very great movement is needed. We have to work very hard to regain just part of the attitude that our great-grandmothers and great-grandfathers once had. The Jewish street was *mamash* saturated with *yiras Hashem*.

Q If I had a fire in my house, does that mean I should think about doing *teshuvah*?

If a fire took place, *chalilah*, in somebody's house, does he have to think about *teshuvah*? Absolutely. Not only if a fire took place. Even if a person touched a hot pot by accident and burned a finger. Of course, you should run to the sink and keep your finger under cold water, too. That's the first thing. But you have to think, "Why did this happen to me?"

We learned, "If one sees any sort of trouble coming upon him, he should search out his deeds and do *teshuvah*" (*Brachos* 5a). Certainly he should think that. Maybe I was pointing at somebody and talking *lashon hara* with my finger. Or something else. Of course you have to. That's why Hashem sent it.

We forget about Hashem, so He reminds us. If you had been thinking about Him in the right way, it could very well be that He wouldn't have burned your finger. Anything that happens in this world is to make us think about Him. And ignoring these things is ignoring the reason that you're in this world—to become more and more aware of Hashem.

Q If a person is still doing *aveiros*, is there any sense in doing *teshuvah*?

Absolutely! And he should ask Hashem for help that he should stop. I'll explain that. When a person does an *aveirah* and he's happy with it, it's a much greater sin. If a person does an *aveirah*, but he's ashamed and sorry that he's doing it, it's subtracted from his punishment. Yes, even though he still does it.

The Chofetz Chaim, *zt"l*, wrote a *sefer* for Jewish soldiers. In those days, when they were drafted into the Russian army, they had to eat *treifah* foods. He said, "If you must eat *treifah* food, then don't suck the juice out of the bones." Which means, don't show you enjoy it. You're only eating it to save yourself from starving.

When a person does a *cheit*, a sin, even a big *cheit*—say he was *mechalel Shabbos*, but he's sorry he was *mechalel Shabbos*, it's already a *madreigah*. To be sorry is a *madreigah*. He has achieved something. Of course it's not *teshuvah sheleimah*. It's very far from it. But it's still a very big thing. Therefore, it pays even for sinners to ask Hashem to forgive them. Only they should add, "… and please, Hashem, help me do *teshuvah sheleimah*."

SUMMARY

- This *brachah* follows the previous one because we need *da'as* to understand how to do *teshuvah*. Without learning Torah and gaining clarity, we might think we're doing *teshuvah* but instead head off in the wrong direction.
- We address Hashem as *Avinu*, our Father, to inspire us to try to connect to Hashem with love and yearning, like a son who has become estranged from his father.
- We mention Torah to appreciate the love Hashem has for us, evidenced by the fact that He gave us the Torah, the greatest gift in the world.
- We address Hashem as *Malkeinu*, our King, because fear is an important component of our relationship with Hashem. Love of Hashem must be balanced with fear of Hashem. Fear should also motivate us to return to Him.
- We have to work on humbling ourselves before Hashem, like an *eved* before his master.
- Real *teshuvah* means returning to the level we achieved at Har Sinai, when we all loved and feared Hashem wholeheartedly, without reservation. We're asking Hashem to help us achieve that to whatever degree possible.

- Nevertheless, any step closer to Hashem is extremely significant in Hashem's eyes.
- If we don't bother to improve ourselves even in areas that are easy, Hashem has a big *tainah* on us.
- *Teshuvah*, at its most basic level, means to get better.
- The best strategy to do *teshuvah* is to make small, clear-cut commitments to change. Vague, general commitments don't accomplish anything.
- The best time to do *teshuvah* is when everything is going well for you, and you want to come closer to Hashem out of gratitude for all He does for you.
- A very important aspect of *teshuvah* is to focus on separating ourselves from the non-Torah world.
- Every misfortune, no matter how small, should spur us to do *teshuvah*.
- If one is still committing an *aveirah* and is not yet able to stop, the fact that one feels bad about it is considered a certain degree of *teshuvah*.

S'lach Lanu

Q Why is *S'lach Lanu* important?

There are ways, unfortunately, for a man to lose his portion in Olam Haba. Korach lost his Olam Haba. Others, too. And we weep for them. It's a great loss for us. But if you do certain serious things, no matter how great you are otherwise, you lose your portion in the World to Come.[30]

Therefore, the only answer is *teshuvah*! *Teshuvah* will help save you from being in Gehinnom forever and ever. No matter what you've done, *teshuvah* can save you. It's very important to keep in mind that as long as a man is alive, he can still change himself.

30 See *Rav Avigdor Miller on Olam Haba*, pp. 167.

That's why he should always be in contact with *teshuvah*. Always! The *brachah* of *S'lach Lanu* is an opportunity. Think about your sins. Don't be *yotzei* by just saying the words. Use the opportunity to think about your past sins. Were you ever insulting to your father or mother? Think about that. "I forgot about it" isn't an excuse. Try to remember the various things you've done wrong when you say, "*S'lach lanu, Avinu*—Our Father, Hashem, please forgive us."

Were you a bully to your younger brother? Sometimes you may have been very mean to your relatives. Think about that. Even now, are you honoring your father and mother sufficiently? It's a very important subject! It's such an important subject to always be doing *teshuvah* for your sins.

S'lach Lanu is a golden opportunity to purify yourself by doing *teshuvah*. By being sorry and regretting, you're cleansing your *neshamah*. You can't just gallop through it.

You have to use the brief opportunity of being alive. Only while you're alive can you say, "*S'lach lanu, Avinu, ki chatanu*," and think about a certain specific thing you did. Sometimes you're amazed about how serious the sin was that you did. Therefore, when a person thinks when he says *S'lach Lanu*, he's accomplishing a tremendous achievement.

Q **What if a person can't think of sins for which he needs to ask forgiveness?**

David Hamelech said, "Of what should I be afraid in the days when there is cause to fear?" (*Tehillim* 49:6). David said he's not afraid of the perils that confront him, of enemies and those who seek to hurt him. What is he afraid of? He fears only one thing, "I fear my sins."

When David was confronted by some danger, he was afraid that at that moment of peril, during the time of difficulty, his sins would rise up and accuse him. They wait for the opportunity, as it states, "When a man is in peril, that's when the accuser brings up his accusations" (*Tanchuma, Vayigash*). When you're already in trouble, you're likely to be accused of your misdeeds in *Shamayim*.

However, pay attention to the words of David, because he specified that it was a specific kind of iniquity that he feared. Of course David was afraid of any sin he might have done, but he was mostly in fear of a certain class of sins. In the time when it is necessary to be apprehensive, when a man should have a certain sensation of fear, of which sins should he be afraid? The *passuk* continues, "Of the sins under my heels."

The Gemara explains it as follows, "*aveiros she'adam dash b'akeivav*—the sins that a man tramples under his heels." They are the ones that "rise up and surround him on the Day of Judgment" (*Avodah Zara* 18a). It means that when a man is cognizant of wrongs that he has done, when he is aware of his sins, to a certain extent he's capable of confronting them. At least he can feel regret. Having regret is already a step toward rectification. It means you're facing in the direction of *teshuvah*. Being sorry is at least a first step. It's a big thing to know that you've done something wrong. Of course, the best thing is to get busy repairing the harm you did, to change your ways. But at least when a man knows that he's guilty, and he has *charatah*, his heart aches, he is worried, that is already a form of *kaparah*. It's not a full *selichah umechilah*, but it's certainly important.

But what should a person worry about? Those sins that he's not concerned about, the sins he commits without thinking. He doesn't consider them important; he may not even consider them as anything wrong. Then suddenly, on the Day of Judgment, he is confronted with enemies he didn't expect. He has fingers pointed at him by opponents that he didn't know existed. "*Avon akeivav m'subin lo*—The sins under his heels rise up and surround him." They'll ambush him, and he won't know what to say because he wasn't prepared for such a confrontation.

Now, there are various kinds of *avon akeiv*. One is the things people consider permissible. Or even if they don't consider them permissible, at least they think they're not serious. He knows it may not be right, but he imagines it's not serious. We have to know, however, that even if it was true—that his judgment was correct that they are lesser *aveiros*, and even if they are at the bottom of the scale of severity, the most lenient of all kinds of sins—nevertheless there is no such thing as a small sin if a person doesn't have regrets. Without *teshuvah*, no sin is small. Every sin is a catastrophe if a person doesn't regret it.

It's like that famous *mashal* of a man trying to go to sleep in a comfortable bed, but that there's a bean under the sheet. It's only one bean, but it presses into his side. It pushes in this direction and that direction. Unless he takes it out, he may not sleep at all that night. That's what you can look forward to from a small *aveirah*. It will make trouble for you no end, like that small bean — unless you pull it out by doing *teshuvah*. As the *Chovos Halevavos* says, "There's no *aveirah* that is big with *teshuvah*, and there is no *aveirah* that is small without *teshuvah*!" Therefore, these unsuspecting enemies are going to ambush a man on the Day of Judgment. From a corner that he didn't expect an attack, suddenly there will come a very big attack.

Not only is he lacking an attitude of regret, of feeling sorrow that he had committed that act, but there's another consideration. Chazal explain that people may start out with deeds that seem as unimportant as spiderwebs. They're "thin" — nothing to be worried about, they think. But when they are added together and become twisted into one big cord, the sins eventually become like the heavy ropes you use to pull wagons (*Sukkah* 52a). Rabbeinu Yonah explains in *Sha'arei Teshuvah* that a small *aveirah* repeated frequently becomes as serious as *chayvei krisus* and *chayvei misas beis din*. Even the smallest sin, if it's committed again and again — its severity is compounded, and eventually it becomes a very big sin, almost like *chayvei krisus* and *chayvei misas beis din*! So we begin to understand that *avon akeivay*, the small sins under my heels, the sins that I'm not even thinking about, are something that should be taken seriously.

PRACTICAL ADVICE

Can you provide an example of a common sin people take for granted?

Passing somebody on the street with an unfriendly face. Now, you might think it's only a small thing. "What?!" you'll say. "Am I obligated to be an actor and smile to him?" Listen to what the Gemara says. "Showing your teeth to someone with a smile is a greater accomplishment than giving him a drink of milk" (*Kesubos* 111b). Suppose a fellow Jew is passing you on the street and he's thirsty, and you have a big case full of bottles of milk. What does it cost to save a fellow Jew from privation? Let's say he's a *meshulach* from Eretz Yisrael or from Williamsburg, and the man has been walking around all day trying to collect a little money for his family or his institution. Would you begrudge him a drink of milk? It's unthinkable. Certainly you'd be happy to offer him a glass of milk because you know how important it is for a thirsty man.

But the Gemara is telling us that this man is even more thirsty for a smile than for a cup of milk. Of course, he's looking for money. He's not walking around knocking on doors for smiles. But when you encounter another Jew, you should know that no matter how wealthy or poor he is, he is hungry and thirsty for your smile.

And don't think it's a small matter. Let's say you pass an acquaintance, and you have a glum face. Now, it could be that you're thinking about your own worries. It's not because you hold that person in low esteem, or because you despise him. But why should he suffer just because your wife yelled at you? It's bad enough that you have to suffer. Therefore, the fact that you deprived him of what he needs most urgently is considered as if you have robbed him of what's coming to him.

It's a Mishnah in *Avos*, "Greet every man with joy" (*Avos* 3:12) Show him that you're happy to see him. That doesn't mean you have to be happy. Maybe you're not. But you have to *show* a happy face. We learn this again and again. "*Hevei mikabel es kol ha'adam b'seiver panim yafos*—Receive people with a pleasant countenance (*Avos* 1:15). "*Seiver panim yafos*—a pleasant countenance" includes three elements. First, it includes *panim*. Show your "face" to a person, not your ear. When you come into your house tonight after the lecture, and your mother is in the kitchen standing over the stove, show her your face. Don't show her the back of your head or your ear. And when your father walks in at night after working all day for you — for you! — do him that benefit of turning around and showing him your face. Not your profile. The front of your face!

Second, show a face with *seiver*. The word *seiver*, from the word *s'vara*, means "thinking." *Seiver* means that you have an expression of interest on your face. If you merely show a deadpan face, that's not enough. Let's say you pick up a pan as someone goes by and you show him the bottom of the pan. Sometimes your face is like that — nothing more than the bottom of a pan. You have to show that you're thinking about him, that you have some interest in that person.

Thirdly, *yafos*. It has to be a "pleasant" countenance. It should show caring and concern. What could be more pleasant than a warm smile that shows you're thinking about him?

Don't underestimate what a smile, a pleasant face, can do for others. You're giving them a lift. A smile goes into the *neshamah* of a person. It gives the recipient *chiyus* — life *mamash*! When you look at somebody with a pleasant face, it's the biggest compliment. It shows that you take him seriously, that he means something to you. That's everyone's deepest desire. All he wants is happiness. And he loves you for it. So flash a smile at somebody as you pass by, especially if he greets you first. Once you see how easy it is to make people happy, and how you can light up a person's face, you'll never stop.

"*Bemiddah she'adam moded modedin lo* — The way a person behaves to others is the way Hashem behaves to him" (*Sotah* 8b). If you cause your countenance to shine on others, if you turn on the sunshine by smiling at other people, Hashem is going to turn His sunshine on you as well. He's going to smile at you, because you're doing exactly what He wants to be done in this world. You're making His children happy. When you activate that *middah* of smiling at people down below, you're going to activate an action from above. You'll be rewarded in the same measure—only that Hashem's measure is much bigger.

There's no easier and more productive career than smiling at everyone. A friendly smile, a face of *simchah*, is often the greatest gift you can bestow on another person. Now, if you're not sure whether you're doing it right, I'll give you a *heter* to stand in front of a mirror and practice it. Or practice on your wife or mother. It's not pleasant to live in the same house with a grouch. They could do with a little bit of happiness from you once in a while.

We shouldn't think that these are commandments only for great *tzaddikim*, for *anshei ma'aseh*, and if we neglect them we've done nothing wrong. No. This is considered *aveiros she'adam dash b'akayvav*. It rankles you when you pass somebody on the street and he doesn't bother to smile at you. Sometimes he doesn't recognize you at all. Even though he knows you and looks at you, he doesn't make the slightest movement with his head. Sometimes you even wish him a good morning and he doesn't answer. He's living in a cloud. That man has committed a serious error. And that's one of the things that he has to be afraid of on the Yom Hadin. These things add up until they become like a heavy rope of many individual threads.

When you come home from work, why are you looking for a fight with your wife and making a tragedy out of the calm home? They need you home for that?! You could have just as well stayed on the subway! Or a woman who picks a fight with her husband and tries to find something to criticize when all he needs is a little rest and consolation. Husbands and wives are constantly committing the worst errors toward each other. With just a few kind words, soft words of encouragement, positive words, you could have done real *teshuvah*.

And it's not only on the Day of Judgment in this world, on Yom Kippur, that you will be surprised by all the sins you trampled on. But on the great Yom Hadin when you come to the next world, you'll be shocked! You'll think of all the people you wronged.

Maybe neighbors, maybe relatives, maybe others. But your own husband or wife certainly was the last one you would have wronged, you think. Absolutely not! Those you sinned against most were the ones closest to you. Husbands and wives are going to be held accountable in the next world for heaps of *aveiros*, mountains of unkind words and glum faces they showed to each other.

When a man is stingy with his words, stingy with giving his wife kindly words, that's a thousand times worse than being stingy with money. When he says or even hints that other women are prettier, it's a knife in her heart. I know one fool who said that to his wife. She called me up and complained. A man should never express such a thing. His wife should know that she is the most beautiful woman in the world to him. And if he can't say it, let him at least keep quiet.

But he's constantly sticking daggers in her, and she in him. These daggers are going to rise up on the Yom Hadin. They're going to be the most dangerous, fearsome opponents. Because of what husbands and wives said to each other, what neighbors said to one another, what friends said to each other — a person will be amazed to find that all the fingers pointed at him on the Yom Hadin.

Q Do I have to say the *tefillah* before going to bed in which I forgive anyone who wronged me?

You're not obligated, but if you want to do it, it's good business. It's a good business opportunity. As the Gemara says, Hashem will forgive one who is willing to forgive others (*Rosh Hashanah* 17a). If you forgive those who sinned against you, Hashem will forgive your sins.

So it pays. If you don't want to, you don't have to say it. But it's good business. It pays to say it. But you have to mean it. You have to put thought into it. Just to mumble the words because it's in the *siddur* won't do any good. You have to think about what you're saying. Think about the neighbor or the co-worker who wronged you and forgive him. But do you have to say it? No. You don't have to say it.

Q **If Torah is a *kaparah* for sin, does it mean that his Torah merit is lost, because he used it up?**

The answer is no. Torah is not merely the *mitzvah* of the Torah. Torah is the frame of mind. When a person has Torah in his mind, it'll remain there forever. As long as he continues to review. Therefore, even though he uses Torah to forgive his sins, the Torah is still in his heart. That man remains a *ben Torah*. And a *ben Torah*, after all, is what Hashem wants us to be. Therefore, the fact that Torah is *mechaper* on certain things will not deduct from his *madreigah* as a *ben Torah*.

SUMMARY

- This *brachah* is an opportunity to think about specific things you've done wrong, even far back in your past, and ask Hashem to forgive you. Try hard to remember—because Hashem doesn't forget.
- In particular, we need to search out the sins that we treat lightly, that we don't consider serious. Even though something may be a small sin, when it's done repeatedly it is considered like the worst sins.
- One example is the sin of not smiling at others, or, more generally, the simple, everyday interactions with the people around us. The sins of not being careful to behave pleasantly with other people can be frightful accusers against us.
- If we forgive others for their sins against us, Hashem will forgive us as well.

R'eih V'anyeinu

Q What does it mean that Hashem "sees our affliction"? Doesn't He see everything?

Here it says, "See into our affliction." Although He sees everything at all times, there's an especial "seeing" of compassion. As is said of Moshe, "He went out to his brothers and 'saw' their burdens" (*Shemos* 2:11). Just as a man may know of his brother's affliction yet isn't agitated until he actually sees it with his eyes, so also the mercy of heaven does not become activated until there's an especial "seeing," so to speak. This type of "seeing" is activated by our supplication. More precisely, this "seeing" is brought about by our awareness that Hashem sees, and this awareness is gained by saying these words and by reflecting on them.

Q Why do we ask Hashem to "fight our fight"?

We don't say "Fight for us," which could imply that we ourselves make no attempt. Rather we say, "*V'rivah riveinu* — Fight our fight," because we have to exert ourselves with effort and valor. But even when we exert ourselves, we look to Him for aid. We look to Him, and Him alone. We are entirely aware that whatever success results from our efforts is due solely to Him.

PRACTICAL ADVICE

Q What does Hashem want from me by making me suffer?

What does Hashem want of you more than anything? More than anything, He desires that you should cry out. Not once and not twice — over and over again. You should cry out with all your heart. Pour out your heart to Hashem. That's what Hashem wants for you.

If subsequently He grants your request and you're redeemed from your tribulations, and from then on you live a tranquil life, don't think that you've achieved the purpose of life. No! Your success was already achieved when you were in the midst of the *tzarah* and you called out to Hashem. The more you called out, the more you thought about Hashem, the more successful you were.

Q **Can't Hashem find a way other than suffering?**

It's very important to realize that the pressure, the squeezing of the grapes, is a tiny portion of a person's experiences.

Most of people's lives are spent happily. Most of our days are spent without headaches, without aches and pains. Most of our days, we're able to function. Inside our body, everything is working. There are so many different parts that must work perfectly, and everything is functioning smoothly. The great majority of mankind, most of their lives, are given the opportunity to call out to Hashem in happiness and become aware of Him that way. You can squeeze out awareness of Hashem that way, too. Unfortunately, most people aren't doing it most of the time.

When the grape doesn't yield its wine readily, it has to be crushed. Even good people sometimes have to be crushed by *tza'ar*. I don't want to translate *tza'ar* as "misfortune," because it isn't a misfortune. But it's a *tza'ar*, a "distress," and it causes a person to grow in *emunah* and awareness, and that's the greatest benefit a man can achieve in this world.

Hashem presses us with all kinds of pressure. One pressure might be trouble with *parnassah*. Another might be trouble with children or trouble having children, *chas v'shalom*. Many single people need *shidduchim*. Many people are crowded in small apartments. Whatever it is, when they cry out to Hashem, that's the good wine of awareness dripping from the good grapes of their *neshamah*. When their heart is torn in anguish and they turn to Hashem for His help, that's already a success. When they weep and pour out their hearts in *tefillah*, that's the good wine Hashem wants. Sometimes He might press again and again and again. Good grapes will keep on giving good wine.

When a man has trouble — he's being threatened with bankruptcy or illness or some other peril — he has to understand that it's sent from Heaven as an incentive to become great. No matter what happens, the results will be good, but there's no better outcome than the achievement of awareness of Hashem.

And not only big perils. Little ones, too. Ask Hashem for everything. "*Harchev picha* — Open your mouth wide" (*Tehillim* 81:11). It doesn't refer to opening the freezer for some ice cream. It means, "Open your mouth in *tefillah* to Me." The more your mouth is open wide to ask Hashem for help, the more of a success you are.

We can apply this to every endeavor. No matter what you do, you won't overdo it. When the lady of the house makes a cake, let her show she recognizes that Hashem is the One who gives success to all her efforts. She should talk to Him in the kitchen. Ask Him for *hatzlachah*. Many things can go wrong when you're baking a cake, and you need His help more than you can imagine.

When a man sets off on a journey out of town, he says *Tefillas Haderech*. That was in the good old days when the only perils were outside of town. Today, even in the city, you should say a prayer before you set out on any kind of trip. Even without a car. When you walk into the street, it's a good idea to say a prayer. We don't say a *brachah* because of a technicality in *halachah*, but you must ask Hashem for help to get to your destination safely.

It's a very good idea to turn to Hashem for every need. If you're in college and have to take an exam, don't be bashful. Hashem listens to you there, too. He's not so happy about you being there, but He listens to you. If you have a cut and want to apply an antiseptic, bother Him. Don't show him that you worship the antiseptic. Show that your trust is not in chemicals. Of course, you should use them. That's what He wants. "*V'rapo y'rapei*" (*Shemos* 21:19). You should heal yourself, but first call out to Him.

That's the way to live a successful life. If you're going to buy a car or a home or a refrigerator or an air conditioner, first say a *tefillah*. "Ribbono Shel Olam, it shouldn't be a mistake. Please guide me. Please help me succeed." You should bother Hashem in all the details of your life. Because that's what He wants. The more we bother Him, the more beloved we are to Him.

Q If a person already believes in Hashem, why does Hashem send suffering his way?

Even though we live our lives with this Torah principle of *emunah*, of belief in Hashem, it actually has a very faint effect on our minds. More than anything, Hashem desires that we turn to Him in *tefillah*. Not once or twice. Over and over again. Pour out your heart to Him. That's the success Hashem wants for you. If He subsequently grants your request and you're redeemed from your tribulations, all the better.

Now that He answered you and you live a tranquil life, don't think you're finished. Living in tranquility is also the time to cry out to Hashem, to thank Him for everything you once thought you'd never have. But success in life doesn't necessarily mean a tranquil life blessed with wealth and prosperity. No! Success is squeezing the juice of awareness of Hashem out of your existence. Your greatest success may be achieved when you're in the midst of the *tzarah* and you call out to Hashem. The more you call out, the more you think about Hashem, and the more successful you are.

No one had greater *emunah* than Avraham. The *Midrash Rabbah* at the beginning of *Lech Lecha* comments on the words, "*Vayomer Hashem el Avram*—And Hashem said to Avram" (*Bereishis* 12:1), which was the first time Hashem spoke to Avraham. The *midrash* offers a parable. A man was walking and came to a large building that was illuminated. As he looked at the building, he saw no sign of inhabitants, but everything was in good order and the lights were on. The man exclaimed, "Is it possible that such a building should not have someone in charge?" When the man said that, the owner of the building suddenly stuck his head out of the window and said, "I am the owner of this house!"

By his labors, Avraham had become so convinced of the presence of Hashem that all he lacked was to hear the voice of Hashem. Finally, after laboring so long and coming so close, he attained the ultimate—the Almighty spoke to him, *Vayomer Hashem el Avram*. "Yes, Avram, here I am!" He communicated to him in prophecy and said, "*Lech lecha*—Get up and go." That was when Avraham was in his seventies.

Despite his great awareness, at that time Avraham lacked something—he had no children. And he would be denied children for thirty more years. Hashem wanted to get thirty more years of prayer out of him. "Hashem desires the prayers of *tzaddikim*" (*Yevamos* 64a). Even before these thirty years, Avraham and Sarah poured their hearts out to Hashem for a child, but these thirty additional years were a towering accomplishment, a crowning achievement.

We see how deep his sorrow was that he was childless. After Hashem promised him great things, he said, "Hashem, what are You going to give me? I am childless." Avraham and Sarah didn't have a desire to clutch a baby and fondle it like a doll. Avraham and Sarah lived for one purpose—to raise up a people who would serve Hashem. This was their dearest aspiration. Despite that, Hashem kept pressing them more and more, trying to squeeze out more and more. Avraham and Sarah prayed day in and day out. They shed tears and tears for many, many bitter years. Our Sages question why Hashem so afflicted the man and woman He loved most. Who else deserved to be happy if not Avraham and Sarah?

The answer is that Avraham and Sarah were like grapes in a winepress. Hashem wanted to press more prayers out of Avraham. The "wine" of a great man is his prayers. The more precious the grapes, the more precious the drops that are extracted from them.

Q If Hashem desires the prayers of *tzaddikim*, and urges them through suffering, are *tzaddikim* consigned to a life of misery?

No! Avraham was one of the most successful men who ever lived. First, he was extremely rich. He had livestock, gold, and silver in abundance, as it says openly (*Bereishis* 13:2). In addition, he was extremely well respected. The gentiles said, "You are a prince of *Elokim* in our midst" (ibid. 23:6). And he was a successful general and military strategist, if that means anything to us. Avraham won battles. With only a handful of men, he chased the four powerful kings all the way up to Syria and defeated them (ibid. 14:15). When he came back, he was given a hero's welcome. All the kings came out to greet him and give him their blessings (ibid. 17–20).

The Rambam states (*Hilchos Avodah Zarah*) that tens of thousands of men congregated around him. He spoke to audiences that we would envy today. Josephus, quoting ancient sources, writes that Avraham composed books. Ancient gentile writers declare that Avraham was the one who taught mathematics and astronomy to the Egyptian priests.

He was a man who had success in everything. The *passuk* says of him, "*Retzon yerei'av ya'aseh*—Hashem does the will of those who fear Him" (*Tehillim* 145:19), which means that *even if they don't say a word,* He will do their will as soon as they feel a certain desire. But there's a contradiction. The next part says, "He hears their outcry and delivers them." He hears, and then He saves them. That means they have to cry out. Which is it? Does Hashem fulfill the desire of those who fear Him *without* their crying out, or does He fulfill it only after they cry out?

The answer is that in all Avraham's successes, in all his achievements, he didn't have to pray. Even before uttering a word, Hashem granted him success. "*Retzon yerei'av ya'aseh*—Hashem performs the will of those who fear Him." Avraham didn't need to open his mouth to ask—with one exception. Except for being given a child. "He hears their outcry and delivers them" doesn't mean that *tzaddikim* are pressed in everything. It doesn't mean that *tzaddikim* must suffer. *Tzaddikim* don't suffer in this world. On the contrary, in most cases *tzaddikim* in this world are quite happy. They live wisely and are more capable of enjoying Olam Hazeh. Hashem gives them His blessing. *Tzaddikim* sit home at nights and know where their children are, while non-*tzaddikim* are turning over in their beds late at night, worrying where their children are.

It's a big error people commonly make when it comes to the subject of "*tzaddik v'ra lo, rasha v'tov lo*—bad things that happen to the righteous and good things that happen to the wicked" (*Brachos* 7a). There's a very great misconception, but that's a separate subject. There's no question that Avraham and other *tzaddikim* in general live happily. Non-*tzaddikim* in general are not happy, even if they seem to have all the trappings that people equate with happiness. It's a big subject, but not for now.

Avraham was successful in every area without the need to ask. Hashem didn't have to wait for him to ask. Hashem did Avraham's will because he feared Him, which means that he was supremely aware of Him. But in one area Hashem helped him as a stepping-stone to greatness—in the area of children. In that area, the second part of the *passuk* applies—"He hears their outcry and delivers them." Hashem forced him to pray and pray, for many years. Finally, when he was great enough even to satisfy Hashem, He granted his wish and gave him children.

From this we understand that if something that seems a misfortune occurs in the lives of righteous people, there's one reason we can generally assume. It's for their benefit—that they should be brought to *tefillah*. Not *tefillah* by rote said rapidly, but a *tefillah* that's squeezed like the good wine, when the heavy beam of the winepress comes down on the grapes. The grape doesn't yield its wine readily unless it's crushed. Even good people sometimes have to be crushed by some *tzarah*, some distress, and that causes them to grow in understanding and *emunah* and awareness. The *tzarah* brings about the greatest benefit. To become more and more aware in this world is the highest achievement. That's what Hashem desires for His righteous ones.

SUMMARY

- By making ourselves more aware that Hashem sees our suffering, we enable Hashem to help us.
- When we put in efforts to resolve our difficulties, we must know that any success we have is from Hashem.
- Hashem sends us difficulties in order to get us to cry out to Him, so we will internalize more and more that we are entirely dependent on Him.
- Every difficulty in life, no matter how small, is an opportunity to call out to Hashem and become more aware of Him. Ask Hashem for help with every detail of your life. But also recognize that most of your life is filled with happiness, that most things in your life are working perfectly.
- The greater the person, the more Hashem expects from him, which is why sometimes great people suffer the most in life. Despite that, the lives of *tzaddikim* are full of happiness, much more so than those of non-*tzaddikim*.

Refa'einu

Q **Why did Hashem create illness?**

Rashi asks the question: Why is there illness in the world? Illness, he answers, comes to make people request Hashem to help them. It's a remarkable statement. Troubles come to make people ask Hashem to help them. The first objective is *tefillah*. Troubles are just a way of coaxing people to achieve the first objective.

If you have a cold, *chalilah*, pray to Hashem. Again and again, every day. In addition to the Afrin and other good medicines, ask Hashem constantly to help you. Even when you're taking medicine, say, "*Yehi ratzon mil'fanecha shey'hei eisek zeh li lirefuah*—May it be Your will that this medicine should help me. "

When a person has an operation, *chalilah*, as he's lying on the operating table, he shouldn't just lie there like a dummy, like a bag of straw. The first thing is to ask Hashem, "Please, Ribbono Shel Olam, guide the surgeon's hands. Make the operation successful and give me a *refuah sheleimah*." Of course, it's better to ask Hashem when you're well, so you shouldn't ever have to get on the operating table at all.

Rashi tells us that when people are negligent in this duty of asking Hashem, He sends them reminders in the form of illness. That's how to understand what illness means. It's a message to remind you that Hashem is in charge.

And not only illness. It's all the troubles in the world. If you lost a dollar, it's to tell you to wake up and ask Hashem for help. You might find it, you might not, but if you don't, you found something better—*tefillah*. That's an accomplishment worth more than the dollar.

Illnesses big and small, as well as all troubles big and small, are wake-up calls. Now you have to put in your request and intensify your requests. That's why *tzaros* happen.

It's the same thing with *simchah*s. Let's say you just had a son or a daughter. You call up all your relatives. *Mazel tov! Mazel tov!* But don't forget the most important thing. "Call up" Hashem and say to Him, "Thank You for this child." How many people are still waiting for a child? How many people don't have even one child? *Baruch Hashem*, you just had one, so the first thing is to thank Hashem. That's why there are *simchah*s in the world. The purpose of *simchah* is *tefillah*. The *simchah* greases the wheel. It stimulates us to partake in the first objective—*tefillah*. *Tefillah* includes *hoda'ah*, thanking Hashem. *Tov l'hodos laHashem* (*Tehillim* 92:2). Do you know what's *tov*, what's "good," in this world? *L'hodos*, "to give thanks."

Tefillah is one of the most important purposes of life. It's of the utmost importance to keep in mind at all times. *Simchah*s and *tzaros* are both stimulants. "*Kos yeshuos esa uv'sheim Hashem ekra*—When I lift up the cup of salvation, I call in the name of Hashem" (*Tehillim* 116:13).

When David was victorious, he cried out to Hashem and thanked Him. "*Tzarah v'yagon emtza uv'sheim Hashem ekra*—If troubles come upon me, I cry out to Hashem" (*Tehillim* 116:3–4). Everything that happens in this world is for one purpose—to make us cry out to Hashem. We cry out this way or that way, but we must cry out. Of course, it's better to cry out for happiness, so you don't have to be reminded the other way. But the purpose is "*B'sheim Hashem ekra.*"

Whatever happens is to remind you of the most important fact in the world—that Hashem is in charge. That's *tefillah*. David Hamelech taught this to the world. All *Tehillim* is devoted to that great principle. It's a very big subject.

Q If everything is in the hands of Hashem, why should we pray to Him to be healed?

"*Refa'einu, Hashem, v'neirafei*—Heal us, Hashem, and we shall be healed." This introduces the element of *bitachon*, of confidence that Hashem is the source of all well-being, which means only by Him can we be healed.

Now, if someone wounds his fellow man, the Torah states, "*V'rapo y'rapei*—He must heal him" (*Shemos* 21:19). And the Gemara says, "From here we learn that the physician has permission to heal" (*Brachos* 60a). Actually, although it states that we have *permission* to seek a physician, it's more than mere permission. It's our *duty* to seek healing. It's our duty to seek remedies. It's our duty to live by the dictates of good sense to maintain our health. Nevertheless, we should never lose sight of the fundamental intention—that Hashem should grant success to our efforts, meaning that He is the healer.

When you take a medicine, even putting antiseptic on a little wound, it's advisable to think that Hashem is the One healing you. You should say, "*Yehi ratzon mil'fanecha shey'hei eisek zeh li lirefuah*—May it be Your will that this action leads to healing." We don't trust in the antiseptic. We have to do it, but we don't put our trust in it.

The farmer must plow to get bread, but we bless Hashem as "the One

Who brings forth bread from the earth." *Hamotzi lechem min ha'aretz.* It's Hashem, not the plow. The same is true with every endeavor. It must be accompanied by the fundamental awareness that we're not doing anything except our duty. Only Hashem makes the outcome. We must go to the physician, but Hashem is the only One Who heals.

That's easy to say but not easy to do. Some people spend a great deal of time guarding their health, so it drives out of their heads any other consideration. After a while, it seems to them that only their efforts are giving them success. That's why it's so important to always accompany every effort to heal yourself with the thought: "*Refa'einu, Hashem, v'neirafei*—Heal us, Hashem, and only because of You will we be healed."

Q **Why do we add "*Hoshi'einu v'nivashei'a* — Help us and we shall be helped"? It sounds redundant.**

In addition to the healing process, it's imperative to prevent illness. We forestall sickness by asking Hashem to make our efforts at prevention successful.

Sometimes illness is caused by enemies, or by constant fear and apprehension. Sometimes illness is caused by poverty—insufficient nutrition, unheated homes, or other forms of deprivation. Sometimes the climate isn't favorable. A sudden cold spell can catch people unprepared. Sometimes it's emotions, as it states, "Envy kills the fool" (*Iyov* 5:2). Many people become ill or even die because of envy. Many people die suddenly in a fit of anger. Sometimes illness is brought on by intemperance in food and drink—eating the wrong things or eating too much; drinking the wrong things or drinking too much. Sometimes some part of the body suddenly stops functioning properly and causes serious issues. Therefore, we ask Hashem before anything happens—"*Hoshi'einu,* help us" against every cause of an illness. "*V'nivashei'a*—and by means of You, we shall be helped."

The root of *nivashei'a* is *yosha,* to "save," to have a *yeshuah.* And another root is *sha'ah* (שעה), which is the word the Torah uses to describe Hashem's reaction to Kayin and Hevel's offerings. "But to Kayin and his offering [Hashem] didn't turn (שעה)" (*Bereishis* 4:5). "And Hashem turned (וישע) to Hevel and his offering" (ibid. 4:4). Then there's the word *l'hishtashei'a,* which means to enjoy oneself, to delight in something. It too has the root *shin ayin* (שע), which is the fundamental root. What is the common denominator?

The common denominator is "to be together," "to join," or "to be with." In the case of Kayin, it means that Hashem didn't "join" him when he brought his offering. He wasn't with him. In the case of a *yeshuah*, salvation, it refers to the help that comes from having someone who is "with" you. The common root of these words is "to be with us." Therefore, we say, "*Hoshi'einu*—You, Hashem, should give us Your salvation," which means Your presence should be with us, and that's going to be our *yeshuah.*

It's only when Hashem steps in that we can hope to successfully achieve our desires. Otherwise, things are going to constantly go off track. Unusual things will happen, one after the other. The purpose of these accidents—sometimes mishaps, sometimes illnesses—is to remind us of Hashem. *Don't forget Me*, says Hashem.

Everyone comes to this world for one purpose—to gain awareness of Hashem. Awareness with a capital "A." The more you become aware of Hashem, the more successful you are.

When a person forgets Hashem, he needs reminding. That's why misfortune actually is a blessing in disguise. When misfortune comes upon a man, he must turn to Hashem for help. "Oh," Hashem says, "now you're thinking about Me? *Shalom aleichem!*"

It's like the son who went away to yeshiva and didn't write letters to his father because every day he received a little check. One day the checks stop coming, so the son starts calling up long distance. "Pa, how are you? What's the matter? All of a sudden, I'm not getting your check."

Oh, now you remind yourself about Me, Hashem says. That's the purpose of all these mishaps in life—to be reminded that we have a Father.

When we say "*Hoshi'einu*—give us Your *yeshuah*," it means give us Your presence, be with us, and that's going to be our salvation. Then Hashem says, "Because you asked Me, I'm going to be with you."

Q If Hashem sent the illness upon us, shouldn't we accept it and let things run their course?

How can we ask Hashem to remove the misfortune? After all, we believe *be'emunah sheleimah* that He sent the illness, or any misfortune. Just because we don't like it, are we going to ask Him to change His will? Where do we get the impudence to propose such an idea? If Hashem sent the illness upon us, why don't we just accept it and let things run their course? How can we ask Him to change His will?

And the answer is that it's Hashem's will that we be aware of Him. He sends illness not because He wants us to be sick but because He wants us to wake up and become aware of him. So when we say, "Please Hashem, heal us," what are we saying? "Don't You see we're aware of You now? We're asking You to heal us. Because of this awareness, please grant our request." So we're doing exactly what He wants from us.

"Oh, you're talking to Me now?" Hashem says. "You're aware of Me? Now I'll help you."

But there's one thing you must add to your request. "Hashem, I'm going to continue to be aware of You even when I wake up in the morning and I see nothing hurts."

Does your head hurt? No, not today. Do your teeth hurt? Not today. Does your stomach hurt? Not today. Do your ears hurt? Not today. Nothing is hurting. I thank you, Hashem, that nothing hurts. I'm aware of You. I don't need any reminders.

Some people aren't reminded unless something hurts them. Unfortunately, there are a lot of people who aren't reminded of Hashem *even* when something hurts them. So He sends them another reminder. If the post office has a package to deliver but you weren't home, they leave a notice. If you don't respond, they leave another notice. Hashem sends notices until we pay attention to Him.

We have to say to Him, "Hashem, please stop sending us notices because now we're going to send notices to ourselves. Every morning when we wake up, we're going to leap out of bed with joy."

Don't leap out, by the way. It's not healthy. But get out of bed with joy and say, "*Modeh ani l'fanecha*—I thank You, Hashem," that nothing hurts today.

"Oh," Hashem says, "as long as you're doing that, you don't need any reminders."

Q How can we overcome the habit of taking our health for granted?

The word *tehillah* comes from the word *hallel. Hallel* is a word that we translate as "praise," but it really means "to go wild." It's from the word *holel. Holellim* means "wild people," people who are out of control. When we speak about *hallel* to Hashem, it means not merely that we appreciate what He's doing for us, but that we're extremely enthusiastic.[31]

If you have good health, even just for today, it deserves extreme enthusiasm. Do you know what it means when a person is suffering in constant pain, and one day of blessed relief comes? Just one day of rest. He'd give a lot of money for that one day. Even if just for one day, the pounding in his head or that tearing sensation in his side would cease.

So we have to appreciate that one day. And a second day just as much. When we cry out in joy, it must be in enthusiastic joy. That's our function. We have to do it when we have pain, and we have to do it when we're well.

If that's all you're going to learn tonight, you didn't waste your time. You have to cry to Hashem when your health is good. You have to cry out with *tehillah*, with wildness! You walk in the streets, not in a wheelchair. You're breathing air, not with an artificial respirator. *Ah, Baruch Atah, Hashem!* What a wonderful world You have given us.

---

31 See the section on Hallel, p. 465.

Even if a sick man is partially healed, he's thrilled. He'd pay a physician a lot of money just to feel a little better. How much more enthusiastic he'd feel if he'd be fully healed. So how much more enthusiastic *we* should be that at the moment we're healthy and don't have pains.

That's why after we say, "*Hoshi'einu v'nivashei'a*—Help us and we shall be helped," we add, "*Ki sehilaseinu Atah*—because You are our praise." As long as we're enthusiastic in our praise to Hashem, as long as we're addressing Him with *tehillah*, Hashem will be our *yeshuah*. He'll be our salvation and help us always.

Q **If we *daven* for health, why do we also need to live in a healthy way?**

It's of the greatest importance to understand the necessity to beware of hypocrisy in prayer. You have to mean what you say, as it says, "*Karov Hashem l'chol kor'av*—Hashem is close to all those who call out to Him..." but with a condition: "*l'chol asher yikra'uhu be'emes*—to all those who call out to Him in truth" (*Tehillim* 145:18). You have to call to Him in truth.

You might say, "Isn't that superfluous?" If a person isn't well, he's surely asking for good health from the bottom of his heart. Do we think him guilty of hypocrisy, of calling in falsehood?

The answer is yes. Here is a sick man, or a sick woman, who needs help. What should be the very first thing? The very first thing is to take care of yourself. But suppose that person persists in going to bed late just because he was reading something interesting. He can't put down that book or newspaper or turn off that infernal device. That's not calling out in truth. If he meant business, he would hit the hay early.

Here's another person. He likes to munch before going to bed, so he takes a bag of peanuts, sits down, and munches and munches and munches. He munches away his life. That person isn't taking care of his health. When he asks Hashem to make him well, his words are empty. We must act in ways that demonstrate that our prayers are genuine.

When somebody prays for the health of his children, he can't let them get into all kinds of dangerous situations. Little children must play only under supervision. It's so easy to swallow something or start a fire, G-d forbid. Many people pray and yet are negligent. It means they're not sincere. Their prayer isn't "in truth."

Anyone who walks regularly, goes to sleep on time, drinks a lot of water every day, does not eat too much, and does not talk too much—by the way, talking a lot is very bad for the health: *Lo matzasi laguf tov mishesikah*, "I never found anything better for the body's health than keeping quiet" (*Avos* 1:17)—is going to be healthier. And because he's doing his part, when he calls out to Hashem—whether to heal him or prevent him from losing his health—Hashem is close to him. "*Karov Hashem l'chol kor'av*—He's close to all who call out to Him," with the condition—"*l'chol asher yikra'uhu be'emes*—to all who call out to Him in truth."

Q **Why do we ask Hashem to heal our "wounds," rather than our illnesses?**

We say, "*V'ha'aleih refuah sheleimah l'chol makoseinu*—Bring perfect healing for all our wounds." Why does it say "wounds," not "illnesses?" What about a cold, or other kinds of illnesses? They're not the results of a blow. Why wounds?

But we must understand that every illness is actually a blow inflicted by Hashem. He is the One Who is inflicting the wound. That's important. You have to always keep in mind that it's not an accident.

And we ask for a "perfect healing." Why a "perfect healing"? It means it's not enough that the symptoms merely disappear. When some people have a cold, they do things to relieve the discomfort, but that's not a healing. Those treatments just make you feel better temporarily. They relieve the symptoms.

Sometimes a physician prescribes both things—an antibiotic to heal and something to relieve the distress. But we have to realize that when we pray for a *refuah sheleimah*, we want Hashem to remove the *causes* of the illness, not just the symptoms. It's not enough to remove the fever or the weakness. We have to attempt to combat the illness itself.

We must realize that any illness is a symptom of some character flaw. The external symptoms always hint at something internal. It's not enough even to be healed entirely of the symptoms if the illness is not healed internally. That's not a *refuah sheleimah.*

Therefore, we're really asking Hashem to aid us in repentance. That's the *refuah sheleimah.* We're asking Hashem to improve our souls, our thoughts, our habits, our character traits, our *middos.* The illness of the body was intended to help us repair our flaws in all these matters.

The Gemara says, "If a man sees that adversity comes upon him, he should search into his deeds" (*Brachos* 5a). But "if he searched and couldn't find"—that doesn't mean us, by the way; we're not on that level; if we search even a little, we'll easily find—"then let him attribute it to not learning Torah." It means he didn't learn enough Torah. Torah is the source of all healing of the soul. How can you know what good character really is if you read only newspapers or listen to the chatter of people on the street? You must come to the source.

I'll give you an example of how you cannot recognize good behavior, good character, without Torah. There was a time when I used to take a taxi every day. I had to go from one school to another to talk. I used the same driver every day. He was an old American Jew, an eighty-year-old man. He didn't know how to learn. He didn't even know the *siddur.* He knew nothing. But one thing he did know—he knew that Orthodox Jews were no good. He was describing to me how his old daughter finally got married, and he hired a *chazenta* to put on a *tallis* and a *yarmulke* and sing, "Oh, Promise Me." A big fat *chazenta* singing her heart out. When I smiled, he said, "You Orthodox Jews don't have any beauty in your ceremonies."

Finally, we crossed the parkway and came into Flatbush. There was a long way to go yet but he closed his meter. "Why are you closing the meter?" I asked.

"Because my boss earned enough today. The rest of the fare will go to me."

Now, he didn't dream that he was a crook. That's how it is. The unorthodox don't even know that they're crooks. All they know is that the Orthodox are crooks.

You can't acquire good character if you don't learn Torah. You can never be good without Torah. So if you searched and you couldn't find any character flaws in yourself, attribute it to *bittul* Torah, to lack of learning Torah. Without Torah, you won't be able to find anything. Without Torah, you'll think that everything you do is fine and virtuous. Without Torah, you'll never suspect yourself of doing something wrong.

There are many things that people don't realize are wrong because they didn't learn. Therefore, to have a *refuah sheleimah*, it's necessary to get to the root and begin learning how to behave according to the will of Hashem, not according to the will of the *New York Times*. Not according to the will of the columnists who teach you good manners. Here's a woman columnist who gives advice to women how to be successful in their homes. The columnist is divorced, and no one wants to marry her because she can't get along with anybody. That's an advice columnist. Like the Yiddish saying goes: "*Shusters gein borvus*—Cobblers go barefoot."

When a person learns Torah, he rids himself of many flaws. If he doesn't rid himself of the flaws, Hashem sends reminders, *makkos*, for him. The illness comes because of character flaws, and the study of Torah helps remove the character flaws.

Q What do the adjectives describing Hashem in *Refa'einu* mean?

At the end of the *brachah* we add, "*Ki Keil Melech rofei ne'eman v'rachaman Atah*—For You are G-d, King, Healer, Trustworthy, and Merciful." We describe Hashem in five ways: G-d, King, Healer, Trustworthy, and Merciful. These are five reasons why we trust in Hashem's healing.

Keil—aleph-lamed—means G.O.D. It means power. Hashem does

not lack medicines. He doesn't lack agents. He has physicians. He has antibodies. He has nutritive materials. He has processes of Nature. Hashem is in charge. He has everything.

Why do people go to medical school? Because of their ambition? No, Hashem sends them there because He wants doctors in the world. They think it's their own ambitions, but He has other ideas in mind. Why do apothecaries open drugstores? To sell toys to children? No, Hashem has other ideas in mind. They'll sell aspirin and fill prescriptions. He arranges that.

Even more, the body itself is a drugstore. The body has so many secretions that help people and save their lives. The body is full of medicines. It's remarkable how many forms of healing the body creates. When there's a cut in the skin, why doesn't the blood drip out endlessly? If you make a hole in, say, a container of milk, it will continue to drip out until it's all gone. Why shouldn't the body continue to drip all its blood through that cut in the skin?

The answer is that Hashem created the body to be self-healing. The blood contains fibrinogen, a certain material that clots when exposed to air. As soon as the blood comes to the surface, it begins to make a plug and close off the wound.

However, just stopping the flow of blood is not enough. You have to repel all the invaders that came through that gateway into your body, all the germs that came in from the outside because of the cut. So from all parts of the body white corpuscles converge on the wound. They come from everywhere, even from your marrow. The marrow in your bones starts discharging extra corpuscles, white corpuscles. They start traveling throughout the entire body, even straight through the tissues of the organs. It's remarkable how these things travel in the body and arrive on the scene in precisely the right spot at precisely the right time.

When they arrive, they look for the culprit. Now, the blood is a very busy street. There are all kinds of things in it. Nutritional materials, waste materials, and all kinds of other secretions are conveyed in the blood. How do these corpuscles, these antibodies, discover who are the invaders and who are the friends? Yet unerringly, without being told, they go straight to the culprits.

It's like picking out a criminal on a busy street who looks just like everybody else. He's not holding a gun. He's not wearing a mask. How can you recognize who he is? But these antibodies unerringly go directly to the criminal, the germs. Then they swallow them up. They don't arrest them and escort them to jail. They swallow them up on the spot.

That's only the beginning. The body begins to manufacture all kinds of secretions to help you heal a cut in the skin. Hashem doesn't need outside apothecaries to supply medicines because He has a whole chemical manufacturing complex within the body.

Therefore, we begin by calling Him *Keil*, because He possesses absolute power. He doesn't need any instruments. In most cases, illness is cured by itself. In most cases, even physicians rely on the healing processes of the body. That's *Keil*. You, Hashem, have all the power to heal. You have all the resources to heal. And by believing in that, we're already on the way to healing.

Second, we call Him *Melech*. *Melech* means He has the sole jurisdiction over everything. Let's say a good physician is trying to heal someone, but outside the physician's office there's a mugger waiting who beats up the patient as he walks out. Now he has to go back to the office again. The physician can't control whether the patient will get home in one piece. But Hashem has sole jurisdiction over you. Nobody can harm you except Hashem. And nobody can interfere if you have Hashem on your side. That's why we say *Melech*—He is the King Who is the sole ruler over everything.

In addition, *Melech* means wisdom, from the word *nimlach*. *Milka* in Aramaic means "wisdom." Sometimes even the best physician makes a mistaken diagnosis. It happens. You see them being sued all over America. Even people with the best intentions. But Hashem never makes a mistake. *Melech* means He knows the source of the illness and the cure for the illness. So, we appeal to Him because He is the *Melech* who has sole jurisdiction over us, and He knows exactly what to do.

Next we say, *Rofei*. He is a "Healer." It means He has established His reputation as a healer. He is the One Who has healed us all of our days.

Is this the first encounter we've had with illness? Since we were babies, we had problems. Everyone becomes ill occasionally or suffers from some minor ailment—yet Hashem is the One Who always stood at our side and healed us. Not only did He heal us, He healed our parents, He healed their parents, and so on. Therefore, because He established a reputation from the beginning, we can put our full trust in Him. That's why we say that He is the *Rofei.*

Ne'eman denotes "steadfast"—standing in one place, never weary, never disheartened, never changing His profession, which is the profession of healing and helping, and He remains always what He is ("I shall be what I shall be"—*Shemos* 3:14). Therefore, we can trust in Him with all our heart. He is truly proficient and totally reliable.

Rachaman, Merciful—even though we are not deserving. Despite a man's continued sinfulness, Hashem heals him again and again. This is an essential requirement for One in Whom we trust. Otherwise, we would constantly fear that because of our unworthiness, our trust would not be requited. But He is merciful (*Rachaman*), which denotes the "permanent profession" of mercy (the suffix *-an* denotes "profession" or "occupation"), always, despite our sins; and therefore, we always continue to hope for His healing.

The literal reading is: "For a G-d, King, trustworthy, and merciful healer are You." By putting "are You" at the end (instead of at the beginning) the intention is: "You alone."

Q **Why do we conclude *Refa'einu* by specifying the *cholim* of Klal Yisrael?**

It says in *Pirkei Avos* (5:3), "Until Avraham came and took the reward of all of them." From Avraham's time onward, his seed is the center of Hashem's interest. Now, that's a big shock to the liberal frame of mind, but the Torah is very far from liberalism. The Torah teaches that Hashem made the world for a righteous people, and since Avraham stepped forward and volunteered, Hashem made him and his seed chosen forever.

If it's alien to your way of thinking, you have to change your way of thinking, because that's Torah. Wherever you look in Torah that's the fundamental thesis—we, the people of Hashem, are the main attraction. Everything else is scenery and backdrop and the supporting cast. The main actor—the one whom all the universe is for—is the Am Yisrael.[32]

When Hashem created natural processes, He didn't make it merely for the purpose of making mankind comfortable. Of course, He wants not only humans but animals to be comfortable, too. You see that the wounds of animals get healed. When a dog gets a bite from another dog, it heals eventually. Hashem even heals lizards. Even fish heal. Even a tree heals. All of Nature is so planned that it should exist in the most

---

32 Rabbi Miller ties this theme to the second verse in the Torah (*Bereishis* 1:2). "And the spirit of G-d hovered over the face of the waters." Did the spirit cease to hover when dry land appeared? Does the spirit prefer dry to wet? But we learn here that the spirit seeks the person or the group that would seek to know Him, and until that person or group appears His spirit hovers and waits. When Abraham came and chose to recognize G-d, the spirit came to rest on Abraham and his seed, forever. "And I: this is My covenant with them, said Hashem, My spirit which is upon you and My words that I have put into your mouth; they shall not depart from your mouth and from the mouth of your seed and from the mouth of the seed of your seed, said Hashem, from now until forever" (*Yeshayah* 59:21). This is "the spirit of G-d that hovered over the waters" (see 17:22, 6:3). One testimonial that this Spirit came to rest upon the Fathers and their offspring: "A man such as this one, that the Spirit of G-d is in him" (41:38), when Joseph became the leader of his people. Subsequently, the Torah relates that the Spirit of G-d came to rest on the Fathers. "Behold, the heavens and the heavens above them belong to Hashem your G-d, the earth, and all therein. (But) only in your Fathers did Hashem delight to love them, and He chose their seed after them, you above all peoples, as at this day" (*Devarim* 10:14–15). The Spirit which hovered finally chose to rest upon the Fathers and upon their seed after them. This same principle is stated by Nechemiah (*Nechemiah* 9:6–7): "You are Hashem alone; You made the heavens (and) the heavens of the heavens and all their host, the earth and all that is on it, the seas and all that is in them, and You give life to all of them, and the host of heaven bow down to You. You are Hashem G-d that chose Abram and You took him out from Ur Kasdim." The Spirit of G-d found no resting-place in the vastness of Space or on the earth, until Abraham appeared; and Abraham's seed created the final resting-place when they accepted the Torah and erected the Mishkan: "And I shall dwell in their midst" (*Shemos* 25:8). Later we see that Hashem said to Jacob: "I shall go down to Egypt with you" (46:4), meaning: "Wherever you go, I go." (*The Beginning*, pp. 13–14)

beneficial manner. But we have to realize that everything good in this world is made only because of a purpose—to facilitate the existence of a virtuous people, a people that lives for the service of Hashem.

If there are processes of healing in this world, if there are physicians, hospitals, medicines, if there's anything in this world that helps people become well, Hashem has done it first and foremost for the Am Yisrael. Therefore, we say "*Rofei cholei amo Yisrael*—You are the One Who heals the ill of His people, Yisrael." Of course, once there are drugstores, chemicals, and physicians that help His people, why should Hashem deny it to others? In the merit of His people, He allows others also to get a ride along with us and enjoy all the good things He has prepared in the world. Therefore, when you walk out and breathe the fresh air, know that the fresh air is for the people of Yisrael. When you see a beautiful moon in the sky, when you see the sun shining, know that these blessings are showering down on everybody, even non-humans, because of us. If not for the Torah, which we accepted, the world would have no cause for existence (*Yirmiyah* 33:25; *Avodah Zarah* 3a). Now, I know it's difficult for us to imagine that the world wouldn't exist, but there was once such a situation—when Hashem brought the Flood on the world, everything was destroyed. The purpose was to demonstrate that Hashem isn't committed to Nature. If He so desires, He can cause the cessation of the usual processes of Nature.

All the phenomena Hashem created for the well-being and healing of the entire world is in the merit of the Am Yisrael. That's why we say, "*Rofei cholei amo Yisrael*—He heals the sick of His people Yisrael." If others are healed, too, it's in the merit of "*Amo Yisrael*."

When you say this *brachah*, you shouldn't be thinking only about yourself. You have a right to mention your own name, too, to pray for yourself and your wife and family, too. But you must also think of all of the sick of the Am Yisrael. Think of all the hospitals in New York City alone. They're full of Jews—undergoing all kinds of operations and suffering from all kinds of illnesses. And all the doctors' offices are crowded with patients. Think about them when you say, "*Rofei cholei amo Yisrael*."

PRACTICAL ADVICE

Q If someone is ill, what should he do first?

The first thing is he should immediately ask Hashem for help. Second, he should immediately get the best assistance from experts. Third, *yeilech eitzel chacham*—he should go to a *chacham* and ask him to be *mispallel* for him. That's a Gemara (*Bava Basra* 116a). I'll repeat these three things.

Number one—he should immediately ask Hashem without any delay. *Tefillah* is number one. If a man doesn't have *tefillah*, he's putting his trust in physicians or medicine. "Accursed is a man who trusts in human beings and makes flesh his strength; his heart turns away from Hashem" (*Yirmiyah* 17:5). At the very outset, you must speak to Hashem.

Number two—"*V'rapo y'rapei*—He must pay the victim's doctor bills" (*Shemos* 21:19). The Gemara says, "We learn from here that the physician has a right to heal" (*Brachos* 60a). The physician is not trespassing on Hashem's domain when he tries to heal, because Hashem Himself gave that command.

Number three—he should seek competent *tefillos* from somebody whose words are heeded by Hashem. *Yeilech eitzel chacham.*

Q Why are some people not healed, even though they ask Hashem every day for a *refuah*?

When we say in *Ashrei* every day that "Hashem is close to all those who call out in truth" (*Tehillim* 145:18), what does it mean to call out "in truth"? Let's say a person who's not feeling well goes to *daven* and says in a formal way, "*Refa'einu, Hashem, v'neirafei*—Heal us, Hashem, and we are healed." He certainly wants to get well, but the question is: Does he feel that he is speaking to the right address, that Hashem is the One Who can make him well? If he does it half-heartedly — if he's thinking that, in reality, he has to go to physicians and that davening to Hashem is a formality — then it's not *be'emes*, "in truth." *Be'emes* means he has the *emunah* that Hashem is the *Rofei cholei amo Yisrael*, "the Healer." It's going to a physician that's the formality.

We're required to look for a good physician and to pay the physician. The Gemara (*Bava Kama* 85a) says you should pay a physician, because "a physician who heals for nothing is worth that much." The example in the Gemara is of a man who wounded his fellow man and is obligated to pay him for several things, including his doctor's bills. If the man says, "I have a friend who's a doctor and he'll heal you for nothing," the wounded man can say, "A physician who heals for nothing is worth nothing." A person has to find a good physician and pay. But at the same time, he has to know that it's only a formality. *Bitachon* requires him to understand that Hashem is the One Who heals. That's *asher yikra'uhu be'emes*. You have to call out in truth, with *emunah*.

The Koreans write their prayers on a scroll and wrap it around a spindle; then they put it on a greased axle and give it a twirl. It goes around many times. Each time it goes around, they get credit for a whole *tefillah*. What do the really pious ones do? They have a whole row of them and walk back and forth, spinning each one. And they are joking and laughing while they do that. The rich ones buy spindles along two rows and spin each one as they pass so they have all these wheels praying for them. The wheels don't stop for even a second, because they keep walking back and forth, giving them a twirl each time. That's what these pious men do to serve the demons to which they pray.

That is really praying by rote. But it's a genuine tragedy to pray by rote even when davening to Hashem. A person must have the attitude that each time he *davens* he tries to *daven* better. Each time he says, "Hashem," he tries to actually think of the Shechinah. Each time he says, "*Atah*, You," he tries to picture what "You" means. "You" means you're talking to Someone.

Then, as the days and months go by, it's like polishing his *neshamah*. First, he polishes off the dirt that's encrusted on the mirror of his *neshamah*. Then, little by little, his *neshamah* begins to become clear, bright, and transparent—and finally the *emunah* starts coming, starts shining through. After much labor, he's able to call out *be'emes*. There is a great deal of progress to be made from *saying* the words to *feeling* the words, and most people aren't doing it. They're busy with other things. That's why it says, "Hashem is close to all who call out to Him *in truth*." It's a great accomplishment for a person to call out to Hashem honestly.

"Heal me!" "Give me *parnassah*!" "Help!" "*Shema koleinu*!" Cry out for anything you want. If you call out to Him, then He's close to you, and that's what He wants—the awareness, the real *yiras Hashem*. If you feel that He is the One to Whom to direct your requests, then He becomes close to you. But there is a condition. "*L'chol asher yikra'uhu be'emes*—to all those who call to Him in truth." You have to call to Him sincerely, Him and only Him.[33]

Now, there's another point here. It says, "*Hamelech ya'aneinu b'yom kareinu*—The King answers us on the day that we call out" (*Tehillim* 20:10). That means there's no such thing as your prayers not being answered. It says, "*Ashirah laHashem ki gamal alai*—I sing to Hashem because He has already bestowed it upon me" (*Tehillim* 13:6). You have to know that as soon as you pray, you're already a lucky person. But sometimes the good fortune comes in ways that you don't know about or you don't want.

I'll give you an example. Here's a boy who needs an operation. Let's say he has to have his appendix removed. The doctors are about to strap him onto the operating table, but this boy has other ideas. As soon as the doctor turns his back, he leaps off the table, streaks through the door, and is running down the street, straight to the candy store. Now he's buying a big ice cream a mile high, walking in the street, licking it. That's life! Who needs an

33 See also *Praise, My Soul*, #405–408.

operation when you can be licking ice cream? But then his father comes along, throws the ice cream into the gutter, and drags him straight back to the hospital. That's going to save his life. He'll be able to eat a lot of ice cream cones later in life because of that.

Hashem isn't necessarily going to give us exactly what we want. We can't write our own prescription. He knows better what's good for us! But this you have to know—that your *tefillah* helped. You're never a failure when you pray. Even the *tzaddik* who prayed and soon after that a misfortune came upon him, *chalilah*, should know that his prayers were answered. Maybe not the way he wanted. Sometimes, the best thing is to be taken out of this world just at that moment, pure and worthy. He'll discover in the Afterlife how lucky he was that he left the world at the right moment.

However, you can never tell. Maybe Hashem is waiting for your prayers. Maybe He'll say to you, "My boy, since you prayed to Me, I'm going to tell the doctors to take you off the operating table." Then they'll take a look at your chart and say, "It was a mistake. Wrong diagnosis. Off to the candy store you go!" It happens sometimes that way. Many times it's a wrong diagnosis. Sometimes it's a fatal disease and yet people survive. Doctors make mistakes—only, they rarely say so. Even when the patient perishes under the scalpel, they say, "Everything went well, except the patient died." Sometimes the doctor says he'll live only three more weeks, but he goes on living for another thirty years. It happens again and again. So keep praying, and Hashem might make that diagnosis turn out to be wrong.

Q **What should one's reaction be when he hears that his friend's child is very sick?**

The first reaction should be to ask for the child's name and make sure to be *mispallel* for him. Ask Hashem to help him. That's a *chiyuv*. Shmuel Hanavi said, "And also I, *chalilah,* far be it from me to sin against Hashem and refrain from praying on your behalf (*I Shmuel* 12:23). Shmuel called it "*chalilah*" to not pray for a person who needs help. It's so important!

Take his name and pray for him. Your friend doesn't need to hear it. Stand in a corner somewhere and speak to Hashem. Or find a telephone booth. You can even take the receiver in your hand if you want. Then pray to Hashem: "Please, Ribbono Shel Olam, send a *refuah sheleimah* to so-and-so, *b'soch sh'ar cholei Yisrael.*" Not just once. Many times! It's very important! You should carry around papers with you that have the names of *cholim*. Carry these papers and from time to time look at them and be *mispallel.* In Shemoneh Esrei, too. And any other time—say these *tefillos* again and again. It's a very important *mitzvah*. A very important opportunity. It's *gemilas chassadim* to be *mispallel* for someone who is sick.

Some say that one who smokes will be protected from danger based on the *passuk*, "Hashem guards the foolish ones" (*Tehillim* 116:6). What do you say about that?

This gentleman wants to know why Hashem wouldn't protect a fool who smokes.

That statement means that Hashem guards the people who are persuaded because they don't know any better. The word *pesi* (foolish ones) means someone who is persuaded. I'll give you an example of a *pesi*. When King Louis XIV of France was ill, he had the very best physicians in Europe caring for him. They took melted pearls and poured it down his throat. Melted pearls were considered the best medicine in those days. So, when the very best physicians came to heal King Louis XIV, they melted pearls and poured them down his throat. And that's what killed him. He was a *pesi*. He couldn't help himself. That's what people believed in those days. Now, when people don't know, Hashem says, "I'm going to help *most* people who are persuaded to do foolish things. There will be a general *shemirah* on people who are doing things that are dangerous if it's not known that there's a danger."

But when you *know* there's a danger, you must be careful. That's why in the olden days, when people didn't know how harmful smoking was, the results were not so evident. But today, when we know that smoking is dangerous—the package itself tells you that it's dangerous—you're not a *pesi*. You're just a *meshugener*. It says on the package that it's dangerous for his health but he's puffing away! He's a *meshugener*! Therefore, today when it comes to smoking, this *passuk* doesn't apply. Hashem will only guard people who are not to blame. Today, if you smoke, you're to blame. Anybody who ignores good advice is no longer a *pesi*. He's a *meizid*, and whatever happens to him is his own fault.

Q **Is there anything wrong with drinking beer?**

For Havdalah you can drink beer. Otherwise, I suggest H_2O. Water is the best drink. I'm not saying it's *assur* to drink beer, but what's the benefit of it? It's just dirty water.

Many people don't drink enough water. That's one reason why they have health issues. Drink plenty of water every day. Sixty years ago, I suffered from constipation. One day, I was walking home from yeshiva and a young man told me to drink a glass of water every day before davening. I started doing it. Only I did it twice—two glasses of water every morning. *Baruch Hashem*, it was a wonderful piece of advice.

You need water to loosen up your digestive system. You must drink enough water, and most people don't.

The body needs lubrication, and one of the most important elements in regular bowel elimination is enough liquid in the body. I cannot overemphasize that necessity. Even though it's not *ruchniyus*, this is important *gashmiyus*, and it's a *chessed* for people to know.

The older you get, the more your body needs liquids. You should drink more and more as you age. You hit sixty or seventy? You should drink at least six big glasses of water every day. You need it for your eyes. Your eyes are lubricated with liquids. You need it for your blood. Your blood is liquid. You need it for your joints. It helps lubricate the joints. Every part of your body needs water.

When people understand the great gift that Hashem gives in the form of water, they'll thank Him for life. Water is life itself.

Q How can I alleviate stress?

Sleep eight hours a night, without exception. Eight hours every night! No *chasunahs*, no other *simchahs*. No excuses. If you start sleeping eight hours every night, and you do it for a long time, you'll discover a great change in your nervous system. A great change! If you take my advice, and you're consistent about it, you'll never want to go back to your former sleeping habits. You'll be a different person.

Now, that's not the only thing. But it's one of the first things to do. Most people, you'll discover, are suffering from stress and other nervous disorders due to lack of sleep. Sleep is one of the greatest gifts of Hashem. It's a pleasure to put your head down on the pillow and drift off into a sweet sleep. A pleasure!

Sleep is a blessing and you have to thank Hashem for it. And say it with your mouth: "*Ah geshmaka* pleasant night's sleep!" It's better than eating the most delicious things! In the morning you get up and you're refreshed. You're a new person. "*Modeh ani l'fanecha*—I thank You, Hashem." So make sure not to neglect this gift.

Q Is there anything wrong with eating candies, cakes, and things like that?

The Rambam states that one who is wise will eat what's healthy for him, what's beneficial. He says, "Don't eat only things just because your palate desires them, like the dog and the donkey do" (*Hilchos Dei'os* 3:2). You're not an animal that eats only what it thinks is delicious. "Eat only the things that are beneficial for you" (ibid.).

We see that following your desires means that you lack sense, like a donkey or a dog. Are candies and cakes wrong for you to eat? Sometimes it's not wrong. Sometimes people are down and need a lift. Then it's recommended to enjoy life a little more than the regular routine. Take a nosh, if that helps. Yes, sometimes you can do things that are not recommended but that raise your spirits.

Ordinarily, however, things full of sugar will cause your teeth to rot, unless you brush after eating them. And sometimes they take the place of the nourishing foods that you should be eating. Therefore, it's not sensible to waste your efforts on *nosherei*. However, we're not going to say that you can't eat candies or cake. It would be foolish to make such a rule. Sometimes a candy or a piece of cake is important to give you a lift. And for happy occasions, sometimes people can be stimulated to a little more joy because of these things. Therefore, the answer to your question requires discretion.

The wise man is the man who chooses a diet that's healthy and nourishing. That's how a wise man should eat. You don't need me to tell you that. You know it yourself.

Q **How can one avoid getting cancer?**

Every day do what the Gemara says, "A person should always plead for mercy from Hashem that he shouldn't get sick" (*Shabbos* 32a). Which means that every day you should pray for good health. Every single day of your life! Don't rely on Shemoneh Esrei. It can be done outside of Shemoneh Esrei, too. Or if you wish, you can add it when you finish Shemoneh Esrei, before you take three steps back. Beg Hashem! Even if you've prayed all your prayers by rote, like a record, say at least one little thing with *kavanah*. Say, "Please guard my health and my well-being. Guard me against automobile accidents and other accidents." You have to always pray to be saved from accidents.

The reason there are accidents in the world is to be a spur, to incite people to pray. If you don't pray, He might have to send an accident, *chalilah*, to make you aware. Therefore, "*L'olam*—always!" a man should always seek mercy from Hashem not to be sick. That's one of the most important pieces of counsel you'll ever hear.

Q Should a *yeshiva man* spend time exercising?

Everybody needs some physical exercise. Exactly how much time depends on his circumstances. I wouldn't give any general advice. But I would say that everybody should do some walking. It's a very great benefit. People cannot live a sedentary life and allow themselves to deteriorate physically.

SUMMARY

- Illness is for the purpose of making us cry out to Hashem.
- Despite all our efforts to heal ourselves or maintain our health, we must always know that Hashem is the One making it happen. Hashem is the real Healer, and all our efforts are just a formality.
- We must always *daven* to Hashem to keep us healthy.
- We can prevent illness by always thanking Hashem when we're healthy, and we should praise Him with enthusiasm by contemplating the alternative.
- We also must do everything possible to maintain our health if we want Hashem to heed our prayers to keep us healthy.
- Illness comes because of character flaws. When we ask for a *refuah sheleimah*, we're asking Hashem to help us rid ourselves of our character flaws.
- We appeal to Hashem as the One Who has absolute power, absolute control, absolute knowledge, a perfect track record, Who is totally reliable, and Who heals us despite our sins.
- All healing that happens in this world is only for the sake of the Am Yisrael.
- Think of all your fellow Jews who are ill and ask that Hashem heal them.

- Even if Hashem doesn't send a *refuah* the way you want, you must know that your prayers were answered—just not necessarily the way you wanted them to be answered. Hashem knows what's best for each person.

Bareich Aleinu

Q **Why are we asking for *gashmiyus*, material good?**

In his *sefer Emunos V'deyos* (9:6), Rabbeinu Saadia Gaon makes a remark that enlightens us about the nature of Olam Hazeh. He says that this world was made for food. All the systems of this world were designed with the goal of supplying food. The world is a food-making machine!

It's an observation we don't usually pay attention to, but Rav Saadia wants to make sure we don't miss it. The world is working *tamid*, all day and all night, for the purpose of producing food. The vast phenomena of the winds, the sun, the rain, the atmosphere, and thousands of other factors are all cooperating with each other in the mighty function of disbursing food to all the living. The world is working to supply you with your breakfast, lunch, and supper—and all the snacking in between.

If you open your eyes, if you open your mind, you'll see it all day long. Even a man in the city who never saw a cow or a wheat field can see what Rav Saadia is speaking about. All day, trucks are driving back and forth on the streets bringing all types of food to the stores. Some are loaded with fruits and vegetables. Others with milk, cheese, poultry, meats, and loaves of every type of bread. And it's *tamid*! From early in the morning, before you're even thinking about getting up, these trucks are on the road loading and unloading cases of food. There's something here! The whole *briyah*—the whole *ma'aseh bereishis*—is working to bring you food! When you walk in the street and see hundreds of people, it is 100 percent incontrovertible proof that everybody is eating.

And it's all *nisei nissim*. Everyone knows what the Gemara says: "A person's food is as difficult as the splitting of the Yam Suf" (*Pesachim* 118a). Now, making a living can be difficult, but almost everybody is doing it. You're making a living, aren't you? But you still can't split the Yam Suf. What the Gemara is telling us is that the subject of food in this world is one of the greatest demonstrations of the greatness of Hashem that we'll ever witness—and every piece of bread is as miraculous as *kriyas Yam Suf*!

Chazal tell us that at the Yam Suf there were 250 *makkos*. That means there were at least 250 open miracles when Hashem split the Yam Suf. And when you're eating food, you're expected to realize that every bite is at least 250 miracles. The truth is that it's much more than that. It's *elef alfei nissim*! It's deep beyond comprehension. You need millions of details to cooperate to make bread.

"You open up Your hand Hashem and feed the whole world" (*Tehillim* 145:16). How does He accomplish that? By harnessing the sun to evaporate the water from the seas to create clouds, and then by moving these water-filled clouds inland by means of the wind. It's like a big conveyor belt moving water from the sea to the farms. Then He opens the clouds and causes the rain to fall upon the fields. Hashem is feeding us all the time by keeping the air in constant motion, bringing a never-ending supply of carbon dioxide to the plants, and by the miracles of photosynthesis and the water cycle. The stupendous phenomenon of supplying countless kinds of foods to countless kinds of diverse creatures, the never-ending process of recycling the waste and the dead plants and animals to replenish the constant supply of food, demands of us the very greatest expression of admiration and gratitude!

That's why when you're sitting at the table and somebody says, "Can you give me that piece of bread?" you can't throw it to him. "*Ein zorkin es hapas*—You can't throw bread" (*Brachos* 50b). *Derech eretz!* You must hand him the bread with the greatest *kavod*. Be polite with the bread! "I'm passing you Hashem's miracle." Would you throw the *Lechem Hapanim*?! If the Kohen Gadol said, "Hand me the *Urim V'tumim*," would you throw it? No, you would lift it with the greatest *derech eretz*, with the greatest *hachna'ah* and *yiras Shamayim* and hand it to him.

But a piece of bread is more *nissim* than the *Urim V'tumim* — much more! The *Urim V'tumim* was a rare miracle, but bread is bigger, much bigger. Only that we're accustomed to it. Hashem says, "Is that My fault? I'm giving you bread every day. Is that a reason you shouldn't be excited?! Would it be better if I gave it to you once every ten years?"

When you see a piece of bread on your table, you have to train yourself to be excited about it — no less excited than if you found the *Urim V'tumim* on your table. Say with your mouth, "You, Hashem, are feeding the whole world. And right now You're feeding me with favor and kindness and mercy." Don't rely on the *brachah*. Don't wait for bentching. Say it now! Because what's the purpose of all those miracles, after all? What's the purpose of that bread on your table? It's for the same purpose as the bread that sat on the Shulchan in the Beis Hamikdash — it's all for the sake of His Great Name! How are we supposed to react after eating a piece of bread? We have to talk about His Great Name! That was the purpose of the *Lechem Hapanim* on the Shulchan — and that's the purpose of the *lechem* on your *shulchan*, too!

Be enthusiastic about food. When you eat breakfast, a little piece of bread and a glass of water, be very excited about it. And when you thank Hashem for breakfast, that's only the beginning. All day long, you're walking and working from the energy this food gave you. All day long, you must think about what you had for breakfast. If you had more than bread and water, you'd better think about it. Maybe you had an egg, too. Oh, an egg — what a luscious bundle of food that is! It comes wrapped in a beautiful package. You just crack it open and it's ready to eat with a small preparation. It's easily swallowed and easily digested. And it's nourishing, full of protein and other important ingredients to maintain the health of the body.

Maybe you had a glass of milk, too — milk is a miracle! Where does milk come from? A cow doesn't drink milk. It eats grass and makes milk out of it. That's beyond the ability of science today. They can't compete with the cow. A cow turning grass into milk is quite a feat. It's a miracle.

If you stand in the great market in downtown New York, you see trucks are coming all night, huge trucks loaded with food, one after the other. Mountains and mountains of food are brought in every day. Mountains of fish and mountains of meat and mountains of vegetables — every day of the year without stop.

When Rav Saadia Gaon says it's a food world, we have to study that.

Q Why did Hashem create us with the need to eat food?

The Gemara (*Pesachim* 118a) speaks about "*Hallel Hagadol*— the Great Hallel" (*Tehillim* 136). Now, we know that everything in *Tehillim* is *gadol*. *Ashrei* is very great. If you say it three times a day, you're a *ben Olam Haba* (*Brachos* 4b) That's how important it is. Why, then, is this chapter singled out to be called "*Hallel Hagadol*"? That's the Gemara's question.

Now, in that chapter it says the phrase, "*Ki l'olam chasdo*" twenty-six times, enumerating the *chasdei Hashem*. He took us out of Mitzrayim, He brought us through the Yam Suf, He destroyed our enemies — a whole long list of *chasdei Hashem*. And what's the pinnacle, the final thing on the list? "*Nosein lechem l'chol basar*— He gives food to all flesh."

The Gemara explains that Hashem sits in the heavens and distributes food for every living creature. The Rashbam (ibid.) says that's the "*davar gadol*— greatest thing of all." The Rashbam is telling us that the phenomenon of Hashem providing food for all living creatures is so important that it's the *davar gadol*. And that's why this chapter is called *Hallel Hagadol*. The *davar gadol* that we see most prevalent in this world is the food that Hashem is feeding everybody. That's why, after a long list of *chasdei Hashem*, the last one — the grand finale, the pinnacle of all of the *chasdei Hashem* — is that Hashem is feeding the world!

That leaves us with a glaring question: What is the purpose of all this? Why is so much going on in this world, all for the purpose of food? Such a wondrous and remarkable production — for what purpose did Hashem do this? And why is it called the *davar gadol*, the most important of all the *chasdei Hashem*?

We find an answer to this question in Chazal (*Chullin* 4b). They tell us that the most effective way to persuade a person is not with words, but with food and drink. Rashi explains that since we live in a world of *gashmiyus*, a physical world, the way to a person's heart is through good food. When you want to make that big sale to an important customer, take him out to a good restaurant. Of course, you'll be talking about how your prices can't be matched, about the quality of your goods, about how the deal you're offering him is a no-brainer, but you still need to put that good steak in front of him to convince him to close the deal.

Now we can understand why Hashem gives us food. We thought that it's merely because we have to live. But no, that's not the real purpose. Nourishment could have been tasteless, colorless, and without aroma. Hashem could have made food with all the materials needed to regenerate your worn-out tissues without taste and without color. And you'd enjoy it as much as you enjoy the gasoline you put into your car. You'd chew them anyhow, because you have to refuel. But instead, Hashem gave you apples that are red, or golden delicious, with all different types of flavors and sweet aromas.

But who needs apples at all? Hashem could have given us white pills without taste. With no other option, we'd swallow white pills. And we'd have been happy to ingest the life-giving materials that would supply us with energy. It would keep us going. Like vitamins — they don't have taste. Sometimes they're bitter. But we'd eat them because we would have to.

Instead He gives us "pills" that taste good. He feeds us "*b'tuvo, b'chein, b'chessed uv'rachamim* — in His goodness, kindliness, grace, and mercy" (Birkas Hamazon). Hashem made eating into a considerable pleasure by bestowing on our food a wide variety of tastes, colors, and aromas. The large variety of fruits, each in various flavors and shades of color; the varieties of poultry and fish and meat; varieties of grains and vegetables and fruit; and various spices and condiments—what's it all for? Why is there so much variety of foods and tastes? The Gemara is teaching us the reason: Hashem is trying to persuade us. He is doing His best to persuade us to perfect ourselves in awareness of His kindliness, of the *chessed* He's doing for us, so that we should tangibly feel His *chessed* all day long and fall in love with Him. All day long, Hashem is trying to seduce you with the endless variety of good, tasty foods. So after every meal, you should be a different person. You should feel an even greater love and appreciation of Hashem, Who just took you out for supper!

That's the real reason this world is a food-making machine—so that we should rejoice in this endless variety and appreciate the infinite kindness of Hashem. It's all for the purpose of inducing us to love Him. That's the reason we're eating and enjoying these things! And that's what we say in Birkas Hamazon, *Ba'avur shemo hagadol*, "for the sake of His great name," so that we should appreciate what He's giving us and feel an actual love, a tangible love. When you eat for the purpose of His great name, even though you're eating it with joy—it's fun eating *kneidlach*—you're becoming a new person, because besides the extra weight you put on, you're also putting something into your mind.

The function of eating is very important in gaining a knowledge and love of Hashem. The person who eats like an *eved Hashem* is supposed to make *brachos* like an *eved Hashem*, so he comes closer and closer to Hashem all the days of his life and achieves the perfection that he came to this world for.

"*Nosein lechem l'chol basar ki l'olam chasdo*—He gives bread to all flesh because His kindness is forever." That's the climax. It's called *Hallel Hagadol* because Hashem distributes food to every creature and does so constantly without end. The supply keeps on coming. It's not merely the volume of the food. It's the volume of the *chessed* that Hashem is doing. He could have given a person an apple a day. You wouldn't be robust, but you wouldn't drop dead, either. Yet Hashem gives a lot of things besides apples. He gives so much that it's called *Hallel Hagadol*, the great praise.

With this in mind, we go back to the *brachah* of *Bareich Aleinu*. In the olden days, the first day that a child went to *cheder*, they used to put a *tallis* on him and give him candy or cake. The candy and cake were only to persuade him to understand that *cheder* is much better than that. So, too, Hashem gives us all the sweets of this world so that we should recognize His great name. That's the purpose of all the *gashmiyus* in this world — to recognize the greatness of the *chessed* Hashem.

Q In *Bareich Aleinu*, why is the emphasis on "us"?

"*Bareich aleinu, Hashem Elokeinu, es hashanah hazos* — Hashem, our G-d, bless upon us this year." Why do we say "*aleinu*"? And why do we add Hashem "*Elokeinu*, our G-d," which we don't say in most *brachos*? Why the emphasis on "us" and "our"?

And the answer is that the prosperity of the year depends on the activation of all the forces of Nature and on the arrangement of many circumstances. We need the sunlight, rain, wind, proper soil quality, protection against parasites, and more. Since there are so many circumstances of a general nature, it's not only the Am Yisrael who's going to benefit from this arrangement, but the entire world. When Hashem bestows *parnassah* in abundance upon the world, all the nations benefit.

The question then arises — if Hashem judges the world in general to see if it deserves to have a year of *brachah*, a year of abundance, shouldn't it be decided after the merit of the majority of people? But if the gift of abundance to the world depended on the merit of the *umos ha'olam*, we would be left out of *parnassah*, because many of the nations are unworthy. Therefore, we say to Hashem, "*Bareich aleinu* — bless *us*." Bless us for *parnassah independently* of them. Disregard whether the world deserves it or not. Give it to *us* in any case. We are Your people.

Hashem has a special estate in the world—His people. We're His "*nachalah*," His estate, as it says many times in the *kisvei hakodesh*. Therefore, we beg Him, for the sake of His *nachalah*, even if the rest of the nations are undeserving. That's why we say "*Bareich aleinu*."

Of course, once it comes down to us, all the nations are going to benefit, as it states, "Because of you all the peoples of the world will benefit and be blessed" (*Bereishis* 12:3). When Hashem showers abundance on the world, it's because of the Am Yisrael. When it rains, it rains for everybody. When there's abundance, everybody has plenty to eat. Through the Am Yisrael all the nations of the world will benefit.

Now, the nations don't realize this. But in the future, when Hashem will redeem His people, we'll be recognized as the bearers of the truth. Then all mankind will be happy, too. They'll be full of joy. It will be a great new period, an era of happiness. Not everybody will be worthy of that. Some nations won't continue to exist when the great Day of Judgment comes. Not everybody will participate. Only those nations that are innocent and have nothing on their record that deserves destruction will continue to exist. Of course, the Am Yisrael will be the aristocracy, as the *navi* says, "You'll be called the *kohanim* of Hashem" (*Yeshayah* 61:6). The nations will be like laymen, but they'll be happy to help out in that great period of happiness. Therefore, when we say *Bareich aleinu*, we actually mean, "bless *because of* us." It's a *brachah* for the rest of mankind, too.

Then we add, "*Hashem Elokeinu*—Hashem our G-d." Sometimes asking for our sake isn't enough. The truth is that it's never enough to ask for our sake. Who says we're worthy? Hashem doesn't owe us anything. So we say *Hashem Elokeinu*—it's because of *You* we're asking. It's for Your sake, not ours. "You are the One Who feeds and supplies everyone" (Birkas Hamazon), because "You love to do kindliness" (*Michah* 7:18). It's a *chessed* You do, not based on our merits. No matter how much we do—and we should do everything we can to deserve merit—it's never enough to pay for all the bounty Hashem gives us.

Q Why do we add details to our request for *parnassah*?

Why do we add, "*kol minei svu'asah*—all the species of its produce"? The answer is that when Hashem grants us our *parnassah*, we need to acknowledge all the details.

Let's say you're a wealthy man and you married off your son or daughter and gave them a nice home as a *chasunah* gift. And not merely bare walls. You put in furniture, too. And you stocked the kitchen with all kinds of dishes and utensils. It's a house in move-in condition. So your son or daughter says, "thank you," and moves in.

Is that the way to say, "thank you"? Oh, no—they should enumerate every detail. They have to thank you for the rugs. Not just for rugs in general, but for the rug in the dining room and the rug in the hall. Each one cost a lot of money. Even if you didn't provide a rug, linoleum also costs money. They have to thank you for the dishes—for the *milchig* dishes and the *fleishig* dishes. They have to thank you for the cutlery. They have to thank you for everything separately.

Some people never express gratitude. They don't even say, "thank you." If they feel compelled to say a weak "thank you," they think they're *yotzei*, that they've fulfilled their obligation. They say, "*Baruch Atah, Hashem, mevareich hashanim*"—and now, don't bother us anymore. We did our obligation. But no, we have to thank Hashem for "*kol minei svu'asah*—*all* the species of produce."

You have to thank Hashem for cherries, for strawberries, for pineapples, for bananas, for peaches, for everything. You have to thank Him for rye, for barley, for oats, and for spelt. Every separate species. When you thank Hashem for apples, it's not enough to say apples in general. You must thank Him for Winesap apples, golden delicious apples, and Cortland apples. You're eating all of them, right? You don't eat only one species. If you're eating all of them, you must thank Hashem for all of them.

That's not a joke—it's an obligation. Of course, when you say this *brachah*, you can't think of everything. Otherwise the *shamash* will lock up the shul with you inside. But at least once in every *brachah*, think of one thing specific. Today think of Winesap apples. Tomorrow think of Cortland apples. The next day think of red delicious apples. The next day yellow delicious apples. Next think of New Zealand apples—also very good apples, by the way. If you like Granny Smith apples, thank Hashem for them, too.

And that's why we say in the winter, "*V'sein tal umatar livrachah al p'nei ha'adamah*—Give a blessing upon the face of the earth."

Because the more we specify the various kinds of produce, the more we appreciate the gift. Not like the son who walks into the house and says to his father a plain "thank you." No, we're going to speak about every detail. When Hashem gives a blessing, you have to talk about it.

When you walk in the street and see soil in the gardens, you're looking at one of the most valuable resources in the universe. Soil isn't simple, not at all. It's more valuable than gold, than diamonds. Nothing can equal the dirt. The soil, the face of the Earth, is invaluable. The Earth's surface is very thin compared to the thickness of the entire planet. Imagine a big dictionary six feet high, and let's say it has a hundred thousand pages. Proportionally, the top page of that dictionary is thicker than the surface of the Earth in proportion to the Earth itself. That's how thin is the surface on which we live. Yet it possesses the ability to maintain all life on this surface. That's the *p'nei ha'adamah*. It's remarkable. Therefore, we have to appreciate that. One of the greatest gifts that Hashem gave us is soil. You don't find soil anywhere except on this Earth. Don't listen to the fairy tales they tell you that maybe out in space there is soil like this. No. This soil—and only this soil—is alive. First, it has microscopic plants (fungi) and tiny animals (bacteria). There are more living organisms in one spoonful of earth than there are people in greater New York. The earth has the ability to take chemicals out of the air with sunlight and transform them into food, clothing, houses, furniture—and people.

Not only can this wondrous substance use materials for the maintenance of life, but it can recycle everything, too. In the end, everything goes back to the earth. The leaves that fall are broken down into reusable components. A little bit of the leaves become earth and the rest becomes water vapor, carbon dioxide, and other things that go into the atmosphere and are ready to begin the cycle again. Bodies of animals decompose in the same way. What we eat was once bodies of animals that lived and walked on the Earth and have since been reconstituted and recycled by the earth.

Soil is a wonderful machinery. So when we say, *p'nei ha'adamah*, we have to appreciate what Hashem did. Then, in winter we say "*v'sein tal umatar*" because it's not enough to merely speak in general. *Tal*, the dew, accomplishes things that the rain doesn't accomplish. Sometimes the dew can cause things to grow more fortuitously, more successfully.

Hashem gives us this great variety for this purpose. There's plenty to think about and thank about. Think of something different every day. And not only the fruits, but also the things that help the food go down, like ketchup, mayonnaise, mustard, horseradish, onions, and garlic — all the things that make life happier for you. Whatever it is, you're obligated to think about it.

That's called *avodas Hashem*. *Avodas Hashem* means thanking Hashem. *Tefillah* is called, "*avodah sheb'leiv* — service of the heart" (*Ta'anis* 2a). But you must thank Him with your mouth, too.

Q **Why do we add "*l'tovah*, for good"?**

Let's say things grow well but you don't have the money to buy them. Crops are excellent but they're expensive. Or sometimes there's plenty of food but you can't eat because you have sensitive teeth, an abscess, and you can't chew anything hard. Some people have no teeth. All they can do is eat puree. We need *parnassah* that helps us; you need "*l'tovah*." We want to enjoy these things. So we're asking Hashem to make all those things available for us in such a way that we benefit.

Some people are allergic to particular foods. Some can't drink milk. Some are allergic to wheat. If you're not, you're a lucky fellow! So ask Hashem to let it continue. Sometimes there's a change to a person's metabolism. Until a certain age he didn't have allergies, but now something happened and he has to stop eating certain foods. Isn't that a pity? Therefore we ask Hashem that all the abundance He created and put before us like a set table should be "*l'tovah.*" We should be able to use it and enjoy it in the very best manner.

Q The Rav has said that prosperity can ruin a person, so why do we *daven* for it every day?

We *daven* every day that rain, the source of prosperity, should come down "*livrachah*—for a blessing." If the rain came down in too much abundance, it would not be for *brachah*. It would ruin the crops. There's even a special *tefillah* for when it rains too much. Farmers used to say *tefillos* when there was too much rain.

When we say "*livrachah*," we're asking Hashem to help us utilize our prosperity as a *brachah*, not necessarily to give us prosperity. Sometimes when people have abundance, they fall into the category of "*Vayishman Yeshurun vayivat*—Because they were satiated and became fat, they rebelled" (*Devarim* 32:15). That's what happened in America. Why is American being ruined? Because there's too much abundance. When a boy goes out of the house in the morning to yeshiva stuffed with food—holding an ice cream in one hand and a chocolate bar in the other—he's starting out on the wrong foot. "*V'achalta v'savata... hishamru lachem pen yifteh l'vavchem*—You will eat and be satisfied...watch out or your heart will become foolish" (*Devarim* 11:16). The Torah constantly warns us against eating all that we want because it's going to cause rebellion in the heart. We don't realize how dangerous that is.

"*Ein ari noheh mitoch kupah shel teven ela mitoch kupah shel basar*—A lion roars not when he's given a basket of hay, but when he's given a basket of meat" (*Brachos* 32a). A lion roars when he's arrogant, not when he has to eat hay. He roars when you give him a basket of meat. All over America today, you hear the roar of the *meshuga'im*, of the youth in the colleges and high schools. They're going crazy looking for things to do, for thrills. They're ruining their lives and other people's lives because they have too much, because of all the abundance and idle time.

That's why we ask that the rain should be "*livrachah*." We want prosperity, but we ask Hashem to please help us use it properly.

Along the same lines we say, "*v'sabeinu mituvah*—and satiate us from the goodness." Actually, there are two versions. The other version is "*sabeinu mituvecha*—satiate us from Your goodness." We're reminding ourselves that all this goodness is from You, Hashem. The other version, "*mituvah*," means from the goodness of the earth that You gave.

Either way, food alone doesn't satiate. "*Ki lo al halechem l'vado yichyeh ha'adam*—A man doesn't live just because of food" (*Devarim* 8:3). Why is it that when you put food in your mouth it helps you? It shouldn't help you at all. Suppose you'd make a cut in one of your blood vessels and start pouring in milk. You wouldn't live long. In a few minutes you'd be finished. But when you put food in your mouth, something amazing happens. It's changed into tens of thousands of different materials that are transported by the blood to various destinations. At each stop, the blood leaves exactly what's necessary for that limb, for that organ. Where you need calcium, it leaves calcium. Where you need something else, it leaves something else. It doesn't make any mistakes, not like the delivery services. It's accurate.

So we ask Hashem, "*sabeinu mituvecha*—satiate us from Your goodness" because many times people have houses full of everything and it's not beneficial to them. Rockefeller was one of the richest people ever, but he had to eat crackers and milk. When a butler came along and asked, "What will you have this morning, sir?" he replied, "Crackers and milk." His wealth didn't help him.

"*Sabeinu*," we ask Hashem. "Satiate us. Let us have enjoyment and benefit from what You're giving us. No matter what it is, how much or how little. Of course we'd like much, but whatever You give us, may it satiate us."

Q **Why do we ask Hashem to bless us "like the good years"?**

We want to get a feeling for what we're asking for. Remember when there was a big bumper crop back in such-and-such a year? We want it now like that year.

But that's not enough—we want *parnassah* like the years long ago in Eretz Yisrael, when they needed eight people to carry an "*eshkol anavim*—a cluster of grapes." That's what we want. Why not ask for that? As it says, "*Harchev picha va'amaleihu*—Open up your mouth and I will fill it" (*Tehillim* 81:11). You have to ask for it.

The Gemara interprets this *passuk* differently: "*Hahu b'divrei Torah k'siv*—It refers to *divrei Torah*" (*Brachos* 50a). However, if you open your mouth properly, Hashem will not only put Torah into it, He'll put other good things in as well. Therefore, we ask Him for the good years, for the years of happiness in the ancient times.

PRACTICAL ADVICE

Q What practical advice can the Rav offer for being enthusiastic about an everyday "miracle" such as food?

There was a *minhag* in Yerushalayim. I don't know if they do it there today, but in the olden days there was a *minhag* that *chachamim* came together the night of Chamishah Asar B'Shvat and ate *peiros*. But eating is only a superficial act meant to awaken the mind to thinking thoughts of Hashem. Because that's what fruits are for—to remind you about Hashem.

The Gemara (*Brachos* 44a) says that Rabbi Yochanan and Reish Lakish used to go out to Ginosar and eat *peiros*. They ate so much that they almost fainted. Rabbi Yochanan ate so much that his forehead became slippery. If a fly tried to land on his forehead, it slipped off. Reish Lakish, it says there, ate so much that he became almost drunk with happiness. Maybe it was from the grapes. Whatever it was, he was wild with thoughts of the *chessed Hashem*. He was so wild that Rabbi Yochanan had to ask the Nasi to send policemen to take Reish Lakish home!

Now, we're talking about great men here. The Gemara is telling us something. We have to know that *peiros*, fruits, are one of the wonderful creations of *emunah.* "*V'nechmad ha'eitz l'haskil*—Fruit is desirable because it brings wisdom" (*Bereishis* 3:6). Look at a beautiful orange or apple. Why is it colored so? Is it an accident? It wasn't beautiful when the fruit was still green, when it was sour and unripe. Only when it became fit to eat did it turn into a beautiful yellow or a beautiful red. Doesn't that say something?! The fruit is a demonstration of the *chessed Hashem.*

Tosfos (*Brachos* 37a) explains the *brachah* of "*Borei nefashos rabos v'chesronan*—Hashem made many different creatures and supplied them with all of their needs." In addition to that, we thank Hashem, "*al kol mah shebarasa l'hachayos bahem nefesh kol chai*—for all that He has created to enliven the spirit of every living thing." This means that He also provided luxuries. Besides the things we need, He also gave us things just to give us pleasure. What luxuries? *Tosfos* says, "Apples, for example." You could get along without apples. Apples are like a dessert. They're an extra *chessed.*

Now, the truth is that everything is *chessed.* The piece of bread is also *chessed,* but apples are an added *chessed.* Hashem isn't merely satisfied that you shouldn't go hungry. Let's say a guest came to your house to eat. Would you just give him a big mountain of bread? No, you'd give him something to add to the bread, maybe butter or jam. And maybe eggs and orange juice. Whatever it is, you'd give him something else, not just bread. And since you have a good heart, after the meal you'd give him some dessert, too. That shows that you're a real *ba'al chessed.* So, too, Hashem gives us fruit. He's giving us desserts all the time.

When you pass a fruit stand, don't walk by like a horse walks by. Take a look! Those delectable fruits are resplendent testaments to the *nifla'os haBorei,* the wonders of Hashem. A fruit is a miracle! Every fruit has a skin that protects it, that keeps it fresh for some time. And when you finish eating the delicious content of the fruit, you find a coupon that entitles you to another package—the seed! The inside of that seed is remarkable! It contains more information than the most sophisticated computer!

Fruits are a wonderful opportunity to gain *emunah* and *ahavas Hashem*. That's how to eat fruit on *Chamishah Asar B'Shvat.* And that's how you should be eating fruit all year long as well.

Q **Does everybody have to work?**

"You should eat bread by the sweat of your brow" (*Bereishis* 3:19). Now, some people who learn Chumash think it was just Hashem telling Adam something, some vague statement about the sweat of the brow. But He's talking to all of Adam's descendants. "You want to eat bread? You'd better work for it." Which means everyone should be prepared to work in this world. Whether he's a businessman or a baker—whatever it is, he has to work for his bread. It could be that you work with your head. A *melamed* is also working. It's not easy work. The boys don't always listen. A *kollel* man must also work hard. In the *kollel,* you also have to work by the sweat of your brow. Whatever it is, wherever you are, it means you have to be busy working.

From the beginning, the Torah is constantly reiterating "*Elokim* made this [*vaya'as*]." It's a world of "doing." "*Hayom la'asosam*—today to do them (*Devarim* 7:11). It's a doing world. You'll tell me that the Gemara interprets "to do" as *mitzvos* (*Eruvin* 22a). No question. Absolutely, you have to do *mitzvos*. And one of the *mitzvos* is, "Six days a week you should be doing" (*Shemos* 20:9). It's not giving you "permission" to work. It's not saying that for six days you're *allowed* to work. It means, six days you *should* work. You have to hustle to make a living.

That doesn't mean you have to stay overtime. It doesn't mean you have to take extra jobs. It doesn't mean you have to stay up until late at night and get an ulcer, *chalilah*, and risk your life. But you have to work! And it's not supposed to be easy. "By the sweat of your brow" will you make a living.

Don't think that it's merely a *gezeirah min haShamayim*, a punishment. No! It's advice for healthy living! The human being is so constructed that he must keep busy. For your mind to be healthy, you have to be busy. You must be accomplishing something. It's like breathing air. You have to breathe air to live. Hashem put into our *teva*, into our nature, that just as we need air, we need work. To be healthy, to live long, you must be a working person.

Now, I know that some people think they can get by without following this Torah advice, but trust me—there will always be side effects. You ignore Torah advice at your own peril. It could be that you'll be able to loaf all your life, but one day you're going to look back and see how much distress and how many troubles that caused. The Gemara (*Kesubos* 59b) says, "*Habatalah meviah lidei shiamum*—Idleness leads to insanity." Not always do you go stark raving mad. You don't necessarily become a maniac, but it brings you to a depression, a sickness of the mind.

Q **Does one get *s'char* (reward) for working?**

I'll explain that on two levels. Hashem rewards those who do things in the proper way, even though they don't do it *l'shem Shamayim*. So you must work. It's like eating. Hashem rewards those who eat. If you won't eat, then you won't be able to live. If you eat, you are rewarded that you live, even though you didn't eat *l'shem Shamayim*. However, if you eat *l'shem Shamayim*, you get more reward. You sit down at breakfast and say, "I am now going to eat in order to have strength to serve my Creator." Is that hard to do? Try it tomorrow morning. It's a whole *siman* in *Shulchan Aruch, Orach Chaim*. I'm now going to eat in order to have strength to serve my Creator. That's certainly even greater.

Therefore, you get reward for working. If you go to work like a decent person—you don't say, "I'm sick," or "I'm too nervous to work," "Let my wife support me..." You have to work. Let your wife stay home. There's plenty to do at home. She has to bake bread; she has to take care of the children. You go to work!

A man once told me that he'd like to stop working and go into a *kollel.* I said, "Go away every Sunday from home and go into a *kollel.* Every Sunday, pack up a lunch and sit in the *kollel* all day long." He never did it. It showed that he didn't want to sit in *kollel.* He just wanted to stop working.

A man who doesn't work becomes sick. He becomes a nervous wreck. He becomes mentally disturbed ("Idleness leads to mental disturbance"—*Kesubos* 59b). "*Gedolah melachah*—How great is work!" (*Nedarim* 49b) Work keeps you alive. It makes you healthy. It makes you mentally well! It's a big tragedy that people don't work as much as they once used to. Once upon a time, people worked all the time, except Shabbos. When Shabbos came, they were weary, and they appreciated the rest. All week long, they had no time for mischief! They worked from early morning until late at night. And it was a blessing! Work is a blessing!

"*Gedolah melachah*—How great is work!" In many ways it's great. *Shemechabedes es ba'aleha*—it makes you respectable (ibid.). You don't have to go beg. You have your own income.

Another *ma'amar*— *Gedolah melachah shemechamemes es ba'aleha*—Work warms you up (*Gittin* 67b). You get exercise when you work. Working keeps you healthy.

There are other benefits of work. Certainly you must work. Even though you don't work *l'shem Shamayim* you'll get reward, no question about it. But when a person works *l'shem Shamayim*, and he has that in mind, how much greater is his reward. After all, he was *mekabel kinyan* on the *kesubah* when he married his wife, and he obligated himself to support her. And he has children to support. He's raising up *ovdei Hashem*—*frum* boys and girls. He has to pay *s'char limud.* He has to feed them. He has to emulate Hashem Who feeds every living thing— *nosein lechem l'chol basar.* He also wants to feed his children like a messenger of Hashem. And when he does it *l'shem Shamayim*, there's no question that this man gets even more reward.

Q How should one curb his desire and the desire of his family to always "keep up with the Joneses"?

Let him listen to these tapes. Play the tapes of these lectures in your home, to your family. It's of the greatest importance to create an atmosphere of independence in your family. We don't follow the crowd! It's very important.

Here's a man who is in dire straits financially. He's on the verge of bankruptcy. But he has to marry off a child. And it costs $50,000. He can't help himself because his wife is pressing him, "How can we have less? We'll be ashamed to face our friends. How can we not have this or that?" This man thinks that he's a prisoner of circumstance, so he goes even more deeply into debt. He borrows to make an expensive wedding.

But who cares what the relatives say?! You can make a wedding even without a smorgasbord. Oh, of course, it's *apikorsus* to say such a thing. But what if you were a German Jew? German Jews don't make a smorgasbord. Therefore, you have a good model to follow.

In every aspect of life, we have to learn to be independent—independent of the foolish pressures from outside the home, because we're constantly pressured to spend money, to keep up with relatives, and with friends. You're running on a treadmill. You're a prisoner of foolishness, of false ideals. You're laboring and spending your substance for something that Hashem never required you to do. That's called wasting. You won't get reward for it—in this world or the next world. You won't get reward for keeping up with the so-called Joneses, or the Levys, either.

Q Does striving to be successful and comfortable detract from Torah and *yiras Shamayim*?

Now we come to a subject that has to be explained. How foolish are people who don't understand how to harmonize Olam Hazeh with *ruchniyus*, with spiritual things! To succeed as a decent Jew, you must have a decent level of *gashmiyus*. A Jew must have a profession. Now, that doesn't mean you have to be a medical doctor, but you have to have some way of making a living. Just to be a *shlep,* a failure, is no way to succeed as a Jew.

Now, if you're a man who can succeed in learning—if you're capable of learning all day long—it's possible you'll find some people who will support you. There are *kollelim* where you can go. But most people don't do that. Therefore, you must live a normal life and learn a trade. You must learn some calling. You must have a home and a wife. You must earn your own way. You cannot live on welfare. Anybody who lives on welfare is a flop, a failure, and his life is ruined, too. Even his *ruchniyus* is ruined.

Let's not deceive ourselves. The Gemara says that a man must teach his son an *umnus,* a profession (*Kiddushin* 30b). "See life with a woman you love" (*Koheles* 9:9). The Gemara says "a woman you love" means the Torah. The Torah is the woman you love. The Jewish nation loves the Torah. But it says that you must "see life with the Torah." It means learn an *umnus.* That's what the Gemara says. You need to learn some kind of livelihood.

Again and again we've seen tragedies of people who neglected to learn a livelihood. There's a man in Crown Heights whose wife is an idealist—she's a *giyoress,* a *ger tzedek,* a big idealist. And she tells me she met this Jewish young man. She made him *frum.* She loves him, she tells me. So I asked her, "What's he doing?"

"He's a writer," she tells me.

"Has he published something?"

"No."

"What does he do?"

"He lies in bed all day long."

I said, "A man like that—why doesn't he do something?"

"Oh," she says. "He's a great idealist. He's thinking up plans. He's drawing up plans for some great work."

Well, a little time passed by, and the next I heard she had left home with three little children because he was beating her up—this "great idealist" was beating her. That's the ruin of an idealistic marriage — a *giyoress*, a righteous convert. She was an idealist, and she was beaten up by this bum, this writer, because he never learned a *parnassah*.

There are a lot of people like that, ruined people. You can't live in a cellar. You have to live in a decent home. Only I must put in a word of warning — you shouldn't put all your efforts into beautifying your home. But you must have a fitting frame for the right kind of a picture. You must make a living. You must guard your health. You can't neglect your health and just be a *shlepper* who is run down in health. You need fresh air, you need exercise, and you need the right diet.

Now, this is a subject that deserves a lecture by itself. I don't have time for it now. I just want to sum up. To live a decent Torah life, you must have a proper and decent material life. The two go together. And that's the *retzon Hashem*, and it can be proven by many statements in the Torah.

Should I try to get a job that involves *chessed* — like a grocer or baker, who is involved in feeding the Jewish nation — rather than another job where no *chessed* is involved?

You should get a job that pays the most money. That's your job — to earn money. You'll be doing the biggest *chessed* by bringing home a decent paycheck for your family.

Now, if you happen to be a baker or a grocer, it's not a bad idea that when you hand the bread over to the customer you think, "*Nosein lechem l'chol basar ki l'olam chasdo* — He gives bread to all flesh, for His kindness is forever" (*Tehillim* 136:25). Nothing wrong. Nothing wrong at all. You're a *shliach*, a messenger of Hashem, feeding His people. Nothing wrong with thinking that. On the contrary, why not utilize the opportunity? You can achieve greatness if you apply your mind and use your thoughts in the right way.

A mother who is serving food at the table should think that she is doing it as a *shliach* of Hashem. If she thinks that way, it will transform her actions. All of us, men and women, must train ourselves to transform the actions that we are already doing by putting the right thoughts into them.

Make sure to get a job that pays the most money, and while you're working in that place, use whatever opportunities you can find to think about Hashem and to become great. You don't have to be a baker or a butcher or a grocer to serve Hashem at work. The opportunities for greatness are endless at any job you have, but of course it will take some effort on your part.

Q Does the Rav recommend reading Dale Carnegie's books?

Some people might not know who Dale Carnegie is. He is a man who wrote a few books with advice on succeeding in life. For example, *How to Win Friends and Influence People* is a very good book to help you learn basic skills in getting along with people.

Now, just as you're going to read a book that tells you how to be a success with computers or accounting or anything else you have to do, you also have to read some books about how to succeed. In *How to Win Friends*, Carnegie tells you how to be a success in dealing with customers and dealing with people in general. Very practical advice. And I can tell you that there is no harm at all in reading those books. His book on public speaking will help you be a successful speaker and his books will help you succeed in general. No harm at all.

Now, that doesn't mean that you'll get *shleimus* or Olam Haba from reading his books. It's like anybody who works hard to make a living. It doesn't mean you'll get Olam Haba for being a successful businessman. But it's something you must do to support your family.

Therefore, if a person wants to benefit from expert advice in learning how to deal with people and with customers, there is no reason that he shouldn't read Dale Carnegie's books. In general, for the practice of dealing with customers and dealing with people in general, he has good advice.

Q What should a man do when he loses his job?

The very first thing is to look for another job. That's number one because nobody should be idle. Idleness causes illness (*Kesubos* 59b). Therefore, even if you haven't found a new job yet, you must find something to do. Now, if somebody is capable of utilizing his time properly, then idleness is a very great blessing. He's being given a sabbatical by Hashem, so he can retire for a little while and learn a *masechta* or learn *sefarim* until he regains his job. But most people are not capable of utilizing idleness and as a result they contract illnesses.

It's very important to be busy. In case you don't know what to do, do *mitzvos*. There are plenty of good things to do in this world, plenty of *mitzvos* to keep you busy. But the main idea to keep in mind is that a person should not be idle! He should always have something to do, even if just for the sake of his own health.

Q What should we be thinking about when we hear the stock market has reached an all-time high?

Well, you should be thinking that the market prices are very high right now, but it's very possible for them to fall and become very low again. Many people have been ruined by the stock market. Therefore, I would say to put your money in the bank, in a savings account. And *daven*. Always be *mispallel*.

I want to tell you something. One of the most important reasons the stock market fluctuates is just for that — so that you should call out to Hashem. When it's high, you should be calling out to Him in gratitude. When it's low, you should be calling out to Him that it should go up. If you don't, the whole experience was a waste. Even if you made a lot of money, you wasted a valuable opportunity. And if you lost money, *chas v'shalom*, but you were forced to *daven*, then you gained. You gained *da'as Hashem*, awareness of Hashem, which is more important than all the money in the world.

Who knows what can happen?! I know a man who has been losing tremendous sums in the stock market. He told me that he lost over $300,000 so far. So I said to him, "What about stopping maybe?" He said, "No, I'll get it back. I'll get it back," he said. The poor man is still hoping.

Q Is there anything wrong with buying lottery tickets?

In Europe there were state lotteries, and it wasn't considered wrong to buy a lottery ticket, even for *frum* Jews. However, some Jews go overboard, and that leads to trouble. It's like drinking wine for Kiddush. It's a good thing, but drinking too much wine, or drinking all the time, is not good.

People start hanging around these places and putting all their money into it. You even have fools who think they have perfected the system and know how to win. There are actually fools like that! I know about it because I have to deal with them. I argued with one. His wife called me up and said that all their money is going down the drain in lottery tickets. I spoke to him and he told me he has a system! He's following a system and he's bound to win. Only that it didn't happen yet. It's always right around the corner. A fool!

Let me tell you something. If you buy one lottery ticket and then get busy davening to Hashem that He should help you, there's nothing wrong with that. But don't buy more. Once you get into that intoxication, it's like drinking whiskey. You'll get drunk and you can get lost in it. One is enough. You can do one in ten years, if you want. And each time, be *mispallel*. Ask Hashem to help you. And if it's *bashert*, you'll get it.

Q Should a young man retire at a young age, even if he won't be learning most of the day?

No! Either you retire to learn, or not at all—and even then I don't know if it's always advisable to do it when you're young. But surely if you won't learn all day long, you had better work because, "*Yegias shneihem mashkachas avon*—Working for a *parnassah* while laboring in Torah helps prevent a person from sinning" (*Avos* 2:2). If you have idle time on your hands, you'll be hanging around the house, looking for ways to argue with your wife. You'll stick your nose into the kitchen constantly. No, that's no good.

A man shouldn't be in the house too much. You have to be either in the *beis medrash* or a place of work. That's the healthiest atmosphere.

Q How should the yeshivas today prepare students to earn a living?

That's a very good question because many times there are boys who are not going to become outstanding in the field of teaching Torah. It's important for parents to think about the future of their children because the Gemara says everybody must teach their son an *umnus,* a trade (*Kiddushin* 29a). Now, if I would talk about that in a plain way, many people would criticize me because today it's the style not to think about that at all.

Of course, it's very useful for young people after they're married to continue a yeshiva career. If he can remain in yeshiva for at least one year after marriage, it transforms his family into a *kollel* family. Even though later he goes into *parnassah*, it makes a big difference if he and his wife first lived a *kollel* life at least for a year. If they have enough money to continue longer, *mah tov umah naim* (even better).

However, eventually, every person should look for a *parnassah.* Not *Toraso umnaso*—unless he's capable of being chosen, of being prepared, for some career in Torah. If he can be a *melamed*, why not? If he can be a *rosh yeshiva*, why not? If he can go into *rabbanus*, yes. There are other fields, like *hashgachah*. He can be a *mashgiach*, yes, or other related forms of *parnassah* in *ruchniyus*. But there are some people who are not built for that, and therefore they must make up their minds that when the time comes, they must find a *parnassah*. You must support your family! There's no such thing as being a loafer who hangs around the *batei midrashim*, not fit to do anything. You're not a *melamed*. You're not a *rosh yeshiva*. First of all, many times people who don't support their families have trouble with *shalom bayis*. Many times they become ill, *chas v'shalom*, due to unhappiness. It's a misfortune to live a life where it's not *mesudar* with a regular program of *parnassah*.

Now, there are all kinds of *parnassah*. I'm not going to tell you what to do. But the main point is that everybody must make up his mind. If he's not going to be a *chovesh beis hamedrash*, a person who is successfully learning, then he should choose some *parnassah*.

There are plenty of things to do. This man is in the carpet-laying business. This man is a plumber. This man is a painter. Another man opens a grocery store. There's no end of *parnassah* opportunities. Take the yellow pages, look through all the kinds of professions and trades available, and learn some kind of *parnassah*. It's very important not to loaf and not to be a hopeless person.

Now, some people are capable of learning all their lives, of being *kollel* people all their lives. However, on one condition — that their wives are satisfied with that kind of a life. Otherwise, he should remember he promised in the *kesubah* to support her *k'hilchos guvrin Yehuda'in*, in accordance with the laws of Jewish men. He has to support his wife. He has to take care of the children. He has to support his family. If he sits and learns in the *kollel* and his wife is very unhappy, then he's not fulfilling his promise. If his wife is willing to work all her life or he has other means of support, why not? Many people learned all their lives successfully because they had wives who were dedicated to that.

Otherwise, *parnassah* is a very big *mitzvah,* a big *chiyuv,* and I have seen cases where people neglected this principle and lived lives of unhappiness as a result.

What kind of *parnassah,* I can't tell you. How should the yeshivas prepare their students? I think that if boys in the high school will at least get a high school diploma, they'll know enough later in life to be able to do many things. If you're a very good *ben Torah* and you want to learn instead of going to *limudei chol*—that happens too today. Some don't go to high school at all. That's because they have good heads. They're succeeding in learning. But suppose you're not such a *metzuyan*? I think it's better to finish high school in the yeshiva and be prepared to go out in the world and take some kind of job. There are plenty of jobs available if a person makes up his mind that he wants *parnassah.*

Q **Is it important to save money to leave for my children?**

It's permissible to save for yourself. You have to have money to live on. However, when it comes to saving for your children, it depends. If you can save without sacrificing the purpose of your life, that's all right. Why not? But people who give away the time that they should be devoting for their own betterment—time they should be spending making something out of themselves—but instead give that time toward saving for their children, it's a hundred percent waste. Your first job in this world is to make something of *yourself,* to achieve *shleimus.* When your child comes into the world, he brings along an allowance—it's from heaven. Everybody is born with an allowance. My parents didn't set me up in business. They didn't leave me any money. Yet, *baruch Hashem,* I never had to borrow money my entire life.

Instead of working to save for your children, take off your evenings to study Torah, and give money to charity. Don't try to leave wealth for your children. Of course, if you want to leave them Torah wealth, and it costs money to send them to yeshivas, and to keep your married children in *kollel*—it's an investment for your own self to a certain extent. Whatever you do for them is for you.

But even that, you have to know what and when and how much. Suppose you're capable of sitting in a *kollel* and learning, but your son would like you to keep slaving away so he can learn in *kollel*. You should tell him, "If you wish, if you like this idea so much, you can do it for me. I'll let you slave and support me in *kollel*." Why not? The father has a right to be in *kollel*, too. Sometimes the father has a better head than the son. The Gemara says, "If there's a question as to who should learn, him or his son, he goes first" (*Kiddushin* 29b).

You don't give away your soul for your children. But if you can do it without big sacrifices of your time and you'll be able to make something out of yourself—but at the same time leave a little bit for them—there's nothing wrong with that. Why not?

Q **When should one begin training his children to be enthusiastic for the food Hashem provides us with every day?**

At the earliest age possible! Now, you won't be able to teach them the details of what the words mean. They're too young. But tell them the ideas. For instance, tell your child, "Do you know how good it is to make a *Hamotzi* on a piece of bread? Making a *Hamotzi* is a very big *mitzvah*! You're thanking Hashem for giving you this bread and Hashem is going to pay you back just for thanking Him. It's like money in the bank." Let him know that he's talking to Hashem, that he's not just saying words. Explain it to him on his level. Later, he'll take the thoughts you planted in his head and put them into the words.

How does bread come out of the earth? It's a *neis*. It's more of a *neis* than the *Mann* that fell in the Midbar. At least the *Mann* came down from the sky. But the wheat comes out of the earth! Nobody can really explain it, that large stalks of wheat should grow out of dirt?! It's a *neis!* The *yetzer hara* tells you, "Well, it's the process of photosynthesis and the absorption of nutrients from the dirt by the roots and so on." Do you think that if you use words from the science books and explain the processes it makes it any less of a miracle?! Not at all! Studying those processes teaches you even more how many miracles are needed to make the wheat kernel grow!

But first make sure to teach yourself to appreciate the *Hamotzi*, and then you'll be able to teach your children. You must know *yourself* that food is a tremendous miracle, and then the child will feel it. Don't think that he doesn't understand it. Even little children who seem to ignore what you're saying—it's going into their heads. They'll remember what you said. I still remember what was said to me when I was two years old. [Rav Miller was ninety years old when he gave this answer in 1998!] You'd be surprised. It stays with you. Children don't forget. So start as early as you can. It's not a waste of time.

SUMMARY

- When we ask Hashem for food, it's not a simple request for *gashmiyus*. We're working on acquiring an awareness of the endless miracles that Hashem does for us by providing every creature in this world with the food that it needs, without end.
- The reason Hashem makes us dependent on food is to persuade us to love Him. He demonstrates His love for us with the endless variety of food He provides us, and all their associated pleasures.
- We ask for *parnassah* for the Am Yisrael, because if we asked Hashem to send *brachah* on the world based on the majority (the nations), the world wouldn't merit it. So the nations receive *parnassah* in our merit, through us.
- We also ask Hashem to send *parnassah* for the sake of His great name, because He is the One Who supports the entire world with His kindness. We know we don't really deserve it on our own merit.
- Every time we say this *brachah*, we should have in mind a specific detail to thank Hashem for. Since Hashem provides us with so much

variety, it behooves us to recognize that great kindness by thanking Him in detail.

- We ask Hashem to give us *parnassah* in a way that enables us to enjoy and benefit from it—"*l'tovah.*"
- We ask that Hashem give us *parnassah* "*livrachah,*" that it should satiate us and not cause us to rebel against Him.
- We should ask for *parnassah* without holding back, that it should be as abundant as Eretz Yisrael was fruitful at the time when B'nei Yisrael conquered it.

Teka B'shofar Gadol

Q **Why should we yearn for the Geulah?**

When the Beis Hamikdash was destroyed, it wasn't just one tragedy. It included several. The Beis Hamikdash alone was a tremendous benefit for everyone, even for the nations of the world. And for us especially. It was our heart. Its destruction was one of the causes for our weeping.

But in addition to its destruction, the fact that we were sent into exile was a separate catastrophe. At that time, Hashem exclaimed, "Alas that I destroyed My house *and* dispersed My children among the nations" (*Brachos* 3a). Therefore, among the reasons we yearn for the restoration of the days of old is the desire that the whole Am Yisrael, the entire Jewish nation, should once more be together.

Q **What are the reasons for the *shofar* and the *neis* (banner)?**

First, it states, "*Teka b'shofar gadol l'cheiruseinu*—Blow a great *shofar* for our freedom." The *shofar gadol* tells the nations of the world, "Let My people go!" The time has come to set us free. Eretz Yisrael has to be restored to us. We must be liberated from any pressure — not just political or physical but also ideological pressure.

It's like Yetzias Mitzrayim. First, Hashem told Moshe to go to Pharaoh and say, "My firstborn son is Yisrael" (*Shemos* 4:22). Many of us are bashful to say that, but it's one of the most important teachings of the Torah. We have to gain the proper frame of mind, or we won't be ready for the Redemption. We must understand our function in the world as Hashem's chosen people. We're "*mamleches kohanim* — a nation of *kohanim*" (*Shemos* 19:6). Our function in this world is to serve Hashem. All of us, not just the *kohanim*. And we're a "*goy kadosh* — a holy nation" (ibid.). We must gain that attitude before we're ready for the Redemption. If we don't accept that attitude, how can we expect the gentiles to accept it?

Once the nations get the message that they must liberate the Am Hashem, Hashem turns to the Jewish people and says, "Raise up a banner to gather in our exiles." The banner isn't for the gentiles. It's for the Am Yisrael. Whether we understand the raising of the banner in a figurative or physical sense, there will be some great demonstration that the time has come. We have to get ready for that. We have to make peace with that idea in our minds. You won't always live on Long Island. Make up your mind that you'll have to move out of New Hampshire eventually. That's not your final place.

The banner will be raised like Yirmiyah Hanavi says, "*Se'u neis Tzionah* — Raise up a banner to come to Tzion." Then he adds, "*Ha'izu, al ta'amodu* — Come together; don't delay" (*Yirmiyah* 4:6). When the time comes, you'll have to quickly grab your hat and your coat and run. You're going to have to get rid of your real estate, your holdings, and your furniture. "*Se'u neis Tzionah*" is a test. Don't miss the boat. If you miss it, you might have to stay here. And if you think that's a good thing, you'll discover it's not. "*Ha'izu* — Come together," the *navi* says. "*Al ta'amodu* — don't remain standing." Don't tarry, don't delay.

Now, the nations of the world are not happy about this. They don't want to recognize the Am Hashem as distinguished. They've been fighting against that throughout history. They've been trying to downgrade us, to teach just the opposite of what the Torah — the entire

Tanach—teaches, that we're Hashem's children. That's the second most important teaching in Tanach. The first most important is that Hashem created the world and is in control of the world, but the second is that Hashem chose Klal Yisrael. Open the Chumash and see that Hashem doesn't talk about other nations. There were great nations at that time—Aram, Bavel, Ashur, Mitzrayim. All the nations—even the greatest empires—are now just dim background. Sometimes they're introduced for a moment, but the spotlight of Hashem's attention is "*Ami*—My people" (*Shemos* 3:7,10; 5:1) and "*Banai*—My sons." "*Banim atem laHashem Elokeichem*—You are sons of Hashem" (*Devarim* 14:1). And "*B'ni bechori Yisrael*—Yisrael is My firstborn son" (*Shemos* 4:22). That's the second most important teaching in the Torah.

The world was afraid that this teaching might get a foothold, so they started a massive campaign of denigration, slander, and calumny to belittle the Am Hashem. That's why one of the oldest and biggest forms of literature in world history is anti-Semitism. Two thousand years ago, Josephus records the great abundance of anti-Semitic literature produced by the nations up to his time. He wrote *Contra Apion* against a famous anti-Semite, Apion.[34]

Church writings are filled with it. Anti-Semitism made its way subsequently into European literature. England was full of anti-Semitic books, not to mention Germany, Russia, and everywhere else. In France, anti-Semitic literature filled the libraries at the time of the Dreyfus Affair.[35] Those books didn't go out of existence. When

---

34 Apion was a Greek scholar who lived in the Roman-controlled city of Alexandria. He wrote a book that said Jews drink the blood of non-Jews; that it was a commandment for Jews to cheat non-Jews—all the classic canards and libels, which would find their way into anti-Semitic Christian, Nazi, Islamist, and other writings. In Apion's time, his books and speeches stoked the fire of civil war between Jews and non-Jews in Alexandria, a civil war that would continue on and off for the next century until the Jewish community there would be completely destroyed. Josephus's book, *Contra Apion* ("Against Apion"), debunked the claims of Apion. (See Rav Miller's *Torah Nation* #591.)

35 The Dreyfus Affair centered around the false accusation that Alfred Dreyfus, a Jew, was a traitor, who caused France to lose the Franco-Prussian War in 1871. Only in 1906—twelve years after the initial trial, and many years after two

Hitler came along, he took them out and used them. And they're still there. Open *Roget's Thesaurus*, turn to the word "Jew," and see the synonyms — usurer, cheater, dishonest, and more. There's a new edition of *Roget's Thesaurus* that leaves out these synonyms, but they were there in the original. I have the old one.

In America we're not so aware of it, and it's a great mercy of Hashem that here it's nowhere near what it was like in Europe. But don't deceive yourself that it's disappeared. Anti-Semitism plays a very large role in the world's literature.

Why this tremendous torrent of literature against the Jewish people? What's behind it? The answer is that they could never acknowledge the principle of the election of the Am Yisrael.

Even when the great banner will be unfurled, they'll try to avoid publishing anything about it. The Orthodox papers will mention it, and the time will come when even the mainstream papers will have to mention it, but at the beginning they'll try to ignore it. What will Hashem do? He'll blow the *shofar gadol*. It will be so loud that it will be impossible to ignore it. Seeing is powerful, but hearing is even stronger because you can't close your eyes to sound. To get the point across, Hashem will blast a *shofar*.

What exactly is that *shofar*? I'm not able to tell you. *Shofar* doesn't necessarily mean a horn of an animal. *Shofar* means there'll be a very great blast in such a way that the entire world will be shaken. Whatever it is, it's going to be a sound that will wake up the world. The blast will go around the world and won't stop. It will say, "*Shalach es ami v'ya'avduni* — Let My people go so they can serve Me" (*Shemos* 7:26). The nations will have to take heed. It's a warning blast that *Hashem Elokei Yisrael* is on the march.

When that shofar is blown, all the nations of the world will be frightened into action. The entire world will begin to cooperate in the plan of *l'cheiruseinu* — to give us our full independence. There will be

---

non-Jewish French officers had been exposed as the guilty parties — did a commission of French army officers exonerate Dreyfus.

great conferences the world over, and the nations will come together to see what can be done to help facilitate the reestablishment of the Am Yisrael as a nation on its own land. It will be a big job. Entire communities will have to be transplanted to Eretz Yisrael. And you must have *parnassah* in Eretz Yisrael, too. In Mashiach's time, you still have to make a living. "The world will follow its accustomed nature" (Rambam, *Melachim* 12:1). We'll need homes, too. It will be complicated, but it's all included in the word "*V'kabtzeinu*—Gather us." It's a big request!

Q **Why isn't the *"shofar gadol"* intended for us?**

We don't need the *shofar gadol* to wake us up. A Jew has to have in his heart a desire to return. As the *navi* says, "*Simchu es Yerushalayim v'gilu bah kol ohaveha*—Rejoice in Yerushalayim and have happiness in it, all you who love it" (*Yeshayah* 66:10). You must love Yerushalayim. That's why it's important now in exile—while you're dwelling among the nations—to learn to love Yerushalayim. Make up your mind now that you love it. Otherwise you won't qualify to come back to Eretz Yisrael. You have to prepare that love right now. You have to learn what Yerushalayim means—what it meant to have ancient Yerushalayim.

What a glorious existence it was to walk down the streets of Yerushalayim in the days of Rav Yochanan ben Zakai, in the days of Hillel, in the days of Shmayah and Avtalyon, in the days of Shimon ben Shetach, in the days of Shimon Hatzaddik. To walk in the streets of Yerushalayim meant breathing the air of *kedushah.* There it was possible to fulfill your life's purpose—to develop your character, to understand your place in the world, to gain the insight the Torah wants you to have. We have no idea of the happiness of the ancient Jew in Yerushalayim. It could be that some people became accustomed to it and didn't appreciate it, but when they lost it, they looked back and saw what they had. The happiness of living a truly Jewish life is the greatest fulfillment of the yearning of the soul. That's what our *neshamah* wants.

In exile, we try substitutes. If you have a yearning, you go to a park, to a restaurant. Some people go to the movies, *l'havdil, chalilah*. But you'll never fulfill that yearning with substitutes. There's only one thing a person wants, "*Yismach leiv mevakshei Hashem*—Those who seek Hashem are happy" (*Tehillim* 105:3). That's what we really want in this world—to get as close to Hashem as possible.

That's why we have to study now and gain that love for Yerushalayim. Don't just say the words. Think about what you're saying when you're saying, "*V'lirushalayim ircha b'rachamim tashuv*—And to Jerusalem Your city with mercy You will return" (Shemoneh Esrei). Spend time on that. Talk about it with the greatest yearning. Ah, Hashem! Restore us to our ancient Yerushalayim!

"*Sisu itah mesos, kol hamisablim aleha*—Rejoice with her, all who are mourning over her" (*Yeshayah* 66:10). Who's going to rejoice with Yerushalayim? Those who mourned for her. You have to mourn for Yerushalayim. Not only on Tisha B'Av but all year round. On Tisha B'Av, you have to sit on the ground and shed tears. Shed tears out of pity for yourself, pity that you're deprived of that greatness you could have had if you had Yerushalayim. Our forefathers mourned every night for Yerushalayim. Many people got up late at night, washed their hands, sat on the ground, said *Tikkun Chatzos*, and mourned for the *churban Yerushalayim*.

The Lelover Rebbe was a famous *tzaddik* as a little child already. They asked his mother how she merited to give birth to such a *tzaddik*. Did his father [who had passed away] have any special *middos tovos, middos chassidus*, special practices? She couldn't remember anything except that when he used to say the *brachah* for Yerushalayim in Birkas Hamazon, he would get up and bang his head against the wall and say, "Ah, Ribbono Shel Olam! Ah, Ribbono Shel Olam!" and break out in tears. That's what she remembered.

The Jewish nation in general had Yerushalayim in its heart. We're not patriots, like the gentiles are patriots for their nations. No. We're patriots of Hashem. David Hamelech built Yerushalayim only for *avodas Hashem*. We have to understand what a great opportunity the ingathering at the time of the Geulah means for us. What a great blessing it's going to be for us. We have to study that a little now to appreciate what we have to look forward to.

Q What's so bad about this *galus* today that we need to be redeemed?

Even when we live in peace and nobody molests us, living among the nations is a tremendous loss. We don't realize what we lose. I'm not talking about a Jew who's already assimilated. Living in a non-Torah society is a tremendous injury to our character and *neshamah*. You can't be anything in this world if you're under non-Torah influence. It's like buying good expensive kosher meat and putting it into a kosher pot, but in the same pot is a piece of ham. If you have foreign teachings in your head alongside Torah, it won't make the rest of the thoughts kosher.

Very often, the influence is subtle. You don't even realize it at first. But after a while, you become enslaved mentally. Becoming enslaved mentally is the greatest form of *avdus*. There's no slavery like mental slavery. What's more important—the mind or the body? The mind. If the body is enslaved but the mind is not, at least you're intellectually free. However, if your mind is enslaved, then you're really enslaved.

That's what happened in Europe. European Jews resisted the outside influences for many centuries, but finally they collapsed and became admirers of the surrounding civilization. Before World War I in Vienna, Sigmund Freud said that every Jewish young man in Vienna thought he was a real German. He didn't think of himself as a Jew at all. He was so proud of being part of German culture. Once that happens, that's the real slavery.

I remember when families first came to America in the early 1900s. I was a little boy then, but I saw what was happening. Jews came from small towns in Europe where they didn't have automobiles. Some had never even seen one. Now for the first time they saw automobiles. To us today, it wasn't a real automobile. The old Fords, the Flivvers, were more like carriages on wheels, but to those freshly arriving Jews they were remarkable. It overwhelmed them.

Streetlights overwhelmed them! They had never seen electric lights before. Ooh ah! Streetlights! The streetlights in the stores were burning on and off, on and off. *Ooooh, America, ah gevaldigeh place!* They went crazy for America. Most of all, you were a free man in this country.

At least, that's what they thought. They thought they were free.

The influence was subtle at first. When the European Jews first came here, they spoke Yiddish. Even when they began speaking English, it was a broken English, with a *trop*. But for many of them the most important thing was to be able to speak English They were proud of that. They were embarrassed by Yiddish. If they sat on a bus and wanted to talk Yiddish to somebody, they spoke quietly because they were ashamed. No one should hear them speaking Yiddish. When a man with a big beard came onto the bus wearing a *kapoteh* and speaking Yiddish, they would think, *Why can't he be more American?*

Their children, of course, grew up with English and forgot Yiddish entirely. The influence was subtle, but the slide was fast and almost impossible to reverse. They gave their children American names, like Morris or Irving or Hyman. The women? Fanny, Gertie. No more Jewish names. Even if they spoke in Yiddish, they would say, "Morris—*kum aher*, Morris." Jewish names were erased when they came to America.

All the benefits in America, including freedom, so enslaved their minds that they didn't have any ability to resist. They couldn't think like Jews anymore. They were so overwhelmed that all their principles collapsed. They forgot everything that they ever learned and became assimilated.

We must know that what we lost in Europe was tremendous. The Jewish small town, or even the Jewish big town, was such a unique arrangement. I was *zocheh* to see it. The entire atmosphere—the very air—was Jewish. Of course, when I saw it, the Jews were already trying to get out. But try as they might, their small towns were still Jewish towns.

Let me tell you about these towns. I once took a hike for five days with another yeshiva *bachur*.[36] We walked down a dirt road for miles and miles. Finally, we saw a wire across the road—an *eruv*! That's how we knew we were approaching a Jewish town. The cobblestones began at the *eruv*. Inside the town, all the stores were owned by Jews. The gentiles were the vast majority, but they lived outside the town. It's a remarkable thing. All the gentile farmers lived outside the towns. They came into the Jewish town during the weekdays to buy merchandise from the Jewish stores, but they lived in a different place. The town was Jewish. The streets were Jewish. It had a *beis hamedrash, a beis haknesses*, a *kloiz*. It had a *shechitah shteibel*, a *mikveh*. And not far away was a Jewish cemetery. It was literally a Jewish town.

The problem was that they had lost their admiration for the Jewish self-contained culture and had their minds on faraway places. They wanted to emigrate. Now, I can't blame them much because there was poverty, lack of opportunity, and persecution. Nevertheless, it was a form of existence you couldn't find anyplace else. There, you could live your whole life as a Jew and nothing but a Jew!

But they desired to be part of the world at large. They looked longingly at Berlin. They dreamed of being in Vienna. They thought of the glories of Paris or of London. So Hashem said, "If you're not appreciating this great gift of the Jewish town, you're going to lose it. I'll have to scatter you to America, England, South Africa, and Australia, because that's what you desire."

---

36 Rav Miller is referring to Rav Yehudah Davis. Rav Miller once said of him, "Ay, Reb Yehudah, I owe him my entire life, because he was the one who encouraged us to go learn in Europe." This trip is described in Rav Miller's biography, *Rav Avigdor Miller—His Life and His Revolution* (Judaica Press). "When they were single, Rabbi Miller and Rabbi Yehudah Davis went on a five-day trip to the cities and towns surrounding Slabodka. The piety and simplicity of the Jews there made a tremendous impression on them, and Rabbi Miller often talked about the splendor of these Jews. When they passed the outskirts of a town that appeared orderly and neat, or a cemetery that was well kept, they knew it was Jewish. Despite the poverty and harshness of their surroundings, the Jewish communities carried themselves with a certain dignity that clearly distinguished them from their neighbors."

That's where we find ourselves today. That's how we got here. We lost what it meant to live in a Jewish town, to live a Jewish life. I hope this situation won't last forever. I hope Jews will have the *seichel* to reestablish Jewish towns before we go to Eretz Yisrael in the days of Mashiach. It was such a big privilege. You didn't have to worry about your children because children in Jewish towns saw nothing but Yahadus, nothing but Judaism. In the streets there was nothing but *yiras Shamayim*. There wasn't a Jew who didn't have his head covered.

But when I went to Europe, it was different. Oh yes, it was different! But before then, about fifty years before World War I, every Jew had a kosher home. They used to say, "If his name is Mendel, you could eat from his *fendel* (pan)." Every Jew had a kosher home. Every single Jew! Every Jew had a Jewish name. There wasn't a single Jew with a gentile name. In Hungary, yes. But not in Poland, Lithuania, or old Russia. No Jews were named Ignaz or Adolph.

Now, it wasn't so easy to live among gentiles there. They weren't very friendly, and the Jews didn't have full rights as citizens, but what they had was something so precious that it was worth it. And many of them decided to remain because of that. They refused to emigrate. But because so many desired to be emulate the surrounding culture, Hashem scattered them among the *umos ha'olam*. That was a great loss.

Even today, even among those who stand strong against the tide, some part of the mind goes lost to the surrounding society. To some extent, everyone is influenced by the world culture. That's why we want Mashiach. That's the Geulah we look forward to most. We ask Hashem to take us out of the gentile lands — even the best lands, where they're polite and civilized. We ask Hashem to be saved from the bad influences and attitudes that surround us on all sides.

"Why do we desire Mashiach to come?" Well, you'll say, "It's a *mitzvah* to desire it." Very good. That's a good reason. But there must be a reason for the *mitzvah*, too. Why should we desire it? Others say, "*Kevod Shamayim*! The Shechinah is in exile. It's not an honor for Hashem that we're in exile. The honor of Hashem requires that we should all be together serving Him in the Beis Hamikdash as a united Jewish nation." Also very good.

But let's listen to what the Rambam says in *Hilchos Teshuvah* (9:2). We want Mashiach to come so that we can be "liberated from subjugation to the nations." When you're among people with anti-Torah attitudes, you're limited in your opportunities. We want to be freed from the *umos ha'olam* because, to a great extent, we're not able to live true Torah lives if we live among negative influences.

You hear that? We want Mashiach because we want our lives, our minds, to be free to serve Hashem. Even if we live in a land where we're totally free to do as we please, it's not enough. There's still something more than that, much more than that. Every nation comes with its own attitudes. That's why even in the good old days, when Jews lived Torah lives, they still needed Mashiach. Even in the Jewish town with its *beis haknesses, beis hamedrash*, and Jewish street, where Jews spoke only Yiddish, it was still *galus* because on all sides we were surrounded by foreign influence. Even though we tried our best—and succeeded greatly in negating the influence of the environment—it had a certain effect on us. We were living in a sea of gentiles, drowning in their influence! To keep our Jewish heads above water and not to go under is an exceedingly difficult task. Almost all of us are drowning. It's not pleasant to say, but we are drowning. We speak their language. We usually look like them. In almost all cases—and this is the worst part of it all—we think like them. Once we think like them, we're thinking the opposite of the Torah.

Therefore, the most important *geulah* we look forward to is the opportunity to be free of even the most subtle influence of the *umos ha'olam*.

Unfortunately, today it's not so subtle. I remember when I was a boy the library had no immoral books. The gentiles were very strict about that. Gentile women fifty years ago in America wore long dresses with long sleeves. On the beaches, policemen went around and measured if the bathing skirts were long enough. Women had to have long bathing skirts on the beach. The newspapers were already poking fun at the police, but those were the rules and the police tried to enforce them. If not, she got a summons. That's how the world was. But today everything is much worse.

Fifty years ago, there was no immorality in the newspapers, no dirty words in books. And there was no TV. The TV is a big sewer main coming right into your home. It's a big pipe of stupidity and filth that leads directly from the broadcasting rooms and empties directly into your living room. If you have a television, the least you can do is chuck it out the window. Look below first to make sure no one is there, and then give it a heave.

But even back then, fifty years ago, the Am Yisrael was a little island of decency surrounded by a huge ocean of depravity. Our big test was then and is still today — as the ocean waves of outside influences rush up on the beach, as they roar and splash, will they wet us as well? Or will we retain our purity despite the overwhelming numbers and power of those who stand against our ideals? That's our big test to be worthy of the Geulah. Are you going to be influenced by the majority? Are you going to drink in their culture and become intoxicated with it? Will you go to their schools and become transformed into one of them? Or are you going to fight back and become more and more identified with the Jewish environment? That's the real Geulah. That's the real Redemption — to redeem the *neshamah*, to redeem the mind from the surrounding culture.

The Jew who understands this principle knows that one of the most important careers in life is to remain loyal to the Jewish people — in body and soul. Loyal Jews, who desire the real Geulah, will be taken out of the *galus* when the time comes. The *navi* (*Yeshayah* 26:2) says, "Open the gates wide open!" And who will come in? "The righteous nation, who remain loyal." Our job is to be loyal Jews and rid ourselves as much as possible from non-Torah influences.

Why do we add the word *"yachad"*?

When we say *"V'kabtzeinu* — gather us," why do we add the

word "*yachad*—together"? *V'kabtzeinu* already implies "together." The word *yachad* seems unnecessary.

It's added because, as difficult as it will be to gather us in from "*arba kanfos ha'aretz*—the four corners of the world," the bigger problem will be do it with a feeling of togetherness and camaraderie. Therefore, we ask You, Hashem, that it should be *yachad*, with togetherness and camaraderie.

Now, pay attention. There's a *machlokess* in the Gemara (*Sanhedrin* 91b) as to what will happen at the time of Mashiach. One opinion is that it's going to be a supernatural existence, not what we are accustomed to today. It will be an entirely different kind of existence. I won't go into that, because the other opinion is the one the Rambam follows: "*Olam k'minhago noheg*—The world will be the same as today" (*Hilchos Melachim* 12:1). It will be a natural existence. You'll have to eat to remain alive. You'll have to go to sleep to be healthy. The difference will be that we'll be free from "*shibud malchuyos*—subjugation to the nations." The nations will recognize the Am Yisrael as the "*mamleches kohanim v'goy kadosh*—kingdom of *kohanim* and a holy nation" (*Shemos* 19:6). That's the opinion the Rambam follows, and that's the consensus.

Now, that's not necessarily such good news, because when we come together in Yerushalayim under Mashiach, we'll still have our differences. There will be Lubavitchers, Satmarers, Belzers, and all types of *chassidim*. There will be Sephardim—Sephardim from Syria, Sephardim from Egypt, Sephardim from Teiman, all kinds of Sephardim. From America there will be Lakewood, Chaim Berlin, the Mirrer, and all kinds of yeshivas. Jews will come from Williamsburg, Flatbush, Boro Park, Monsey, Baltimore, and Alaska. They'll come from South Africa, Russia, and England. They'll come from places where we didn't even know there were Jews.

The Teimanim [Yemenite Jews] will come with their robes and turbans. The *chassidim* will come with their *shtreimelech* and *bekeshehs*. Some will come wearing only a *yarmulke.* There will be all kinds. And each will come with his own *minhagim*, customs. Even *minhagei Torah* are different—*minhagim* of Teimani Jews are very different than the *minhagim* of Lithuanian Jews. And the *minhagim* of the Lithuanian Jews are different than the *chassidishe minhagim.*

There will be a lot of work to do to achieve "*yachad.*" Maybe some of you are hoping that such a thing will come about by fiat, by a command of Hashem, or that it'll just happen by itself. Well, I'm sorry to be the bearer of bad news, but it won't be that way. Somehow the differences will have to be overcome. Don't think it will be different than today. There will be trouble then. All will be pressed together in Eretz Yisrael. There will be opportunities for disagreements and arguments. We'll have to figure out how to get along "*yachad,*" together. And we have to *daven* to Hashem now to help us with this.

One of the purposes Hashem had in mind when He exiled the Jews from the Old World to America was that for the first time in a thousand years, Syrian Jews would live shoulder to shoulder with Jews from Poland. It would never have happened otherwise. Over time each began to think of themselves as a separate nation. Let's say if a Polish Jew came to Paris and encountered an Egyptian Jew. It was like encountering a complete stranger. But that's not the plan of Hashem. The plan is for Jews of all backgrounds to feel connected—"*chaverim kol Yisrael.*"

America is a rehearsal. When the time comes and we'll arrive in Yerushalayim, there will be cliques. There'll be a quarter where the Ashkenazim will be by themselves. And don't think all the Ashkenazim will automatically be united. They'll also be fractionalized. There'll be North American Ashkenazim and South American Ashkenazim. In addition to the Ashkenazim, there'll be Syrians from Aleppo and Syrians from Damascus. There'll be different groups that would never naturally amalgamate into one people.

In the Yemos HaMashiach, we'll all rub shoulders together. Against your will, you'll be sitting next to a Persian Jew or a Jew from China. You'll be sitting next to Jews from all over the world, so practice now loving all Jews. Practice right now. Don't feel that if he wears a black hat and has a big beard, he's a stranger to you. Don't feel that if he doesn't talk English with your accent, he's a stranger. Practice *yachad* now. Once we're accustomed to living with and loving Jews, we're ready for Mashiach.

To get ready for the Geulah, right now we have to work on "*V'ahavta l'rei'acha kamocha*—Love your fellow man as you love yourself" (*Vayikra* 19:3). Even though he may *daven* with a different *nusach*, speak with a different pronunciation, or have different *minhagim*, clothing, mannerisms, and so on—*V'ahavta l'rei'acha kamocha!*

Employees and employers must learn to work in harmony with each other. Also your business competitors—you must love the man who has the same business down the block. Once a man is a business competitor, human nature begins finding faults in him.

Tenants must learn to love their landlords, and landlords their tenants. Neighbors must love neighbors. You must love the person next door even though you and he want to park in the same spot. Of course you each think you're right. You have arguments. But you must overlook things. The Torah says about your fellow Jew, "*V'ahavta.*" "*V'ahavta*" means you must *love* your fellow Jew, not merely tolerate him. You must start finding good qualities in him, in every person. It's not just a nice thing to do. It's a Torah obligation. You must love every person here. You must look at him and say what a beautiful face that is. It's *tzelem Elokim*. Every Jewish face is *kadosh*. That's not a simple matter. You must work on that right now. That's not an easy thing. It's a big job. All the problems we have now will be problems then, too. "*Olam k'minhago noheg.*"

But Hashem doesn't want to bring us to Yerushalayim to fight among ourselves. It's the greatest benefit for Klal Yisrael to be together. Do you know what it means when each one contributes his qualities, his ingenuity, his abilities, his character, all together to become the perfect unit? It's just like a body—you need arms, legs, eyes, ears, a stomach, a heart, a pancreas. You must have so many different parts to create a body. Similarly, to create a nation you need very many different kinds of people, each one contributing to Klal Yisrael all of his abilities. We need the people who *daven* with a special *bren*, with a *hislahavus*. We need people who concentrate on learning Torah all the time. We need people who are busy with *tefillah*. Some people pray for hours and hours. We need people who learn *mussar*, who learn *chassidus*. All the great expressions that were created in the many centuries of our *galus*, all these contributions will come together then. And we need them all.

What an excitement it's going to be when all the B'nei Yisrael flock to Eretz Yisrael. Therefore, before the Geulah we must get ready and learn to live together. And not only neighbors — but husbands and wives, too. Today there's so much trouble in domestic life. Husbands and wives must learn to live in harmony. That's also part of the *yachad*. We must practice living in harmony at home. It's not a simple matter. A husband and a wife are different nationalities, the Gemara says (*Shabbos* 62a). "*Nashim am bifnei atzmam.*" Hashem created women different than men.

If you really want Mashiach to come, you must be ready for him because it's going to be a very big *nisayon*, a very big test. It won't be easy. We need a great deal of preparation for the Geulah. Therefore "*yachad*" isn't superfluous. It's telling us an especially important message — get ready *now*!

Q

What will unite us?

Even with Mashiach leading us and the whole nation finally together, how can so many people from so many different environments with so many different *minhagim* be welded together?

Our nation is only a nation because of the Torah (Rav Saadia Gaon, *Emunos V'deyos* 3:7). Hashem gave us the Torah. That's what made us His people, and that's what still makes us His people. Who are the Am Yisrael? Those who keep the Torah. We are a Torah-nation. That's the cause of our existence, and that's the only thing that binds our nation together.

Just as the binding of the book keeps the pages from falling out, Jews bond with each other through Torah, through *avodas Hashem*. Whatever differences seem to pull us in different directions, they're overcome by the glue of *avodas Hashem*. We're connected to each other in the bond of serving Hashem.

Even though we each have our differences and our separate lives, there always remains this glue of service to Hashem that binds us together in the kinship of brotherhood. It's much more than a blood line. It's a real bond, a bond of the mind that ties us together. We're not merely connected to each other by blood, by DNA. It's much more than that.

When Yaakov Avinu was on his deathbed and saw how different his sons were, he was full of anxiety. What's going to happen to the future of our people? All the sons understood their father's concern and made a declaration, "*Shema, Yisrael, Hashem Elokeinu Hashem Echad*—Hear, our father Yisrael... Hashem is One." We're all servants of the One G-d. And that's going to keep us together. Hashem told Moshe to put those words in the Torah. That's why you say them every day when you go to sleep and when you wake up. It's of the greatest importance to realize the glue that keeps us together—that we have one Hashem and He gave us one Torah. It's the greatest necessity, the greatest urgency. We must always remember that we're all one nation.

And not only Polish Jews and Persian Jews and Jews from all over the world, but men and women should realize they're one nation. Even though Hashem made a number of natural things to keep them together, nature isn't enough. They need something supernatural to keep them together always. And that's the *Toras Hashem*. It's the strongest force in maintaining the unity of the family. When husband and wife are united in serving Hashem, all their petty considerations fade away. There are a thousand things that can pull people apart. This one wants to go to the country, and this one wants to go to the seashore. After all, he's a man and she's a woman, and their interests are different. But when they have one Hashem and one Torah, that bond ensures the stability of the Jewish home.

When we are *yachad* in our dedication to Hashem's service, to His Torah, we transcend all the forces that can pull us apart. To prepare for the coming of Mashiach, we must practice the principle of *yachad* even now. So practice up!

Q **Won't Mashiach *force* Jews to become *chaverim* with each other?**

Absolutely not. Although Mashiach is going to inspire everybody, it's still going to be *"olam k'minhago noheg"* (*Hilchos Melachim* 12:1). We follow the Rambam's decision. It'll be a world of free will, and there will still be people who misuse their free will and refuse the opportunity.

Certainly, the great revival of the Am Hashem on a grand scale will be miraculous. Wonderful things will take place, things that will stir the hearts of many people. But let me tell you something—there are some *resha'im* of Yisrael today who are so hardened in their hatred of Torah that nothing will help. They have devoted their lives to stamping out the Torah. They're real *sonei Hashem*. When the time comes for us to gather together, they'll be kicked out of Eretz Yisrael.

Not everybody will choose properly. And it won't be so simple to choose. Therefore, it's necessary now to prepare for the coming of Mashiach.

Q **Why thank Hashem now for the Geulah? It hasn't happened yet.**

If you wait, you'll get no credit for thanking Him. Naturally, everybody will thank Hashem when they see the Geulah with their own eyes. The real credit for thanking Hashem for the Geulah is right now, thanking him for the benefit He's going to give us then. Now is the time to grab a reward for thanking Him.

Who knows how long this world as we know it is going to last? One day it will come to an end. It could happen quite suddenly. Hashem will give a summons and we'll have to hurry up, grab our hats and coats, and run. Those who aren't ready will miss the boat. Or the airplane. There won't be more flights after a certain time.

Of course, it's not easy to thank Him for something you don't have yet. But that's what we're doing—what we should be doing—when we say, "*Baruch Atah, Hashem, m'kabeitz nidchei amo Yisrael*—Blessed are You, Hashem, Who gathers the scattered members of His nation Yisrael." We're thanking Him now for what's going to happen later.

It's the same thing with *Mechayeih meisim* [the second *brachah* of Shemoneh Esrei]. When the dead will be revived, we won't have free will anymore. If you'll say, "*Baruch Atah, Hashem,*" then, you won't get credit for thanking with free will. You'll just be expressing what your *seichel* tells you. We will absolutely bless Hashem when He revises the dead, but we won't be doing it with our free will. Therefore, we thank Hashem today for the *Techiyas Hameisim* that will happen someday later. And when we do so, we're using our *bechirah* and will get rewarded for it.

Q **What does "*galuyoseinu*" refer to?**

"*V'sa neis l'kabeitz galuyoseinu*"—the word *galuyoseinu* means "those who are in exile." It refers to people who live in an exiled community. This is an important point, so pay attention. It does not refer to people who *chose* to be in exile, who voluntarily went away from the Jewish people. It's talking about Jews who were *sent* into exile. For example, a hundred years ago there was persecution in Russia and Jews fled to America. They were forced to leave. But suppose a Jew who was on the Lower East Side or in Brooklyn decided to go live in a place like California, Nevada, or Arizona. He didn't leave out of necessity. Nobody was persecuting him. He left to run away from the Jewish people. He's not included in "*galuyoseinu.*"

You must understand that the banner that's going to be raised to summon the Am Hashem is not for everybody. It's only for people who were forced into exile. If someone voluntarily left, he's not going to be summoned back. Only those who were forced into exile will be summoned back. Those who exiled themselves from the Jewish people will remain lost.

A Jew who ran away and changed his name from Cohen to Cowan or O'Connor so that his name should sound Irish and he shouldn't be recognized as a *kohen* shows his disdain for his people. A Jew has to be proud that he's a Jew. He has to stick with his people. In America, many Jews chose to move out of Jewish neighborhoods and into gentile neighborhoods. Then, if other Jews followed them into that neighborhood, they moved again. They're constantly running away from Jews. The *passuk* says, "*Va'avadetem bagoyim*—you'll go lost among the nations" (*Vayikra* 26:38). On that Rava comments, "I'm afraid of that *passuk*" (*Makkos* 24a). To disappear among the nations is the worst thing that can happen to a Jew.

"*Kol Yisrael yesh lahem chelek l'Olam Haba*—All Israel has a portion in the World to Come" (*Sanhedrin* 90b). If you're together with Yisrael in this world, you're together in the next world. The Am Yisrael is one eternal entity traveling through history—"This people I have created for Me that they should relate My praise" (*Yeshayah* 43:21). All other nations fade away—the ancient Egyptians, the Babylonians, the Persians, the Greeks, the Romans, etc. Only the entity Yisrael survives. We survive in this world and we survive in the next world. Therefore, only an individual who is identified with and connected to Yisrael has a *chelek* in Olam Haba. If he does something that disconnects him, he loses his connection with Olam Haba. That's why Rava was afraid of that *passuk*.

Q Who are the *"nidchei Yisrael"*?

The *brachah* concludes, "*Mekabeitz nidchei amo Yisrael*—He gathers together the dispersed of His people Yisrael." We're adding a new word here—"*nidchei*," as opposed to "*galuyos*."

Many Jews aren't aware of the necessity to come together with the Jewish people. They were born far away from Jewish communities. Their parents may have already been lost souls, but they *chose* to be lost souls. Their children didn't. Even though the children are *nidchei*, lost souls, it's not their fault. Many Jews are lost out of ignorance. It's a tremendous pity on them. It's not their fault. Their parents put them into public schools. They lived in neighborhoods far away from *frum* communities. It's a tragedy.

Therefore, Hashem will give them a chance. He'll have pity on them and give them an opportunity. There will be remarkable opportunities then. Of course, if someone rejects the opportunity and remains where he is, he'll go lost. But very many of the *nidchei Yisrael* at that time will hop on the wagon and come back again. Very many.

You see today many Jews who have come back. It's a remarkable thing. Thirty years ago, it was hard to find a *ba'al teshuvah* in America. Today, the synagogues are full of *ba'alei teshuvah*. Wherever you go, Jews are coming back. Not enough, by any means. But they're coming back. They're coming back here in America, in Eretz Yisrael, in England, in Australia. Maybe it's a beginning for the Geulah. Let's hope.

Whatever it is, the time will come when Hashem will raise up the banner. "*Se'u neis Tzionah*—Raise a banner and come back to Tzion" (*Yirmiyah* 4:6). Then there will be a great movement of *ba'alei teshuvah*. Masses of Jews will throw away all the idols of the nations. They'll start fighting to get out of Russia.[37] Jews from Fifth Avenue [in New York] will change their minds about wasting their lives in the foolishness of the surrounding culture. Jews will flock to the banner of the Torah. It's going to happen. It'll be a great excitement, a great *simchah*. Some will be left out, however—the tough old assimilationists, liberals who identify so much with America that they cannot tear themselves loose.

But those who have some loyalty in their hearts should now use the opportunity and prepare for that great day when the great trumpet will sound, and the banner will be unfurled, and Hashem Himself will summon us to come and live lives of fulfillment of the greatest joy together in Yerushalayim.

---

37 This is exactly what happened in the Soviet Union by the late 1980s. See *The Underground* by Yaakov Astor (Judaica Press).

Q What proportion of Jews will remain behind?

That I'm not able to tell you. There's a *s'vara* that maybe more will come along [in Mashiach's time than those who left Egypt]. It could be. Who knows? Maybe big masses will not remain behind. I'm not able to say.

Let's hope more and more people wake up before it's too late. When the signal is given and the airplanes begin leaving, don't think a person will be able to go whenever he wants. After the airplanes leave, some will be left behind. And they'll be very sorry, but the gates will be closed.

Up to a certain amount of time, Hashem waits for people. After that, no more. He closes the gates of *teshuvah* on people who wait too long. The gates don't remain open forever.

PRACTICAL ADVICE

Q Practically speaking, how can we work on unity now?

As you walk the streets and see Jewish boys with yarmulkes and black hats coming out of the yeshivas, or you see buses carrying children to yeshivas, your heart should overflow with happiness. You must feel a great respect for your fellow *ovdei Hashem*. You're looking at your people! If you see a group of *frum* girls dressed *b'tzniyus* coming out of the Beis Yaakov schools, walking with decency and wearing long skirts, your heart should be full of happiness. Those girls are your people!

As you walk through blocks and blocks and see fathers with children going to the *beis haknesses*, let your heart swell with pride and happiness. Some who survived the war weep with joy when they see Jewish children. All of us should feel that way, all the time.

But you must work on the feeling. That's why it's a very good idea to walk through Boro Park and look at the big *mezuzos*, one after the other, on all the doors. Blocks and blocks of Jewish houses. Whenever I come to Boro Park, I feel a reverence. It's the truth. I rarely go, but when I turn off Ocean Parkway down Eighteenth Avenue and start approaching Boro Park, I feel a *yiras hakavod.* I'm thinking, "It's such a great happiness to be a part of a nation of *tzaddikim.*"

That's what we should be thinking as we walk. "I'm walking among my people. They're my people and I love them. I don't care what hat he wears or what group he belongs to. They're all my people! These are the people in this world whom I identify with."

Q Must one first undergo a special spiritual preparation before going to Eretz Yisrael?

And the answer is, absolutely! Yirmiyah Hanavi said, "You came and you defiled My land" (*Yirmiyah* 2:7). Therefore, it is of the utmost importance to be ready to behave if one wants to go to Eretz Yisrael. He should learn how to conduct himself perfectly *al pi haTorah* before he goes. Even if he is good here, he must resolve to be even better there. There are no two ways about that. It's Eretz Hakodesh and it's only for Jews who live *b'kedushah.*

It's of the utmost importance that a Jew, before he goes to Eretz Yisrael, make up his mind to be there *b'kedushah*. Even if just for a visit. Nobody should go unless he'll go *b'kedushah.* If he takes along his wife, he must make sure that she's dressed completely properly, because Eretz Yisrael is a land that will vomit out the people who live there if they don't suit its taste. "The land will vomit out its inhabitants" (*Vayikra* 18:25). Eretz Yisrael is finicky. It's a delicate land, and only those people who behave properly can please the land.

Q Should every Jew in America consider *aliyah*?

The answer is this—absolutely. But he has to do it in the right time. *When Mashiach comes*, he should be ready for the *aliyah*. Everybody should be preparing for Mashiach. Whether he should jump the gun and do it beforehand depends.

If you have a place to live in Eretz Yisrael, and you won't have to look for charity, and your children will have a *frum* environment, why not? But if your children will have to go into the army—watch out. The army is a slaughterhouse for Jewish boys and Jewish girls. It's a big error to go to Eretz Yisrael and to entrust your children to the army.

Jewish girls in the army don't become *tz'nuos*, decent girls. Don't deceive yourself. Everybody knows what happens in the army. Tens of thousands of abortions take place every year in the army. Tens of thousands of abortions! And how many don't abort?

Therefore, whether you should go to Eretz Yisrael today or not depends. If you'll have to beg for dollars, it doesn't pay. If you have some kind of a livelihood or you have money, and you move into a good neighborhood and can guarantee that the children are always only in good environment, and your girls will get married early, and your sons are always *b'nei Torah* and will never be drafted into the army, then certainly. Why shouldn't you consider it? But in general, we are waiting for the time when Hashem will summon us to go.

Q **Are the Ten Tribes still around?**

Now that's a question based on a misunderstanding. Some people think that somewhere in the world the Ten Shevatim are concealed and we don't know where they are. Don't believe it. There was a time when this was true, when the world didn't have communication. You could live in a certain village and not know what's in the next village. There were places that were isolated. Back then, there could have been a place where some of the Aseres Hashevatim lived.

Today we know the entire world. And there are members of the Aseres Hashevatim mixed among us. That needs explanation.

Yirmiyah Hanavi spent time bringing back people from all the *shevatim* wherever they had been exiled to (*Megillah* 14b; see *Behold a People* #516). Therefore, we have among our people today representatives of every *shevet*. So it would not be correct to say that these tribes went lost *entirely*. Individuals still exist, but you will not find them as a group today.

The *navi* says, "*Uva'u ha'ovdim b'eretz Ashur v'hanidachim b'eretz Mitzrayim*—And those who were lost in the land of Assyria as well as those who were pushed away in the land of Egypt will come" (*Yeshayah* 27:13). Then "*V'hishtachavu laHashem b'har hakodesh biYerushalayim*—They will bow to Hashem on the holy mountain in Yerushalayim." It means that when we'll all come together, Hashem will point out which of us is from Asher, from Reuven, from Shimon, and so on. But today it's impossible to accept that a complete *shevet* should be hiding someplace. If a *shevet* is so mixed among the gentiles that they don't know who they are, they really are gentiles.

In the times of the early Rishonim, it was still possible that there were communities unknown to the world. Columbus didn't know about America. There were other places no one knew about. Eldad HaDani reported that he had met certain *shevatim* who had no contact with the rest of the world and maintained all their loyalty to Hashem. Yes, in his time it was very possible. But now it's impossible.

All the *shevatim* are mixed among us today. They were the *ovdim b'eretz Ashur* and the *nidachim b'eretz Mitzrayim* that the *navi* spoke about. They and we will all come together *b'har hakodesh biYerushalayim.*

Today, unless you're a Kohen or a Levi, we don't know clearly from which *shevet* we come. But this we do know—Hashem will come and purify the gold from the dross in the times of Mashiach. Each individual will be singled out and separated, each according to his *shevet.*

Q Why did Rashi and others miss out on the Geulah?

That's a big question. It's bothered me many times, for years and years. When the time comes—who knows when, maybe tomorrow—the *shofar gadol* will blast, a great blast that will cause a tremendous disturbance in the world. All the nations will tremble and say something is happening. The Melech HaMashiach has appeared. They won't make fun of us any longer. He will be the *real* Mashiach. It'll be a tremendous experience. Everyone will be shaken to his roots at that time.

But isn't it a great pity that Rashi won't be present? Rashi missed all that fun. I think it's a big *kashya*. And Rabbi Akiva missed it, too. They're in Gan Eden, but after all, this is something they wanted in this world. It's a very big *kashya*. The poor Rambam. He was waiting for Mashiach. He didn't live to see it. How could that be? All these great people lived and waited and waited and weren't *zocheh* to see it. They have Olam Haba, no question, but *bi'as haMashiach* is something special.

And the answer is, as the Rambam tells us, that this world is not made for fun. Of course, good kosher enjoyment can be found in the world. And *bi'as haMashiach* will certainly be a *simchah*. "*Az yimalei s'chok pinu*—Then our mouths will be filled with laughter" (*Tehillim* 126:1). No question, we're going to open our mouths as wide as we can and laugh, a big, joyful laughter. However, we have to realize that the purpose of all this is to prepare for Olam Haba. If that's the case, it's not the happiness of it that's important—it's what you use that opportunity for.[38]

The Rambam was *zocheh* to *bi'as haMashiach* because the Rambam used every minute of his life for perfection. But plenty of us—if we'll

38 "The Sages and the prophets did not yearn for the Messianic era to have dominion over the entire world, to rule over the nations, to be exalted by the nations, or to eat, drink, and celebrate. Rather, they desired to be free to involve themselves in Torah and wisdom without any pressures or disturbances, so that they would merit the World to Come" (Rambam, *Hilchos Melachim* 12:4).

be *zocheh* to Mashiach—won't use our lives for even a fraction of what the Rambam achieved. The Rambam covered so many subjects. Besides the *Moreh Nevuchim,* his *Peirush* on *Mishnayos,* and *Sefer Hamitzvos,* the Rambam's *Yad Hachazakah* is an entire bookshelf by itself. It's remarkable what this brilliant man did. He didn't sit down and copy it. He thought out each *halachah* and decided between the different opinions. And the Rambam was a busy man, by the way. He worked for his living. He was a doctor, and whenever the Sultan of Egypt had a toothache or a headache, he called him. Nevertheless, the Rambam used every minute of his time for his studies in Torah. I'm sure he spent a lot of time on Shemoneh Esrei, too. Did the Rambam fail to use anything of his life? I'm sure he used his life perfectly. Therefore, he didn't need Mashiach.

Every person is going to be asked when they come to the next world, "*Tzipisa liyeshuah*—Did you look forward to the *yeshuah?*" (*Shabbos* 31a). Were you waiting for Mashiach? Were you worried about My glory, the *kevod Hashem*?

The whole world is full of idolatry, and the truth about Hashem is buried. Aren't you worried about that? *Tzipisa liyeshuah*—Aren't you looking forward to a time when "*bayom hahu yiheyeh Hashem echad ushmo echad*—on that day Hashem will be One and His name will be One"? Don't you want that?

The answer is that they certainly wanted it. The Rambam wanted it. Rashi wanted it. Rabbi Akiva wanted it. All the great *tzaddikim* wanted it. Not only that, but they worked for it. They spread *da'as Hashem* with their *sefarim,* with their teachings. Therefore, they were *mekayem bi'as haMashiach.* They did everything possible to bring Mashiach. So don't pity the Rambam. He succeeded.

And that's our function, too—*tzipiyah liyeshuah,* waiting for *bi'as haMashiach.* If we're really waiting and doing whatever we can to make use of our lives as if it were already here, we're successful. We have to use our life the way they used their lives. *Bi'as haMashiach* is not the end in itself. It's only a means toward the end. And the great final goal for all of us is the happiness of Olam Haba.

Now, I'm going to explain something about Olam Haba. The Gemara says that Olam Haba is compared to a ring dance (*Ta'anis* 31a). The difference between a ring dance and dancing in a straight line is that when you dance in a straight line, you come to an end. At some point you come to a wall and stop. A ring dance never stops. What does that mean? The happiness of Olam Haba will never come to an end. That's the difference. In this world, everything eventually becomes tiresome. You lose sight of the happiness. But in Olam Haba, the happiness doesn't stop. On the contrary, the longer one is in Olam Haba, the greater the happiness is.

And the Gemara says that the first time the *tzaddikim* go around in their ring dance they say, "*Zeh Elokeinu kivinu lo*—This is our G-d Whom we hoped for," and the second time they say "*Zeh Hashem kivinu lo*—This is Hashem Whom we hoped for" (*Yeshayah* 25:9). During the first time they say "*Elokeinu*" and the second time they say "*Hashem.*" Hashem is a higher degree of recognition, a clearer recognition, which means that each time they go around, the *simchah* becomes greater and greater.

Now, it's disappointing to hear that the great happiness is in Olam Haba. We would like to have it all in Olam Hazeh. But still, we have to face the truth that whatever we have in this world comes to an end sooner or later. Even during Yemos HaMashiach we won't live forever.[39]

The main point right now is that the coming of Mashiach is in itself not the fulfillment of our desires. It's our attitude and our preparation that matter. Like the Rambam, Rashi, Rabbi Akiva, and all the great *tzaddikim* of past generations who were not *zocheh* to see Mashiach and nevertheless fulfilled all the ideals that would have been carried out had Mashiach come in their day, so, too, if we live with the right idealism, then it's like Mashiach came in our days. It's as if the *kibbutz galuyos* took place and our prayers were answered.

39 See *Rav Avigdor Miller on Olam Haba* for more on this subject.

SUMMARY

- We ask Hashem to restore the Beis Hamikdash and with it all the benefits it brought to us and the world. We're also asking that all Jews be brought back to Eretz Yisrael, so we can live all together as one nation.
- We *daven* for the time when Hashem will make it known to the entire world that the Am Yisrael is His chosen people. But we must work on ourselves now to internalize that truth. Hashem will make it known to the nations, but we must labor now to make it known to ourselves, or else we might not be worthy of redemption.
- We have to realize what a terrible harm it is for us to live in *galus*, in an anti-Torah society. Even if we're not harmed physically, the environment is very detrimental to our *ruchniyus*. Being in *galus* enslaves our minds to their ideas. We want to live true Torah lives, free from foreign influence.
- We have to work on ourselves now to love all different types of *frum* Jews, so that when we come together again in the Yemos HaMashiach, it will be in a spirit of love and camaraderie.
- The Am Yisrael is a nation only by virtue of its loyalty to the Torah. We can learn to love each other despite our differences by internalizing the fact that the Torah unites us.
- Thank Hashem for the Geulah now, before it comes. If you wait until it happens, you won't get any credit for having *emunah*.
- If we want to personally merit the Geulah, we must remain proud Jews, loyal to our people, and not try to run away from Jewish communities so we can live among gentiles.
- Those who are lost among the nations through no fault of their own, but due to the choices of their parents or grandparents, will have the opportunity to rejoin the Jewish people. But the opportunity to answer Hashem's call to return will be limited.

Hashivah Shofteinu

Q **Why do we ask for "*shoftim*, judges," rather than for kings?**

First, we have to understand what a Jewish king was. David Hamelech said, "*Aromimcha, Elokai Hamelech*—I will exalt You, My Hashem, the King" (*Tehillim* 145:1). David himself was a king. He was every inch a king. He was a conqueror, and a very successful one. He was so successful and beloved by his people that to this day we look back with longing to the *Malchus David*. It was the most powerful and successful reign we ever had. All the nations were subjugated. All the other kings were afraid of him and sent him tribute. Nobody would lift a finger against or say something against a Jew because they knew that David's warriors would take revenge. If the nations harmed a Jew, they knew right away there'd be reprisal. Either David marched out himself, or he sent Yoav and took stern retribution.

Yet, even though David was an extremely powerful king, he didn't feel he was a king. He felt he was sitting on the throne of Hashem. Even when his son Shlomo took the throne, he felt he was an intruder. They had to push him onto it. It was *kisei Hashem*, Hashem's throne. "Sit down on it," they said to him, "because you're Hashem's representative." That's a Jewish king.

That's how David could be such a powerful ruler and still say he was a nobody. "You, Hashem, are the King." What's more, the entire Jewish nation felt that Hashem was their King. It's a remarkable fact. If you study Tanach, you see that everybody understood that. For instance, when they came to Gidon—who fought battles and won great victories over their oppressors—the people said to him, "Be our king—you, your son, and your son's son" (*Shoftim* 8:22). Listen to what Gidon replied: "I'm not going to be your king because Hashem is your king" (ibid. 8:23). Isn't that a remarkable statement? Throughout Jewish history, the Jewish nation felt it in their bones. They actually felt that Hashem was their king.

David was speaking for his nation when he said, "I'm going to exalt You, the King." Even though he was a great king in every sense of the word, he recognized that he was nothing. Hashem was the king. Nobody else could say that with the same impact. No king was greater, more successful, or more powerful than David—yet he ascribed all his power to the King of Kings.

In *Hashivah Shofteinu*, we say, "*Umeloch aleinu Atah, Hashem, levadcha*—And You, Hashem, alone should rule over us." At Kriyas Yam Suf all the people said, "*Hashem yimloch l'olam va'ed*—He is our King forever" (*Shemos* 15:18). That's the way it should be. And that's the way it was when we had kings like David Hamelech, Chizkiyah, Assa, Yehoshafat, Yoshiyahu, and the other good kings. They had a tremendously positive influence on the nation. In those days, when the Am Yisrael accepted Hashem's word, Hashem ruled over them—alone.

The was especially true in the early days of the *Shoftim*. All the *Shoftim* minimized themselves. A *shofet* didn't have a palace. He wasn't a man who rode on a horse. He usually walked or rode on a little donkey. He was looked at like an unimportant personality if you didn't know better. You had to imagine how great he was to have respect for him. And that was so that people should not have any *mechitzah* between them and Hashem. In that way, in the olden days, Hashem ruled over them alone.

This stopped as soon as they made a king over themselves. A great change took place then. When they insisted on a king in the days of Shmuel Hanavi, it was considered a break with that great promise that they had said, "*Hashem yimloch l'olam va'ed*—May Hashem reign forever." When the people asked for a *melech*, Hashem said to Shmuel Hanavi, "*Lo os'cha ma'asu ki im Osi ma'asu*—They have not rejected you by asking for a king; they have rejected Me" (I *Shmuel* 8:7). Even though the righteous kings continued with the understanding that "*Hashem yimloch l'olam va'ed*," as a general rule it came to an end.

Now, it didn't come to a complete end because we're still saying that *passuk* today. But it wasn't in the sense that it was originally understood. So when we pray to Hashem that He should restore "our judges" as at first, and reign over us once more, it means we want to come back to that happy state when we were supremely aware that Hashem and only Hashem was our King.

Q **Why should we yearn for the "days of old"?**

It's important for us to know that we are different from all the nations of the world. The nations generally make progress, become more civilized, more experienced. They start at a low point and are climbing, even though it may not seem so sometimes. But we started at the highest point—Har Sinai. So the further we go away from our past, the lower we become. We yearn to regain the past, not to move past it. When we ask for "the" days of old, we mean the time when we had the greatest people in Jewish history.

"*Lo kam od navi b'Yisrael k'Moshe*—Never again will there be a prophet like Moshe" (*Devarim* 34:10). The Torah has stated that he was a leader with no equal. It was the generation when Aharon was an advisor for people. He was "*Oheiv shalom v'rodeif shalom*—He made peace among people" with his good advice (*Avos* 1:12). And Miriam was a very important factor in the greatness of our nation. Never again did we have such personalities. We have to learn what was said about them and continually review it in our minds, to serve as models. What is there to learn about Aharon, about Miriam? A great deal. We have extensive literature—*midrashim, ma'amarei Chazal*—that speak a great deal about these personalities. Whatever you can learn from them is valuable for all future history. That's why we say, "*k'varishonah*—as at the beginning," during the best period of our history. We should look back and say those were the days when it really paid to be alive.

The happiest days of our history were the days of our past. It's not like among the gentiles, *l'havdil.* They might imagine the olden days were better, but it's just nostalgia. With us it's not imagination. We have to accept it as a principle—those were the days when it paid to be alive. We should feel sorry that we weren't born in the *Dor Hamidbar*. Not only did the greatest personalities live then, but the nation was very great. It was filled with *tzaddikim.* The *midrash* calls them the *Dor De'ah*, a nation that witnessed the *Makkos* on Mitzrayim. The *Makkos* taught *de'ah.* They saw the *Makkos* with their own eyes. They were present at Kriyas Yam Suf and sang *Az Yashir* when they were rescued. They were present at Kabbalas HaTorah. It was a once-in-history experience to stand at Har Sinai. They ate *Mann* for forty years. All the things that they saw in the Midbar are things we can only dream of. That generation was the greatest generation. And we long to be like that generation. Make no mistake about that.

Q How will the restoration of our Torah leaders "remove our sorrow"?

"*V'haseir mimenu yagon va'anachah*—And remove from us sorrow and sighing." It means that when things happen to people, when their lives are disrupted and sometimes ruined, many times it's because they lack the guidance of the great teachers of old.

The *Shoftim* and the *yo'atzim* brought happiness upon the nation. The Torah is described as "*Deracheha darchei no'am v'chol nesivoseha shalom*—Its ways are ways of pleasantness and all its paths are peace" (*Mishlei* 3:17). Torah is the pleasantness of life. It's sweetness. It leads to success and tranquility in life. *Shalom* means tranquility of life. When we had our great teachers and we followed them, our lives were sweet and tranquil.

"*Yagon va'anachah*" didn't exist in the days of old. It was a life of *simchah.* Even when there were difficult times—nationally and personally—their lives were filled with happiness. Even when they were tested with a *nisayon*, the general framework of life was entirely different. That's because they had leaders who taught them how to make progress in spiritual achievements, and that no matter what was happening on the outside, they were accomplishing and coming closer to Hashem in their life. Whether an open *brachah* or a *nisayon*, they understood that it was all *avodas Hashem.* And that filled them with *simchah*, with a very great happiness.

We have to study the days of old to know what we're missing. And so we say to Hashem that we look forward once more to the restoration of our great leaders so that we be restored to the state of happiness that they caused the nation to enjoy.

Q **If the generations have declined, how can we hope for greatness at this time in history?**

The Gemara tells us that someone complained that they didn't have a Moshe in their generation (*Rosh Hashanah* 25a–b), and that if he had been born in the generation of Moshe, he would have been something. It's true. No question about it. If we could take one look at Moshe, it would be worth as much as sitting in a yeshiva or in a *kollel* for fifty years. No exaggeration. As one of the Sages said, "Do you know why I'm better than my fellow in learning? Because I saw the back of Rabbi Meir" (*Eruvin* 13b). He didn't even see Rabbi Meir's face. He only saw his back, yet that's why he was greater than his peers, he said.

Suppose you could see Moshe, just one glimpse. It would transform you. You would never be the same. His face was glowing with a light *min haShamayim* (*Shemos* 34:29–35), and when that light entered your eyes and your *neshamah*, you were transformed. The *kedushah* of Moshe's face alone would have transformed you.

Let me tell you more. Even if you would have seen Kalev ben Yefuneh, you wouldn't be the same person.

When Moshe passed away, the *ziknei hador* looked at Yehoshua and were wringing their hands at their loss. They said, "*P'nei Moshe kip'nei chamah, p'nei Yehoshua kip'nei levanah*—Moshe's face was like the sun; Yehoshua's face was like a moon" (*Bava Basra* 75a). The moon is also good, but "*Oy l'osah bushah*—Alas for that embarrassment!" We lost Moshe. The generation wept and wept for Moshe. After they lost him, they realized what they had once had.

Now, many people think that because we don't have Moshe, it doesn't pay to follow anyone today. At least if we had Yeshayah Hanavi around, they say, they would be happy. Or they would settle for Rabbi

Akiva. Rabbi Akiva, yes—that would be a rabbi they would follow. In truth, these people would follow Rabbi Akiva maybe half a mile to hear him. Maybe they would go if he gave a speech. Maybe.

Maybe we would settle for Rashi. If Rashi would have a *beis hamedrash* where he was teaching Chumash, maybe. I don't know. I'm very much in doubt if we would go. Rashi was a quiet man, I imagine. He said everything *al pi p'shat* and was careful with what he said. Even when he said a *ma'amar Chazal*, it was very *pashut*, very straightforward. Although Rashi was a deep thinker, as you know, he said it in a simple way, and I'm sure a lot of people would probably go listen to somebody else.

Suppose we agree a certain Rebbe is a *tzaddik hador*. First, look at how many people ignore him. Only the people who belong to his persuasion go to him. Others don't bother. He's not their Rebbe. Second, even his own followers come around once in a while, but do they sit and review his words? We have great *roshei yeshiva*, but they're ignored by the masses. Even their *talmidim* often exhibit a relatively limited kind of devotion.

Therefore, we're told that we have to consider the *gedolim* of our generation "*k'Moshe b'doro*—like Moshe in his generation" (*Rosh Hashanah* 25b). That's your opportunity. You have to utilize the *gedolim* we have, because they were put into your life to help you make something of yourself.

Korach, Dasan, and Aviram made the same tragic mistake. They said, "Moshe isn't Avraham, Yitzchak, or Yaakov." They saw faults in Moshe and disputed his authority. They weren't *apikorsim*, but they thought he didn't measure up to the great men of antiquity. Therefore, they failed to utilize him, and as a result they went lost.

The same with us. Korach, Dasan, and Aviram were made examples. They were put into this world as a warning for future generations. There are Korachs, Dasans, and Avirams today, I'm afraid. They don't accept the authority of the *gedolei Yisrael*. Don't be like them.

Q What if a person doesn't have access to *gedolim*?

Can we claim that we're not who we should be because we don't have the great leaders of old with us anymore? And the answer is — they're here right now. They're on the shelves — the *sefarim* are your great leaders.

Of course, they could have more influence on you if you knew them in person. On the other hand, if you're a small-minded person and wouldn't respect them, they would have *less* influence on you in person. Therefore, in case we're not big enough to live with our leaders and appreciate them, at least we have their *sefarim*. We have great teachers who are waiting for us to listen to their words.

The *Chovos Halevavos* in *Sha'ar Habechinah* enumerates various forms of kindnesses that Hashem bestows. Included in this list is always thanking Hashem for the practices, institutions, and inventions of the nations of the world. If you see a fire engine coming down the street, know that Hashem did that *chessed* for our benefit. Appreciating that is a form of obligation.

We have to thank Hashem for traffic lights. It allows you to cross the street with a certain amount of safety. Of course you have to look on all sides, but *baruch Hashem* there are traffic lights. And for building codes, too.

That's an important idea he's teaching us. We're accustomed to think only in terms of natural things, of thanking Hashem for *nifla'os haBorei*. But the obligation of *bechinah* is more than that, the *Chovos Halevavos* teaches. We have to also be thankful for the things that Hashem inspired people to invent and institute. He is the One Who gave ideas to the nations of the world. Thank Hashem for that. When you say "*Modim anachnu lach* — We give thanks to You," include all of the benefits of a civilized nation. That there are bridges, police, and certain good laws. It all comes from Hashem and is part of "*gomel chassadim tovim*" that we say every day (in the first *brachah* of Shemoneh Esrei) — "He bestows good kindnesses upon us."

Among the many things you must thank Hashem for is the

invention of printing. Printing revolutionized the entire subject of the study of Torah. Of course, *l'havdil,* it was also used to print silly literature and useless books. That's Hashem's way. He lets people have their way as long as we get the benefit of that invention. In the ancient times, a *sefer* cost as much as a house. For a scribe to sit down and write the whole Gemara from beginning to end was a very big task. It took years. If he had to write Rashi too, it was an even bigger task. *Tosfos* didn't have a whole Shas. Many times *Tosfos* wants to refer to a *mishnah*, say, in *masechta Erchin*, but says to find it cross-referenced in one of the more common Gemaras like *Bava Kama* or *Bava Basra.* That's because *Tosfos* didn't have a whole Shas.

This all changed with the advent of printing. Now *sefarim* are available to everybody who is willing to learn. And Hashem did that for a good reason—the generations were becoming weaker and weaker. In the days of the Rashba, the Rosh, and the Ran, the *gedolei Yisrael* taught Torah with a few handwritten *sefarim* in the great yeshivas, where great *lamdanim* were able to follow them. But when the generations became weaker, Hashem caused a German to discover the idea of printing so that from then on everybody could obtain *sefarim.* Therefore, one of the things for which we must thank Hashem is the invention of printing.

Of course, the invention of printing was also a great misfortune to the world. Printing caused the downfall of European Jewry. In Europe, the press was in the hands of the irreligious Jews. They took newspapers and began ruining the nation. Only the *resha'im* published newspapers. The *Magen Avraham* said that it's forbidden to read the newspapers. He called it the "Gazette." All the newspapers are a *moshav leitzim*, he said. In the course of time, their poison spread throughout the entire nation. However, the plan of Hashem was to rescue us from the generations becoming weaker and weaker by making *sefarim* affordable for everyone.

Therefore, when you ask Hashem in this *tefillah* to restore the days of old, and you think you have no access to any of it except in your imagination, think again. There are *sefarim* available. Hashem introduced the idea of the printing press and even allowed people to use it for worthless or wicked purposes, just so that you should be able to open a *sefer* and learn. Do you appreciate what a concession that was?

So, are you listening to the words of our *shofteinu v'yo'atzeinu* in the *sefarim*? They're available now. You don't need to use your imagination.

Of course, it would be a much greater benefit if we could be alive together with them and hear these great men's advice personally. Our lives would be transformed into lives of fulfillment and happiness. Nevertheless, to a very great extent, the happiness that comes from good advice and great leadership is still available in the *sefarim*.

Q What does it mean that Hashem loves *"tzedakah umishpat"*?

We conclude, "*Baruch Atah, Hashem, Melech*"—You're our real King. We have to obey You as in the days of old, and know that everything comes only from You, and accept You as our Judge. But then we add, "*Oheiv tzedakah umishpat*—Hashem loves righteousness and justice." That's a very important principle.

"*Oheiv tzedakah*" means that He loves when people follow the laws of *bein adam lachaveiro*. And "*mishpat*" means living according to the *halachah*. *Bein adam lachaveiro* means *gemilas chassadim* and correct behavior. To gain favor in the eyes of Hashem, we must have leaders who will influence us to fulfill this ideal of living with *tzedek umishpat*.

We must understand that "*Torah t'chilasah gemilas chassadim v'sofo gemilas chassadim*—The Torah begins and ends with kindliness" (*Sotah* 14a). It begins with how Hashem clothed Adam and Chavah (*Bereishis* 3:21) and concludes with how He buried Moshe (*Devarim* 34:6). The entire Torah is kindliness. What does that mean? It means a person can gain a life of real happiness by paying attention to the counsel of the Torah. We're not talking about reward now. When people are willing to listen to the counsel of the Torah, they're going to have a great happiness in their lives.

"*Ki heim chayeinu*—The words of the Torah are our lives" (Maariv,

Blessing of the Shema). When we hear these words, we think we know all about it. "*Ki heim chayeinu!* Torah is our life! Yes, it's *chayei olam*. It's eternal life! It's Olam Haba." Certainly, we'll have Olam Haba because of the Torah. In the next world, Torah is very, very important. Torah means eternal life. But along comes the *Chovos Halevavos* (*Sha'ar Cheshbon Hanefesh* 30) and tells us something we might be surprised to hear. He says that *ki heim chayeinu* means that the Torah is our life *in this world*! Of course, there's the next world, too. That day will come, no question about it, and the Torah will be our *hatzalah* in that world, too. But meanwhile, we're not in any rush to get there, and the *chassid gadol*—that's what they all call the *Chovos Halevavos*—wants us to know that the Torah will save you right now in this world. The Torah is our success by rescuing us from all types of trouble in Olam Hazeh!

This needs an explanation, with details and examples. We have to understand that people who learn are able to ward off all kinds of troubles that people who don't learn don't know about. The Gemara states, "*Assur l'adam l'ha'amid sulam ra'ua b'soch beiso*—It's forbidden to have a rickety ladder in your house" (*Kesubos* 41b). If you have a ladder that's rickety, a weak ladder, you have to smash it. It's *assur* to keep it. How many people have fallen down from rickety ladders and as a result remained in wheelchairs for the rest of their lives? I remember a story like that. Had that person learned Torah, he would have saved himself a ruined life.

The Gemara (*Beitzah* 34a) said about a certain man who had a *shor*, an ox. The *shor* fell and was injured. The law is that in such a situation, you can't slaughter it right away. You have to wait at least twenty-four hours to see if it's able to endure. Otherwise, if you *shecht* it quickly, it's considered a *treifah*. Now, this man didn't know, so he slaughtered it and lost a *shor* that cost him a lot of money. The *chachamim* said to him, "Had you learned, you would have known to wait twenty-four hours before you slaughtered it." So we see that when a person learns, he can save himself money.

Whether it's the Torah *sheb'al peh* or Torah *shebiksav*, the Torah is a storehouse of good counsel for life. It's crammed with good advice on all matters of practical living. "*Mi ha'ish hechafetz chaim, oheiv yamim liros tov*—Who is the man who wants to live long and experience good?" (*Tehillim* 34:13–14). What should you do to live long? "*Netzor l'shoncha meira*—Guard your tongue from speaking evil." Don't speak *lashon hara*, and don't quarrel. "*Shomer piv ul'shonav*—Guard your tongue and mouth" (*Mishlei* 21:23). "*Shomer piv*"—First, keep your mouth closed. If you must speak, then "*l'shonav*"—guard your tongue. Don't open up your mouth. But if you must open it, then guard your tongue not to say many words. That's good advice. That's a way to live long.

I visited a man living by himself. His wife left him, and he was blind. What happened? This man fought with his wife a long time, became a diabetic, and then lost his eyesight. Because of that, his wife left him. Now he was all alone and blind. A tragedy. If this man hadn't argued with his wife constantly, he would have remained in good health and married. But because he fought all the time, because he couldn't keep his mouth closed, he became sick and blind, and his wife left him. It even shortened his life.

"*Mi ha'ish hechafetz chaim*" is common sense. Listen to the advice not merely because of reward and punishment but because it's common sense. If people would pay more attention to the simple advice of the Torah, it's a fulfillment of "*shofteinu v'yo'atzeinu*," of living with the great teachers and advisors of old. We have them right here in *Tehillim*.

There's commonsense advice on all sides, in the Torah and in the Gemara. People can benefit a great deal by listening to such advice. That's why we say, "*Deracheha darchei no'am v'chol nesivoseha shalom*—Its ways are ways of pleasantness and all its paths are peace" (*Mishlei* 3:17). That refers to the advice of Torah. It's very important for us for everyday life.

The Torah is full of advice for succeeding in this world. It teaches you how to deal with your parents and your children, how to handle a wife or a husband, and in-laws, too. From the Torah, you learn how to deal with your Italian neighbor. It teaches you how to be *matzliach* in business and how to succeed in your own inner life. Not only in your private life. How to react to public issues, how to make public policy—how to deal with the mayor and the governor. It's full of advice on how to deal with the surrounding nations. Even health! The Gemara is full of advice on how to take care of your health. The truth is, the number of people who have lost their lives for lack of taking counsel from the Torah has yet to be counted. Even the stickiest problems can be resolved by listening to the Torah's advice. Many times it seems like there's no way out, that there's no solution to a problem, but when you hear the counsel of the Torah, immediately the problem can be solved. In every phase of life, the Torah stands by a man's side and offers him practical advice for how to live successfully. The Gemara is full of wisdom on how to live—only, you have to learn it!

I had a *rebbi*, *zichrono livrachah*, who learned in Volozhin. Volozhin—the mother of the yeshivas! He knew how to learn! When he said a *shiur* in the Gemara and came to something that gave him an excuse to talk *divrei derech eretz*, *middos tovos*, and *emunah*, he always stopped and spoke about it. I remember how he taught a *mishnah* in *Nedarim* (72b). At first glance the *mishnah* doesn't appear to be giving any advice. It says "*Derech talmidei chachamim* ... The way of *talmidei chachamim* is ..." and goes on to say that if they want to find out whether their wives or daughters have obligated themselves with *Nedarim*, they have a way of investigating. My *rebbi* explained it like this—I remember his shining face to this day—"*Ahh! Zolzain a lichtiger Gan Eden,*" he said. "*Derech talmidei chachamim*, it's the way of *talmidei chachamim*.... We see that *talmidei chachamim* have a *derech*, a different way in life!" That's how he learned the *mishnah*. It was telling him that you must have a *derech* in life. Then he gave a whole talk about a *derech* of *talmidei chachamim*. He spoke to us about a way of thinking differently, of acting differently. The *mishnah* was talking about something else entirely, about the technicalities of *nedarim*. But he uncovered a gem of advice in the words of the Torah because he knew all the advice you need is in the Torah. The trouble is that people become hardened. They become habituated by reading the

Torah constantly in a superficial way, and they don't seek its advice.

The advisors of old are here with us, and they're full of advice. Yes, it's better to have living advisors. I know a number of great men right here in Brooklyn, *talmidei chachamim* and *tzaddikim* who are capable of advising people. But we also have great advisors from our past, and their precious advice is literally at our fingertips. We just have to open our eyes. They're alive and well in all the beautiful *sefarim* that give us guidance in life. Are we utilizing them? Are we utilizing those great teachers whose teachings are available to us today? That's the question. At the very least, when we ask for good advice, we should ask Hashem to open our eyes to the advice readily available to us now.

Hashem is saying to the whole world that's praying to Him — "You ask Me to restore the *Shoftim* and the *yo'atzim k'vatchilah*. What about the ones you have here? And what about the *sefarim* that contain the advice of all the *Shoftim* and *yo'atzim* from the days of old?" That's a question.

However, we ask Hashem to bring back our great leaders of the ancient times, and we hope that this time we're going to use them to the fullest, making the best out of ourselves under the leadership of our great men.

PRACTICAL ADVICE

If you were elected the leader of a country, what policies would you pursue?

I would call together all the *chachmei haTorah* and tell them, "Make policies for me." Whatever the *chachmei haTorah* would say, I would follow. Only you have to know which *chachmei haTorah* to call together. That's a different story. But I would call together the *chachmei haTorah* because they would know what to do, what policies to pursue. They have experience.

The Gemara is full of experience, full of *eitzah*s. It's a very big Shas. The *chachmei HaTorah* sit and deliberate. They'd think it over for weeks and months. Then they'd give their advice. And that would be the most fortunate government, the most fortunate people, if we ever had such a thing.

"Please, Hashem, bring back our judges as we had in the past and our advisors as in the days of old." We say it every day in Shemoneh Esrei. "And remove from us all sadness and sighing." All troubles come from the wrong people leading us, people who have no business giving advice to the Jewish nation. They're causing us a great deal of trouble, all these so-called leaders.

Therefore, we ask Hashem, "Remove from us sadness and sighing." Bring back our leaders, our great Torah leaders. Even though they're not *nevi'im* anymore, still, they're the ones to lead us.

Then, "And You, Hashem, should rule over us alone." When you have politicians—selfish, ambitious people—they're there for their own glory. They do things for their party, their own success. They don't care for the people. They're a *mechitzah*, a partition, between us and Hashem. They actually block out Hashem from our sight. But when you have *tzaddikim*, *talmidei chachamim*, who are interested only in *retzon* Hashem, doing only what is right, they're transparent. Our great men always felt they were nothing, and therefore they weren't a *mechitzah* between us and Hashem. In the days of old, when our leaders were the Torah people, there was no partition between us and Hashem. Therefore, to have a successful administration, you need the policy of the *chachmei HaTorah*.

I would tell even our new president the same thing. Of course he doesn't have enough sense to realize that. After all, what is he? He has no *seichel*. He should have called together all the great men of the Am Yisrael. "Make a policy for me. Think of a policy." And they'd win over the Congress as well. There are ways of winning them over. He could do it. The *chachmei HaTorah* could do it.

I could give you a list of the *chachmei HaTorah* right now. It would include all shades of the Torah world. And you can be sure that they would come up with very good ideas, excellent policies, that would help his administration succeed. But what can I do? He won't listen to my suggestions.

SUMMARY

- We ask Hashem to bring us back to the level we were on during the time of the *Shoftim*, when we understood that Hashem was our only King and we were under His direct rulership.
- The further back in time we go, the closer to Har Sinai, and to the perfection that the generation of the Midbar achieved. We long to return to their level of *da'as*.
- We ask Hashem to restore to us great leaders and advisors as we had in the early generations, so that they can help guide us to lead lives of *simchah* and accomplishment.
- At the same time, we must recognize and respect the *gedolim* of our own generation and listen to them. We can't excuse ourselves from doing so by saying that they're not as good as the *gedolim* of previous generations.
- We should recognize that we still have access to our great leaders from past generations, through studying their *sefarim*. And we should ask Hashem to open our eyes and help us recognize the great Torah advice that's available to us, both from *sefarim* and from living *talmidei chachamim*.

V'lamalshinim

Q Why was the *brachah* of *V'lamalshinim* added to Shemoneh Esrei?

In the days of the first *galus*, Bavel had treated the Jews equitably and had even elevated several to high office. But after the second *Churban*, Rome burned with animosity against Klal Yisrael. The

Greek and Roman writers and orators poured out a constant torrent of hatred upon the Jews. Even before the destruction, in Egypt, Syria, and Eretz Yisrael there were fearsome massacres against Jews in numerous cities.

After the *Churban*, Rome was in an ugly mood. Rabban Yochanan ben Zakai had visited Vespasian at Caesarea before the commencement of the siege of Yerushalayim and petitioned that Yavneh be spared together with all the Sages. He also requested that the family of Rabban Gamaliel be spared.

From then on, the Sages convened in a national Torah-assemblage at Yavneh. The Mesivta of Yavneh (and afterwards at Usha, Shefaram, and the other stations of its wanderings) was the successor of the Great Sanhedrin. This was the seat of government, where the conduct of the entire nation was decided. The Sanhedrin at Yavneh was entirely unlike any other governing body by reason of *its being dedicated to the knowledge and practice of the Torah.* Never was any government even remotely similar. At the head stood Rabban Gamaliel (now referred to as Rabban Gamliel of Yavneh).[40] Now the nation gained a central authority to conduct its affairs. The entire people, in all the places of their dispersion, considered themselves united by the twofold phenomenon of a central Torah-assemblage and the central authority of a Nasi of the seed of Hillel, representing the house of David that had from ancient times upheld the service of Hashem and the loyalty to His Torah.

At first the Romans disregarded all this. They viewed solely the exterior political aspects. And since Yerushalayim was desolate, they saw nothing wrong in the religious teachings and rites that were carried on at Yavneh. All this was due to the great strategy of Rabban Yochanan ben Zakai. Gradually the wounds of the nation could have healed, and they could look forward to rebuilding the Beis Hamikdash. Now, after being rid of the plague of the Tzedukim (Sadducees) and

---

40 To distinguish him from his grandfather, Rabban Gamaliel the son of Rabban Shimon.

Herodians (who forsook the nation in its hour of travail), they were in the position to regain the confidence of Rome.

But Hashem willed otherwise. The Christians, who mingled with the Jews (and still considered themselves Jews), were instrumental in preventing a return to the old order. They constantly alarmed Rome with reports of the regrowth of the nation, and they kept Rome in constant expectation of a revolt by the Jews.

At first, the Romans failed to notice the process of healing of the nation's wounds, and the gradual unification and centralization of the people. But after a few years, it became more difficult to conceal. In addition, the Christians had become more and more disloyal to their people. They kept Rome supplied with reports of the progress of the Sanhedrin at Yavneh, and Rome began to make its displeasure felt.

The chief target of Rome's suspicions and of the denunciations by the Christians was Rabban Gamaliel, who was now the official head of the remnants of the nation and therefore its unifying force. It was now, at Yavneh, that they instituted the prayer (*Brachos* 28b) against the slanders of the enemies from within.

The Shemoneh Esrei had been initiated in remote antiquity and had received its final form at the hands of the Men of the Great Assembly (*Megillah* 17b). The fact that a nineteenth *brachah* was added is a testament to the urgency of seeking Hashem's intervention against the machinations of the internal foes.[41]

Q **When was this *brachah* added?**

The Gemara says, "Rabban Gamaliel said to the Sages, 'Is anyone able to institute (compose) a prayer concerning the *minim*?' Shmuel Hakatan arose and instituted it (*tiknah*)" (*Brachos* 28b).

The Shemoneh Esrei was not composed at Yavneh. It was composed by the ancient Sages, and their final version was fixed by the Great Assembly four hundred years *before* Yavneh. At Yavneh, Shmuel

41 See *Exalted People*, #133–135.

Hakatan added only the *brachah* of the *minim* (*V'lamalshinim*). And even this he didn't compose alone, but with the collaboration of the Sages. "In the presence of Rabban Gamaliel (and the Sanhedrin) at Yavneh" (ibid.). The eighteen *brachos* were merely *edited* by the Sages under the direction of Shimon Hapekuli.

There were compelling reasons for this editing of the Shemoneh Esrei now, after the destruction of the Second Beis Hamikdash. In addition to the fact that the destruction had made some minor changes necessary (for example, "Restore the service to the Sanctuary of Your house"), a variety of versions had developed. No *siddurim* existed, for it was forbidden to write anything of a public nature other than Tanach. Therefore, in the course of time, because of the nation's dispersion and especially because of the numerous catastrophes they had undergone, some minor variations had appeared in the version of the prayers. Under the leadership of the Nasi and his Sanhedrin, now at Yavneh they restored the ancient authentic version that united all Jews everywhere in a uniform expression of prayer.

Shmuel Hakatan was one of the elderly Sages who survived the destruction and came to participate in the assemblage at Yavneh. When a new *brachah* needed to be added to the ancient eighteen *brachos* (the Shemoneh Esrei) composed by the Men of the Great Assembly four hundred years before, Shmuel Hakatan volunteered to undertake the task. This certainly was not accomplished in a moment. Every word was weighed by him and his collaborators, and the completed composition was then presented to the body of the assemblage for approval. Just as the original eighteen *brachos* were composed with the participation of the last surviving *nevi'im*, together with the leading Sages, so also was this additional one (the prayer against the *minim* and defamers) composed by the survivors of the era of *ruach hakodesh* together with the Torah leaders. A *bas kol*, the prophetic voice that had sometimes been heard in the old era of the Second Beis Hamikdash, had proclaimed that Shmuel Hakatan would have been worthy of the presence of the Shechinah had he lived in a greater generation (*Sanhedrin* 11b). At his death, he foretold the War of

Betar (ibid.). Therefore, he was worthy to lead the task of creating a nineteenth blessing.

Q Who are the *"zeidim"*?

The word *zeidim* refers to *minim*, people who aren't merely misguided or deceived. They could be people who recognize the falsehood of their contentions, but their wickedness (*zadon*) and desire for malicious mischief causes them to advocate their systems.

When the Bolsheviks seized power in Russia, many Jews there became Yevseksia, Jewish communists. They turned into ardent communists and began helping the Bolsheviks stamp out the Torah from the Jewish people. They sent many Jews to their deaths. It's an important chapter in Jewish history that many don't know. The Yevseksia were the ones who stamped out Yiddishkeit in Russia. They were worse than the Russian atheists. In the end, the Yevseksia were all shot by Stalin. Whatever his reasons were, we see how much their "idealism"—for false ideals—stood them in good stead.

When Jews lose their sense of solidarity—which is the minimum that a Jew should possess—and defame their fellow Jews to the gentiles, that's considered the worst that can happen.[42] Even if a Jew lacks Torah or *yiras Shamayim*, at least he should have a feeling that he belongs to his people. Once he loses that, he's lost everything.

Q Are today's atheists included in *V'lamalshinim*?

Although this prayer is against the defamers who bring false information to the authorities, it is also aimed against the falsifiers who seek to mislead Jews by false dogmas, including evolution and atheism.

"All who come to her shall not return" (*Mishlei* 2:19). "This refers to *apikorsus*" (*Avodah Zarah* 17b), from which it is difficult to turn

42 "The son of David will not come until informers proliferate..." (*Sanhedrin* 97a).

back. Therefore, because they rob men of hope, "*al t'hi sikvah*"—they deserve to be deprived of hope in all their affairs.[43]

"Do not turn to the idols" (*Vayikra* 19:4). The word here for "idols" is *elilim*, derived from the root *al,* meaning "not" or "nothing." "All the gods of the nations are nothing-gods (*elilim*)" (*Tehillim* 96:5), even of the nations that understand that there is a Superior Power. Those that deny any deity, such as evolutionists, are guilty of worshiping an even emptier religion than that of the idolaters, and their theories are the lowest form of *elilim* or "nothingness." "Atheism is worse than idolatry" (Rambam, *Moreh Nevuchim* 1:36; *Ma'amar Kiddush Hashem*).

In this *brachah*, it's noteworthy that the word "*m'heirah*—speedily" is used, in addition to the expression "*k'rega*—in one moment." This signifies the urgency that our *tefillah* be granted without delay. The expression of "*m'heirah*" is used only in connection with the Geulah in Shemoneh Esrei, but in *Es Tzemach David*, the word "speedily" is used only once. Here it appears three times! We learn from this how great is the harm caused by the *minim* who speak against the truth, and that every additional day they exist poses a great peril to the world. Although we eagerly await the Redemption, before the Redemption we hope even more eagerly that the falsifiers should cease poisoning the minds of men. Even those falsifiers who apparently speak the praises of G-d, yet they speak against His Torah or against the Sages of Israel or against His people, are enemies of Hashem.

Q **Who are the Jewish people's biggest enemies?**

The Rambam wrote his *Igeres Teiman* (Letter to the Yemenite Jews) when there was a *shmad* in the land of Teiman. He wrote this to encourage them to persist in their loyalty, in their *emunah*. The Rambam states that there are three enemies the Am Yisrael confronts. Who are they?

---

43 See *Praise, My Soul*, #1238.

The first is the group who try to force us to forsake our *emunah* by means of *shmad*—brute force. This happened again and again in our history. The Romans made a *shmad*. Much earlier, Antiochus in Syria made a *shmad*. The Rambam calls that group the *Anasim*, those who try to "force" us. Again and again they have tried. In Portugal, they dragged thousands of Jews to the baptismal altar against their will. They tore away Jewish children from their parents. The Russian czar took away Jewish boys from their parents and tried to bring them up as gentiles. Those are the *Anasim*.

Another group are those who argue against us, who attack our minds. These include the philosophers of Greece and the so-called scientists of today, all the newspapers, and all the schools. They are called *To'anim*, the group who try to convince us to forsake Hashem with their *tainos*, their "arguments" against us.

The third group consists of those who "imitate" us. It means the Christians and the Muslims, the imitating religions.

It's these three groups we must face throughout our history. The Rambam says that all of them will go lost. All of them! If you see that they have some power for the time being, you should know it won't continue forever. It's a temporary victory, which will come to an end one day. That's what the Rambam says. "Hashem promised Yaakov Avinu that even though the nations will oppress his children, Yaakov's children will remain, while those who persecuted them will eventually go lost and disappear." And it's not just the Rambam. The world knows it, too. Mark Twain said, "The Jew walks on the graves of all his oppressors." Hashem promised us that whenever enemies will rise against us—whether it's a *shmad* or any other kind of attempt against us—He will cause them to disappear.

We see how it's already happened with idol worship. The *navi* says, "The idols will disappear entirely" (*Yeshayah* 2:18). At that time, it was extremely difficult to accept that statement. There were certain people who just couldn't believe it. Even the best of our people had a hard time accepting such a statement. And yet if you look back, we must admit that today idolatry is already dead. There are certain forms that persist in parts of the world, but nobody considers that a temptation any longer. The *yetzer hara* of *avodah zarah* has been slaughtered entirely. Not only among us, even among the nations. Today, as far as most of humanity is concerned, idolatry is dead. And the Rambam says that all the others will disappear as well—all the philosophers and the academicians of today, all the universities, the press, and the literature. All will come to an end.

Evolution will someday be ridiculed. The truth is that evolution is as silly as can be. It's only for one reason that it has any power—because there are great numbers of those who advocate it. Anyone could ask, "How could non-life become life?" To this day there is no answer. They're twisting their minds trying to find ways how it could have happened. In all the laboratories they're trying their best, but they have no answer. The simplest form of life must have at least a trillion bits of data recorded on it. Again—the simplest cell must have at least one trillion bits of data to function. You know what a trillion is? More than all the *letters* in the biggest library in the world. Not *books*—letters! And each bit of data is necessary. A trillion essential bits of information for the simplest form of life. So how can a piece of iron, or a piece of copper, or an oxygen atom turn into life?

Most of the evolutionists dodge that question. They'll say, "In some way—we know not how—life originally appeared." But how did it appear? They try not to answer that question because there is no answer. But because so many people are upholding that theory, it's accepted. It's today's *avodah zarah*. I had a *rebbi* who said that because in ancient times they were wiser than today, they couldn't have preached evolution. Today the world has turned silly. Therefore, a silly *yetzer hara* is being preached to a silly world.

PRACTICAL ADVICE

Q Does *apikorsus* take on different forms?

There's always something new. When I was a boy, all the *rabbanim* used to thunder against Reform. Every synagogue Jew was trained to abhor the falsities of Reform. But then Conservative "Judaism" came around, and these same Jews entered the Conservative synagogues. How could that happen?

The answer is because these Jews were conditioned to withstand the temptation of Reform, but not Conservatism. When the *yetzer hara* saw there was no use knocking his head against the wall, instead of using the old label of Reform that had already been discredited, he adopted a new label, and many Jews eventually went lost.

If someone would come along today and preach socialism to the Jewish masses, we would just smile at him. Socialism is a dead ideal. We've been through it already. It's a flop. But when I was a boy, socialism was the wave of the future. I once had a fistfight with somebody because I was fighting to defend socialism. I retired from that debate with my nose bleeding.

In those days, there were European rabbis with beards who preached in the synagogue and showed with *pesukim*, "Socialism *min haTorah minayin*," that socialism was the Torah way. At the same time that the socialists were tearing down Torah and *mitzvos* and belief in Hashem, the *yetzer hara* was cunningly pulling the wool over our eyes.

That's how it is. The ideals of Olam Hazeh are composed of falsifications. It's *sheker*—with millions of adherents. A tremendous amount of humanity today subscribes to the *sheker* of humanism. All the evolutionists are full of *sheker*.

Believing in false ideals goes back to the very beginning, to Adam and Chavah. The function of the *nachash*, the serpent, is to mislead, test, and tempt—and that's what it did in its first appearance in the Torah. The *nachash* represents a great power the Creator put into this world. We call it the *yetzer hara*, the evil inclination. It's a certain force that exists in order to put us through ordeals and test our virtue.

To punish the *nachash*, Hashem sentenced it to forever crawl on its stomach. "You will go on your belly" (*Bereishis* 3:14). That sentence wasn't a mere technicality. It teaches us a very important lesson about the *yetzer hara*. If you go walking in the woods behind your bungalow colony, you must be careful where you step. If you step over a log, make sure to take a good look before you put your foot down. And when you walk in the meadows, in the deep grass, make sure you're wearing high boots because Hashem gave the snake an opportunity to attack its victims with stealth and surprise.

Now we understand why the *nachash* was sentenced to crawl. It's a *mashal* for the *yetzer hara*. The *yetzer hara* is the one entity in this world that doesn't look for *kavod*. Everybody wants recognition, publicity, but the *yetzer hara* prefers to remain unseen and unnoticed, because that's his greatest tool! Hashem made the *yetzer hara* like a snake that crawls in the grass. He crawls up to you and you don't see him. He's talking to you and crawling around your thoughts, but he's camouflaged among everything else in your head. That's why most people are enticed by the *yetzer hara*, even though they don't dream that they have any contact with him. It doesn't even enter their mind because he's concealed in such a manner that nobody who is ensnared by him realizes what's taking place.

The *yetzer hara* doesn't bother with the form of a snake. He has other forms, new ways of appearing to man—all of them incognito. Today he can appear in the form of a college professor or a neighbor. Sometimes he'll even come as a man with a beard and long *peyos*. It has to be that way, because if the *yetzer hara* would have continued to exist in the form that it was in the time of the first *cheit*, we would already know to watch out for him.

But you must learn his ways in order to overcome him and succeed in your purpose in this world. You don't see him? That means he's doing his job well. But you should know he's very busy. Falsehoods fill the world today. Big buildings, libraries, universities. And they have the media today to spread their falsehoods. If you don't look beneath the facade, you'll never see the truth. *Sheker* fills the world today because the *yetzer hara* is choosing the most effective forms possible. Wherever you go today, you can no longer say the truth—you have to use "politically correct" speech. A tremendous tolerance of *sheker* was erected under our noses. The *yetzer hara* crawled and slithered along, and the world is full of falsehood.

The *yetzer hara* didn't retire when he was sentenced to crawl on his belly. He didn't go out of business. He just came up with new forms, different words, new temptations. The *yetzer hara* is still alive and well. He's not crawling on his belly—he's crawling in our minds.

The stealth of the *nachash* means that there's always something new, always something that slithers into our minds. Of course, people don't realize they're prey for the *nachash*. You buy the newspaper and think, "What's so bad?" But it's a bite from the *nachash*. Turn the page—another bite. A man goes to the movies—it bites and bites and bites. He's swallowed up by the *nachash*! If you bring a TV into your house, you're bringing a very big snake into your house, a poisonous snake to attack your children. Even if you don't do that, outside the home, just walking in the street, the snake is lurking everywhere. In the windows of the stores, in the advertisements. If you adopt the ways and mannerisms of those around you, the *nachash* is doing a job on you.

We certainly cannot do justice to the subject with a couple of hours together. Each disguise must be spoken about because the snake is very cunning, and it's important to unmask him.

Q Given all the infiltration of secular culture into our lives, how can we hope to defeat the *yetzer hara* for false ideals and attitudes?

The Gemara (*Kiddushin* 30b) says, "If Hashem wouldn't help a man, he couldn't overcome the *yetzer hara*." It's impossible to contend with the *yetzer hara* on your own. You must have supernatural help—and that help is always ready. Just ask for it. Without help from Hashem, all is lost. With Him, everything is possible. We must ask for His aid against this otherwise insuperable enemy that's stationed in our midst and participating in all our counsel.

The Gemara says that if somebody is a *ba'al ga'avah*—if he's too arrogant to ask for help—Hashem will not help him, and he'll be left in the power of his *yetzer hara*. But when a man is humble and asks Hashem constantly to save him from the *yetzer hara*, which is constantly lurking, those *tefillos* are among the most important ways of exposing the *yetzer hara* for what it is—a *dimyon*, an imagination. The degree to which you turn to Hashem is the degree to which you're recognizing the danger you're facing.

In the Midbar, when "the spirit of the nation became impatient because of the journey" (*Bamidbar* 21:4), Hashem sent poisonous snakes to attack them. "*Hanechashim hasrafim*—fiery serpents" were suddenly slithering everywhere, and "*vay'nashchu es ha'am*—some of the people were bitten" (21:6). Hashem then commanded Moshe, "Make for yourself the form of a poisonous snake and put it on a high pole, and anybody who was bitten by the serpents—let him look at that pole and become healed" (21:8). And that's exactly what happened. "If a serpent had bitten a man, he would stare at the copper serpent and live" (ibid. 21:9).

Why did they have to raise their eyes to the serpent? Couldn't it just have been any tall pole with nothing on top, and when they looked at the top of the pole they'd see the sky and be reminded of "*Yosheiv baShamayim*—Hashem, Who sits on high" (*Tehillim* 4:2)? That could have been the way to be healed. But what's a snake doing on top of the pole? And why is the snake colored like copper? Why not silver or gold? Or maybe wood?

But Moshe made a copper snake because desert snakes are most often copper-colored. And that color is very important to its function. That's how it performs its job in this world—it camouflages itself. Unpolished copper is beige. It's inconspicuous. It's a color that allows the snake to blend into the background. That's why *nechoshes*, "copper," and *nachash*, "snake," share the same root. The snake wants to hide himself from you. That's how he accomplishes his task best—by not letting you know he's getting close.

How does it happen that instead of being full of happiness, you're dissatisfied with your station in this world? Why is it that all kinds of wrong ideas come into your mind, and complaints come constantly out of your mouth? It happens by stealth. It doesn't happen openly. It happens without you even noticing. That's what causes you to think that something imaginary is real.

That's why Hashem commanded Moshe to put a snake very high up on a pole—because it's the opposite of what the *yetzer hara* wants. He wants to be as low as possible, so that nobody should see him. That's when he's most effective. He says, "Don't talk about me. I'm an *anav*. I don't want publicity. I'm successful when I'm incognito."

So Hashem said, "Put him on a high pole. Let everybody see the peril, the *sakanah*, so that they can overcome it." That's what Moshe told the Am Yisrael when he raised up the copper snake and commanded everyone bitten to look up at the top of the pole. "Look at this copper-colored snake camouflaged among your thoughts. I'm lifting it up high for you so you'll notice it. The fact that you're not satisfied, that you're thinking you'd be better off in Mitzrayim, is nothing but the wiles of the *yetzer hara*."

By exposing the wiles of the snake, the *yetzer hara*—through our *tefillos*—we lift the copper snake from the brush where he hides. In proportion to your *tefillos*, Hashem steps in. He helps you to the extent that you desire to be helped.

Q Wouldn't it be beneficial for us to gain from what the nations have to offer?

When you see an airplane take off for Eretz Yisrael carrying many Yidden who are going to learn in yeshivas in Eretz Yisrael, that's an example of how we take advantage of what the world has to offer us. Rabbi Akiva Eiger didn't invent an airplane; neither did the Vilna Gaon. Gentiles invented it. So we say, "Absolutely! Utilize all we can from the inventions of all people. Even the scientific knowledge that has been discovered—make use of everything."

We're like the bee. The bee takes nectar and turns it into honey. When the bee takes nectar from a plant, he doesn't merely take the nectar and leave it as is. By means of enzymes, he transforms it into honey. We take from the nations of the world whatever they have and utilize it for *devarim shebikdushah*, holy purposes. No question about it. That's why in all our homes today we don't have torches or gas lights. We have electric lights. They use lights in yeshivas to learn Torah. By all means, use everything the world has to offer for good purposes. Certainly!

Now, I think that when Mashiach comes, we'll still use automobiles. The world will continue to run the way it does today. The Gemara says that (*Sanhedrin* 91b). And if there will be automobiles, there will have to be traffic lights, too. Traffic lights were invented by the non-Jews, but there will be traffic lights, too.

In Mashiach's times, I'm sure they'll use radio to let people know *dinim*, *halachos*, and other important information. People will listen to Torah on the radio. In those days there will be a kosher TV. Kosher TV means people will sit in their homes, look at the TV, and see *tzaddikim* teaching Torah and explaining things like *halachos*, *middos tovos*, *halachos* of *yom tov* and Shabbos. They'll show the *yad Hashem* in Nature, the *yad Hashem* in history. It will be much more effective than words or printed pages. I'm sure all the modern inventions will be utilized in the days of Mashiach.

Therefore, certainly we want to make use of the benefits the gentiles bring to the world.

After saying all that, however, it depends what we're discussing, because there's also a lot of wickedness in the world. We have to be careful what we take from them and what we keep far away from. Our *gedolim* are the ones who should introduce us to all the good things of the world.

Q Should we get a radio?[44]

First, why not listen to my tapes? Second, I want to tell you, "Blessings upon your home for not having a radio!" You don't know how lucky you are. Let me tell you a *mishnah* in *Sanhedrin* (100b) that everybody knows. "The following have no share in the World to Come — one who reads in 'outside books' (*hakorei b'sefarim hachitzonim*)..." The *mefarshim* generally classify *sefarim hachitzonim* in two categories. One is those that corrupt the mind — love stories, romances, immoral tales; also, books that advocate atheism or disbelief, *leitzanus* of the *emes*. That's one class. But there's another class, which is *devarim b'teilim* — idle things that in themselves are no harm but are also of no benefit.

Regarding the first class, there's not much to be said. On the radio today, you must be selective. If you do have a radio, you cannot listen to everything. The truth is that there's very little to which you could listen today. There's a lot of poison being disseminated on the radio, but when you're accustomed to it, you're not aware of what you're swallowing. And movies are even worse — anybody who goes to movies today should know that it's the worst poison for the *neshamah*. If a person says that some

44 The full question: "For the past three years we haven't had a radio. We feel it's our responsibility to be up on the news, but perhaps, in addition I would like to listen to another voice while I'm here in the kitchen all day taking care of the children. My husband says that this is a change in policy that shouldn't be done without consultation. Should we get a radio or not?"

movies are okay, they should know that once they step through those portals of infamy, they're wallowing in a spiritual *beis hakisei*, a big chamber pot, and they're smearing their *neshamah* with the worst kind of excrement. Their *neshamah* is polluted, and they must do a very great *teshuvah*. No question—movies are out of bounds for anybody who wants to have any connection with Judaism.

But now we'll go to the second category—books that have no harmful influence but are a waste of time. What's the *cheit*? We could say the *cheit* is *bittul Torah*, that you're losing time from learning Torah. That's true. *Bittul Torah* is a big *cheit*. Every word of Torah is happiness and success. It's Olam Haba; it's perfection. There's no question that it's a great tragedy to waste time.

But suppose women want to read books. Women don't have an *issur* of *bittul Torah*. So what's the harm?

Still, you must know that books that don't deal with Torah aren't written on a Torah foundation. There's no such thing as harmless books because the *devarim b'teilim* are full of concealed poison. If you read *Time* magazine or *Newsweek*, the poison is obvious. Unfortunately, there are plenty of people who don't know that, either. *Time* and *Newsweek* are obviously wicked periodicals. The *New York Times* is obviously a wicked newspaper. The ads alone tell you the story. Movie ads glorify immorality. Therefore, if you ask my opinion, I'd say if you're hoping for Olam Haba, don't bother to buy the *New York Times*.

But let's say you have something that was written a hundred years ago. *Ivanhoe* doesn't have any open immorality, and no *apikorsus*. I think it even has very little *avodah zarah*. It may have some *avodah zarah*, but very little. There are some books from a hundred years ago that have none at all. They have no religious connotations. And yet, they're full of poison. Only the poison is subtle. It's concealed.

What do I mean by poison? The poison is that if you read them, you'll become exactly what the author was. You are what you read. Once, every Jewish woman had in her head a picture of all the great teachings. Maybe she couldn't quote some, but she had a competent composite picture, a sum total of all the good things of Torah. Her outlook on life was a Torah outlook. But if you read secular books, even harmless ones, you must know it's going to make an impression. It will impress upon you that everything is materialism and that things happen by accident. All the great principles of your *emunah* are subtly omitted or contradicted. After a time, your mind becomes transformed.

No, I'm not going to force anybody when it comes to reading materials. I'm not going to make you *nezirim*. But since the subject came up, you should know that if you don't have a radio you are most fortunate. You are *b'nei Olam Haba*. Any home that has no connection with the surrounding world I say is a happy home, and the blessing of Hashem will be on that house forever.

Q **Doesn't a person need to keep up with the news?**

You don't need the news because all the news is cooked. You think that the radio, the newspapers, and the television are *reporting* the news? That's a great error. They are *making* the news. You don't realize that. The news is not what they report. They take certain items and magnify them. They emphasize them, make them prominent, and let other things pass by. Either they put them on the back pages, or sometimes on no page at all. There is a lot of important news, but don't expect to get it in the newspaper or on the radio or TV.

Suppose a man passed away, a righteous gentile. Let's say it's someone who conducted business with principles his entire life. That's big news. "So-and-so passed away. He was the head of a big company and was famous all his life for probity, honesty, and sterling work. He succeeded in business, and everybody respected him." That should be big news — but not for the newspapers. What's news for the newspapers? The opposite of virtue. Crime is news; wickedness is news; confrontation is news. You don't sell newspapers if you talk about decent things. Newspapers are built on lies and exaggerations, and the foolish public thinks they're getting the news. They're getting falsehood and distortion. Why should you be a sucker and pay money to read their ads and patronize the liars who are exploiting you?

Q If everything happens because of the Jewish nation (*Yevamos* 63a), isn't it important to read newspapers to know what happens?

I'll tell you a simple answer. We are so backed up on our homework that we can stop taking any more assignments. There are so many lessons in past history we haven't studied yet that we shouldn't worry about learning new ones.

I'll explain to you. You could dispense with understanding why [a recent headline reported] that a certain mafia man was shot down in a restaurant in Green Point. That certainly happened for us, but we could dispense with that information. Let's first know what happened in the time of Moshe Rabbeinu. Do you know that most yeshiva men don't know that? Most yeshiva men don't begin to know what's in the Chumash. Sometimes they know a little bit because they look in the Chumash during *kriyas haTorah* but they don't begin to know what happened in *sefer Yehoshua*. Let's study that history. That history is well-analyzed in the *midrashim* and in the Gemara. Let's study what happened in *Shoftim*, *Shmuel*, *Melachim*, and *Divrei Hayamim*.

There's so much to study before we'll be finished with this, we'll be so old, that we wouldn't have any time to read the newspapers. If you'll finish all these great subjects, you'll be an *adam gadol*, and then you'll be able to analyze the news. You'll know the news without reading the newspapers. Did you know that? The *gedolim* know the news without reading newspapers. How do they do it? You have to be a *gadol* to know. I can't tell you. Someday you'll be an old sage; you'll have gone through all the great incidents of our history, and then you'll study why this mafia man was shot down. You'll say, "Aha! That's a *mussar haskel*. It comes to teach us such-and-such. It teaches us that you shouldn't put your trust in money, in bodyguards, and so on." You'll become more pious as a result of studying that.

Q **The Rav said we must use common sense, but how can we do that, given that you've also said that our minds are so influenced by the outside world that we don't have common sense any longer?**

There was a lecture given here called, "The Torah of Common Sense." Now really, it's a Gemara: "Why do we need a *passuk* to teach us something that we can figure out on our own?" (*Kesubos* 22a). We have to learn to follow our *s'vara*, which is common sense. So this man is asking: How can we follow common sense if our mind is full of wrong ideas we've absorbed? And the answer is that you can't. You can't.

Once upon a time, the world didn't have newspapers. There was no literature. It was possible for a person to think on his own and have common sense. But today, if you read garbage, all that trash fills your mind. It's very hard to have common sense unless you try very hard to launder your mind. If you wash your mind by putting in Torah thoughts and by thinking pure and noble ideas, maybe after a while you'll get some common sense. But until you do that, you'll certainly be lacking it.

Today, when somebody says that he's using his common sense, it means he's using what he read in the *New York Times* or what he heard on the radio. That's not common sense. If you walk in the street and you hear people talking, you have to know that your mind is being poisoned. All the foolishness of people is going straight into your head. And once it's in your head, it's terrible. It's a poison.

Don't talk to fools. If you see a fool, keep away from him. It says in *Mishlei* that if you see a fool coming toward you, you should know that it's worse than a she-bear coming toward you. An enraged she-bear is less dangerous than a fool. "It's better for a person to encounter an angry she-bear than to encounter a fool with his foolishness" (*Mishlei* 17:12). You hear that? An angry she-bear is less harmful than a fool. Because when a fool talks to you, his foolishness goes into your mind—and it stays there forever.

If you have to go to college, be aware that you have a big job ahead of you—the job of cleaning your mind of all the garbage that fell into it. Of course, there's useful information as well, but there's so much garbage, so many lies and so much wickedness, that you have to do a lot of work to get rid of it. If you went to school—even to yeshiva—the English department can fill your mind with much foolishness and much garbage, I'm sorry to tell you. If the teachers would utilize the time to show the *yad Hashem* in Nature, and in history and current events, they could strengthen your *emunah* just from that. But they don't do it. Instead, you learn garbage in the yeshivas, too. So we have a big job ahead of us.

SUMMARY

- The *tefillah* of *V'lamalshinim* was instituted after the destruction of the second Beis Hamikdash, to protect us from the slanders of the early Christians, the enemy within our midst.
- It is directed against Jews who willingly promote false ideologies or persecute their fellow Jews.
- We ask Hashem *with the utmost sense of urgency* to do away with such people, because they pose such an intense spiritual danger to Klal Yisrael.
- We should know with confidence that all those who try to oppose us will ultimately disappear.
- We must guard ourselves from all the false ideologies of the world. From every side, they're trying to enter our minds to poison us. Without Hashem's help, we will never succeed in keeping them at bay.

Al Hatzaddikim

Q Why is it important to pray for *tzaddikim*?

Tzaddikim are important to pray for because they're our wealth. "*Tzaddik yesod olam*—The *tzaddik* is the foundation upon which the world stands" (*Mishlei* 10:25).

When Nevuchadnetzar took some people of Yehudah into exile in Bavel (during what's known as *galus Yechanyah*), at first he took only one thousand of the best people, "*hacharash v'hamasger*—the craftsmen and the locksmiths" (II *Melachim* 24:14). They were the scholars and men of prominence, who were so named by the people for their skill in Torah (*Yerushalmi, Nedarim* 23b). Nevuchadnetzar took them to Bavel before he exiled the rest of the population. Rather than despoil Eretz Yisrael of its material wealth, he took away their wise men. Among them were Yechezkel Hanavi, Mordechai, and Daniel, as well as Chananyah, Mishael, and Azaryah. They were among the one thousand sages, young and old, whom Nevuchadnetzar chose to enrich his own land eleven years before he returned and destroyed the Beis Hamikdash.

It's remarkable. A conqueror who wanted to despoil a nation of its *tzaddikim* and wise men! But he understood that they would be of supreme benefit to his empire. It wasn't merely because he thought their righteousness would help him. It could be. I'm not saying he wouldn't think that way. But he certainly recognized their usefulness. He made them officers in his regime. At one time, Daniel was the second in command (*Daniel* 2:46). Mordechai became a "*mishneh lamelech*—second in command" to Achashverosh (*Esther* 10:3).

When we speak of *tzaddikim*, it's a general term. It includes all the precious people who maintain our nation. "*Hashem oheiv tzaddikim*—Hashem loves *tzaddikim*" (*Tehillim* 146:8). He has compassion on *tzaddikim*. But before we ask Hashem to have compassion on them, there's one condition we ourselves must have—*we* must have compassion on the *tzaddikim*. We should feel how precious they are to *us*.

Q **Do we know who the *tzaddikim* are?**

That's a good question. The *navi* said, "*Hatzaddik avad v'ein ish sam al lev*—When the *tzaddik* passes away, people don't take it to heart" (*Yeshayah* 57:1). They say *hespedim* and mourn for him, but the *navi* says that's insufficient. People don't appreciate what they had in this *tzaddik*. Before you can appreciate *tzaddikim*, you have to know who they are.

The Gemara (*Sotah* 48b) states that in the early part of the second Beis Hamikdash era, the spirit of *nevuah* didn't exist but they still had the *bas kol*, which was a minor form of *nevuah*. The Gemara tells of two instances of a *bas kol* during that era. One was when the Sanhedrin was seated together and they suddenly heard a voice say, "One among you is fit to receive the spirit of *nevuah,* but the generation does not deserve it." They looked around and decided it must be Hillel. Now, they knew Hillel was a great man. They made him the Nasi; they had already recognized his excellence. But Hashem made a demonstration to show them they didn't recognize it enough. This Hillel who you honor and made leader—you don't realize who he is.

We see that it was necessary for the generation to be made aware of what they possessed. If you had, say, a gold mine beneath your basement floor but didn't know it, you could live that way all your life and still be a poor man. It's the knowledge of what you possess that makes you wealthy. When Hashem let us know we had a Hillel, then everybody understood he was the wealth of the nation.

The Gemara (*Shabbos* 31a) says that once two men made a wager of four hundred *zuz*, a lot of money, to see if one of them could make Hillel angry. The first man came to Hillel on *erev Shabbos*, when time was short, and tried to make him angry by asking strange questions. He went away, came back, and asked another question. Then he came back again. Each time Hillel received him with a *sever panim yafos*, a friendly face, and said, "You're asking good questions." In the end the man was so exasperated that he said, "There shouldn't be many like you." "Why?" Hillel asked. "I lost four hundred *zuz* because of you!" the man said. Hillel responded, "It's worth losing four hundred *zuz* and another four hundred *zuz*, and Hillel will not get upset."

Pay attention to what Hillel said. He said, "It's worth it that every Jew lose eight hundred *zuz* as long as we have a Hillel." It's strange that he should say such a thing, boasting in such a way. But the answer is that Hillel wasn't boasting. He was letting them know that they must appreciate the benefit of having a man among them who will not get angry. It's worth it for each person to contribute eight hundred *zuz* in order that there be a Hillel. That's why the *bas kol* came — to let the people know what they possessed.

We too must know what we possess and who the *tzaddikim* among us are. Now, I can't tell you because today we're not united in one big *kehillah*. There are *tzaddikim*, say, that the Teimanim would recognize but not the Polish Jews. The Litvaks may call a certain person a *tzaddik* while the Sephardim may know nothing about him. Therefore, it's not so easy today. But there's no question that we have *tzaddikim*. We know by tradition that there's no generation with less than thirty-six *tzaddikim* (*Sanhedrin* 97b). Who these thirty-six are is a good question.

Reb Shlomo Feldman was a *mocher sefarim* but every Chol Hamoed he called together hundreds of boys when they were off from *cheder* and taught them Torah, dispensing prizes. He did things like that constantly. I don't think you can appreciate how great was his *tzidkus*.[45]

45 From Rav Miller's biography: "A major catalyst was Reb Shlomo Feldman, a *chassid* who lived in Boro Park. Reb Shlomo was enamored by the life-altering quality of the lectures, and when he met Rabbi Miller he was awestruck. He made it his mission to draw people to the Rav. Reb Shlomo had a *sefarim* store in Boro Park, which was more a center for disseminating Torah than a business. He begged Rabbi Miller to let him sell the tapes in his store, and he did. Reb Shlomo kept the price at $2. He was a consummate salesman for the tapes, always getting people to buy them or try one for free ....

"Over time, he influenced countless *chassidim* from Boro Park, Williamsburg, Monsey, New Square, and elsewhere to buy the tapes. He would also encourage them to go in person to hear a *shiur*, and many did.

Not long ago there was a *tzaddik*, Rav Asher Zimmerman, *zecher tzaddik livrachah*. He didn't look like a *tzaddik*. He looked like a plain man. But I knew him personally for at least fifty years. He never spoke *lashon hara*, even *avak lashon hara*. He was a man who could answer any questions in *halachah l'ma'aseh*. People called him constantly with questions and he always answered. It was a great loss when Reb Asher passed away but when he was among us, he wasn't appreciated. I'm not blaming anybody because the generation didn't have *ruach hakodesh* or a *bas kol* to point him out.

When I was a boy, there was a young man I admired as a *tzaddik*. He learned all the time, was always polite, an *anav*, and he respected you when you asked him questions. In my mind, he was a *tzaddik*. I lost touch with him when I went to Europe, but when I was in America, I looked at him as a *tzaddik*.

I had a *rebbi* who taught me the whole *masechta Kesubos* privately in his house, along with every *Tosfos*, and he didn't ask for a penny. I consider him a *tzaddik*.

You'll meet *tzaddikim* in your lifetime, certainly. But you won't know all the *tzaddikim*. It's a great loss for us if we don't appreciate them, so right now we have to get busy thinking that we love all the *tzaddikim*, whoever and wherever they are. As you walk down the street in Williamsburg or in Boro Park, you should suspect that

---

"He was so successful that on one Chol Hamoed, after a special *shiur* delivered in the shul in honor of yom tov, Rabbi Miller said to Reb Shlomo, "What did you do to me? I was almost the only one without a *shtreimel*!"

Also in the biography: "The children of Reb Shlomo Feldman relate that when they were sitting *shivah* for their father, Rabbi Miller came over. For ten minutes he sat and described for them their father's situation in Olam Haba. He described how their father was sitting in a garden, in Gan Eden, on a royal throne, with a crown decorating his head, bejeweled with all the various *mitzvos* and meritorious deeds he brought with him. His face was shining, with a tremendous smile, looking down at his progeny. Rabbi Miller continued with this description, all the while emphasizing that this was reality, not theory. As they recalled, it did not sound like a discourse; rather it made them feel as if they were actually experiencing what he was describing."

Rav Miller dedicated lecture #999 to Reb Shlomo.

maybe there are *tzaddikim* here. I'm sure there are *tzaddikim* there. Wherever you go in a Jewish *kehillah*, you have to know that there's a possibility. Are you thinking about them?

We have *tzaddikim* among us today, and we should prize them more than we prize our own property. Here, in *Al Hatzaddikim*, we ask Hashem to please spare the *tzaddikim* whether we know who they are or not. But first, before asking Hashem to think about them, are you thinking about them? If Hashem loves *tzaddikim*, so should we.

Q **When we mention the word "*tzaddikim*," does that exclude the rest of us?**

By no means. There are *tzaddikim* here. No question. Plenty of Jews who mean business with their Judaism. They're bringing up their children as good Jews. They're sacrificing for Yiddishkeit. We have, *baruch Hashem* — not hundreds — we have tens of thousands of *tzaddikim*! Men and women, boys and girls.

Once upon a time, an American boy who was a *shomer Shabbos* was an anachronism, a curiosity. I remember that. Today we have a golden youth, an idealistic youth. Married people today — not only *kollel* people — a lot of professional people, too. They were brought up in *mesivta*s and they mean business with their Yiddishkeit! Flatbush, Boro Park, other places. They mean business. And we're proud of them!

Q **Are women also included in the prayer for *tzaddikim*?**

Tzaddikim includes not only men. *Tzaddikim* includes women, too. I can point out one or two without hesitation. Rebbetzin Kaplan who founded the first girls' seminary is without question one of them. She had fourteen children of her own and taught thousands of girls. She raised up *doros*, not only of teachers but *balebusteh*s who brought up *frum* families of *b'nei* Torah. No question she is among the *tzaddikim*. Rav Aharon Kotler, *zt"l*, said that without her the *kollelim* wouldn't exist in America. She prepared girls to marry *kollel* boys.

Going back further, Sarah Schenirer was a *tzaddeikess*. No question. She started Bais Yaakov in Poland. I remember that the *menahel ruchni* of our Slabodka yeshiva once went to Poland for a visit. When he returned, we sat around his table and he told us that in Poland he saw girls who were like *fartzeitige rebbetzin*s, old-time *rebbetzin*s. I heard that from him sixty years ago. She planted in their hearts such deep *emunah*, such great *ahavas Hashem*. I once passed a home in Flatbush and overheard a little girl sitting on the steps saying to her friend, "A *bas Yisrael* doesn't do that!" It was a beautiful thing to hear from a little girl in Flatbush. But where did that come from? From Sarah Schenirer.

Every woman — in the privacy of her home, even in the kitchen — can grow in *shleimus*. To a great extent, it was David Hamelech's mother who was responsible for the *gadol* he became. He said, "*Ani avdecha, ben amasecha* — I am your servant, the son of your handmaid" (*Tehillim* 116:16). His mother! His mother didn't have a yeshiva. Her *kitchen* was where she became great. When little David used to totter into the kitchen, she spoke to him and inspired him. That's how David grew up. "I'm Your servant," he sang to Hashem. Why am I Your servant? "Because I'm the son of your handmaid." She was serving You in the house! In the kitchen, when I was a little boy, she was serving You. She served You by bringing me up this way.

Many women have become tremendously great in the home just by how they raised their children. There's no greater mission than raising Jewish children! Sometimes a woman calls me on the phone to tell me that she feels unfulfilled with her duties in the home. But the truth is that a man can be sitting and learning Torah and writing *chiddushim* and also feel unfulfilled. We must remember why we're doing what we're doing. A woman who forgets what she's working for, what greatness lies in building a Jewish home, will of course feel unfulfilled. You have to constantly remind yourself that you're working in the greatest endeavor available to the human race. You're raising up a living Shas! A mother in her home is actually filling the world with Torah.

Suppose *masechta Brachos* was alive. Imagine it had blood, bones, skin, and hair, and could talk. At first he's a little toddler, a mischievous fellow who breaks things. But what wouldn't you do for *masechta Brachos*? In the beginning, you'd have to change his diapers and a lot of things like that. It's a nuisance. When he's bigger, he's a bigger nuisance. Big boys are also nuisances. There's always going to be trouble in the house when there are boys around. It's human nature to be a nuisance. Now, suppose it's not only *Brachos*—it's the whole Shas toddling around in your house! Even though he turns on the water in the bathroom and floods it, for Shas you'd do anything. And your daughters are even better. Your daughters are going to be a whole lot of Shassen. You're creating *tzaddikim* and *tzidkaniyos* in your home.

Certainly women are included in this *tefillah* about *tzaddikim*. They may be hiding with *tzniyus* but there are women—great women. They're very important, whether we recognize them or not. So when you're saying this *tefillah*, keep them in mind. It's a special *bakashah*—"Please, Hashem, keep the *tzaddikim* alive among us."

Q **Is it enough to love *tzaddikim* in our hearts?**

You shouldn't just love *tzaddikim*; you should give them *brachos*. That's a profitable business. The more *brachos* you give the *tzaddikim*, the more returns you'll get for your investment because Hashem promised Avraham, "*Va'avarcha mevarachecha*—I will bless those who bless You" (*Bereishis* 12:3). Not only for Avraham, but also for any Jew. Certainly, if you bless *tzaddikim*, you're going to be blessed.

Tosfos in *Chullin* (49a) cites a story from the *Yerushalmi Brachos*. A certain gentile was walking on the road when he encountered Rabbi Yishmael and said to him, "*Al-salam aleikum*—Peace upon you, Rabbi." Rabbi Yishmael answered, "My blessing to you is already said." In other words, "It's not necessary for me to respond to your blessing with a blessing of my own because it's automatic. It's done already." Since Hashem told Avraham, "I will bless those who bless you," Rabbi Yishmael was saying, "As soon as you blessed me, you were already blessed by Hashem." *Tosfos* makes a point of telling us that this rule of "I will bless those who bless you" applies even to a gentile who blesses a Jew. After all, it was an Arab traveler who was blessing Rabbi Yishmael. It wasn't a *kohen*. It wasn't even a Jew. "Even a gentile who blesses a Jew is going to be blessed." If a gentile is rewarded for blessing a Jew, imagine what blessings Hashem showers upon His own children when they bless each other. Another lesson from this story is that this *brachah* of "I will bless those who bless you" isn't only applicable if one blesses the whole nation or intones the special blessings of *Birkas Kohanim*. No! Even someone who blesses an individual Jew, as the gentile in our story did, has already secured himself a *brachah* that comes directly from Hashem.

If you bless *tzaddikim*, you're certainly going to be blessed. Even when you don't know who they are, you should *daven* that they live long, be healthy, have good *parnassah*, have *nachas* from their children, and succeed in all the things they do. If you know someone who is a *tzaddik*, you should think about that person specifically. And don't wait for the *brachah* of *Al Hatzaddikim* in Shemoneh Esrei. When you leave here tonight, on the way home, say, "Hashem, please bless all the *tzaddikim*." And when you come to the *brachah* of *Al Hatzaddikim*, exert yourself even more.

Q **Is it too ambitious to try to become a *tzaddik*?**

If you're ambitious to make yourself a *tzaddik*, don't be afraid. Don't be ashamed. Don't say, who am I? "*B'derech she'adam rotzeh leileich, bah molichin oso*—In the way a man wishes to go, he is led" (*Makkos* 10b). Anybody who sincerely desires to make progress will find help coming his way. Surprising help. Doors will open. New thoughts will pop into his mind that never occurred to him before.

When all is said and done, you might not become a *tzaddik*. But the desire itself is worthwhile.

And why are you doing it? You're doing it because you want to help Klal Yisrael. The better you are, the better your generation will be. It will prosper and be blessed because of you. If there's another *tzaddik*, that's another additional *brachah* for the Am Yisrael. If you're the one who can be it, Hashem will reward your efforts.

Q **What's the difference between *tzaddikim* and *chassidim*?**

There's a big difference. They're two different classes of people. *Chassidim* are greater than *tzaddikim*. A *tzaddik* is someone who fulfills the Torah. He won't talk *lashon hara*. He won't say any words of *ona'as devarim*. He won't hurt anybody's feelings, whether his wife's or his neighbor's. He's careful never to hurt anybody's feelings. He's *mekayem* the entire *Shulchan Aruch*. That's a *tzaddik*.

A *chassid* goes beyond the line of duty. A *chassid* is a person who has a great deal of wisdom. People don't know that. The *Mesillas Yesharim* explains that a *chassid* needs a great deal of learning, a great deal of wisdom. As a *mashal*—a boy is walking with his father in the street and they pass a fruit stand. The father stops to look at the apples and then keeps walking. The boy thinks, *My father likes apples. I'm going to buy nice apples for him. He didn't ask me, but I'm going to buy them for him anyway.* From then on, he always stops off to buy apples for his father. His father never asked him to do so, but he saw that his father is interested in apples, so he goes ahead and does it on his own.

"*V'achalta v'savata uveirachta*—You will eat and be satisfied and bless" (*Devarim* 8:10). After you eat bread and you're satiated, you're obligated to say Birkas Hamazon. That's a *din* of the Torah. Hashem is our Father. He wants us to say thanks to Him. Now, if He wants us to say thanks to Him, why should we wait until we eat? So, we make a *brachah* beforehand—*Hamotzi lechem min ha'aretz*. He asked us to say a *brachah* afterward, but we also say one beforehand. The Jewish nation are thereby acting like *chassidim*. They made a *takanah* to bless Hashem not only after they ate, but before, too.

And not only on bread, but even on apples and peanuts. If Hashem, our Father, likes to hear our *brachos* thanking Him, we follow that model to thank Him even when He didn't ask us specifically. We thank Him for our clothing, *malbish arumim*. We thank Him for our shoes, *she'asah li kol tzarki*. We thank Him for a nice black hat, *oteir Yisrael b'sifarah*. We thank Him for everything.

Now, you have to be careful. Sometimes you might learn the wrong lessons. You might go in the wrong direction. You need what the *Mesillas Yesharim* calls *mishkal hachassidus*. He has a whole chapter on it. You must know how to weigh things. True *chassidim* are *maskilim*—they have great wisdom. They understand the *derech Hashem*.

When a *chassid* walks in the street and has *hana'ah* from the trees, he says, "I thank You, Hashem, for the beautiful trees." He says it quietly. If someone else would hear him, they'd think something was wrong with him. But he's a *chassid*, so he acts *lifnim mishuras hadin*, beyond the letter of the law.

Avraham Avinu was a *chassid*. Avraham understood that this world was an inn, a hotel that Hashem made for guests. We're all the guests here. In this hotel, He gives us all good things. Avraham decided to emulate Hashem, even though He didn't tell him to. He made a grove of trees like a hotel and invited guests who passed by to sit under his trees so he could give them good things to eat. That's *chassidus*.

When the guests finished eating, they wanted to thank Avraham, but he said, "Don't thank me. Thank the Proprietor." "Who's the proprietor?" they asked. "Hashem," he said. So they all thanked Hashem. That's how Avraham spread *hakaras tov* and *avodas Hashem* in the world.

When Avraham saw guests coming, he ran out to meet them. He was an old man, and very wealthy and powerful, but he not only welcomed every guest, he *ran* to meet them. Even on a boiling hot day! Even then, he was afraid words alone wouldn't persuade them to stay, so he fell on the ground and begged them. Can you imagine such a thing! He lay down on the ground and begged them, "*Al na sa'avor mei'al avdecha*—Please don't pass by your servant" (*Bereishis* 18:3). If you were looking at him, you'd think, *What's wrong with him*? But Hashem saw it and thought, *That's the one I chose*. Avraham went out of his way because he knew that My principle was to make a world of *hachnasas orchim*, and he wants to emulate My ways even without being commanded to do it. If that's the case, then he's the man I want.

The same applies to Rivkah. When Eliezer came, she had a heavy pitcher on her shoulder. Eliezer asked, "*Hashkini na m'at mayim mikadeich*—Please give me a little water from your pitcher" (*Bereishis* 24:17). Now, Rivkah was a young girl, and it was a heavy pitcher. She could have pointed and said, "There's a well over there, mister." She could have said, "You can take the pitcher off my shoulder." But she said neither. Rather, she took the pitcher off herself and gave him water to drink. As he drank, she said, "Allow me to give water to your camels, too" (ibid 24:19). Camels? One camel can drink enough for thirty men! But Eliezer said yes. He wanted to see just how "*meshuga*" she was for *chessed*. She ran back and forth and back and forth, back and forth, drawing water for the camels. "*V'ha'ish mishta'eh*" (ibid. 24:21)—he was "amazed" at her. It was a wild thing to do. Someone else would have said she's *meshuga*. She's not a good *shidduch* for Yitzchak. But when Eliezer saw that, he knew she was the one, because Hashem loves the *chassidim*. He loves *tzaddikim*, but He loves *chassidim* even more.

Q **Can anyone become a *chassid*?**

Everybody is a candidate to become a *chassid*. But that doesn't mean that you can immediately practice *chassidus*. We're not talking about being *machmir*. Being *machmir* is easy. We're talking about being a *chassid*. It's not so easy because first you must learn and understand the *derech Hashem*. When you learn the *derech Hashem* and become convinced by *haskalah rabbah*—that's the wording in *Mesillas Yesharim*; *haskalah rabbah* means "great wisdom"—what Hashem wants, and you add effort to go beyond what you're required to do, then you become a *chassid*.

Let's take the case of a man like Rav Avraham Kalmanowitz. He was a Rav in Tiktin, a small town. He came here and was active in the Vaad Hatzalah. During the war, he received a telegram that Jews from the Mir Yeshiva and others were stranded and needed a large amount of money immediately to buy tickets for traveling. If they didn't get it, they'd be stuck, and who knows what would happen. So, on Shabbos he got into an open car and drove through Williamsburg back and forth, crying out, "Bring money! *Pikuach nefesh!*" People ran to his house and brought him money on Shabbos. Thanks to his efforts, the entire Mir yeshiva was saved from destruction. Now, that's a *chassid*. He knew that "*Pikuach nefesh docheh Shabbos*"—you can violate Shabbos to save people from a life-threatening situation. Some people might have rationalized that maybe they'd be saved without violating Shabbos. But a man who's a *maskil* knows not to fool around when it comes to *pikuach nefesh*. You must be *mechalel Shabbos* even for a possible *pikuach nefesh*. Therefore, his *p'sak halachah* was to be *mechalel Shabbos* in order to save them. And he did. He saved the Mirrer Yeshiva. Eventually, he brought them here and founded the Mirrer Yeshiva in America, and it became a lighthouse. Generations and generations of *bachurim* have been trained in that yeshiva. Looking back, we see he was a great man. I'm not sure whether people who knew him at the time thought he was a *tzaddik*. A long beard, an old-time *rav*, but nothing particularly exceptional. Only now, when they look back, do they see that he was anything but usual. He not only saved the Mir, but all the generations that followed. This neighborhood was completely changed thanks to him. Not just Ashkenazim. Sephardi Jews have moved in and are influenced. A very great change has taken place in the Sephardi *kehillah* because of him. So we look back and see now that this was a great man.

Once upon a time, I lived in Williamsburg. But Williamsburg has changed tremendously since then. It was transformed into one of the best *kehillos* in the world. And it was the work of one man—the Satmarer Rav made Williamsburg a different kind of *kehillah*. He turned Williamsburg upside down. It became better than Satmar in Hungary. Anybody who could take thousands of people and shape them into very observant, loyal Jews, was a *tzaddik*. No question about it.

Rav Aharon Kotler, *zt"l*—because of him there is a Lakewood. And not only Lakewood. From Lakewood, they traveled all over

America and opened *kollelim*. That couldn't happen through just an ordinary person.

Rav Shraga Feivel Mendlowitz turned the world upside down. Not only did he build Torah Voda'as, he also built Camp Mesivta, the first *frum* summer camp. He made Monsey. He made Torah Umesorah. And he refused to be called "Rabbi." "Mr. Mendlowitz, that's my name," he'd say. At the time, many people didn't think he was such an extraordinary person.

I'll take the liberty of giving one more example. When I was in Lithuania, a friend of mine visited the yeshiva of Telz. He said he was walking with a *bachur* through the old country farms just outside the Telz yeshiva, and said, "*Es shmekt zach funn Ketzos.*" The fields around Telz smelled like *Ketzos Hachoshen*. What did he mean? For generations, people had walked there talking in learning over the *Ketzos Hachoshen*. When the *Ketzos Hachoshen* first came out, it created a storm in Torah Judaism. It was such a *geshmakeit* that the world was captivated by it.

It was written by a poor *melamed*. He didn't even have money for wood to feed the fire in his stove. His hands were so freezing that when he wrote the *Ketzos*, he had to write it under a blanket. And since he was poor, he couldn't publish it, so he wrote it over and over again. That's why it became so successful — because he kept rewriting it until he perfected the language. Others who had money published their *sefarim* right away, and it was sometimes difficult to understand what they were saying. But the Ketzos had to write it over and over again until it was crystal clear. His *lashon* captivated the whole *tzibbur*, and for generations now they've been learning *Ketzos Hachoshen* with a *geshmak* and saying *shiur* from it. Today, the *Ketzos Hachoshen* has *sefarim* written about it, with *kashya*s and *terutzim*. All from a man who was an unknown *melamed* at first. There's no question in my mind that the *Ketzos Hachoshen* is recognized in Gan Eden as one of the great *chassidim*.

Now, I'm going to make another statement. When you see a family of *tzaddikim* — husbands with big beards, wives very *frum*, *frum* children and grandchildren—when you go back to the roots, who started this? The mother. The mother was a Bais Yaakov girl who decided to emulate Rebbetzin Kaplan, marry a *ben Torah* and have a big family. Now, in retrospect, we see she wasn't an ordinary girl. She was an exceptional personality to have such a great *zechus*.

When we say "*Al hatzaddikim v'al hachassidim*," we should think about these people who were *mezakim es harabbim*, who changed our nation and are still changing it today.

People in America today don't know what it was like years ago. Even compared to Europe, a tremendous transformation has taken place. *Baruch Hashem*, we stand surprised at the Torah explosion. Who is responsible for it? The *tzaddikim*. "*Tzaddik yesod olam.*" Therefore, we have to pray for them, even if we don't recognize them.

When you say *Al Hatzaddikim*, think of all these people whose deeds will someday be recognized for what they contributed to our nation—all the great changes they are effecting in our nation, the families they've raised and influenced who have spread out and built Torah institutions. And even not famous people, just *frum* Jews who did certain great deeds of their own. That's number one in this *tefillah*. Have that in mind. They're our wealth, and we're proud of them.

PRACTICAL ADVICE

Q How can one make himself a *tzaddik*?

How to become a *tzaddik*? It's not that difficult. "*Ki karov eilecha hadavar me'od b'ficha uvilvavcha la'asoso*—The matter is very close to you, in your mouth and your thoughts and with your acts" (*Devarim* 301:4). The *passuk* supplies us with a three-step program. First, *b'ficha*—say certain things with your mouth. For instance, ask Hashem to bless the *tzaddikim*. That's easy. Next, *bilvavcha*—don't just say with your mouth, but *think* about the *tzaddikim* sometimes, too. Think how much you love them. Even if you don't, think about it anyhow. Persuade yourself to think that you really love them. That's auto-suggestion. After a while, you'll come to love them. And then, *la'asoso*—after a while, begin to imitate the *tzaddikim*. Emulate them. Become one *l'ma'aseh*. Get busy doing what they do.

Q How can we help our families feel connected to *tzaddikim* and become *tzaddikim*?

Have pictures of *tzaddikim* on the walls of your home. Some very, very pious people have a prejudice against pictures, but we're not like that. We do have pictures.

I like pictures of Nature. You can have that. Why not? While you're looking at the landscape, at a beautiful meadow, think about the creation that Hashem made for our happiness. But why not pictures of *tzaddikim*, too? A picture of the Rambam. A picture of the Vilna Gaon. If you're a Lubavitcher, pictures of some of the Rebbes.

There are so many *tzaddikim* who can adorn our walls. Your children will see that these are your heroes. It's a very big asset in a home when you have pictures of *tzaddikim* adorning your walls. The whole family looks up to them.

And it should be a principle to speak about *tzaddikim*, too—to praise *talmidei chachamim* always. The people who learn Torah, yeshiva people, *rabbanim*, *talmidei chachamim*, *gedolim*—your mouth should be full of nothing but lavish praise for the heroes of our nation. A father and mother should always speak about the great ideal of becoming a righteous man, a servant of Hashem.

Every Jewish home should have *pushka*s—charity boxes. When I was a little boy, I remember how every Jewish kitchen had *pushka*s nailed all around the door—on both sides, up and down. Each represented a yeshiva in the old Yishuv in Yerushalayim. There was a whole ceremony to unlock the *pushka* with a little key and empty out its contents. An elderly Yerushalayimer Yid would come to the home and pour the coins out onto the table, and the family stood and watched as he counted the pennies. Only pennies. A nickel in the *pushka* was a rarity. A nickel in those days was enough for a bus ride. Then the man wrote out a receipt, took out his little hammer, and nailed the charity box back onto the wall. Because of that the whole family felt they were in contact with Yerushalayim, with the *Ir Hakodesh.*

A genuine Jewish home should have charity boxes. The mother should always drop in something before she kindles the Shabbos candles. That's how children should be taught, too. The children should always know their home supports Torah institutions and is in contact with the Torah institutions. From infancy, a Jewish child has to feel a responsibility. When he grows up, he'll feel it's his duty to write checks. He'll be on the Board of Directors for a yeshiva because you raised him to be connected to *talmidei chachamim.*

The home should be a place of *tefillah*, and it's the mother who presents herself as the symbol of prayer, the model of *tefillah* for the Am Yisrael. Now, she can't stand and say long prayers. She's busy with a lot of things in the house. But the mother must be a person of prayer. Our mothers always prayed a great deal. A Jewish mother should pray even more than a man prays. Men have certain circumscribed duties and because of that, some of them gallop through the davening. It's something that has to be done, so they do it. But Jewish mothers don't gallop through davening. A Jewish mother in the home should be turning to Hashem all day long. The old-time Jewish woman had a handbook of prayers—prayers for every kind of eventuality. She would be praying for help in the home, that her supper should come out delicious, for a child who wasn't well, or for a child who wasn't going exactly on the straight path. Today, too, a mother prays constantly that the washing machine shouldn't break down, that her husband should earn a good livelihood, that he should find favor in the eyes of his boss and get a raise.

The first thing in the morning the children should hear when they get up is, "Abba is davening in shul." "Abba's learning." When children ask, "Did Totty come back from shul yet?" the mother should tell them, "Totty is in shul talking to Hashem. He'll be home soon." That's how the Jewish home should start every day. Besides that, the mother should spend her day speaking to Hashem about everything. In the olden days, the Jewish mother was a symbol of prayer even more than the husband. It's something that's forgotten today, but that was one of the greatest achievements in a Jewish home. A Jewish mother should always be praying. The children who grow up with that know that their house is a home where Hashem resides. The aristocratic Jewish home actually became a Mishkan, a Beis Hamikdash.

Now, I'm not saying that the home is the sole criterion, the only place to accomplish. There are other areas besides the home. For a man, there are surely opportunities outside the home. Although the home is extremely important, he has other areas, too, where he must make progress. But the mother, father, and children all must know that the true measure of their success is in the home. What goes on in your tent — between the four walls of your home — is where your greatness is achieved. That's your opportunity to mold a nation. The home is what counts!

Once a man understands this function, he puts his energy into his home. He makes sure to learn Torah in his house, do *mitzvos* in his house, and make *brachos* out loud. He brings up his children with idealism. He and his wife constantly praise good character and kindly words. All day long, whatever they do, they put their *kochos* into their house. Maybe it's a little home, only five people. If you're *zocheh*, if you merit it, it's crowded with ten people there, maybe more. But whatever the size, that's where they serve Hashem. That's where they grow great.

SUMMARY

- We pray for the welfare of *tzaddikim* because we recognize that they are the true wealth of our nation.

- There are *tzaddikim* in our generation, too, though we don't always recognize them. We should try our best to discover them and learn from them, but regardless, we *daven* for them all, whoever and wherever they are.
- "*Tzaddikim*," of course, includes women just as much as men. Women can achieve tremendous *shleimus* by fulfilling their role in the home, and we certainly must have them in mind when we say this *brachah*.
- When we bless *tzaddikim*, we automatically receive a *brachah* ourselves, because Hashem told Avraham, "I will bless those who bless you."
- Crying out to Hashem in davening helps us become *tzaddikim* ourselves, and we should desire to become *tzaddikim*.
- As much as Hashem loves *tzaddikim*, He loves *chassidim* even more, because they go beyond what's required of them to do things that make Hashem happy. But it's not simple to be a real *chassid*—it requires great wisdom to be able to understand Hashem's will.

Boneih Yerushalayim

Q How should we think about Yerushalayim of old?

Just as David envisioned all the details for the Beis Hamikdash and prepared all the materials, so he prepared all the songs that the Levi'im would sing in the Beis Hamikdash. He left out nothing. And this is one of them: "*Samachti b'omrim li, beis Hashem neileich*—I rejoiced when they said to me, 'We shall go to the house of Hashem'" (*Tehillim* 122:1). What does that mean?

All over Eretz Yisrael, people waited for the times when they could fulfill the *mitzvah* of being *oleh regel*. Three times every year, this *mitzvah* was incumbent upon every man. People packed their bags and said their farewells, and then the crier of the town came by and announced, "*Beis Hashem neileich!* We're going to the Beis Hamikdash!" This cry resounded across the entire expanse of Eretz Yisrael, in every town and hamlet.

Everybody now became full of enthusiasm and *simchah*. They looked forward to walking together on the roads and meeting their brothers from different towns and different tribes as they converged on the main road leading toward Yerushalayim. And as they went, they were singing. All the way there, they were singing *shirei David avdecha* (the songs of David, Your servant). Their heads were so high in the clouds that they weren't aware how much distance they had covered. Their *neshamos* were soaring *bishmei marom*, in the heavens above. That's why, when they finally arrived, it says, "*Omdos hayu ragleinu bish'arayich, Yerushalayim* — Our feet were standing in your gates, Yerushalayim." Where were their heads? Their heads weren't at the gates of Yerushalayim — their heads were in the clouds. When they arrived in Yerushalayim, they suddenly realized that they had traveled many miles.

The first important lesson is that before they even left, they cried out and said, "I rejoiced when they said to me, 'We shall go to the house of Hashem.'" Each one rejoiced because the biggest *simchah* is to be close to Hashem. Only when one is distant from Hashem does he become sad and discouraged. When a person realizes that his purpose in life is being fulfilled, he gains energy to accomplish that which he would otherwise be unable to do. When people instinctively realize that they are wasting their lives, it creates an undertone of sadness. Even in the midst of revelry, when people seem to be having a good time, there's an underlying sadness because they know it will all come to an end sooner or later, and there's no meaning in what they're doing. But when they find purpose in their activities, when they know that there's a reason for their endeavors, they gain a new joy and a new energy in life. Therefore, the news that the time had come to start moving and coming closer to Hashem was a great tiding. Everyone was filled with a great gladness and looked forward to the journey.

Of course, this *mizmor* is talking about when everybody went up to Yerushalayim and it was part of their lives. We have to supply details from our imagination. We have to imagine that we are living in those great days and traveling together with our brothers on the road toward the Beis Hamikdash. And we're singing this song, *Tehillim* 122. This was one of the songs they sang on the roads. They felt how fortunate their lot was to be chosen for a life of purpose.

For us today, it means that when we have the opportunity to go learn in a *beis medrash* or *daven* in a *beis haknesses*, it's important that we go with excitement, with a feeling that it's a privilege. If you go to a yeshiva or a *beis haknesses*, you're recognizing that you have been chosen for the function of coming to the House of Hashem to serve Him. You go in happiness, to demonstrate your aristocracy. Let's say, *l'havdil elef havdalos*, when a lord in England went to Parliament to sit in his seat in the House of Lords, did he do it as an onerous duty? No, he was happy to do it. He wanted to establish his status as a peer. Every time he went, it was a demonstration that he belonged to the aristocracy. His father and grandfather before him sat in that seat. The Duke of Wyndham sat in the same seat as his father's father did, all the way back. Therefore, he went proudly, to establish his status and maintain it.

The *shamash* in the towns of Europe used to go around in the morning and cry out, "*Kumu la'avodas haBorei*—Get up to serve Your Creator." That's how they woke up in the towns in Europe for generations. All the Am Yisrael arose with alacrity to exercise their privilege, to thank Hashem "*asher bachar banu mikol ha'amim*—Who chose us from among all the nations." They went happily. They hastened to the house of their peers where all the aristocrats were gathered. Whether you were a peddler or the town rabbi, you went together, shoulder to shoulder. They all sat in the "House of Lords," demonstrating that they were the Am Hashem, chosen forever.

That's what David is saying here. When they heard the proclamation, "*Beis Hashem neileich*," everyone was already full of joy. They felt their purpose keenly and were now about to embark on the path toward achieving it. They were in a state of happiness even before the time arrived.

We can achieve some of that, but we have to imagine the details of the trip. It was like a river forming—first it began with little trickles that came from a spring. Gradually, the trickles converged and became a bigger stream. Then this stream became a tributary of larger ones. Finally, there was a majestic river rolling on toward the sea. That's how it was. First came people in little groups from the small towns, singing as they went. Then they heard behind the hills another group singing. Soon their friends came into sight and they joined each other. As they marched together, the clamor of their singing became louder. Then they heard groups of others from all sides, singing. Groups coming from here and there. They were all converging on the main road. Finally, the main road became so clogged that you had to walk inch by inch. But they all continued singing. By now, they didn't know they were walking. Their minds were in the heavens. They were so enraptured—they were in such ecstasy with the enthusiasm of singing together—that they lost all sense of time and place. Ah, if we could hear that song now! We'd be changed people. Imagine hundreds and thousands of men singing together. They all knew the songs, and they all knew the language. They all were sincere, and their hearts were devoted to Hashem.

So they traveled along the road to Yerushalayim. Suddenly somebody said, "We're in Yerushalayim!" Until that moment they weren't aware. Suddenly—"*Omdos hayu ragleinu*—Our feet were standing, *bish'arayich*—in your gates, Yerushalayim" (*Tehillim* 122:2).

They didn't stop, however. They continued singing. As others came from all sides through different gates, everyone converged on the main streets until there was no place to go, until they were a standing mass in the streets of Yerushalayim. And even then, they didn't stop singing. Yerushalayim was full of song.

Ah! If only we could have seen it. We'd be different people. But we can imagine it.

What does Yerushalayim "*habenuyah*, the built city" (*Tehillim* 122:3) mean?

David Hamelech built it with several purposes. First, it would be a city devoted to Hashem. All the people who converged on Yerushalayim knew that it was the place for serving Hashem. It was the *Ir Hashem*. The city was one big Beis Hamikdash.

As they entered the gates of Yerushalayim, the street was already *kadosh*. The walls of Yerushalayim created in *halachah* a certain boundary of *kedushah*. For instance, if you had a *korban Shlamim* or a *korban Todah*, you could eat it anywhere within the walls of Yerushalayim, but not beyond them. If you had *ma'aser sheini*, you could only eat it within the walls of Yerushalayim. The city itself was *kadosh*.

The streets of Yerushalayim were paved from the *machatzis hashekel* money. After they had taken the *terumas halishkah* to buy *korbanos tzibbur*, the amount left over each year was used for the streets of Yerushalayim because it was *kadosh*.

In Yerushalayim, no visitors paid rent because Yerushalayim didn't belong to any individual. It belonged to all the *shevatim*. The rest of Eretz Yisrael was divided. Each tribe had its own separate territory. But Yerushalayim was like an international property. It belonged to no one, so no one had any property rights. If someone squatted in Yerushalayim in a home, he remained there and didn't have to pay rent. If someone who lived there took in a visitor for *yom tov*, he didn't charge rent, the Gemara says. You couldn't collect any rent in Yerushalayim because it wasn't your property.

David had planned it that way. When he said "*Yerushalayim habenuyah*," he meant *a city that was built for a purpose*. Among his purposes was that it should be a place to bond together all the *shivtei Hashem*. Its purpose was to bring together all Jews, to reunite them as brothers, no matter how different they were or how far they had come.

In the Shabbos Mevarchim blessing for Rosh Chodesh we say, "*chaverim kol Yisrael*—all Jews as brothers." We pray for the time when once more we'll come together in Yerushalayim and everybody will be *chaverim*—whether you're a Jew from Siberia or India or New York or Persia. Jews have varied complexions now. Some are swarthy, some light-skinned. Their languages are different. Even the way they read *lashon kodesh* is so different that it makes it hard to communicate.

Nevertheless, the time will come when they must come together.

Coming together is the first part of the job.[46] The second part is *keeping* us together so we shouldn't *chas v'shalom* split up again. That will be a monumental task. When Mashiach comes, he'll bring all of us to join together into one great nation, but then the great miracle of keeping us together will begin. That will truly be a miracle — but it's a miracle that was first accomplished by David. He set the precedent. When Yerushalayim was built, it was open for everybody. It was *Yerushalayim habenuyah.* It was a city built to bring every part of the nation together.

What will keep us together? The bond of *avodas Hashem.* When Yosef's brothers came to him after their father passed away, they were concerned that Yosef might start thinking of taking revenge for what they had done to him. They threw themselves at his feet, saying, "*Sa na pesha avdei Elokei avicha* — Please forgive the iniquity done by the servants of the G-d of your father" (*Bereishis* 50:17). They understood that the strongest bond between brothers is that they all serve the G-d of their father. That's what keeps them together.

It's only when Jews forget Hashem, severing that bond, that they can split up and forget they're brothers. That's what happened in Europe. The Reform Jews in America forgot they had brothers there. When there was still time to save perhaps millions of Jewish lives, their leader of the Reform, Stephen Wise,[47] and his cohorts prevailed upon President Roosevelt to desist from efforts to help the European Jews,[48] thereby leaving them to be destroyed in Hitler's crematoria.

---

46 See commentary to the *brachah* "*Teka B'shofar*" above.

47 Reform leader Stephen Wise was the most vocal American Jew in the public eye during World War II, and he was a close confidant of President Franklin D. Roosevelt. In August 1942, reports of Nazi genocide reached Wise. Under pressure from the State Department, he promised not to publicize the news — even though millions of lives were at stake! Today, Wise and his ilk are recognized as Roosevelt lackeys who blocked efforts to save the lives of millions of their own people.

48 Many Jews rose to public office in the United States, including Bernard Baruch, Henry Morgenthau, Herbert Lehmann, and Samuel Rosenman, a judge who was Roosevelt's speechwriter during the war years. When a group of Orthodox Jews approached him to help save Jews from the Nazis, he refused to get them an

By contrast, the *gedolei Yisrael* understood that that their bond through *Hashem Elokei Yisrael* united them with all the Jews of Europe. They were the ones who were genuinely concerned. It was the *gedolei Yisrael* who created the Vaad Hatzalah and rescued many Jews, even though they had very limited funds.[49] Had they had more money, they could have rescued millions.[50] If you want to hear more about it, read *Perfidy* [by Ben Hecht].[51]

---

appointment with Roosevelt, saying bluntly, "The president is busy with important war matters. We can't foist this upon him."

49 The Vaad Hatzalah was founded in 1940. After the war, John Pehle, the non-Jewish head of the War Refugee Board (WRB), wrote a letter of tribute to the Vaad: "The Vaad Hatzalah may not have had available to it the largest sums for rescue and relief; it may not have had the greatest impact on public opinion; but for imaginative and constructive ideas, for courageous programs, for ingenuity and singleness of purpose, your organization need bow to none. General [Dwight D.] Eisenhower's stern warning to the German people on his entry onto German soil not to molest those in concentration camps had its origin in a suggestion made by you. Your persistent efforts to bring relief to the refugee group in Shanghai, to the victims of oppression in Slovakia, Poland, Hungary, and elsewhere, testify to the fervor with which you fought to save precious lives. Under almost insurmountable difficulties, you devised a program to finance underground means of bringing endangered Jews from Poland across the Carpathians to the safety that Hungary afforded early in 1944. Significantly enough, this program was approved by this government on January 22, 1944, the very day that the late President Roosevelt created the War Refugee Board. Later, when Hungary was occupied by the Germans, your plans and projects were directed to securing safer places of refuge. Your assistance reached deep into Bohemia itself and brought release from Theresienstadt to many."

50 For instance, Hillel Kook, who changed his name to Peter Bergson while in the States, placed controversial full-page ads in major newspapers, demanding action. On February 16, 1943, the most famous of all Bergson's advertisements appeared in the *New York Times*: "FOR SALE to Humanity, 70,000 Jews, Guaranteed Human Beings, at $50 apiece." This shocking ad notified the world of Romania's willingness to allow these Jews out of concentration camps if they would emigrate to Palestine. Immediately, a barrage of protest came from the established non-Orthodox Jewish organizations and press. They angrily charged Bergson with deliberately and deceptively implying that each $50 contribution would save a Romanian Jew. However, the offer was genuine. Sadly, no American response was forthcoming, and these 70,000 Romanian Jews perished during the war. (See *Miraculous Journey* by Rabbi Yosef Eisen, pp. 515–16, 519.)

51 Ben Hecht was a successful screenwriter-turned-rescue activist. *Perfidy* is his

David's purpose in building Yerushalayim was to unite all Jews through serving Hashem in the Beis Hamikdash. One nation, with one Torah, serving the one G-d.

Let's imagine that we're standing in Yerushalayim now. Our feet are in Yerushalayim, but our heads are in the heavens. We're singing and hearing all kinds of dialects and expressions. Some are singing the songs and dialects of Ephraim, some in the style of Shevet Reuven and so forth. Even though they're all different, it's music to our ears—and it's music to the ears of Hashem. The whole Am Yisrael is singing to Him. Who cares what the accent is! The main thing is that their hearts are united. United in singing praises to Hashem.

Q **What's the real function of the Beis Hamikdash?**

The answer is in the *mizmor* composed entirely to the theme of the dedication of the Beis Hamikdash. "*Mizmor shir chanukas habayis l'David*—A song of a poem of the inauguration of the Beis Hamikdash by David" (*Tehillim* 30:1). Even though this *mizmor* was composed for the dedication of the Beis Hamikdash, you won't find a word about the Beis Hamikdash there except in the title, in the opening *passuk*. Beyond that, nothing is said about it. It's a remarkable fact.

What does this *mizmor* speak about? "*Hashem, Elokai, l'olam odeka*—Hashem, my G-d, I'm always going to praise You" (ibid. 30:13). It talks about the greatness of praising Hashem, of thanking Hashem, of elevating Hashem. "*Aromimcha, Hashem, ki dilisani*—I'm going to exalt You, Hashem, because You rescued me" (ibid. v. 2).

What do we see from the fact the song intended to dedicate the Beis Hamikdash speaks only about the great function of speaking

---

account of the 1953 Kastner Trial, at which Rudolph Kastner, an important member in Ben Gurion's cabinet, was found guilty of collaborating with the Nazis in Hungary, hiding from his fellow Jews the truth about the Nazis' intentions of extermination, and thereby failing to impede in any way the murder of 400,000 Hungarian Jews.

praises and thanks to Hashem? We see that that's the purpose of the Beis Hamikdash.

And that's the purpose of every Jew. *Yehudah*, which means a Jew, means "he shall praise Hashem." When somebody calls you a Jew, he doesn't realize it but he's saying you're a person whose career is to single-mindedly praise Hashem. That's the meaning of the word *Yehudi*. But just as non-Jews don't know what the word really means, I'm afraid most Jews don't know it, either.

When Jews used to go up to the Beis Hamikdash, they had many *mitzvos* in mind. They had to be *mekayem* the *mitzvah* of *aliyah l'regel*, which is a *mitzvas aseih*. There was also a *mitzvah* to bring *korbanos*—*olas re'iyah, shalmei chagigah*. They brought *ma'aser sheini* with them. They brought *korbanos* to fulfill their *nedarim* and *nedavos*, the pledges they had made. A lot of *mitzvos*. Some people had questions in *dinei Torah* to ask the Sanhedrin. They had many things to accomplish in Yerushalayim. But of all the purposes they came to fulfill, the chief one was to demonstrate that the entire nation was united in praising Hashem. Not merely to praise. When a Jew opens a *Tehillim* or a *siddur* in his house and praises Hashem, it's wonderful. It's very important. But when Jews come together in a *beis tefillah*, in a house of prayer, to praise Hashem, that's the real praise that Hashem is waiting for.

That's what David meant when he said, "*Shesham alu shevatim*—There [in Yerushalayim], all the tribes came together" (*Tehillim* 122:4). And what did they come for? "*L'hodos l'shem Hashem*—To make a public declaration of their thanks and praise to the name of Hashem" (ibid.).

Q What should we be nostalgic about when we think of Yerushalayim?

First, it's important to know that we *should* be nostalgic. In *Eichah* (1:7) it states, "Yerushalayim looked back and remembered, in the days of her bitterness and her complaint, all her delights that she had in the days of old." That's what we're supposed to do. In *galus*, we are expected to look back and remember all the delights we once possessed.

David explains what we possessed at that time. "*Ki shamah yashvu kisos lamishpat*—Because there sat the thrones of justice" (*Tehillim* 122:5). And he adds, "*kisos l'veis David*—and the thrones of the house of David." We possessed two types of thrones in Yerushalayim—thrones of justice and thrones of Beis David.

"Thrones of justice" means the Great Sanhedrin, the body of seventy elders, who were the last word in interpreting Torah. If there was a question that couldn't be settled by a local *beis din*, the people ascended to Yerushalayim and asked their question to the Sanhedrin. The Sanhedrin was the representative of Hashem. While it functioned, there were no schisms, no division of opinion, no *machlokess*.

The first unresolved *machlokess* took place during the Second Beis Hamikdash era, when there was great turmoil in the days of Yosi ben Yoezer and Yosi ben Yochanan. It was a question about *semichah*—whether one could do *semichah* (lean) on a *korban* on *yom tov*.[52] And it was considered a reproach. Our nation hung its head in

---

52 *Torah Nation*, #252–3: "The first recorded difference of opinion (*machlokess*) among the Sages took place at the end of the time of Yosi ben Yoezer and Yosi ben Yochanan, when the land was in great turmoil. The question was: Whether to perform *semichah* (putting hands on the offerings before sacrifice) during the festivals. *Semichah* required leaning upon the animal, which is ordinarily prohibited on the Sabbath or Yom Tov; but there arose a controversy whether this prohibition applied to an offering, which had the extenuating circumstances of 1) *mitzvah* and 2) of the Sanctuary (for usually the Rabbinical Sabbath-prohibitions, called *Shvus*, do not apply to the Sanctuary). This difference of opinion was due solely to the great upheaval in the nation caused by Joseph ben Toviah and his network of tyrants who now ruled the nation. ... The great Torah-academies had not been able to continue and were destroyed; now the motto of Yosi ben Yoezer was: 'Let your house be a meeting-place for the Sages' (*Avos* 1:4). It was now that the first *machlokess* took place, as a result of the great disturbance in the Torah-life of the nation. 'Until the death (the last part of his life) of Yosi ben Yoezer, they studied the Torah like our master Moses (without doubtful points and without forgetting)...Up to (the time of) Yosi ben Yoezer, there was no blemish....Which blemish occurred then? The dissension over

shame; it reminded them of what they had in the glory of the days of old, when the Sanhedrin could resolve all questions.

Jews had one Torah because they had one Sanhedrin that issued decisions for everybody on everything. The Sanhedrin was never impartial or weak. It didn't change due to the tenor of the times. Nobody could plead before the Sanhedrin against the established *halachah*. It was a fair and just society. Even Josephus states that, although there were a few malefactors, a few people who transgressed Torah laws, they did not escape punishment. The Torah was supreme. There was no such thing as a person embarking on a career of wickedness without consequences. If a man was wicked or irresponsible toward his wife, he was called to judgment and had to answer. There was no such thing as treading on the rights of others, because the Sanhedrin served as the conscience of the people. Their presence helped everyone stay in line and their wise counsel taught people the proper way to behave.

But in addition to the "*kisos lamishpat*—thrones of judgment," there were "*kisos l'veis David*—thrones of the House of David." What was the function of a Jewish *melech* in the days of old? A Jewish king was the arm that enforced the Torah. That's why the *kisos lamishpat* and the *kisos l'veis David* were next to each other. In one place sat the Sages of the Sanhedrin, and next to it were the palaces of the kings of David.

Even hundreds and hundreds of years later, after the Romans destroyed the Beis Hamikdash and the Sanhedrin, there remained some semblance of the House of David. When Rav Yehudah Nesiyah (the Amora) was told about a certain *kohen* who married a woman who was forbidden, a powerful man who refused to obey the local *beis din*, Rav Yehudah Nesiyah sent his soldiers to enforce the law and forced the *kohen* to divorce that woman. That was the job of the

---

semichah' (*Temurah* 15b). 'When did this *machlokess* take place? At the end of his days, when understanding (of the Torah) diminished' (ibid. 16a) because of the nation's tribulations. This marked a steep descent from the days of old. It was the first instance of disturbance in the hitherto smoothly flowing stream of Torah-tradition.

House of David—to enforce the law. Together, the thrones of the House of David and the thrones of judgment, the Sanhedrin, upheld the name of Hashem among the Jewish people.

Any man who was wronged, even a poor individual, had the right to personally come before the king and lodge a complaint. We know this from a number of instances related in Tanach. Remember the story of the two women who came before Shlomo Hamelech (I *Melachim* 3:16–28)? One of them had smothered her child at night but claimed the child of the other woman was hers. They were the dregs of the people, but they were given an audience with Shlomo Hamelech, a great and powerful monarch, to settle their dispute. And Shlomo was interested. He judged with his unparalleled wisdom.

Every morning, the kings of the House of David sat on their thrones and the gates were thrown open. Anybody could come and cry out, "*Hoshia, hamelech*—Help, O King," and the king's ears would now focus on this man or woman. If people couldn't find redress in their local *beis din*, they had a right to come to the *malchei Beis David* and protest.

In those great days, everybody could find justice. Whether it was a matter of enforcing the Torah or an individual problem of somebody wronging you, you came finally to the *kisos l'veis David*, known as a strong arm that would take up the case for the poor and downtrodden. The purpose was upholding the glory of Hashem. The Sanhedrin, the Sages of the Am Yisrael, taught the ways of Hashem, and the House of David carried out their decrees.

PRACTICAL ADVICE

Q **How do we keep our feeling for Yerushalayim alive?**

"*Yehi shalom b'cheileich*—May there be peace in your walls, *shalvah b'armenosayich*—and tranquility upon your palaces" (*Tehillim* 122:7). David is blessing Yerushalayim. Today, we too must bless Yerushalayim. If you go to Meah Shearim or B'nei Brak, don't go there like a sightseer or a tourist. Go like it's your city. And bless it like it's your city.

As David Hamelech said, "*Sha'alu sh'lom Yerushalayim*—Seek the welfare of Yerushalayim" (*Tehillim* 122:6). Speak well of Yerushalayim when you come home from your visit three times a year. Tell all what a wonderful experience it was. Don't complain that it was overcrowded. Aggrandize it, praise it. Even glamorize the physical setting of Yerushalayim, as it states, "*y'fei nof*—a beautiful district, *m'sos kol ha'aretz*—the joy of the whole world" (*Tehillim* 48:3). Don't make the mistake of ignoring everything besides the city's spiritual value. It's important to speak about the physical beauty of Yerushalayim. The Beis Hamikdash, the Sanhedrin, and the *Malchei Beis David.* It's necessary to praise the trees and the gardens of Yerushalayim. Since it's the city of Hashem, it's our task to glamorize it in every detail. We have to praise the climate of Yerushalayim. We have to speak highly of the beauty of the mountains.

Today, when we don't have the Beis Hamikdash, the Sanhedrin, or the *Malchei Beis David*, we apply this to the yeshivas. We have to speak well of the yeshivas. When you return home, be careful not to say that you saw paper on the floor or that the bathroom wasn't so clean. You must feel a responsibility to uphold the yeshiva's reputation. Love not only the Torah, but also the places of Torah. Love the men of Torah. When a *talmid chacham* passes in the street, you shouldn't feel that he's a stranger. You should feel that he's a close relative of yours. You should love him with all your heart.

It doesn't come naturally. Naturally, a person gravitates toward materialism. But we should labor to acquire the attitude that the yeshivas are beloved places and those who learn there are beloved. There are people who pass by the yeshivas day after day, but to them it's a remote, distant place. Your heart should be there. If you're not in there yourself learning, you should at least feel that a place where people are learning Torah is a place where the Shechinah rests. The presence of Hashem hovers there, and therefore you love it.

By the way, you also have to bless Boro Park. Just because you live in Boro Park doesn't mean it's not an *ir hakodesh.* It's a great pity that people don't appreciate it. Boro Park is crammed with *talmidei chachamim* and *tzaddikim*. They're quiet people. Their names aren't in newspapers. But almost every street has great people. Some are very big *talmidei chachamim.* Bless Boro Park as soon as you alight from the bus. If you don't practice it in Boro Park, you won't do it when you get to Yerushalayim. Don't think that even though you're a cold spectator to Boro Park, you're going to bless Yerushalayim. If the first thing you look for is faults, then you're going to criticize Yerushalayim in the days of Mashiach, too. And you won't remain long. You'll be hustled right out. They'll say, "Get back to New York, back to Brownsville, if you're so happy over there."

You must prepare for Mashiach. One of the ways is to learn to appreciate the places where Jews who are loyal to Hashem assemble. We have to bless Williamsburg. If you ever are *zocheh* to be in Crown Heights, near 770, give a blessing.

Here's a man who comes to Lakewood. He needs a little vacation, so he just goes to a hotel and doesn't bother to visit the yeshiva. That means his heart is really in the dining room of the hotel.

Rav Yehudah Halevi said, "*Libi b'Yerushalayim*—My heart is in Yerushalayim." Every Jew should feel his heart is in Yerushalayim where the Shechinah is. His heart is where the *avdei Hashem* are.

Our hearts must be in Crown Heights, in 770 Eastern Parkway. Our hearts must be in Williamsburg, with Jews who are living a traditional Jewish life, raising big families and living with *tzniyus*. There are no television sets there. They're walking in the paths of their forefathers. They speak Yiddish. That's where our hearts should be.

Our hearts are in the Mirrer Yeshiva, where young men are

sitting all day until late at night laboring in Torah. Our hearts are in Lakewood. Our hearts are in Boro Park. Our hearts are with all those *tzaddikim*, all the people who live a Torah-true life.

If you pass through a Jewish neighborhood in your car, don't miss the opportunity to shower them with blessings. Say. as David Hamelech said—*Yehi shalom b'cheileich, shalvah b'armenosayich.* Wish peace on every one of those Jewish homes. Their families should all be well. They should all have *nachas* from their children. They should all have *parnassah*. They should live *b'shalom.* They should have all the benefits of this world in addition to the benefits they're going to have in the World to Come. Don't be stingy with your blessings.

When you come up to Yerushalayim, David says, don't be wrapped up in yourself and think merely of discharging your obligation. Remember to leave behind your blessings in Yerushalayim. The same is true when a Jew goes to Eretz Yisrael today—he should leave over his blessings. Of course, he should leave over some of his cash, too. Inquire of the yeshiva office—do they have enough money to pay the salaries? When you visit the Ponovezh yeshiva, give your blessings to them. Now, it could be that the secretary won't appreciate your blessings alone. He'll want you to leave over something else as well, but Hashem considers your blessings more important than your money, because that shows where your heart is.

A man can sometimes coldly give a thousand dollars. He has discharged his obligation. He's *patur*. But beloved is the man whose heart swells with love when he sees 500 young men from all over the world laboring in Torah. Sometimes he weeps from happiness. Such a man is particularly beloved. When I was a little boy, I lived in a gentile neighborhood, but one day I took an adventure downtown to the Jewish neighborhood, and I saw Jews—a multitude of Jews—and I wept with happiness. When you come to Ponovezh and see so many people devoted to Hashem's Torah, you should weep with happiness. Say, "*Yevareich es Beis Yisrael*—May Hashem bless the Beis Yisrael" (*Tehillim* 115:12). That's what you should have in mind when you come to Yerushalayim.

I remember a scene in a certain yeshiva on Yom Kippur after Neilah, a *yeshivishe* Yom Kippur. On *motza'ei Yom Kippur*, when they blew the *shofar*, the whole congregation burst out singing, "*Yevareich es Beis Yisrael*" and they didn't stop. They had all been fasting. They were worn out. But with their last *kochos* the entire congregation shouted, "*Yevareich es Beis Yisrael!*" The tears were flowing from their eyes, tears of happiness and tears of love for the Jewish people.

That's what we have to experience even now when we see *frum* Jews, when we see yeshivas, when we see Boro Park, when we see Lubavitcher Jews marching, when we see Satmarer Jews standing on the street corners, busy shopping on *erev Shabbos*. That's *kevod Shamayim*. We have to overflow with love for them and say, "*Yehi shalom b'cheileich, shalvah b'armenosayich.*" That's how we can keep the feeling of Yerushalayim alive.

Q Were the women of ancient Yerushalayim really better than the women of today?

Absolutely. No question about it. What do you think?! If there is a society in which people are striving for perfection, a society in which the men are counting their words, do you think that only the men did it?! Their wives counted their words, too. Their daughters counted their words. Their mothers counted their words. Everybody became better.

You should know that, in general, when men are good, the women are also good. There's no such thing as men having *shleimus* without their wives. *Shleimus* is contagious. All good *middos* are contagious. So you be sure to do your part in making your home a Beis Hamikdash, and be sure to lead yourself *b'derech haTorah* and *b'derech hakedushah*, and you'll see—it will be contagious.

SUMMARY

- To fill ourselves with a longing for the old Yerushalayim and truly desire its restoration, we have to use our imagination to picture the glorious times of *aliyah l'regel*, when all of Klal Yisrael traveled the roads of Eretz Yisrael to go up to Yerushalayim, full of joyous song.
- Yerushalayim was and will be a place where loyal Jews will unite in serving Hashem, despite whatever physical or cultural differences we may have.
- The primary purpose of coming together in Yerushalayim and the Beis Hamikdash was to praise and thank Hashem, all united. We long for that opportunity.
- We also long for the restoration of the Sanhedrin and the kings of David's royal house, so that we will once again have clear Torah guidance, enforced by the power of the *malchus*.

Es Tzemach David

Q **Will Mashiach have supernatural powers?**

Mashiach is a man, a human being who comes from the House of David, because Hashem promised David that he and his seed would sit on the throne of Hashem forever.

Now, this man is going to be of excellent character and great wisdom, but he alone cannot make the Geulah. Don't expect him to bring us back. It's only Hashem Who will do it. "*V'simloch Atah, Hashem Elokeinu, l'vadecha*—You, Hashem, alone will rule over us" (Rosh Hashanah prayers). Mashiach will represent Hashem and organize the Am Hashem. He will enforce the Torah with great wisdom and justice. But don't put too much emphasis on Mashiach. Remember, it's Hashem Who is our redeemer. He is the *Go'el* Who's going to redeem us. If Mashiach is called a *go'el*, it's only in the sense that he's a messenger of Hashem.

Q In what ways will Mashiach stand out among other men?

The Gemara (*Sanhedrin* 98a) tells us that Rabbi Yehoshua ben Levi once asked Eliyahu Hanavi where Mashiach was. He was told that he was sitting in the gates of Rome. Now, the gates of Rome thronged with people. So he asked how he would recognize Mashiach. Eliyahu told him that he would be sitting with the poor and ill, and that he would be fixing his bandages one at a time, not all at once. All the poor and ill had wounds and sores that they needed to bandage up. It's a long process, taking off all of one's bandages, cleansing the wounds, and replacing the bandages. But Mashiach would only change one bandage at a time so he could be ready in case he would be called to redeem the Jewish people. That's the sign Rabbi Yehoshua ben Levi was given to pick out Mashiach among the throngs sitting at the gates of Rome.

Now, this we must understand is certainly not *kipshuto*—although many people learn it that way. Rather, it's all a *mashal*, a figure of speech. And we begin by asking, "Why is Mashiach sitting at the gates of Rome? What business does he have sitting there? And what business does he have among sick people who have bandages and are sitting there tending their wounds?

"The gates of Rome" is a *mashal* for the *galus* of Rome, which we are in today. This is the *galus* of Edom, which is Rome. We went into *galus* when Rome brought about the destruction of the Beis Hamikdash and exiled our people from our land. As a result, the Jewish nation has suffered a number of wounds. These wounds aren't merely physical wounds, although we certainly have suffered physical wounds in *galus*. They're also all kinds of spiritual wounds, all kinds of changes affecting us as a result of living in *galus*.

We had so many beautiful attributes when we lived in our own land under the rule of the *chachmei haTorah*, in a Torah commonwealth. Every detail of Jewish life was pure. For instance, Rabbi Yochanan recalled that when he was a boy, boys and girls of seventeen years old would play together in the streets of Teveriah and nobody ever thought of anything immoral. That's how Jews used to be. It was only when they went among the nations that we had to start separating.

In the olden days, when did a man go to choose his wife? On Yom Kippur and on the fifteenth of Av (*Ta'anis* 26b). These were two days in the year when Jewish young men went to choose a wife. Didn't they have other things to do on those days? But it was like when people buy an *esrog*. They're standing around and examining each *esrog* to make sure they're picking the best and most *chashuv*. That's how they went to choose a wife, too. To them, a wife wasn't romance. In the olden days, the Jewish nation was a pure people, and to them a wife was a *mitzvah* just like buying an *esrog*. Therefore, Yom Kippur was the most suitable day because it was a day of *kedushah*. That's why marriage is called *kiddushin*. It's a holy thing to be *mekadesh* an *ishah*, and the best time for *kadosh* people to go about it is on a day that is *kadosh*. But today men and women can't be trusted to behave with purity of thought, because we lack the inherent purity of the Jewish lifestyle before *galus*. Therefore, it can be said that we have a lot of wounds we have suffered from our environment. We haven't remained unmarred.

Now, Mashiach and others are sitting at the gates of Rome, tying and untying their wounds. We're all suffering from the wounds inflicted by Rome, the spiritual wounds. This one is lacking in *tefillah*. This one is lacking in *tzedakah*. This one is lacking in purity of thought. This one has multiple wounds. But some are busy tending their wounds, which means trying to rid themselves of the ways of the surrounding culture. The one who shows more alacrity than others to divest himself of those negative ways—the person who adjusts himself to the *darchei haTorah* most completely—is the best candidate for Mashiach. When the time comes and Hashem summons him to be Mashiach, the one from the Beis David who is most prepared—meaning he has the least number of wounds—when opportunity knocks will be chosen to be the Mashiach.

I'm sure there's much more than that in this *aggadeta*, but this is one of the things that distinguishes Mashiach. He's counted among the top *tzaddikim* of the generation, and he will be distinguished in the way he prepared for the moment by ridding himself of the influences of the nations.[53]

Q **When Mashiach comes, will we all be happy?**

Actually, when the days of Mashiach come, we'll be sorry—very sorry. That's what the Gemara says. "Remember your Creator before the evil days come" (*Koheles* 12:1). Which "evil days"? The days of Mashiach (*Shabbos* 151b).

Why will that era be "evil"? Because there will be no more reward as in the good old days. "Ay yay yay! Ah, the good old days! It was such a good thing to be a Jew in the good old days when we had to fight against the majority of the world who thought we were crazy and insignificant, and who hated us. Ay yay yay! We used to get so much reward. But now everybody agrees with us! We're in the majority now. Everyone recognizes the truth. No more reward!"

It's a good thing to be a Jew today, to have the opportunity to fight for the *emes* in a world that fights for *sheker*. In Yemos HaMashiach, they'll reminisce about the good old days when we walked in the street and somebody yelled at us, "Dirty Jew!" Oooh! What a *hatzlachah* it was! *Baruch Hashem!* It was better than a million dollars!

I was standing on the street corner years ago. It wasn't the style to have beards yet in those days. Today, everybody wears a beard. Bums also have beards today. But there were no beards in those days. I was standing and waiting for the bus, minding my own business, when a man shouted at me from across the street, "*Meshugener! Meshugener!*" That's an opportunity. It makes you stronger when you laugh it away.

On all sides, the multitudes are yelling at us. The *New York Times*, the universities—they're all belittling the *frum* Jews. Today, they even

---

53 Perhaps we can add that the idea of Mashiach treating one wound at a time teaches us an important strategy in Yemos HaMashiach, in a generation overwhelmed with all types of sins and problems. And the strategy is something Rav Miller emphasized many times—work on perfecting yourself one area at a time. Don't try to perfect yourself in all areas at once.

enlisted irreligious Jews to belittle the *frum* Jews. And we say *baruch Hashem*! We're a minority of a minority! It's *s'char* on top of *s'char*! It's the great opportunity of standing strong.

That's the big test of this world. Atheism, materialism, and false ideals surround us on all sides. We're a small island of truth in an ocean of *sheker*. All the time, big ocean waves are crashing down on our little island! And the question is, as the waves rush up on the beach, as they roar and they splash, will they wet us as well? Will we yield? Will we be influenced, or will we be able to maintain our pride in the truth of Torah ideals? That's the test the Am Yisrael has endured throughout its history! And it's our opportunity for greatness.

"*Avodah zarah* was put into this world for no other purpose than that we should gain reward by means of resisting it" (*Sanhedrin* 64a). The test of *avodah zarah* was only the beginning of our responsibility to resist the world. *B'chol dor vador*, in every generation, *omdim aleinu*, they rise against us to fill our minds with foolishness. Our job is to turn our backs on the *sheker* of the outside world. No matter how many people are telling us we're wrong, we won't budge. All the false religions, all the idols, all the false ideals, the false philosophies—humanism, socialism, and all the other -isms—all the false sciences, all the *to'eivah*s and materialism, it's all a test to try to overpower the "*me'at mikol ha'amim*—smallest among the nations" (*Devarim* 7:7).

You know, they once took a poll among people of different faiths, and it revealed that Orthodox Jews were more resistant to public pressure than any other people. And it's common sense. Orthodox Jews are more liable to resist the pressure of public opinion because they're trained to say no to the multitudes. Otherwise, they wouldn't be Orthodox Jews. They'd be Reform or Conservative. They'd be nothing. Whatever it is, they wouldn't be authentic Jews. We Orthodox Jews have always stood up for our principles in the face of a world that at best hates us and at worst persecutes and seeks to kill us. The poor Orthodox Jew has been kicked around and scorned. But that makes him tough.

All the ideals of the world—entertainment, amusement, sports, money, immorality—the whole culture through and through is *hevel havalim*. Even though the world is busy disdaining us—we're too antiquated, they say—it doesn't sway us in the least. Millions, even billions, of people won't budge us from the Torah ideals. We have no thought of weakening! *Chas v'shalom!*

"*L'fum tza'ara agra*—According to the pain is the reward" (*Avos* 5:26). All the opposition, all the difficulties, are only to test and improve us and give us a merit that makes us much greater. When Mashiach comes, they will all come tumbling down—all the universities, all the stadiums, all the great edifices that were erected throughout the generations. They will all crumble into nothing. The whole world will agree that we have the *emes* and always had it. But we'll be sorry then. We'll regret the lost opportunity of *l'fum tza'ara agra*. There will still be some reward, but not that much.

Yes, we'll be happy when Mashiach comes. "*Az yimalei s'chok pinu*—Then our mouths will be full of laughter" (*Tehillim* 126:2). Our mouths will be full with laughter from all the reward, all the *s'char* we'll be *experiencing*. It will be a delirium of happiness at that time. But we'll also be sorry about all the *opportunity* for *s'char* that we will have lost.

PRACTICAL ADVICE

Do we need the irreligious Jews to do *teshuvah* in order to bring Mashiach?

Absolutely, absolutely! The Orthodox are not enough. We need *all* Jewry. There aren't enough Orthodox Jews. We are judged by the majority of Jews, and the Reformers are Jews. And we're suffering because of them, make no mistake about it. We're all responsible for each other. We have to save them because if they are the majority, then, *chas v'shalom*, who knows what can happen! And they *are* the majority today!

Now, crying out to Hashem always helps, and we should cry as much as we can, but the crying out should not be by Orthodox Jewry alone. All Jews must unite and cry out. Koch [Ed Koch, an irreligious Jew who was the mayor of New York City] has to come to a *beis hamedrash* and stop being an *oisvorf*. He has to become a *ba'al teshuvah*. All the Liberals and Reformers have to do *teshuvah*. You can't ignore them. Their sins are on the heads of the entire Jewish people.

We're talking now, of course, about the requirement that we must be "*kulo zakai*—entirely meritorious" (*Sanhedrin* 98a)—to bring the Geulah. If *chas v'shalom* they don't do *teshuvah*, then Hashem has a different method. But we prefer the first.[54]

Q **Can Mashiach come at any time?**

We're told by Chazal that "In the month of Nissan we were redeemed from Mitzrayim, and in the month of Nissan we will be redeemed from the current exile" (*Rosh Hashanah* 11a). What is *p'shat* in this *ma'amar Chazal*? Only in Nissan? What about the principle that we await him every day? Does that principle contradict this Gemara?

And the answer is this. If we try hard enough, he can come any day. But if we don't try hard enough, he will come anyway. Sooner or later, he will come. And when he comes automatically, he will come in Nissan.

54 From Rav Miller's commentary to *Perek Chelek* (*Sanhedrin* 98a): "Rabbi Yochanan says: 'The son of David will come only in a generation that is entirely innocent or entirely guilty.' The generation will be either all virtuous or all wicked. It means as follows: When it's all virtuous, Hashem will bring it [the Redemption] because that's the generation that deserves it. And when it's all wicked, He'll bring it because He sees there's no use waiting any longer. Now, an 'all wicked' generation can never be, because there will always be a remnant of loyal Jews. That's what the Rambam says in *Igeres Teiman*: 'We will never stop being a pious nation, an *umah chasidah*.' Only, how many will constitute the 'pious nation' is a different question. Therefore, when there's a time that there are so many renegades that the generation can be called 'all wicked,' it's also a time for Mashiach."

Q Should we trust that Mashiach is coming soon? Or should we continue planting anyhow?

What you mean by planting, I don't know. If you mean planting your garden, go ahead. Do you mean building institutions? Go ahead!

I recall, almost forty-five years ago, I was at a banquet in Boston and a Mizrachi rabbi was speaking there. It happened to be my business to be there; I couldn't avoid it. One of the biggest leaders of the Mizrachi was speaking. I won't mention his name because he's long dead. And he said, "You American Jews are making a great error by building big synagogues and yeshivas in America. Go to Eretz Yisrael and build," he said. "That's the only place that has any future."

That was forty-five years ago. In those days there was no Lakewood, no Chaim Berlin, no Mirrer Yeshiva, no Torah Voda'as, no Tiferes Yerushalayim. There was nothing except YU. He was telling the world then that it didn't pay to build in America. It's so silly what he said! During those years, a whole generation grew up of Bais Yaakovs and yeshivas. A glorious young generation!

Even if Mashiach comes tomorrow, start tonight building a yeshiva or contributing to a yeshiva. Don't worry what will happen! You'll get rewarded for your good intentions. Mashiach has nothing to do with our plans. We have to go ahead with all our plans.

And not only plans to build a yeshiva — even plans to make a nice garden. Springtime is coming. It's a good idea. Go ahead and make a nice garden in your backyard. If Mashiach comes before the garden has time to develop, so what! You'll still go to Eretz Yisrael, and you'll still go *b'rinah,* with singing. Who cares what will happen! We'll sing in Eretz Yisrael. There are good gardens there, too.

You can paint your homes in America, too. Of course, don't go all out and overspend on beautifying your homes, but you can have decent homes. You can make a good living and enjoy life.

Don't worry about it. When Mashiach comes, it won't be held against you.

Q If our generation is the *Ikvesa d'Meshicha*, the "footsteps of Mashiach," why are we the lowest of all generations?

Now, I don't know if this is the generation of *Ikvesa d'Meshicha*. But let's say it is. The answer is this. When Hashem sees that all the power is gone from us, and we see there is nobody to help us, He will come to help (*Sanhedrin* 97a). That's what the Chofetz Chaim said. "Please, Ribbono Shel Olam, it's getting late and we're going lost. Please come quickly and help us." That's why Mashiach should come—*because* we're the lowest of all generations.

Of course, it would be much better if Mashiach would come because we're so good. "*Ein ben David ba ela b'dor shekulo zakai o kulo chayav*—Mashiach will come either in a generation that's entirely virtuous or entirely wicked" (*Sanhedrin* 98a). However, nobody knows what will happen, so don't be so sure that this is the end.

Q What's going to happen to the Lubavitcher *chassidim*, the Satmerer *chassidim*, and the Belzer *chassidim* when Mashiach comes?

That's a question that's too big for me to answer. But one thing I will tell you—they'll all be happy. They'll all rejoice! No question about it. They'll all be together in happiness. They'll hold hands and dance together around Mashiach. No question about that! I guarantee you.

The only question is what *nusach* will they *daven*—Sephard or Ashkenaz? I think there will have to be a showdown there. There will be a Sanhedrin then, and the Sanhedrin will say that we should all go back to the original *nusach*. What's the original *nusach*—that's the problem. The Anshei Knesses Hagedolah made only one *nusach*. They didn't make ten different *nuscha'os*, ten different versions of *tefillah*.

Therefore, at that time, we'll come back to the original *nusach*, and everybody will find out that he's been making mistakes. Everybody is saying something wrong. Not much—we're *yotzei* anyway—but in the time of Mashiach we're going to return to one *nusach*. Then, "Everyone will call out to the one Hashem, with the same language"—the same *nusach* of *tefillah*.

Q What are the "birthpangs of Mashiach"?

"*Im ra'isa dor shemisma'et v'holech, chakeh lo*—If you see a generation that's diminishing, await him" *(Sanhedrin* 98b). This means if a generation is dying out—there are fewer and fewer people in the Jewish nation—anticipate Mashiach. Becoming poor in numbers is one of the signs, one of the portents, that Mashiach might be coming.

On this we have a comment from the Chofetz Chaim, *zt"l*, which is repeated in [the essay] *Ikvesa D'Meshicha* by his *talmid*, Rav Elchanan Wasserman. The *Midrash Rabbah* states that when Yaakov Avinu was about to meet Eisav, he sent ahead gifts of livestock and said to his servants, "Leave a space between each group of animals" (*Bereishis* 32:17). The *midrash* finds something prophetic in these words. Yaakov asked Hashem that if troubles were going to come upon his children, there should be a *revach*, a space between the troubles. They shouldn't come one right after the other. There should be periods of tranquility in between.

There have been times lasting a hundred years when everything was quiet, before the next persecution began. However, the closer it comes to Mashiach, the more it will resemble the pangs of childbirth. Just as in childbirth, at first the pangs are spaced far apart but, as the birth comes closer, the pangs come more and more quickly. That's how it's going to be when the arrival of Mashiach comes closer.

The Gemara quotes a *passuk*, "*Ki yavo kanahar tzar ruach Hashem nosesah vo*—When suffering comes like a river that Hashem raises up" *(Yeshayah* 59:19). The word *nosesah* means "raise up high," like a banner. That's the sign that the banner of Hashem is being raised up. That's one explanation. Rashi says another: *Nosesah* is a spirit of Hashem (*ruach Hashem*) that's gnawing away and causing *tzaros* in preparation for the Geulah.

Again, the first explanation is that the spirit of Hashem is being raised like a banner. He's letting you know the time is about to come. That's why the *tzaros* are becoming unbearable, without leaving us any breathing space.

The other explanation is that it's the spirit of Hashem that's gnawing away and causing these endless *tzaros* in order to prepare for Mashiach.

So if you see a generation when *tzaros* are coming like a river—without a break—then you can expect Mashiach.

Q **Can we spare ourselves from the "birthpangs of Mashiach"?**

When Mashiach comes, it's going to be like "*chevlei yoleidah,* the pangs of giving birth" (*Sanhedrin* 98b). After a mother gives birth, it's *sasson v'simchah*, it's *mazel tov* and happiness. But while the baby is in the process of being born, it's *oy vey.* So, too, there will be a big "*oy vey*" just before the advent of Mashiach. The purpose of that "*oy vey*" is to teach people a lot of lessons. We don't have time to describe the lessons now, but there will certainly be many lessons we're going to learn during the *chevlei Mashiach.*

However, the Gemara offers a substitute way of learning these lessons, an easier way (*Shabbos* 118a). And that's when you sit down on Shabbos at the table and eat a fat piece of kugel, drink wine, and sing songs—and you think about what all that food and *oneg* is supposed to teach you. It's supposed to teach you that Hashem made this world out of nothing. That's what you're supposed to think while you're eating the chicken and the cholent. Now, it's not easy. When people are sitting and stuffing themselves, they tend to become drowsy and their brains fall asleep. They're lulled into a happy, soporific state of non-thinking. But if you can force yourself with every bite and every sip to say, "All of this is nothing but the word of Hashem; it's all Hashem's imagination," that means you're already learning the lessons Hashem wants you to learn.

"There's nothing in this world except Hashem's word. He is the only real existence, and everything else is the result of His desire, His imagination"— that's what you should be thinking while you're eating the Shabbos *seudah*. It's fascinating to think about— that the world came into being only because Hashem said, "Let it be." Now, if you'll study this Shabbos at the meals— and three times every Shabbos— you won't need the lessons of *chevlei Mashiach*. And it's much easier than the *chevlei Mashiach*. So you have your choice.

SUMMARY

- When we *daven* for the arrival of Mashiach, we must always keep in mind that Mashiach is only going to be Hashem's *shliach*, but it's Hashem alone Who will actually redeem us from *galus*.
- Mashiach will not only be among the biggest *tzaddikim* of the generation, but he will also be the one who has worked the most to rid himself of non-Torah influence.
- Even though we long for Mashiach to come, we should know that we will lose the opportunity for reward that we have nowadays for fighting against the influence of the surrounding culture. So we should focus now on taking advantage of the golden opportunity we have and maximize our efforts in that regard.

Shema Koleinu

Q Are we justified in asking Hashem to listen to our *tefillos*?

"*Shema Koleinu Hashem Elokeinu*—Please, Hashem, listen to us." He's certainly listening to us, *but are we listening to ourselves*? First, we have to listen to what *we're* saying. Then we're justified in asking Him to listen to us.

What are we saying here? We're thanking Hashem for that great privilege that He—the Creator of the Universe—allows us to speak to Him and He in turn listens to us. It's an opportunity. It's a great opportunity three times a day to work on the feeling that you are really speaking to Someone. We shouldn't miss out. So, first, before we ask Hashem to listen to us, Hashem asks us, "Are you listening to yourself?" That's number one.

Q Are we *tzaddikim* that Hashem should want to listen to our *tefillos*?

I'm going to tell you something—you have a right in this case to be arrogant, to say you are one of the *tzaddikim*, because you have no alternative. You certainly want Him to listen. Therefore, "*Ki Atah shomei'a tefillas kol peh*—For You hear the prayers of every mouth." That's *nusach Sephard* [in *Shema Koleinu*]. You, Hashem, hear everyone's *tefillos*. He listens to everyone's *tefillah*. So, no matter who you are, it pays to cry out to Hashem.

And now I'll tell you a secret—you're not a *tzaddik*. I don't mean *you*—you are a *tzaddik*. But let's say somebody isn't a *tzaddik* and he's crying out. Do you know what crying out does? It makes him a *tzaddik*! So get busy and become one. Cry out from the bottom of your heart and do a lot of it. That's how you become *tzaddikim*.

Q How can we impress upon ourselves that Hashem is really listening to our *tefillos*?

Emunah p'shutah means to be a *ma'amin*, a believer, without having to put in any work. And in most cases, it's a *chalom shav*, an empty dream. There's no such thing. Maybe if you lived, say, two hundred years ago in a Jewish town where the air was saturated with *emunah*. The streets were full of *emunah*—everybody believed in Hashem. It was real; it was tangible. You couldn't help yourself. It entered you by osmosis. It soaked into you from the environment. When you saw a child making a *brachah* two hundred years ago, it was a different *brachah* than we see today.

We don't realize it, but once upon a time, the Am Yisrael had a fire in them. Therefore, in the olden days *emunah p'shutah* was possible. You lived among the *ma'aminim* and it went into your hearts. You would give your life for your *emunah*.

But today, we live in an atmosphere of *kefirah*, of denying Hashem. The whole world is *kefirah* today. Today, to get *emunah p'shutah* is not easy at all. If a person says, "I have *emunah p'shutah*," what it means is that he's dodging his responsibility. Instead of working to get *emunah*, he's looking for an excuse to evade his responsibility. *Emunah p'shutah* today is very, very rare. If you're born into a very *frum* family, you get it a certain degree. But even then, the *kefirah* from the street seeps into the house and nobody even realizes it. Once you come to America—or England or Holland or Eretz Yisrael today—you're soaking in *apikorsus*. Even for the *frummeh*, *emunah* is a very thin veneer. You have to work hard. You must labor to get *emunah* today.

It's so important to listen to these lessons and make up your mind that you're going to dedicate your career to learning to being a *ma'amin*. But you have to learn how to be a *ma'amin* and work on doing it. It's an attitude you have to work on to achieve.

The *Mesillas Yesharim* says, for instance, that when you *daven*, you have to train yourself to feel that Someone is standing in front of you and listening to your words. He says, "And although it is not easy—"

Do you hear that?! "It's not easy," he says, "to think that Someone is standing and listening to you, because your senses don't help you." You don't see anybody. But with a little work, he says, you can train yourself. In his day—that was two hundred years ago—it took only a little work. With some effort you could train yourself to feel that Somebody's listening. But today we need a lot of work.

That's why, when you come to *Shema Koleinu*, it's an opportunity to put in the work. "*Ki Atah shomei'a*—You, Hashem, are listening." You have to say it with *kavanah*. Little by little it gets into your blood. Say it again and again with *kavanah*, three times a day. Slowly it starts entering into your blood. That's how you must work on *emunah p'shutah*. Then it's not called *emunah p'shutah* any longer. Then it's *emunah sichlis*, it's intellectual *emunah*. That type of *emunah* is the result of hard work. You have to work on *emunah* today, no question about it.

By the way, it's true of everything. If you want to really feel it, you have to work on it. "Keep My Sabbaths ... so you will know that I am Hashem Who makes you holy" (*Shemos* 31:13). Shabbos makes us holy. Simply by refraining from working on Shabbos we become holy—but on one condition: that you believe Shabbos makes you holy. As soon as we welcome Shabbos with *Lechah Dodi*, it starts elevating your mind and hallowing your thoughts, making you into an *ish kadosh*, a holy person. When Shabbos is over, it leaves a residue of *kedushah* in your mind that's going to be there forever. As you go through life, every Shabbos leaves layer on top of layer and you become greater and greater in *kedushah*. When a Jew is old, he's filled with the *kedushah* of Shabbos. We cannot estimate how great that achievement is—but it's all based on the condition that he believes that Shabbos makes him holy.

The same with *tefillah*. When we pray to Hashem, "*Ki Atah shomei'a tefillos amcha Yisrael*—You listen to the prayers of Your people Yisrael," we have to believe that Hashem is actually listening to every word. If you don't believe that, your *tefillah* is not accepted. You're speaking to the wall. It's a meditation, but it's not *tefillah*.

Tefillah means *emunah* that Hashem hears your words. It's very important to work on that, and the best opportunity to do so is when you come to the words in *Shema Koleinu* in Shemoneh Esrei—"*Ki Atah shomei'a*—You are listening." You are listening to me. That's a tremendous proclamation. Hashem is listening to me. I'm a Yisrael and there's a covenant. He's listening to our prayers. And he does so "*b'rachamim*—with mercy."

We must work on that. We must train ourselves to feel that Hashem loves us. He is thinking about you more than you are thinking about yourself. Day and night. His mind is constantly on you. We have to labor to really feel that. It's easier said than done, but if it's not said it will never be done. The first thing is to say it, and do so constantly.

Autosuggestion is one of the most powerful tools in a person's life. That's why it is so important to *daven* with *kavanah*. At first the words seem alien and artificial. The concepts are very remote from your mind. But by davening and thinking about what you are saying, little by little you begin to think of Hashem as a reality until finally the day will come when you will be saying, "*Atah, Hashem!*" and you will feel that you are speaking directly to Someone who is listening. If you never try, you will never arrive at that point.

SUMMARY

- The first thing to contemplate with this *brachah* is developing our awareness that Hashem has given us the great privilege of allowing us to speak to Him directly, and that He is always listening to our prayers. Without that awareness, it's unjustified to question why our prayers may not have been answered yet.
- Focusing on the word "*Atah*, You" when davening to Hashem is one of the ideal ways to acquire *emunah chushis*, palpable belief that you are talking to Hashem and that He's listening.
- Hashem listens to all our *tefillos*, even if we're not *tzaddikim*. But we should certainly strive to become *tzaddikim*.

R'tzeih

Q What does "*R'tzeih*, favor" mean?

R'tzeih ("favor") is fundamentally the same meaning as *rutz*, "to run." "*Mashcheini, acharecha narutzah*—Draw me; we will run after You" (*Shir Hashirim* 1:14). One who truly desires something runs toward it. The genuine Jew hastens to his house of prayer three times daily. "To the house of Hashem we go with excitement" (*Tehillim* 55:15).

The word "favor" (*r'tzeih*, *ratzon*) occurs three times in the *brachah* and is the theme of this prayer. This was originally a prayer that Hashem should favor the offerings in the Beis Hamikdash. There are varying degrees of Hashem's favor, and according to the intensity of the favor is the corresponding degree of the Shechinah's presence. That's why this *brachah* begins with the word *r'tzeih* and concludes with the restoration of the Shechinah.

Originally, this prayer requested that Hashem accept the service in the Beis Hamikdash, because the Shemoneh Esrei was initiated by the Anshei Knesses Hagedolah at the beginning of the Second Beis Hamikdash era. Since the Shechinah was absent from it, they prayed for its restoration. After the destruction of the Second Beis Hamikdash, the version of this *brachah* was altered to include, "*V'hasheiv es ha'avodah*—And restore the service." The purpose of our service, and this is our dearest wish, is to draw near to Him in such a measure that we should be worthy of having His Presence among us. Our dearest wish is to do His will and thereby gain His favor. The favor of Hashem really means the happiness of everlasting life. This is the ultimate meaning of "*chaim birtzono*—in His favor is life" (*Tehillim* 30:6).

Although we are absolved today from the service of offerings because we don't possess a Beis Hamikdash, we're not absolved from *desiring and longing* to perform the Sanctuary service. Whatever we're able to do we must do, but whatever we're unable to do we must *desire* and also *pray* that we should be able to do.

Q Is seeking Hashem's favor so things go well for us considered like serving Hashem for the sake of reward?

It says, "Perform His will as you do your own, so that He should fulfill your will as He does His own" (*Avos* 2:4). It sounds like we're doing His will so that we'll be rewarded for it. If you want Hashem to fulfill your desire, you should fulfill His desire. It looks like an exchange.

And the answer is . . . it's not. But first you have to understand that even if it was, it's not bad. It's logical. Why should Hashem not expect people to do His will in return for which He'll reward them? If you want Hashem to listen to your *tefillah* and grant your request, it's only logical that you listen to what He tells you and obey His request. It's only logical that it can't be a one-way street, that you're only sending your requests to Him but not fulfilling His requests. He also sends commandments to you. Therefore, if you do what He tells you, Hashem will hearken to what you ask Him to do.

And this brings us to a fundamental teaching in the Torah that the world is trying its best to ignore — the great principle of sin. S-I-N. *Sin* is one of the most unpopular words in the English language. But we have to realize that there is such a thing as sin, and that it's one of the most important subjects in Torah. A man is responsible for his actions! When Hashem states that something should not be done — whether it's stated openly in the Torah or it arises in a man's conscience — he is fully responsible.

Conscience is not the result of evolutionary development, you should know. Even a wild man who grew up in the jungle without parents has a conscience. Of course, you can't rely on his conscience. His conscience might tell him to have you for supper. But a wild man has a conscience, too.

Now, because of the great principle that a person is responsible for his actions, it stands to reason that a man who does not sin deserves reward and that Hashem should grant his prayers. Nevertheless, it's actually much more than that. It's not just a simple exchange.

It's not merely tit for tat, that because you're pious, observant, or kind-hearted, you'll get your reward. It's more than that. When you do what Hashem wants you to do, you're learning *bitachon*. Therefore, when you want Hashem to give you something beyond what you have now, you must start doing things beyond what you do now. You do it so that your *bitachon* should become stronger. The more you're aware of Hashem's mastery—His control—of the world, the more Hashem is going to reward you for that.

The more you ask Hashem to help you, the more it registers in your mind that He is the only One Who *can* help you. It ingrains in your mind the conviction that Hashem is in charge. The more you try to conform to the wishes of Hashem, the more *bitachon* you acquire.

When a man refrains from doing a *cheit*, not because of habit but because he's aware that he's fulfilling the will of Hashem, that person is gaining an awareness that Hashem is in charge. The more a man fulfills the will of Hashem, the more he becomes convinced of the presence of Hashem and of His power.

Consider the opposite. When a man commits a sin, he's not thinking about being punished. Nobody wants to get killed for his sin. And so, what does he think right away? "It will not happen. I'm still a *ma'amin*, a believer. But for this time at least, it will not happen." If he commits a sin twice, he's even more convinced that it won't happen. The more he sins, the more he loses his *bitachon*, and the more he becomes sold out to the idea that he won't be punished. He's bribed by his sins.

Why do we circumcise Jewish boys? Because that's going to help the father and son recognize Hashem. All his life, a Jew feels that he carries the seal of the covenant on his own body. Why do we put on *tefillin*? *Tefillin* makes a person recognize Hashem. Why do we eat kosher? Kosher means that you're not a gentile; you're a Jew. That's the result of it. "I separated you from the nations" (*Vayikra* 20:26). I gave you different dietary laws. When you eat kosher, you shouldn't eat without thinking about the purpose. The purpose is to remind you of Hashem Who gave you the laws.

Why do we keep Shabbos? It's a pity that people put so much effort into Shabbos yet never think about what Shabbos is. Shabbos is a demonstration that Hashem created the world out of nothing. There was no matter or energy. Hashem willed matter and energy into existence. It's the most important of all teachings. It's the first teaching in the Torah, and that should be paramount in our minds on Shabbos. When you eat *challah* and drink wine on Shabbos, at least once in while think—and say it at the table, too (say it to yourself if your wife is tired of hearing it from you)—that it's all to celebrate and demonstrate that Hashem is the Creator of the universe.

The more you try to fulfill *mitzvos* with the intention of recognizing the will of Hashem, the more you're demonstrating *bitachon*—your awareness that Hashem is in charge of everything—and in that merit Hashem will fulfill your desires. It's not an exchange. At least not in the sense of a reward disconnected from the act. It's a *means*. It's a means to awareness of Hashem. That's the paramount virtue. We live in this world chiefly to recognize Hashem. And by doing His *mitzvos*, we're led to greater and greater recognition of Hashem.

SUMMARY

- This *brachah* was originally a prayer that Hashem should accept our *korbanos* in the Beis Hamikdash with favor. Nowadays, it expresses our desire that Hashem restore the service of *korbanos* to us, so that we will be worthy of having Hashem's Shechinah in our midst.
- We seek Hashem's favor by fulfilling His will. The more we try to fulfill His will, the more we deepen our recognition that He is in control, and the worthier we become of His favor.

Modim

Q **What should we be thinking when we say *Modim*?**

"*Vayar Elokim es kol asher asah v'hineih tov me'od*—And Hashem saw all that He had made and declared that it was very good" (*Bereishis* 1:31). This world is *very good*. Not just good. Even if Hashem said it was just "good," we would understand that it's superlatively good because His good is very, very good. But if He said, "*tov me'od*, very good," then we understand that it's very, very, very, good. When Hashem says *me'od*, it means *me'ooooooooooooooooooooood*! He doesn't give His seal of approval like that unless He means it.

Hashem wants us to understand that as much as possible—and to say it, too. We should also say, "*Hodu laHashem ki tov*—Thank You, Hashem, because You made the world so good" (*Tehillim* 136:1). What's so good? Everything. The luminaries in the skies, the skies—everything in this world is not just good; it's *very* good!

Do you appreciate your ability to chew food? Teeth are very good. Food is very good. Rain is very good. The winds are very good. The world can't exist without winds. It's a big subject, but think about it and you'll see. It's a pity that many people never study these things and think about them.

Clothing is very good. Ears are very good. Everything in this world is very good—and our job is to say to Hashem, "Thank You for all the good things." That's our function. Not only to thank Hashem that everything is very good in general, for the human race as a whole, but the good He bestows on each person—on *you*. No one can say he's never had the benefits of Hashem's *tov*.

Tov l'hodos laHashem (*Tehillim* 92:2). Do you know what's good? "To give thanks to Hashem." It's not merely *a* good thing. It's *the* good thing. In this world, we're here to make ourselves busy giving thanks to Hashem. And not just us. We say in the Shabbos morning prayers, "*Shekein chovas kol hayetzurim*—It's the duty of all creatures" to thank Hashem. Everybody—which means even Eskimos, Fiji islanders, Englishmen, Africans. Everybody is *mechuyav*. It's an obligation.

What must one do to thank Hashem for all the good things? "*L'hodos, l'hallel, l'shabeyach, l'fa'eir, l'romeim, l'hadeir, l'vareich, l'aleih, ul'kaleis*—to thank, to praise, to extol, to glorify, to exalt, to lavish, to bless, to raise high, and to acclaim." There's a whole list of things to do. And it's an obligation on everyone. "*V'chol hachaim yoducha sela*—All who live will thank You." All who *live*—that's why they were given life — must praise You and thank You.

And it says in *P'sukei D'zimrah*, "*Havu laHashem mishpechos amim* — Give to Hashem, you families of the nations." Attribute all glory and strength to Him. Everybody — Greeks, Italians, Irish. Everybody is obligated to spend a great deal of time thanking Hashem. "*Hallelu es Hashem, kol goyim* — Every kind of nationality should speak of Hashem's greatness" (*Tehillim* 117:1). The fact that they don't do it is held against them.

But we, the Am Yisrael, are even more obligated because of what He did for us, which is more than He did for the other nations. "*Ki gavar aleinu chasdo* — For his kindness has overwhelmed us" (ibid. v. 2). We are much more obligated.

So now we know what our function in this world is — to praise Hashem, to thank Him. "*Aleinu l'shabeyach la'Adon hakol* — Upon us is the obligation to praise the Master of all." That's our job in this world. You have to wake up and realize what you're here for. You're here to thank Hashem.

The greatest *yetzer hara* is neglecting to recognize the kindnesses of Hashem. Of course, there are all kinds of *yetzer hara*s, but the most dangerous of all is the one that causes us to overlook what Hashem has done for us. Because that's the chief function for which we were created.

Q **Why do we bow during Shemoneh Esrei?**

To express our gratitude for all that Hashem did, does, and will do for us. There's so much we're grateful for that when we bow to Him, we should never straighten up. The load is too big, so we should really remain eternally bent over.

The Gemara asks why we bow at the first *brachah* in Shemoneh Esrei and at *Modim* but not during the rest of the *brachos* (*Brachos* 34a). Why do we bow only at the beginning and the end? A Kohen Gadol bends over at the beginning and the end of each *brachah*. A king remains bent over the entire Shemoneh Esrei. Why does everyone else only bow at the beginning and the end?

The answer is that we remain bent over in accordance with the benefits showered upon us. Although Hashem gives ordinary people blessings and kindliness without end, it's enough for us to bend over at the beginning and the end. A Kohen Gadol, who is granted very great privileges, is more obligated to thank Hashem, so he bends over at the beginning and end of each *brachah* in Shemoneh Esrei. But a king has even more. Being king is the greatest honor, so he bows for the entire Shemoneh Esrei. He can't ever straighten up. He has such a tremendous burden of gratitude.

We see from this that the more Hashem gives you—the wealthier and more successful you are—the more you must bow down in gratitude to Hashem. Therefore, when we talk about being an *eved* of Hashem and showing our humility toward Him, it's necessary to study in detail all that He has done for us throughout our lifetime as well as what He continues to do for us constantly. That's why we say *Baruch Atah, Hashem*—the word "*baruch*" means "bending the knee." Whenever we say "*Baruch*," we are expressing the emotion of indebtedness by saying we feel we should bend our knees from the great load of gratitude to Him and in recognition of our debt to Him.

It's so important to have *kavanah* when thanking Hashem. It's not enough just to know the translation, to know what you're saying—you must truly feel a debt of gratitude to Hashem. Thank Him for a favor He has bestowed on you. Let's say you're saying "*Pokei'ach ivrim*—You open the eyes of the blind." Oh, what a favor that is! Suppose Hashem didn't give you the ability to see. What a tragedy, *chalilah*, that would be. To live a life in total darkness! So that should fill you with happiness that you can see and help you actually feel a debt of gratitude to Hashem.

And so on with all the *tov me'od*s He gives us. It's a never-ending obligation. It's our chief purpose in life.[55]

So every time you say *Modim*, think of a particular debt that you

55 This is elaborated on in the section on *Brachos* above, p. 71.

have to Hashem and utilize the opportunity you have to actually bend your knees in recognition and gratitude.

What's the best time of the year to help us deepen our feelings of gratitude to Hashem?

The happiest season of the year is the summertime. There's nothing like summertime. In the summertime if you're a landlord, you don't spend any money on heating the building. Think of all the money you save on oil bills! That's a happiness. You think it's silly? It's not silly at all.

Summertime — there are no colds! Unless you sit in front of the air conditioner all the time and drink only cold drinks — watch out for that! But otherwise, you won't catch a cold. Respiratory illnesses? Not in the summertime! No coughing, no sneezing! Summer is a pleasure! What a great blessing it is.

In the summer you get vitamins free of charge. Walk out in the street and the sun is showering vitamins on you. The sun is a vitamin dispensary. In wintertime there are clouds and you don't always get the vitamins you need. Sometimes you have to take extra vitamin pills. In the summertime, you get all you want. *Baruch Hashem* for the summertime!

In the summer, fruits are plentiful. Red apples and luscious cherries and plums and peaches. They're plentiful in the summer so the prices go down in all the fruit stores. Now you're living!

So when you walk out in the street, don't complain, "Oh, it's a hot day." Hashem is giving you so much energy from the sun, free of charge. Millions of tons of energy are pouring down onto this Earth for free. It doesn't cost you a penny to get all that energy from the sun. When you walk out into the street, you have to say, "*Baruch Atah, Hashem, Yotzer hame'oros!*" Don't say Hashem's name, of course. But say *something*! You must thank Hashem for the summertime.

Learn how to sing to Hashem. And don't think it's a small thing. *Tov l'hodos laHashem* (*Tehillim* 92:2). Do you know what's good in this world? To sing to Hashem and thank Him. That's what's good. It's the only good there is.

What do you think was the *avodas Hashem* we were *mekabel* when we accepted the Torah on Har Sinai? The most important service of Hashem is gratitude to Hashem! So we must get busy singing and thanking Hashem for the manifold benefits He's giving us. That's the very great service in the summertime. It doesn't mean you have to stop learning. You can continue learning Torah and doing *mitzvos*. Nevertheless, the *avodah* of gratitude for the summertime—the happiness of the summertime and thankfulness we must feel—is a very important *avodah*, and it's one of the chief purposes of *tefillah*.

SUMMARY

- Our chief obligation in this world is to praise and thank Hashem, and not just in general but in detail. Every person in the world has this obligation, but we Jews have the greatest obligation because Hashem chose us as His people.
- The more that Hashem gives a person, the greater his obligation to thank Him. Every additional day of life, of *parnassah*, of good health, and every other benefit means you're more indebted to Hashem than you were before. So your gratitude to Him should increase in kind.
- When everything is going well, that's the time to thank Hashem for all the many benefits He's giving you.

Birkas Kohanim

Q **What makes a *tzaddik's brachos* especially powerful?**

You have to know that even when you get a *brachah* from a *tzaddik*, the *brachah* is really coming only from Hashem. In the three verses of *Birkas Kohanim*, the *kohanim* utter Hashem's name in each blessing—"*Y'varechecha Hashem ... Ya'eir Hashem ... Yisa Hashem*" (*Bamidbar* 6:24–26). The *kohanim* say Hashem's name in each blessing.

It seems redundant, but this procedure emphasizes the awareness that it's solely Hashem who confers the blessings. It's not the *kohanim*, and it's not the *tzaddik*, or any other cause.

The listeners are expected to pay attention to this repetition of Hashem's name and learn that all blessings are from Him and from Him alone. It's not the words of the *kohanim* that are bestowing the blessings. The *brachos* are a prayer to Hashem, that He should bless the Jewish people.

Nevertheless, a *tzaddik*'s *brachos* are different because the *mechitzah* between him and Hashem is minimal. Great men like Moshe, Aharon, and Shmuel didn't constitute a curtain between the people and Hashem. There was no *mechitzah*. When you looked at Moshe Rabbeinu, you didn't see Moshe Rabbeinu. He was transparent. When you looked at him, you saw Hashem — Moshe was just a conduit. When you looked at Shmuel Hanavi, you saw Hashem. You didn't see Shmuel Hanavi.

Today, the *roshei yeshiva*s are our leaders, and through them Hashem is able to shine directly to us because they're not a *mechitzah*.

Sim Shalom

Q **What is included in the idea of "*shalom*"?**

It means you want all the Am Yisrael to have *shalom*. Some Jews are being persecuted by the government. Some by the IRS. Some Jews are suffering from anti-Semitic attacks. Many Jews have troubles. We want all Jews to have *shalom*. If you add that thought, there is a big reward for that.

We want that all those people who don't have children should have children. All those who haven't found *shidduchim* should get good *shidduchim* quickly. All those who don't have *parnassah* should have *parnassah*. People who are not well should become well. That's what we're saying.

And we say "*shalom rav*,"[56] not just plain *shalom*. *Shalom rav* means that we want "great *shalom*" for Yisrael. And it shouldn't be only a temporary *shalom*, but "*l'olam*—forever and ever."

If you train yourself to think that way, you're going to get a very great reward. Oh, yes! The more you bless the Am Yisrael, the greater will be your reward. "I will bless those who bless you" (*Bereishis* 12:3). By blessing a fellow Jew, you're invoking upon yourself a special covenant that Hashem made with our forefathers and with all of the future generations of the Am Yisrael.

When a person trains himself to always be busy thinking of the Am Yisrael and blessing them, he's going to get a very big blessing from Hashem. Even if you only do it one time, you get a big *mitzvah*. But if you do it again and again, you get more *mitzvos*. That's why the Shemoneh Esrei is such a gold mine. If three times a day, day after day, you say *brachos* for this Jew and this Jew and that Jew—each individually—there's more and more reward each time. The Shemoneh Esrei is a veritable gold mine full of opportunities for greatness.

Q **Do we need to pray for peace if we're not at war?**

When we finish Shemoneh Esrei, we say *Sim Shalom* or *Shalom Rav*, asking Hashem to "give us peace." When a soldier was in Vietnam or in France [during World War II] trying to dodge bullets, he had one dream—that is, if he was able to dream at all; the truth is that he had no time to dream, but if he could put his head down for a moment on mud and snatch a few minutes of sleep, do you know what his dream was? He was dreaming that he was somewhere in a desert in New Mexico, next to a cactus bush, lying on the sand. Now, in the desert there's nothing to eat, nothing to drink, and the merciless sun is baking him. But all around there's *shalom*, peace. That was his heart's desire. No constant buzzing of bullets all around him. No men screaming in pain. No constant fear of instant death. If he

---

56 In Maariv, and for *nusach Ashkenaz*, Minchah as well.

could have *shalom*, even if he could just lie down on a park bench in the Bowery with bums, clothed in lice-ridden garments, without a nickel in his pants, it would be to him the dearest wish of his heart. That's what *shalom* means.

But suppose we remember to pray for *shalom* right now, while we have peace. As you walk down the street in the daytime, there's nothing to fear but traffic. Traffic, by the way, is a serious enemy. Of all "diseases" one can be struck with, the worst is traffic, because it's an ever-present danger. Therefore, pray to avoid a traffic accident, *chas v'shalom*. Never fail to express your thanks to Hashem for avoiding them.

Be that as it may, we live in times of relative *shalom*, so now is the time to pray for it with real feeling and reap reward three times a day. It's a pity people think that this prayer is a formality, that we're keeping it in reserve for the time, *chas v'shalom*, when war comes. Then we'll pray for *shalom*. We should pray then, too, of course, but now is the time because now it's a thousand times more acceptable.

If you haven't davened Maariv yet, pray for *shalom* with all your heart. "*Shalom rav al Yisrael amcha!*" Oh, please give us peace! What do you mean "give us peace"? Don't we have it already? The answer is we don't. As soon as we say we have peace, it means we have removed our trust, our *emunah*, from Hashem.

Q **What does real *shalom* feel like?**

It may be a surprise for you to hear that the happiest time in the history of our people was the forty years they spent in the Midbar. It's true. Am Yisrael's journey in the wilderness is described as follows: "Hashem blessed you in everything you did. He paid attention and supervised your walking in this great wilderness. These forty years, Hashem was with you, and you lacked nothing" (*Devarim* 2:7).

Never in history were they as safe as they were in that camp. The *anenei hakavod* were overhead. They walked in security. And they were expected to find happiness in that security, happiness in *shalom*. Just the fact that nothing bad happens is a very great blessing.

You don't know what a pleasure it is not to have to worry about an invading army coming through your city. In Russia and Poland, for many years, armies flowed back and forth. One day this army occupied the city; the next day the other army occupied the city. There were executions every day! Life hung by a thread. I'm not talking about the Nazis. When the Nazis came, it was the real *malach hamavess*. But even before the Nazis, when World War I raged on for years, the landscape was flooded with dangers. There was no such thing as security. People yearned just for peace, real lasting peace!

Learn to enjoy the absence of war, the absence of insurrection, of rioting. That's the way a wise person studies the world and lives with true happiness. When you're walking in the street in the summertime and perspiring and thinking maybe of some cool place—you'd like to be in Maine, perhaps—remember these words, "You lacked nothing." Think of the peace you're enjoying now! Savor it! You're not famished by hunger? You're not suffering through war? You have it nice and quiet? Then recognize that the regular routine of life is a very great happiness.

You slept last night? You can lie down in your bed at night without being disturbed? That's the happiness Hashem wants you to enjoy! "And you will lie down, and nobody will disturb your sleep" (*Vayikra* 26:6). At night the secret police won't come banging on your door. I was in Lithuania and once, in the middle of the night, the police came banging on the door. Somebody was staying with us in our apartment. He was a foreigner staying there overnight. At half past twelve, there was a pounding at the door. The police were banging and shouting, "Open the door immediately!" They didn't need a warrant in Lithuania. They banged down the door and pulled you out of bed.

Here in America, you can sleep in bed and nobody bothers you. That's a happiness! You can sleep in peace. Bands of soldiers are not roaming the streets. Drunken bums are not banging on your door. Of course, today you must secure your windows at night because the liberals have wreaked havoc upon us. But let's say you have strong bars on your windows. You can fall asleep without being terror-stricken.

In the Midbar, the Am Yisrael learned the happiness of *shalom*, of daily routine. It lasted forty years! That's a long time. Forty years of routine. They woke up, did what had to be done, and went to sleep. No trouble! No excitement! Try to go outside today and convince somebody that he should be happy with the regular routine of life. That's what *shalom* is, after all. He'll look at you as if you fell off the moon. "No," he says. "I want some fun! I think I should get in my car and travel someplace."

So he sits in the car all day long, gripping the steering wheel. He's tense. He can't rest and he's smelling the gasoline fumes of a thousand cars ahead of him. Does it enter his mind that maybe he would have been better off sitting on the porch in front of his house? Or inside his dining room? No, the happiness of *shalom* isn't good enough for him. He has to go to the bowling alley. You know, there's nothing natural about wanting to go bowling. I'm much older than you, and I've never desired to go bowling. Only that when a person is too lazy to find happiness in his own life, the way that Hashem intended, he fans the flames of desire. "Give us meat!" "Give us a bowling alley!"

But all these things are meaningless compared to the happiness of, "I'm going to give you peace in the land" (*Vayikra* 26:6). You hear that? Hashem doesn't promise restaurants and basketball games. He doesn't say, "I'll give you money to travel and eat out. And I'll give you all types of luxuries." No, all that Hashem promises is that He'll give you enough to eat and peace in the land.

Many people get nervous when they hear that. That's all? That's happiness? That's boring! It's monotonous! That's called life?

Yes, indeed! *Shalom* means that life is monotonous, nothing exciting. You're going to live all your life without excitement. No ambulances will come to your house. No fire engines will come to your house. Your daughter is not calling you in the middle of the night to tell you she's having trouble with her husband. That's *simchah*! A nice, quiet life. That's happiness! If you can live quietly, that's the greatest happiness in life. You can go to sleep tonight and appreciate the gift of peace that Hashem is giving you and you'll fall asleep a joyous person, with feelings of happy gratitude to Hashem.

So that's what we have to *daven* for and have in mind when begging "*Sim shalom!*" and when finishing the *brachah*—thanking Hashem for the blessed routine of ordinary life.

PRACTICAL ADVICE

Should we be giving *brachos* to our fellow Jews even outside of the context of Shemoneh Esrei?

Absolutely! By merely wishing a fellow Jew a "*shalom aleichem*," a "good morning," a "good night," a "good Shabbos," or anything similar, you will be blessed. And that's even if you said it without much thought. How much more so will the blessing of Hashem be on one who blesses his fellow Jew wholeheartedly!

Now, better than saying meaningless words, like "Hi" or "Hello," say "*shalom aleichem*," the traditional Jewish greeting. Rav Gustman, a *rosh yeshiva* in America, once heard somebody say "Hello." So he said, "*Vus epess* 'hello'?! "'Hello' doesn't mean anything," he said. "Say *shalom aleichem*, a real greeting." Even if you say it superficially, you've already done a wise thing—you've made a very good investment—because it's going to come back to you. At the very least, you'll be greeted by others!

Did it ever happen that as you pass an acquaintance on the street, he doesn't seem particularly interested in looking at you? You're thinking, *What's wrong with this grouchy fellow?* But maybe he's not acknowledging you because you're not acknowledging him! Maybe it's because you didn't greet him! Being greeted happily by others is a happiness. It's a boon for living healthfully. So train yourself to always greet others first.

However, a proper *shalom aleichem* is much more than that. When you say "*Shalom*" to a person, you should be specific. Have in mind that Hashem should bless him with peaceful things. He shouldn't fight with his landlord. He shouldn't argue with his wife. He shouldn't have a conflict with his boss or with his partner. He should get along with his neighbors and not fight about the driveway. When you put something into that word "*Shalom*," you're giving him a blessing that has meaning to it.

This *yesod*, this principle of "I will bless those who bless you" is really the secret behind the well-known Chazal: "If a man prays for his fellow man and he needs the same thing, Hashem will answer him first" (*Bava Kama* 92b). Most people learn this *ma'amar Chazal* wrong. They think it's some sort of reward, an incentive to pray for your fellow man. But it's really much more than that. It's a direct result of your *tefillah*, because of the great principle of the Torah, "I will bless those who bless you." And that's why the Anshei Knesses Hagedolah established all our *tefillos* in plural form—because every *tefillah* for your fellow Jew ends up being a *tefillah* for yourself as well. This is a practice that true *ovdei Hashem* can do without any effort, and it's available all the time. When you pass someone and say, "Good Shabbos, good Shabbos" don't say it and forget about him. Don't waste the opportunity. Five paces later say again, "Good Shabbos." This time he doesn't hear it, but this time you mean it more. And under your breath add a few *peirushim*! "Your meals should be *geshmak*. You should enjoy the cholent and the kugel. Hashem should help you enjoy your children and your wife. You should have a good Shabbos nap."

The Alter of Slabodka was once walking in the morning with a disciple of his and they passed by a house where one of the *kollel* men lived. The Alter stopped, faced the house, and said to the house, "*Gut morgen*—Good morning. You should have a wonderful day." This *talmid* said, "Nobody's listening!" So the Alter replied, "*Tzu darf ehr heren?*—Does he have to be listening?" You hear that? You hear what the Alter said?! That's from a great man! "*Tzu darf ehr heren?*—Does he have to hear?" The point of the *brachah* is not that he should hear you. What you want *is that Hashem should hear you.*

Anybody, a Jew or a gentile, who takes the trouble to say words of blessing to a Jew must know that Hashem is now mortgaged to him, and He's going to deliver. The man who makes the effort to bless the Am Yisrael should know that Hashem is under contract to deliver.

Q What advice can you give for spouses who argue?

Here's a man who quarrels with his wife. Now, it's possible that both of them are to blame, but he should worry about himself now. So, when he comes home at night, as he's holding the doorknob in his hand, let him think, *No matter what, tonight I'm not going to react. I heard Rabbi Miller say that in a lecture and so I'm going to try it out.* He steels himself for whatever may come.

Then, when he opens the door, he's prepared. "Where were you all night long?" his wife is yelling. "I was left with the children—they were driving me crazy!" And so on and so forth. But instead of exploding and saying, "What do you want from me?! I'm trying to make a living!" he keeps quiet. He has a lot to say but he keeps his mouth closed. "Hashem suspends the whole world for the man who keeps his mouth closed" (*Chullin* 89a). Someone who can keep his mouth closed at the time of a quarrel is so important that the whole world hangs in the balance because of him!

Maybe he opens it just a little to say, "Oh, I'm so sorry you had a difficult day. Tell me what happened." And he says it in a calm, quiet voice.

Now, you won't be able to do such a thing naturally. You have to train yourself and fortify yourself beforehand. That's why you should prepare while you're still standing outside the house. *No matter what happens, I'm not going to react.*

The first time it's not so easy. His blood is boiling, and it's not easy to keep his tongue locked behind his teeth. But he does it and the night passes by *b'shalom*. Then another night passes, and then another and another. After a while, it becomes easier and easier for him.

He should continue in this manner for a long time. The Rambam (*Hilchos Dei'os* 2:2) doesn't say how long, but you have to work on this until the quality of anger is uprooted from your mind entirely. Eventually, you won't even notice those things that cause others to get angry. You'll be able to remain calm under any circumstances because getting angry doesn't even occur to you anymore.

Anger is like dynamite. Dynamite, you know, is a wonderful invention. Let's say you're trying to build a road and you come to a rocky hill that's standing in the way. Now, it's going to be a problem if you have to detour around every mountain, so you take sticks of dynamite and blow that hill out of the way to clear a path for your road. But suppose you come home from work after dynamiting mountains for the Department of Highways and now you're locked out of the house. You can't find your key, and your wife is out somewhere. Will you take a piece of dynamite from your work truck and blow the door open? No, you can't use such extreme means. Dynamite is not meant for that.

Now, let's say this man dynamites the door open and now he's in the house. It doesn't end there. A man like that never knows when to stop. When the door is finally opened, he explodes with emotional dynamite: "Why did you lock the latch from the inside?! I was trying to get in all this time! Of course I tried the key! Don't you have any consideration for me? I'm standing outside in the freezing cold! Don't people here think about things before they do them?!" A man like that is the biggest failure. He's a terror! His wife and his children wish he'd go back to work.

I'm talking now about a man, but the same applies to a woman. If she wants to spend money on something and he feels they can't afford it, she's frustrated. "He's preventing me from buying something I desire!" All her life she was a spoiled little girl whose mother waited on her hand and foot, and now she's angry because she can't get what she wants. Her husband looks on in astonishment. "Is this the lovely woman I married?" Instead of his wife, he sees a raging female. A raging female isn't so beautiful anymore.

Now, of course, every married couple must know that an argument doesn't mean your marriage is over. Even after a person makes an error—a woman or a man might get angry and say or do the wrong thing—it's never too late. You can always make amends. If you listen to good advice, you won't let the matter last too long. You'll try to mend things quickly. Try to forgive and forget right away. The next day, act as if it didn't happen. It may seem a little funny, but what do you care? You want to continue to live normally.

Here's a man who got angry and lost his temper. It shouldn't happen! A wicked thing. A terrible *cheit*. He was shouting at his wife. But the next day, he realizes he made a terrible mistake and wants to make amends. So, he buys her a gift—a box of candy or chocolate. Actually, he should have gone to Manhattan and bought her a diamond. It would have cost him a pretty penny and he'd have to pay it back in installments for five years, but it would be worth it. He should bring a diamond home and not say anything about the night before. Let him keep his mouth shut about the past, about why he's buying it. He should just give it to her. Hopefully, she would accept it.

But suppose a man didn't do that. Instead of a diamond ring, he bought his wife a box of chocolates. Now, is a box of chocolate enough to appease a wife?! No, but if she's a smart woman, she'll accept it anyway. She lets herself be appeased with a little nothing. A woman like that is wise—much wiser than all the fools who call me and tell me about how they're going to court to break up their marriage because of this or that. They're setting themselves up for a life of unhappiness. While they're bemoaning their fate, this wise woman will still be happily married, and she'll dance at her grandchildren's *chasunah*s. She'll be attending *brissim*, birthdays, and bar mitzvahs. Who knows how many happy occasions the foolish woman misses out on because of one careless fit of anger?

If a person trains himself to avoid anger at all costs, he saves himself a lot of trouble. Shlomo Hamelech says, "Remove anger from your heart and you'll remove a lot of trouble from your life"

(*Koheles* 11:10). Train yourself beforehand so when people say something unfair to you, it doesn't make an impression and you remain calm.

Anger is a terrible tool. It's dynamite, and it must be locked away in a cabinet. There is such a thing as anger for a just purpose, but even then, it should be "*ka'as hapanim v'lo ka'as haleiv* — an externality, a show of anger" (Rambam, ibid. 2:3). I told you once about Reb Simcha Zissel, *zichrono livrachah*. He had a *minhag* when he had to get angry. He had a special hat that he kept on his shelf. When the time came to show anger, he took the hat off the shelf and announced to himself, *This is my anger hat*. That reminded him that he was about to put on an act, that his anger was only a *levush*, an externality. It wasn't him. It was just a mask he put on. He made sure never to become angry unless he wore that hat. By doing that, he reminded himself that he shouldn't allow the anger to percolate into his heart.

I once was sent by a *rosh yeshiva* to a Board of Directors meeting for the yeshiva. We had to ask them for money to hire another *rebbi*. But the Board said they didn't have the money to hire another person. I was angry at them! When I came back and told the *rosh yeshiva* what the Board said, he asked me, "Were you angry at them?" and I said, "Yes, very angry. We need that *rebbi*." The *rosh yeshiva* said, "Oh, no — you should have shown just a face of anger. You shouldn't have been angry. It's *ka'as hapanim* you must show, but never *ka'as haleiv*."

Now, I can't tell you all the details — when yes, when no, how much yes, how much no. The situations we face are endless, and therefore the words you're hearing now need to be applied judiciously. Everything you hear in this place is like good meat (at least I hope so). But even good meat can't be eaten by itself. You must have a little bit of onions. You need a little bit of salt and pepper. You need some condiments. If you buy a piece of meat in a butcher shop and try to eat it straight from the butcher's block, you won't enjoy it much.

Everything you hear here needs to be explained and applied in practice. You need a great many other things besides these words alone. What you're hearing here are just generalities or generalizations. We're not talking about waving a magic wand and suddenly everything is transformed. You can't expect to hear something once and think you're now ready to face the world.

You'll have to hear these ideas repeatedly and think about them. Only by dint of studying will you learn how to keep far, far away from anger, and how to use it when needed. You have to get to work changing yourself. Certainly it takes work. Nothing good comes easy. Everything good comes as a result of work! You'll have to go home and practice again and again and again. After years and years, you'll discover that you were rewarded richly for all the effort you invested into *tikkun hamiddos*. You'll become a more and more perfect *eved Hashem* every day of your life, fulfilling the purpose that you came into this world to achieve.

Q **Should we be on good terms with everyone?**

Somebody once said, "A thousand friends is too few, and one enemy is too many." You hear that *chachmah*? It means, get busy making friends. I was once walking in the street when a young Puerto Rican, seventeen years old, approached me and started saying *divrei cheirufim*, calling me names. So I put my arm around his shoulder. "Oh, I haven't seen you for a long time," I said. We started walking down the street like that and he kept quiet. At the corner I said, "It was good seeing you again," and I walked away. That's the way to deal with your enemies.

The saying goes that you can catch more flies with a drop of honey than with a gallon of vinegar. It means if you want to catch flies—"flies" here means "friends"—be sweet like honey. Don't be sour like vinegar because you're not going to get any benefit except getting bitten on all sides.

That's one of the principles of the Torah: "Her ways are ways of peace" (*Mishlei* 3:17). Hashem wants us to live happily, peacefully. You're following the advice of the Torah when you get along with your brothers. "How good and pleasant it is when brothers sit together as one" (*Tehillim* 133:1). Train yourself to be friendly to your entire family. In case they insult you, forget about it. If they wrong you, overlook it. That's why it says not only "*bakeish shalom* — seek peace" but "*v'radfeihu*" (*Tehillim* 34:15). *Radfeihu* means "run after it" — no matter what they did! "You expect me to keep quiet after what they did to me?!" Yes! It's for your benefit to keep quiet. You'll be surprised.

In my first *kehillah*, I was standing in the hall one Shabbos afternoon before I gave my *drashah*. A man came in and passed by. The next day this man brought a claim against me to the Board of Directors that I didn't say "*gut Shabbos*" to him. In front of the whole Board he complained, "The Rav didn't say *gut Shabbos* to me." I was a new Rav, too. The president asked me, "Is it true?" I said, "I think I did say *gut Shabbos* to him." I was surprised. I was thinking, "Such a chutzpah to accuse me for nothing." Before the Board of Directors, too. I didn't say anything, however. It wouldn't help to perpetuate hard feelings.

Three months later, this man gets up at the Board of Directors meeting and makes a motion to raise the Rav's salary. Nobody else thought of raising my salary. He was the first one. A year later he raised the salary again, the same man! So, it pays to listen to the advice in the Torah — make friends, not enemies. It's very important advice, "*Bakeish shalom v'radfeihu.*"

Q What do you think about the election of Jimmy Carter as president?

I haven't the slightest knowledge about Carter [who was elected in November 1976]. But I hope that Hashem will give him His blessings and success. Now that he's been elected, it's a *mitzvah* to *daven* for Carter. It's a *mishnah*, plain and simple—be *mispallel "bishlomah shel malchus"* (*Avos* 3:2). Every Jew has to pray for the benefit of the government. It's a *mitzvah*. Now that he's been elected, we *daven* that he should be well, he shouldn't catch a cold, he shouldn't be bothered by the liberals, he shouldn't have wars in his time. "In his time the Jewish people should be happy and prosperous and Mashiach should come" (*Yirmiyah* 23:6). That's our duty—to pray for Carter.

You have to still pray for Ford, by the way, because he's still president until January. But a Jew must pray for his government. It's very important. Even if you haven't done it until now, it's a good time to begin. From now on, think about it sometimes and say it. When you're on the street walking, say a little prayer for the president and the vice president, and don't be ashamed. Don't worry that you might be ridiculed by somebody. Know that you're just fulfilling the duty of an Orthodox Jew.

You must pray for the government not because you want to show the government that you pray for them. The fakers come together and wave flags. They make an official prayer. That doesn't mean a thing. They're not praying for the government; they're just showing off. Pray for the government quietly, between yourself and Hashem. And you should really mean it. Have in mind that Carter should be well and that he shouldn't have troubles. He shouldn't fight with his wife. He should have peace at home and peace in the government. Congress should cooperate with him. There's no question that if there will be a tranquil government, then Carter will try to make a good name for himself. No question about it. Any president would like to make his term go down in history as a successful term. And so, our best wishes are given to President-elect Carter. Hashem should help him—and us.

When Hashem hears that He says, "I see you mean business. You're blessing My children. Now I'll get busy blessing you."

SUMMARY

- We ask Hashem to grant *shalom*, which includes all *brachos*—*parnassah*, *shidduchim*, good health, and so on—to all our fellow Jews. When saying this *brachah*, it's a good idea to have in mind specific individuals and ask Hashem to bless them with all good things.
- When we have peace is the best time to ask Hashem to give us peace. Doing so demonstrates that we understand that we have peace only as long as Hashem wills it. Most people don't recognize the value of peace until they no longer have it. Don't be like most people.
- The fact that nothing bad happens is a very great blessing. Don't take it for granted. Don't become dissatisfied with your peaceful, regular routine. It's a great blessing.

Elokai, Netzor

Q **Why do we say *Elokai, Netzor* after Shemoneh Esrei?**

The Gemara records a series of personal prayers that various Tannaim and Amoraim said after their Shemoneh Esrei (*Brachos* 16b). Each had his own *tefillah*, and it's not a bad idea for us, too, to say our own *tefillos*. You can add your own words. Each of us has his own needs. Sometimes you have to say a *tefillah* for a sick person or for your own health, or you need success in some business venture. Whatever it is, be *mispallel*. That's the real *tefillah*. When you say what you need for yourself, it's a *tefillah* that comes from the heart. Nobody needs the same things. Therefore, at the end of Shemoneh Esrei, a person should add his own requests for the things he needs.[57]

57 The *Chayei Adam*, quoted in the *Mishnah Berurah* (122:7), says that it's good for a person to *daven* every day expressly for his personal needs. After he finishes the *brachos* of Shemoneh Esrei, he should verbalize his personal requests to Hashem, e.g., *parnassah*, that Torah should never leave his mouth or those of his children and grandchildren, and that his descendants should be *ovdei Hashem be'emes*.

The end of Shemoneh Esrei includes part of the *tefillah* said by Mar b'rei d'Ravina. Here's a brief commentary Rav Miller delivered on it:

"*Elokai*, guard my tongue from evil"—That's the first *tefillah* he added! So we see how urgent it is. One of the greatest perils is a man's tongue, which can say things that hurt. *Lashon hara* doesn't only mean to slander people. The worst part of a "bad tongue" is to hurt people's feelings. When husbands and wives hurt each other's feelings, that's *lashon hara*. You can hurt your neighbors with a bad tongue. Therefore, it's of the utmost importance to ask Hashem to help you guard your tongue from evil. *Evil* means misusing your tongue, whether for slander or to hurt people's feelings, which is even worse.

"And my lips from speaking deceit"—The lips sometimes can make an impression that one is speaking virtuous words when it's actually trickery. Therefore, we have to ask Hashem to guard our lips from speaking deceitfully.[58]

"And to those who curse me"—those who belittle me, make light of me—"let my soul be silent"—don't let me be angry at them; help me ignore what they say—"and let my soul be like dust to everybody"—even if somebody walks on you like dust, the end will be that the dirt will cover him up eventually, so one who makes himself humble, like dirt, will win out in the end.

"Open up my heart in your Torah"—The heart is sealed. It's necessary for the heart to open for Hashem to put in all the good qualities. But your heart won't open unless you learn Torah. Torah is the key to opening the heart. Once the heart is open, Hashem will put in good things, like love and fear of Him. But first you must learn Torah if you want your heart to open up and become a receptacle for love and fear.

"And my soul should pursue your *mitzvos*"—not merely do the *mitzvos*, but run after them as if you are pursuing something you desire greatly.

---

58 Lips are more external than the tongue, so it's a symbol of someone whose speech looks kosher on the outside but isn't kosher on the inside.

Yehi Ratzon

Q How can I learn to mourn for the Beis Hamikdash?

Well, if you never think about the Beis Hamikdash, you'll never be able to understand the loss. So first of all, think about the Beis Hamikdash. Most people don't even think about it. Then the month of Av comes and they ask me how to mourn for the *Churban*.

When you finish the Shemoneh Esrei, make sure to say the last few sentences slowly, with some thought. Most people are already thinking about breakfast when they say these words. These sentences are precious. They're an opportunity. Don't waste them! When you walk back three steps, don't just wait for the *chazzan* to say *kedushah*. Take your time and say it with feeling! "Ah, Hashem, if we could have the Beis Hamikdash again!"

Of course, it's not sincere in the beginning. It's only talk. But train yourself. "Ay yay yay, Ribbono Shel Olam, please give me a Beis Hamikdash once more." Say it with *tza'ar*! Not just with *peirush hamilos*. Say it with regret! "I'm so sorry that I don't have the Beis Hamikdash." Say the words slowly and think about them. Show you understand that it's a loss. If you don't understand it's a loss, there's no use talking. That's number one.

I'm telling you something that's very valuable right now. Most people don't understand it, but every day when you finish Shemoneh Esrei is a glorious opportunity to gain a very big *mitzvah*. "Please, Hashem, bring back the Beis Hamikdash, and there we will serve You as in the days of old."

That's why it's very important for us to study the days of old to know what we once had. We look back now and we're so sad that we don't have the Beis Hamikdash anymore! "Yerushalayim remembers, in the days of her affliction and her sadness" (*Eichah* 1:7). It means that after the *Churban* Beis Hamikdash, she remembers "all of her delights that she had in the days of old" (ibid.).

The Beis Hamikdash was a great opportunity. You would come there and learn *yiras Shamayim* just from looking at it. "So that you should learn to fear Hashem your G-d all the days" (*Devarim* 14:23). Merely by coming there and seeing the *kohanim* doing their *avodah* and hearing the Levi'im singing you'd become inspired. What a terrible loss!

The Gemara says that at the *Simchas Beis Hasho'eivah*, they were "drawing out *ruach hakodesh* like people draw water" (*Sukkah* 50b). They came together on Sukkos and were singing all night. And as they sang, they were gaining *ruach hakodesh* by the bucket. Buckets full of *ruach hakodesh*. *Tosfos* cites a *Yerushalmi* (*Sukkah* 22b) that Yonah became a *navi* when he was at the *Simchas Beis Hasho'eivah* in the Beis Hamikdash. When he first arrived, he wasn't a *navi*, but as he stood there singing with the Am Yisrael all night, the spirit of Hashem suddenly came upon him for the first time. In the middle of the night, the spirit of Hashem came upon him. That doesn't mean that anybody who sings will get *nevuah*. *Nevuah* needs a great deal of preparation of the soul, which Yonah had already accomplished. But at the *Simchas Beis Hasho'eivah* his soul became so elevated from singing to Hashem that the *ruach hanevuah* came upon him for the first time.

When you ask Hashem to restore the Beis Hamikdash, that doesn't mean you want Mashiach. The Beis Hamikdash without Mashiach is also good. Of course, it won't come without Mashiach. But you have to recognize the great gift of the Beis Hamikdash on its own. You have to think, "I want Mashiach to come and build the Beis Hamikdash." We should all come together in the Beis Hamikdash and soak in the *ruach hakodesh* just from being there. We want the Beis Hamikdash to get closer to Hashem.

That's how to mourn for the Beis Hamikdash. Little by little, as you think these thoughts, you'll feel the loss. That's how to begin. You'll never mourn for it if you don't feel the loss. First, you have to train yourself to feel how great the opportunity was when we had it. Then you'll know what it means to not have it, and you'll be able to mourn for the loss.

TACHANUN

Q Why do we fall on our face when reciting Tachanun?

In addition to saying words, we use real physical terms for Hashem throughout our davening. For example, on Mondays and Thursdays, we say a long Tachanun. And in there we say, "*Hateih, Elokai, aznecha ushema*—Hashem, incline Your ear toward me and listen to my words." Open Your ear to hear my words?! "*Pekach einecha ur'eih*—Open Your eyes and see." Open Your eyes?! You're telling Hashem to open His ears and eyes?!

When you're davening, you're not supposed to be contemplating the *p'shat* of the Rambam in these words, the *p'shat* of the Targum Onkelos, that these are all allegories and similes for deeper concepts. No! You should be thinking about real eyes, and real ears.

Yes, that's exactly what you're supposed to be thinking. And picturing! You're asking a loving father to lean over and open His ears and listen to your entreaties. These words were chosen for our *tefillah*—in abundance—for that purpose. We want to talk as graphically as possible, with words that we can understand, so that we achieve the goal of our lives, awareness of Hashem.

And don't think it's foolish. Don't think it's false and immature. No! You're the fool if you ignore all these *tziyurim*, this imagery. Because you're fooling yourself! Your mouth is saying all these physical expressions for Hashem but you're ignoring them completely! You're frustrating the plan of Hashem in this world, the plan of the *p'shuto shel mikra*, the straightforward meaning of the *pesukim*.

We say every day in Shema—"*V'charah af*—the wrath of Hashem is kindled" against those who do idolatry. Now, Hashem doesn't lose his temper. Hashem doesn't have any fury. Hashem is always calm and always happy, and His wisdom always shines like an eternal light. It doesn't flicker. Now, I can't tell you much about Him. We'll have to wait until we get there. But there's no question that to say that Hashem is furious, that He's burning with anger, is applying a physical expression to a Being Who has no connection to physicality at all. But it's still useful to do so. It's needed and it's important.

I'll give you a *mashal*. Here's a person at work. Sometimes he might be a bit lazy, not working up to par. This man must know that the boss will be angry at him. So what do you do? Don't tell him, "It's against the rules if you come late or you do this or that." Don't say, "If so and so happens, I will have to put in a report." No, tell him, "The boss will get angry at you! He'll be furious if he finds out!" Even better, say, "He'll be so angry there'll be smoke pouring out of his nose!" Now you're talking! Now you mean business!

If we're going to fear Hashem at least as much as we fear our boss, if we're going to love Hashem at least as much as we love our children, we must at least be as aware of Him as we are of our boss and our children. So, for the sake of becoming aware of Hashem, it was worth taking the risk of utilizing the pictures that Hashem provided us with.

And when a person makes use of this program, the program that we find in Tanach of making Hashem real, he'll succeed at actually living with Hashem in his life.

When I was in Slabodka, I heard from the older yeshiva men that there was a *mussar shteibel* in Kovno. In Kovno there was a special *mussar* house. So I went there. I left *seder* once, walked across the river, and went to that *mussar* house. They told me it was always locked, but that there was a loose brick where they kept the key hidden. They said that I should pull out the loose brick and get the key. Sure enough, I found the loose brick, pulled it out, found the key, and let myself in.

I was all by myself in the old *mussar* house. I was sitting there and thinking, "What should I do?" Then I thought, "It's an opportunity." I was thinking I should work on this idea: "Hashem is looking at me."

I sat there for an hour. For a full hour I sat there by myself, thinking that Hashem is looking at me. I don't regret that experience. Not at all.

It's so important to find time for such things. The great *tzaddikim* of ancient times spent weeks and months on that. Of course, they did other things, too, but they constantly worked on this attitude, this awareness that Hashem is looking. His eyes are looking at you all the time.

The Gra was once riding on a wagon driven by a Jewish wagon

driver. As they were driving down the road, the driver stopped for a moment to let his horse eat from the grain that was growing by the roadside. Of course, it wasn't right because the grain belonged to the owner of the field. The Gra yelled out to the driver, "*Er kukt!* He's looking!" The driver got frightened, whipped his horse, and quickly the wagon drove away.

When he had gone down the road some distance, the driver turned to the Gra and said, "I didn't notice him. Where'd you see him? Who was looking?"

The Gra said, "*Hashem* was looking!"

"Oh, *baruch Hashem*!" said the driver. "I got scared. I thought it was a gentile looking at me."

He thought it was a flesh and blood human being, not Hakadosh Baruch Hu. That's because you know that the gentile has eyes. But Hashem is somewhere far, far away.

We must learn to be aware of Hashem, not only of the secular authorities. That's an important lesson. You can never overdo it—gaining the great attitude that what you do is being seen every moment. That's why we fall on our face every day in Tachanun. It's not enough to just recite the words. It's a lost opportunity when we mumble the words in the *siddur*. We have to say them with feeling. During Tachanun, we have to cry out. But even that's not enough. *We do real physical actions* to drive home to ourselves that Hashem is watching us, and we're entreating Him to save us from trouble and protect us from ever encountering it.

Q **Are we supposed to cry out even for relatively minor misfortunes?**

Wise is the man who will use even the smallest misfortune to improve by calling out to Hashem and becoming more aware of Him.

You're standing in your store and no customers are coming in. Why are you wasting that great opportunity?! Cry out to Hashem! "Ribbono Shel Olam! Please send me some customers!"

Opportunities like those are endless. Every day, all day long, there are bumps in the road. Just because there's no taskmaster standing over you with a whip doesn't mean you can't use the opportunities of *tza'ar* in your life—from the smallest things to the biggest—to call out to Hashem.

Don't let your Shemoneh Esrei go to waste! You mean to say you're going to spend your years just mumbling your *tefillos* every day by rote and not thinking about Hashem?! Shemoneh Esrei is a gold mine. When you're standing in a gold mine, even if you grab only one handful, you're already a wealthy man. But you must know how to grab!

"If you're not begging Hashem for mercy, if you're not crying out and begging, your *tefillah* is not a *tefillah*" (*Brachos* 29b). You must *daven* like a poor man begging at the door of a rich man (*Orach Chaim* 89:3). It's talking about a man without shoes; he's hungry and cold, and he's begging for something to eat. That's a man who knows how to cry out! And that's how *we're* supposed to *daven*.

When you *daven* Shemoneh Esrei, concentrate on the gold mine of at least one *brachah* to say *b'tachanunim*, with feeling. Cry out to Hashem instead of running through the words. You have a cold? "*Refa'einu, Hashem, v'neirafei!*" Cry out! Trouble with *parnassah*? Cry out, "*Bareich aleinu!*" There's fighting in the house, *machlokess* with your neighbor? *Sim shalom!*

Don't just mumble the words to yourself. Cry out to Hashem! At least in your mind. At least inside you should be crying out. It should be a cry of the mind up to Hashem.

Sometimes things get more difficult. What that means is that Hashem wants even more awareness from you. When things are difficult with *parnassah*, you get desperate. You were hoping this job would work out or maybe this deal would go through, but nothing is happening. You're at wit's end! Your rich uncle won't take your phone calls, the bank won't lend you more money, and welfare won't pay the bills. So you have to cry out to Hashem. Oh, that's a *hatzlachah!* That's more important than your *parnassah!*

Now, once we understand that the purpose of *tefillah* is awareness of Hashem, so you'll see that we're not talking only about *tefillah* when something *already* happened. We're also talking about *tefillah* that bad things *shouldn't* happen. *Tefillah kodem l'tzarah*—how important that is! When you fall on your arm after Shemoneh Esrei and say Tachanun, don't just rush through and mumble the words. Tachanun is *tachanunim*—you're crying out and entreating Hashem for mercy. "*Rachum v'chanun*—Hashem, You're the merciful One." Say it with feeling. Mean it! "Please, Hashem, don't rebuke me in Your anger. Please don't chastise me in Your wrath." Be wise enough to call out to Hashem before the *tzarah* even comes. Why wait, *chalilah*? Maybe it will be too late then. "A man should always pray *before* he needs something, before the troubles set in" (*Sanhedrin* 44b).

That's a real sign of *yiras Hashem*, when you are always aware of what *could* be—so many things can go wrong in a man's life, and you must cry out to Hashem so that He should save you from them all. That's the system Hashem set up for mankind. That's His prescription for the world. So if you say to Hashem, "I'm going to cry out to You even when there's no trouble," you are fulfilling His prescription of *yiras Hashem* in the best way possible.[59]

---

59 In the last year of his life, tragedy struck Rav Miller. His beloved grandson, Yisroel Miller, was killed when his car collided with a bus while on the way to the Kosel with his bar mitzvah son. The news hit Rav Miller like a hammer blow. Living as he did in close proximity to his grandfather, Sruly had the opportunity to serve his *zeidy* in various ways and became close to him. From his youngest years, Sruly had learned privately with him. At the *shivah*, Rav Miller expressed his pain, telling the family, "I feel I should be sitting *shivah* here along with you." When his daughter asked him for a practical lesson the family could derive from the tragedy, Rav Miller responded that he felt that his daily *tefillos* for his children and grandchildren were becoming habitual, so he needed to add more fervor when he beseeched Hashem to protect them. He suggested to his children to add more *kavanah* when they recited the *brachah* of *Hashkiveinu*. (*Rav Avigdor Miller—His Life and His Revolution*, p. 253)

Q What do you think our reaction should be to the crash of the Pan Am jetliner?

The first thing is to thank Hashem that you weren't there. That's very important. That's one of the big reasons that things happen in this world. "Any misfortune that happens in this world is for the purpose of the Am Yisrael." (*Yevamos* 63a). And Rashi says there that it's done to frighten us, so that we should do *teshuvah*.

The first thing to think is, "Did I ever travel on an airplane?" Yes, certainly. "*Baruch Hashem, baruch Hashem*, I'm still here!" Then you'll start saying, "Well, in most of the cases airplanes don't crash, so I don't have to think about that." No, that's a mistake. This incident must be utilized properly to gain more gratitude to Hashem.

Now, if we study more about it, we'll learn there were twenty *frum* Jews who were scheduled to take that airplane, but they were rerouted for a certain reason. That means that *Hashem* was rerouting them. It's a fact. Twenty *frum* Jews were supposed to be on that plane and weren't. It was the *yad Hashem*.

Of course, they themselves should always—all their lives—think about that and sing to Hashem. But we, too, must study that. It's up to us also to see that everyone on that plane was led there by Hashem; they were sentenced by Hashem beforehand.

Why were they sentenced? Only Hashem knows. But we know He brought them all together in one place where all those people were destined to lose their lives, and that's why it happened at that moment. Nothing happens by accident.

We must learn how important it is for us to always be on guard with *yiras Hashem*. Nobody can know when he is being sentenced, *chas v'shalom*. A person may be packing his valise, full of joy that he's going for a pleasant trip. He doesn't know that he's now heading to his death. Therefore, a man must always be ready with *yiras Hashem*. At all times, a person should think, "Who knows what can happen?"

And do you know when you should think about that? When you say Tachanun every day. "*Rachum v'chanun, chatasi l'fanecha*—I sinned before You, Hashem." And "*Hashem, al b'apcha sochicheini*—Please, Hashem, don't rebuke me in Your anger." That's why you put your face on your arm and say Tachanun—you're asking for *rachamim*! Don't tell me you prayed already. Maybe it didn't help. Maybe despite your prayers the sentence was passed. So you have to fall on your face, say Tachanun, and beg. A condemned man falls on his arm and bursts out with *tachanunim*—"Please, Hashem, please don't rebuke me in Your wrath." That's why it's called Tachanun—you're imploring! "Hashem—please, please, recall the decree!"

That's how important it is to say Tachanun with an outcry all the time. It's not sufficient to mumble a little prayer. Cry out to Hashem. Nobody can know what's in store for him. So, it always pays to cry out to Hashem *beforehand*.

ALEINU

Q Who are the *mishpechos ha'adamah* referenced in Aleinu?

When Eliezer the servant of Avraham came to take Rivka as a bride for Yitzchak, at first her family hesitated. They wanted to postpone. Finally, they agreed to let her go. And they gave her a blessing, "*Achoseinu, at hayi l'alfei revavah*—our sister, you should become thousands times ten thousands" (*Bereishis* 24:60). Your posterity should number in the millions. That's a great blessing. Actually, it wasn't their words. Hashem put those words in their mouths. Today, when a father marries off his daughter, just before the *chuppah*, he comes into the room where she's sitting surrounded by family and friends and says, "*Achoseinu, at hayi l'alfei revavah.*" It's a blessing. Then he adds, "*V'yirash zareich eis sha'ar sonav*—And your seed should inherit the gates (or cities) of his enemy" (ibid.). Which enemies? Which cities were conquered by our people? Only Canaan. Our people conquered the cities of Canaan.

But was Canaan really an enemy? Were they bothering our people? Were they harassing us? No. The truth is just the opposite. When Avraham went to live in Canaan, he wasn't bothered. He was bothered by the Plishtim. Avimelech took his wife away. He was bothered by Pharaoh. But the Canaanim didn't bother him. Why, then, are the Canaanim called "enemies"?

The answer is that they were enemies in the sense of existing at the opposite end of the ideological spectrum. Avraham was entirely for Hashem. What was Canaan for? Canaan was "*mishpechos ha'adamah*—the families of the earth." They lived for the earth. I'll explain that.

Hashem wanted His people to come into Eretz Canaan eventually and have a beautiful country, a country full of gardens. A fertile land. The Canaanim were agriculturalists. They fell in love with the land and were busy all the time cultivating it. Canaan was from Cham, and hot-natured. They loved Nature and fell in love with it. Therefore, they cultivated every stretch of earth until it became a garden. Eretz Yisrael was called "*gan Hashem*—a garden of Hashem" (*Bereishis* 13:10). The Canaanim specialized in agriculture. They even cultivated the mountains. They terraced all the hills. Wherever a person went, fruit trees were growing, crops were growing. There wasn't a country in the world that had such expert agriculturists as the land of Canaan.

One of the Canaanite people were the Chivi. The Gemara (*Shabbos* 85a) says that their name comes from the word *snake*. Why were they called snakes? Because "*nachash afar lachmo*—the snake eats dust." It slithers on its belly and earth goes into its mouth. It doesn't eat earth, but all the dust of the earth gets into its mouth. The Chivi also used to "eat earth." They used to taste the soil and discover which soil was more acidic, which more alkaline, and they used to plant crops in each type of soil that they knew would flourish there. They had such knowledge of agriculture that simply by tasting the soil they knew exactly what would grow in it. This patch of land is better for apples. This one is better for dates. This one for wheat. And so forth. They became agricultural experts.

But beyond being agriculturalists, they represented an ideology—an ideology of "*mishpechos ha'adamah*." They viewed Nature as an end unto itself. They worshipped gods that represented fertility. There was a god of wheat, a god of barley, a god of wine, a god that took care of sheep, of cows, and so on. Nature was their god. They loved Nature for itself and worshiped it.[60]

Avraham represented the opposite ideology. The Rambam (*Avodah*

60 Rav Miller explains elsewhere that their materialistic-hedonistic ideology led to terrible moral failings. "In no other lands have the archeologists discovered so many obscene images as in Canaan. In comparison with the idolatry of Egypt and Mesopotamia, Canaan was much more devoted to the cult of immorality. Even the Romans were amazed at the depravity of Carthage (a colony of the Phoenicians, one of the Canaani peoples). The chief god of Canaan was a cruel despot who seduced women, usurped his father's throne, and killed his sons and his daughter.... The archeologists have found remnants of children's skeletons and mounds of ashes around Canaani altars. The sacrifice of children, the cult of prostitutes, and the worship of snakes and wicked gods all degraded them into one of the worst peoples of antiquity...'He arose and measured the land; He saw, and He cast out the nations' (*Chabakuk* 3:6). 'What did He see? He saw how the nations transgressed the Seven Precepts of the children of Noah, and therefore He expelled them from their lands' (*Bava Kama* 38a)." (*Behold a People*, #247)

Zarah 1:3) explains that Avraham also studied Nature, but from his studies he came to discover—and preach to the world—the fact of a Creator. Nature wasn't an end unto itself. Avraham didn't devote his life to eating grapes and enjoying the wheat of the land. Avraham studied Nature, but he used it to teach lessons about the Borei.

So there were two opposite camps—Avraham and the Canaanim. They were ideological enemies. The Canaanim were "*mishpechos ha'adamah.*" Their ideology and outlook opposed Avraham every step of the way, making it very difficult for him to teach the world about Hashem. Avraham waged an ideological war against the Canaanim. They were his true enemies.

That's the *brachah* that was given to Rivka. "*V'yirash zareich eis sha'ar sonav*—Your seed should inherit the cities of his enemy." Those who live for Nature and think only in terms of Nature—*gashmiyus*, materialism—are enemies of the Am Hashem, who use Nature to recognize Hashem. When *we* look at Nature, we see Hashem. When *they* look at Nature, they see accident and evolution. Where they see materialism and hedonism, we see *nifla'os haBorei.*

We study Nature to feel gratitude to Hashem, and to enhance our love for Him. They love Nature for itself—for hedonism, *taivos*, every form of *gashmiyus*. When we talk about love, about marriage, we talk about it in the sense of *kedushah.* To us, marriage is *kiddushin*, something holy. To them, love is a physical thing. It's brutish, rude, animalistic. We look at the world from the viewpoint of the Borei, whereas they look at the world from the viewpoint of the physical phenomena themselves.

The beginning of the Jewish people, of the Am Yisrael, is understanding that we're at loggerheads with the world, with the *mishpechos ha'adamah.* Where their vision stops at the material, we see through the material. The Torah teaches us how to see beyond Nature. Where they see Nature as a system of laws operating automatically, we see it as a creation that Hashem made in six days. The more they see of the world, the less they believe in Hashem. The more we see, the more we believe in Him.

Hashem made the world in a way that it can conceal Him. In some ways, the world is the greatest deception, the greatest snare. It's darkness. "Behold, a darkness covers the world and the thick cloud covers the nations" (*Yeshayah* 60:2). But for us, "Hashem shines on you. His glory will be seen upon you" (ibid.) It shines upon us because we, the Am Yisrael, follow in the footsteps of Avraham who stood in opposition to the values of the *mishpechos ha'adamah.*

Q **Should a Jew have a garden?**

I'm all for gardens, but some people have put their souls into their gardens—and that's where their souls are going to remain. When I was in Europe, in Lithuania, I saw that the Jews didn't have gardens. The little plots of earth in front of their houses were wastelands. The gentiles had gardens. It was understandable. If the Jew had spare time, he had *his* garden to cultivate—the garden of his character. He went to the *beis hamedrash.* The *Chovos Halevavos* offers a *mashal.* There were two brothers who had to work for a living, but whenever one of them had spare time, he went home and worked on his little plot of land to cultivate it, whereas the other one didn't. In time, this brother was able to give up his work because his garden was yielding enough to support him. And what's that garden? That's your character, your soul, the *Chovos Halevavos* says.

You must work for a living, but you have your own garden to cultivate. Therefore, in the evenings, when Jews had a few moments to themselves, they went to the *beis hamedrash* and watered their gardens. They watered them with *Ein Yaakov*, with *Chumash* or *Mishnayos* or Gemara or *Shulchan Aruch.* What did the non-Jew do with his spare time? He poured it all into the earth in front of his house. Yes, he had some decent-looking shrubs and flowers, but when he left this world he didn't take anything with him. When they put him into the ground, all he had to show for his time here was his garden. He lived for the earth and he ended up part of the earth, nothing more. That's *mishpechos ha'adamah.*

But we say three times a day, "*Aleinu l'shabeyach la'Adon hakol shelo asanu k'mishpechos ha'adamah*—It's our obligation to praise the Master of all who did not make us like the families of the earth." Three times a day we say *Aleinu*, praising Hashem for not making us like "*mishpechos ha'adamah*—the families of the earth." Our "garden" work is the hard work of earning Olam Haba. If you *earn* Olam Haba, you're going to walk in those green pastures of Olam Haba, viewing your rolling meadows and your beautiful mansions with their beautiful gardens, knowing you built it all up with your own efforts. You withstood the ordeals of this world and gained perfection by means of your own hands. That's going to give you a happiness beyond description.[61]

61 For more on this topic, read *Rav Avigdor Miller on Olam Haba*.

HALLEL

Q What's so special about Rosh Chodesh that we say Hallel?

There are three elements easily seen in every Rosh Chodesh. If you ignore them or just think about them in a superficial manner, you're wasting a valuable opportunity. And many people do waste this opportunity. Yes, many people.

First of all, we must look back and thank Hashem for letting us live through the past month. Do you think that's a small thing?! Many people didn't survive to make it to this month. *Baruch Hashem*, we're still around. *Baruch Hashem!* So, first, Hallel is to thank Hashem for the past month.

Now, Rosh Chodesh is also a "*z'man kaparah l'chol toldosam*—a time of atonement for all their offspring" (Rosh Chodesh Mussaf). It's an opportunity for a *kaparah*, atonement, for the sins we committed over the past month. Look back and remind yourself of the things you did wrong. Not only the things you did wrong but, even more important—the good things that you didn't do right. What a loss! What a loss! Look back and do *teshuvah*. It's a "*z'man kaparah*," a special opportunity for *teshuvah* and atonement.

The third element is that it's a *yom tefillah* for the upcoming month, a special day for davening. At minimum, you say *Ya'aleh V'yavo*. The words of *Ya'aleh V'yavo* are an important *tefillah* for the coming month.

So those are the three elements. One is to thank Hashem for the past month. The second is to be "*m'fashfeish b'ma'asav*—to examine your deeds" (*Brachos* 5a) over the past month and do *teshuvah*. That's "*z'man kaparah*." And the third is to ask Hashem for help for the coming month. These are very important ideas. That's why Rosh Chodesh is a very important occasion.

You think that a month is a small thing in our lives?! If you look back and see you didn't accomplish much in the past month, you should be worried. Yes, you should worry. And make up your mind that in the next month you're going to start doing all the good things you hear here. At least that. Get busy doing all these good things next month. Make up your mind that a month shouldn't be wasted.

A month is not a day. It's not a week. It's a whole month. That's a big slice of life! Therefore, on Rosh Chodesh thank Hashem for the past month. Do *teshuvah* for the things you did wrong in the past month, and ask Hashem for His help for the upcoming month.

Q What's the idea that Hallel expresses?

The word *hallel* means something more than just praise. *Hallel* means to be excited about Hashem. The word *holel* means "wild." "*Amarti laholelim al taholu*—I said to those who are jovial and wild, 'Don't be wild'" (*Tehillim* 75:5). *Hallel* means to be wild. The word is what you call onomatopoeic. It's a word that communicates its meaning through the sound of the word itself. *Hallel* comes from *holel and holel* comes from *ho*, "to shout." When drunken revelers are dancing and singing "Ho! Ho!"—that's *holelus*. David was saying, "Don't waste your energy." Turn *holelus* into Hallel.

David says, "Yes, you have to shout in this world! You must shout with happiness. But to whom should you shout?" *Hallelu-Kah*! Shout out in wild *simchah* only to *Kah*, only to Hashem. *Kah* is an abbreviation of *Hayah*, *Hoveh*, and *Yiheyeh*—He is the One Who was, is, and will be—the One Who is around always. *Kah* means, "Being, the One Who has true existence." We don't have true existence. We're only the imagination of Hashem. Of course, we like this imagination. We want to keep this imagination going for a long time, but still we're only imagination. He is the only One Who has true existence. He is the One Who is providing you with everything you have. He's the One to express your gratitude to. He's the author of your happiness. He is the One—the only One. Therefore, shout out in happiness and gratitude only to Hashem.

When they brought the ark of Hashem to Yerushalayim (II *Shmuel* 6:16), David—the great monarch—was dancing in the street, jumping up and down wildly, in the midst of the common people. Slaves were jumping, too. And over to the side there were handmaidens jumping, too. They saw a king jump. When you see the king leaping up and down in excitement, the people got excited, too.

Michal bas Shaul, the aristocratic wife of David, looked through the palace window and saw a sight that made her blood run cold. Her husband, David, was jumping and dancing in the street among the slaves and handmaidens! Now, she was a great woman. She wore *tefillin* (*Eruvim* 96a). She was the daughter of Shaul, a great *tzaddik* himself. And there she was standing at the window, wearing *tefillin*, when she suddenly saw her husband, the *mashiach Hashem*, misbehaving. Then and there she decided to tell him something when he came upstairs later—and she did. But David replied to her, "Before Hashem Who chose me…I will dance even more." (II *Shmuel* 6:21–22).

David went wild. The love he had for Hashem is the wellspring of our national inspiration. That's why we *daven* from David's words. As much as we express our inspiration, as much excitement as we muster in repeating these noble words, we will never attain a fraction of what this great lover of Hashem actually felt. But David set the love of his people on fire forever and ever.

It says in *Baruch She'amar*, "*Hamehulal b'fi amo*—He is praised wildly by His people." "*Amo*, His people," means everybody—the wise as well as the ignoramuses. When they mention Hashem, they go wild and shout. This fire of enthusiasm—which is their love for Hashem—burned in the hearts of the entire Jewish nation. Don't think David was the only one. David was the great one, but great men don't come out of nowhere. David came from a great nation, a nation enthusiastic about Hashem. He rekindled them with their own fire.

Q **Aren't our prayers supposed to be reserved and dignified?**

Now, in addition to being enthusiastic, it says (in *Baruch She'amar*), "*Meshubach umefo'ar bilshon chassidav va'avadav*—He is praised and glorified with the tongues of His pious ones and His servants." This is a different story. There's no excitement here. Here they talk calmly, with words of logic. It's only "*bilshon chassidav va'avadav*—by the *tongue* of His pious ones and those who serve

Him." That's a different level, not for the entire people.

There are two ways to praise Hashem. One way is a common denominator—to shout with enthusiasm. This, everybody does. Even the *chassidim* and the *avdei Hashem* shout. On Rosh Hashanah, the people are standing on their feet and shouting, "*Hashem melech! Hashem malach!*" Even the *rosh yeshiva*. He doesn't stand back. He opens his mouth and shouts, too. Everybody shouts, "*Hashem melech! Hashem malach! Hashem yimloch l'olam va'ed.*" We say it all day long. That's our job. We're enthusiastic about being Jews. We're enthusiastic about Hashem.

In addition, the people who have intellect, who study Torah—or even those who've studied only the sciences—can use their intellects for this subject. For them it's "by the tongue." It's not merely the throat. The throat is all that's necessary for shouting, but the tongue is needed to express words and ideas. These great men express words of praise. They speak ideas of praise.

There are two levels, then. On the first level, everybody participates. Whether it's a Rosh Hashanah or a weekday, when you come to shul it's not supposed to be quiet and orderly like a cemetery. Many synagogues are nice and quiet like that. The people are looking in the *siddur* and their lips are barely moving. You don't hear any noise. That's not a Jewish synagogue. A synagogue is a place where you make noise. Do you know what synagogue means? *Syna* means "together," and *gogue* means "talking." All talk together. Not the way they do in other places—all talk while the *shliach tzibbur* is talking. No, that talking is a sin. That's a "sin-agogue."

When I was a boy and there were still immigrants in all the shuls, they used to raise the roof. Every man was doing his thing. This one was singing. This was stamping his foot. Everybody was going to town. They were talking to Hashem. They were enthusiastic. That's what a synagogue is for. But in addition to the excited expression of love to Hashem, the people with intellect were putting something additional into it. Their gears weren't merely turning; they were engaged, and something was really moving there. They were *thinking*. That's

"*Meshubach umefo'ar bilshon chassidav va'avadav.*" Both forms of davening are expected of us.

Q Should we be saying Hallel all the time?

Yes! Not literally, of course. In fact, the Gemara (*Shabbos* 118b) says it's considered very wrong to actually say Hallel every day. But listen to the words of David Hamelech. "The name of Hashem should be blessed forever and ever" (ibid. 103:2). How often should you do this? On Rosh Chodesh? Should you bless Him only once a month? No! You should do it forever and ever." And if you do it in this world, then you'll continue to do so in the next world as well! (*Sanhedrin* 91b)

That's our job as *avdei Hashem*. We have to attribute everything we have to Hashem. Look how many people cannot walk. How many people need wheelchairs? How many people have walkers? Or crutches? Or canes? And you're able to walk! Even those who have canes must thank Hashem. Even those who have crutches must thank Hashem. Even those who have wheelchairs must thank Hashem. As long as you can open your mouth and say something, you must thank Hashem! There are many people who can't even talk—they know sign language, that's all. But even with sign language, you must thank Hashem in sign language. At least you have hands to make the motions.

You have two good eyes? *I'm born with two good eyes*, you think. *They're mine*. No, you're not born with two good eyes! You have two good eyes that are given to you every day by Hashem. Every day is a new gift. Two good eyes! That's how to think if you're an *eved Hashem*. You say every day, "You open up the eyes of the blind." Why don't you say, "I thank You that You gave me two good eyes"? No! You have to act like you're blind, and just now you got two good eyes. Ohhhh!! A blind man who suddenly gets two good eyes wouldn't say "Muh-muh-muh-muh" [Rav Miller mumbled the *brachah*]. No! He would say it with dancing! He would be *meshuga*! He would be drunk with happiness! He would shout! He'd say Hallel! Not half-Hallel—the whole

Hallel! That's how you must say the *brachah* of "*Pokei'ach ivrim*—He opens up the eyes of the blind."

That's the function of *avdei Hashem*. You have to thank Hashem for everything you have. You have teeth? Most of you have teeth, don't you? Your own teeth. Ahhh! Ah, ah, ah! How lucky you are! You have to thank Hashem for that great gift. Teeth are a great gift! People say that's silly. They think, "You came here for such foolish talk?! You came here to say this?! You came here to hear *sodos*, *sisrei Torah*, and *chiddushim*! But such things—thanking Hashem for your teeth—you can't waste your time with that." But you have to know that what I'm telling you now is the biggest *chiddush*. Thank Hashem that you have teeth! If you don't, you're not an *eved Hashem*.

Hallelu-Kah!! Who? Who has the function of *Hallelu-Kah*? *Avdei Hashem*—you, the servants of Hashem. *Hallelu-Kah!!* That's your job in this world. Thank Him for your teeth! It's the first time you heard it?! Then you're lucky you came tonight!

"You servants of Hashem—be wild over Him" (*Tehillim* 103:1). Your job in this world is to "call out in excitement to give thanks to Hashem" (ibid.). In this world, your job is to praise Hashem! All the time! For everything! Attribute everything to Hashem.

Praising Hashem is a career that lasts a lifetime. We have our job cut out for us. It's not just a figure of speech, some nice words to make a *niggun* and then forget about. No, it's a career for your whole life!

Q Are non-Jews obligated to praise Hashem?

Now, pay attention. This is one of the fundamental foundations of Torah. Rabbeinu Nissim Gaon states at the beginning of *masechta Brachos* why the early generations before Matan Torah were held responsible and punished for sins, even though they were not explicitly forbidden to them. Without having been given a Torah, why were they blamed?

And the answer is, "Whatever depends on the understanding of a man's mind—that Hashem gave him *seichel* to understand by himself—that's a Torah he's obligated to keep." Whatever is logical, whatever is rational, human beings are obligated to obey. And the most logical of all things is that the Creator designed everything. "*Gadlo v'tuvo malei olam*—His greatness and goodness fill the world" (Shabbos morning prayers). There isn't an object or phenomenon in the world that doesn't reflect the plan and purpose of an Infinite Wisdom.

If you see a big, fat strawberry, look at the beautiful color. Why is it that when it's ripe it has such a deep red color? It's so attractive that it's begging you to sink your teeth into it. But when it was unripe, it was green. Why is that? Doesn't that show plan and purpose? Why shouldn't it have been red when it was unripe and green when it was ripe? The answer is as open as anything in the world could be. When it was unripe, Hashem wanted it to be green so that it could hide among the grass of the field and you wouldn't see it. But when it was ready to be eaten, it announced its presence—it turns on the light, a big red light, and says, "Here I am!"

How is it that the entire outside surface of the strawberry is peppered with seeds? What are those seeds for? Where do they come from? You know, each seed is a marvel. Each seed is capable of reproducing the original plant in all its details. It has a little blueprint inside, millions of blueprints, and it has all the equipment to carry out the instructions of the blueprints. How can any honest person look at that and not recognize the hand of Hashem?

Of course, if people go to college, their minds get crippled by the lies of the academicians. Instead of getting educated, they get indoctrinated into falsehood. But when people use their native intelligence, the truth is open to all who want to see it. You don't need a Torah to tell you that. "*Lamah li kra, s'vara hu*—Why is a proof from the Scriptures necessary if we can derive it by logic?" (*Bava Kama* 46b). Everybody is obligated to follow common sense.

Therefore, it says, "*Hallelu Hashem, kol goyim*—Bless Hashem, all the nations" (*Tehillim* 117:1). "*Ki kein chovas kol hayetzurim*—because everybody is obligated" to thank Hashem (Shabbos morning prayers).

TEFILLAH B'TZIBBUR

Q Is there anything wrong with davening without a *minyan* as long as I say Kriyas Shema at the right time?

Let me explain something I've said before. When you *daven* with a *minyan*, you're identifying with Klal Yisrael. Our *tefillos* are all plural. We don't say, "*Refa'eini Hashem*—Heal *me*, Hashem." We say, "*Refa'einu* Hashem—Heal *us*." And we say, "*Baruch Atah, Hashem, rofei cholei amo Yisrael.*" We *daven* for *all* the *cholei Yisrael.* That's such an important element. It must be emphasized. It's a form of identifying with the Am Yisrael. We are together. We're all one.

Even when you put on your hat in the morning and make the *brachah,* "*Oteir Yisrael b'sifarah*—Thank You, Hashem, for crowning Yisrael with glory," or when you put on a belt and say, "*Ozeir Yisrael bigvurah*—You crown Yisrael with power," you mention *Yisrael.* Again and again we mention Yisrael, Yisrael, Yisrael. You're identifying with your people. We're all together.

Therefore, when it comes to *tefillah*, not only should the words show togetherness, but you should be together physically. The least you can do is go to a *minyan.* The *minyan* represents Klal Yisrael. To a certain extent, the Shechinah is there, too, and you're joining with the Am Yisrael. When you *daven* in your home, that shows that you're not interested in identifying with them.

Now, there might be extenuating circumstances why you can't make it to a *minyan*, such as when you have to get to work at a certain time. But there's no question that davening with a *minyan* ought to be a regular part of a loyal Jew's routine because it's an important form of showing he belongs to Hashem, by means of identifying with those people who are gathering together serving Him.

It's not merely important to *daven* with a *minyan*, it's an obligation. It's a *chiyuv. Tefillah b'tzibbur* is a *chiyuv.* If people neglect it, they should know they're not doing their duty. If you can't help yourself because of *parnassah*, that's a different question. But absolutely it's a *chiyuv* to *daven* with a *minyan.*

However, I must point out that it depends on what kind of a *minyan.*

If the *minyan* is so rushed that if you cough then you're already lost, don't bother with that *minyan*. Sometimes you can walk into a synagogue and see a person put on *tallis* and *tefillin* and finish davening in twenty-five minutes. Twenty-five minutes! So you think maybe he skipped parts. He must have started from *Yotzer Ohr* and walked out after *Oseh Shalom* of Shemoneh Esrei. No! He said everything. He even said *Adon Olam*. And *parshas ha'Akeidah*. And all the *Ani Maamins*! And I'm afraid he got in a little conversation, too. He got everything in. That's a caricature of *tefillah*. It's a tragedy.

If you can *daven* with a slow *minyan*, it's a valuable gift. *Davening* with *kavanah* is very important. Very important! "*Utefillas yesharim retzono*—Hashem desires the *tefillah* of righteous people" (*Mishlei* 15:8). He wants to hear *tefillah*. "*Hakadosh Baruch Hu misaveh litfillasan shel tzaddikim*—Hashem wants to hear the *tefillah* of *tzaddikim*" (*Yevamos* 64a). So you need to allow yourself the time to understand what you're saying.

By the way, it's a very good idea to learn the *peirush* of the *tefillah*. People who never spend any time thinking about the *peirush* of the *tefillah* are missing a great opportunity. The words of *tefillah* are a gold mine of Torah ideals, and the more you *daven* with *kavanah*, the more your thoughts eventually follow your words. Once you accustom yourself to saying the words of davening with understanding, you'll begin to live with the great ideals expressed in the *tefillah*.

Is it proper to sacrifice the *mitzvah* of davening with a *minyan* to be able to *daven* with *kavanah*?

Now, I'm going to be the last one to tell you yes. You could, if you wish, come earlier and start a long time before the *minyan* starts, so that by the time you reach Shemoneh Esrei you're saying it at the same time as everybody else. You allow yourself a long time before they begin, and your Shemoneh Esrei can continue for a long time afterward. There's no need to lose *tefillah b'tzibbur*.

I know that's going to sound ridiculous to some people. So, be ridiculous! Anybody who shows he's a little more *frum* than people expect him to be is considered a crank. If you want to become something, you must set out on the path toward Hashem by yourself. It's a path that's sparsely traversed. There are only a few travelers on it. You know, on a mountain there are a lot of people at the bottom of the mountain. The higher you go, the more rarefied the atmosphere and the fewer people you'll find there. Very few people actually reach the summit.

However, this question deserves more attention than that because sometimes the environment doesn't permit you to *daven* with *kavanah*. And so I'm not going to answer. I'll leave it to *gedolei Yisrael*.

Q **Should a person *daven* loudly?**

You must *daven* somewhat quietly if you're in public. If you *daven* loudly, people will be disturbed. I was once told to shut up. I was in a certain *shteibel* in Williamsburg. I wasn't shouting loud, but a man turned around with a complaint that I'm not letting him *daven*. So I piped down.

Now, my one davening took three *minyanim* of theirs. Three *minyanim* finished while I was davening there once. I wasn't davening that fast, so you understand why I was disturbing him.

Q **Is it preferable to *daven* in a good *minyan* where there's no *rav* or in another *minyan* with a lesser clientele but that has a *rav*?**

It depends. Sometimes even when there is a *rav*, the people act like he's not present! In that case, you're better off in the other place. But suppose all things are equal, and one place has somebody who has a certain responsibility, authority. No question that's better.

There's another reason. I must tell you something that happens all the time. A woman calls me up. Her husband is terrible. "Does your husband have a rabbi?" I ask. "No, he has no rabbi. He goes to one shul Friday night, another shul Shabbos morning, and another place for Minchah. During the week it's someplace else. He doesn't have a rabbi."

If there were a *rav* to whom he felt a certain attachment, that could help very much. Otherwise he's an orphan. Who should she talk to? You shouldn't marry a man who doesn't have a *rav*, a *rebbe*, or a *rosh yeshiva*. Otherwise, who knows what's going to happen? If he has someone who can influence him, there's a chance. If you have a man who's proud that he's "self-made," that nobody tells him what to do, then he's a self-made nobody!

That's why it's very important—very important!—to have somebody. The mere fact that he is somebody—somebody you'll listen to, somebody you're embarrassed to disappoint—already makes a *mensch* out of you.

Q **Is it a good idea to *daven* at a Vasikin *minyan*?**

There are *tzaddikim* who *daven Vasikin*. They get up very early. Now, it's excellent, but I must make one remark. On Shabbos they also *daven Vasikin* and they miss the opportunity to hear a little bit of *yiras Shamayim* from somebody who speaks. They come together for a *minyan*, and they *daven* fast and go home instead of davening in a place where there's a *rav* who sometimes shares some *divrei mussar*. It's a valuable opportunity. It's more important than *Vasikin*.

"*Aseih l'cha rav*" (*Avos* 1:6) means you should always be in a place where there is a *rav*, somebody who will tell you something. Don't think that you know everything. There's no end to the amount of information that we require to know the *derech Hashem*. The people who go early Shabbos morning to *Vasikin* come out without any kind of lesson. They're not any better than they were last week. Nobody is telling them anything wrong about themselves, and that's a problem.

A person walks in blindness all his life. Do you know how many faults people have?! Somebody has to criticize you. Your wife is not enough. You need some kind of instruction. How else will you know the truth? We are living in a world of darkness. "*Hineih choshech y'chaseh aretz*—Behold, darkness covers the Earth" (*Yeshayah* 60:2). The world is covered in darkness. We are walking in darkness, and we're blind to the truth. Only if someone is teaching you can you hope to see through the darkness. You have to have someone to tell you. At *Vasikin*, there's nobody to tell you anything. They probably think it's the very best thing. But I don't.

Q **In my shul, people are always talking. Should I complain about it or find a different shul?**

The best thing to do is to leave that place altogether. Unless you're a very important personality there. Otherwise, you're not going to change them.

It's a great tragedy, this tragedy of talking in the synagogues. It's a *bizayon*, a disgrace for Hashem. If a gentile would come into a shul and see what type of place it is, he'd lose all interest, all respect. You have to realize that it's a great cancer of our nation, *Rachmana litzlan*. It's a terrible cancer. And if you cannot heal it—you can't go and get into a fight with them—then find a better place and at least rescue yourself.

Q **What's the idea behind saying "Amein"?**

The Gemara (*Shabbos* 119b) makes a comment on the *passuk*, "*Pischu she'arim v'yavo goy tzedek shomer emunim*—Open the gates wide so the righteous nation who are loyal will come" into the arms of Hashem (*Yeshayah* 26:2). The Gemara says don't read it as "*shomer emunim*—a nation that guards its loyalty," but "*shomer ameinim*—a nation that guards the Ameins." The people who say Amein all the time are the ones for whom the gates will open.

Amein?! What's that got to do with it? Answering Amein is only a small detail. Are Chazal going to take that great statement of Yeshayahu Hanavi about a nation that kept its loyalty and limit it to the simple act of answering Amein?! To reduce such a grand idea to such a minute point?

And the answer is yes. Loyalty is composed of many things. It's not enough to just say, "I'm a Jew." You have to *live* like a Jew—you have to fulfill all the *d'Oraysa*s, all the *d'rabbanan*s, and all the *minhagim*. That's a loyal Jew.

However, because loyalty is such a tremendous quality, the *navi* is telling us that even a little bit is priceless. It's like a diamond—even a tiny diamond chip is precious. Many little diamonds are surely worth something.

Therefore, the Gemara is telling us that we should treasure our loyalty even down to the smallest detail. Even when it comes to backing up the *chazzan*. When the *chazzan* is saying a *brachah*, we must muster enough interest to say Amein. Amein isn't a formality, a meaningless word. Amein means "Yes, we're behind you 100 percent!"

Here's a man who never misses saying Amein. He sits in shul listening obediently and carefully to his fellow Jews praising Hashem. Everything is Hashem, Hashem, Hashem, and he's answering Amein, Amein, Amein. Amein, after all, is only a word. It's not an act. It's easy to say Amein. But he always makes it his business to chime in, "Amein." He wants to show "I'm loyal!" Not only won't he talk in shul, but he won't even slack off a drop in his loyalty to Hashem. He won't miss saying Amein for anything. "Yes, Amein!" And again, "Amein! I'm as loyal as ever."

Now, it's an easy thing to do. You're not sacrificing your life for it. But even such a small thing is precious. It might be only a small act of loyalty, but it's the persistence and consistency that makes it so great. You should try it once—try sitting quietly and attentively in shul, listening to every word and answering Amein. Every Amein is a precious diamond of loyalty.

Like saying Amein, there are many things that, when done with the proper intention, can be the greatest demonstration of loyalty. Every step of our lives is *emunah*. It's not only in the once-in-a-lifetime sacrifice that the loyalty of our people is recognized. It's in the dedication of our daily lives that our greatness lies. Our days are filled with acts of loyalty. Of course, without thought it's worth much less, so try to think when you walk down the street with your *tzitzis* out or with your *sheitel* on your head. Think when you call out, "*Amein! Y'hei sh'meih rabbah*," or when you stop in the middle of your day to *daven* Minchah. Think during the hundreds of other things you're doing all day long. That's your opportunity to be found "*ne'eman l'fanecha*—loyal before Hashem."

That's the way to tread the path of life, with thoughts of loyal dedication to Hashem. It's valuable beyond your imagination.

Q **What's the minimum a Jew has to do to earn Olam Haba?**

The Gemara (*Sanhedrin* 110b) says that as soon as a little child can say "Amein," he belongs to us and joins the congregation of those who live forever. If he lived only to say Amein, he accomplished something in this world. That's the minimum participation of a Jew.

There are a lot of things a Jew has to do to be loyal, but the easiest is to say Amein. Even if a Jew isn't much of a Jew, but he's proud of being a Jew, he's already a loyal Jew. Even if a Jew is wicked, but he's not ashamed to say Amein to all good things, then he already deserves that the gates of Olam Haba should open for him (*Yeshayah* 26:2). Amein is the minimum. It means, "Yes, I agree." If he says "Amein," even that low level of loyalty is enough to give him a share in the eternity of the Jewish nation, which means Olam Haba.

Now you see how important it is. If an irreligious Jew who doesn't keep anything—who even forgot all about his Judaism—reminds himself once, just once, to walk into a synagogue where they're davening, just for the chance of saying one Amein, he has already accomplished the difference between existence and non-existence. He has registered his presence with the Jewish people. Just to come in and say, "Amein! I'm with you!" is enough. So once a little child says Amein, he's already a *ben Olam Haba*.

Q Why is one who says Amein to a *brachah* greater than the one who makes it (*Brachos* 53b)?

When somebody else makes a *brachah*, it's a bother for you. He's troubling you to say Amein. It was his idea and he's forcing your hand. Now you're forced to say Amein to his *brachah*. So you're thinking, "Why didn't he make the *brachah* quietly? He shouldn't have bothered me to answer Amein!" You're somewhat annoyed. But no! You overcome your *yetzer hara* and say, "He made a *brachah*, and I want to join in with him and participate in praising Hashem." You're *misgaber* and you say, "I'm joining in. I'll say Amein."

In a certain sense, you're greater than he is. He did what he wanted to do, but you're going along and doing what *he* wanted. That's why you get more reward. Therefore, when you see someone doing something good, don't say, "Well, let him do it. I won't help." No, if he's doing something good, join in, and you'll be mightily rewarded. When a person is *kovesh es yitzro,* when he overcomes his nature, he's greater than the one who didn't.

THINGS TO PRAY FOR

OVERVIEW

In Lecture 108, "What to Pray For," Rav Miller analyzes a Gemara and uses it to explain things that require our special attention when it comes to *tefillah*.

The Gemara (*Brachos* 8a) offers a certain counsel based on a *passuk* in *Tehillim* (32:6). "*Al zos yispallel kol chassid eilecha l'eis m'tzo*—For this, every pious man should pray to You, Hashem, at the time of finding."

First, we need to understand what "*al zos*—for this" means. The truth is that you must pray for everything. Even if you're going out shopping for a pair of shoes, it's proper to pray to get the right kind. If they're too small, you're going to have a great deal of discomfort and maybe you won't be able to wear them after a while. Sometimes the wrong shoes can bring on headaches or back problems. Not only is it a demonstration that you have *emunah*, that you know the affairs of this world are in the hands of Hashem, but it helps, too. It pays to *daven* for everything. From the biggest to the smallest things, it pays to turn to Hashem for help.

Here, however, "*al zos*" means "for this" *especially*. This is something every pious person must especially pray for. What is it that he must pray for especially? The *passuk* doesn't tell us what he should pray for. The Gemara, therefore, offers several explanations.

Rav Miller then goes through each of them one by one. We will add related explanations from other lectures and writings of Rav Miller.

Marriage

Q Why does the Gemara say specifically that a man has to pray for a wife?

"For this, let every pious man pray to You in the time of finding, that the overflowing waters may not reach him" (*Tehillim* 32:6). Rabbi Chanina said: The time of finding refers to a wife, as it says, 'He who finds [*matzah*] a wife finds [*matzah*] good and obtains favor from Hashem' (*Mishlei 18*:22)." (*Brachos* 8a)

What should the pious man (*chassid*) pray for? Rabbi Chanina says a wife. Of course, when we say every *chassid* must pray for that, it's self-understood that every *chassidah*, every pious woman, also must pray for that. She also must be *mispallel* to Hashem to find the right one.

All unmarried people are urged to turn to Hashem and invest time on this matter. It pays to devote time to *tefillah*. If you're already married, you must pray that you make the best of what you have. Before you go back the three steps after Shemoneh Esrei, after you say *Yiheyu l'ratzon*, put in a request for this. You can do it in the middle of the day, too, not just during Shemoneh Esrei. When you're going to meet a marriage prospect, ask Hashem to guide your footsteps. If she's not the right one, ask Hashem that she should turn you down.

The Gemara cites a *passuk*. "*Matzah ishah, matzah tov*—If he finds a wife, he finds good" (*Mishlei* 18:22). "Good" means happiness and success. As you begin to reach the years when you must be serious, men and women, boys and girls must pray to Hashem. If they're a *chassid*—if they have some connection with *yiras Hashem, bitachon, emunah*—they shouldn't merely rely on their own efforts. They shouldn't think that things will just happen. They shouldn't merely say it's foreordained, that it's *bashert*. "Whatever happens will be good for me." No, the Gemara says. You should pray because it could be that what's foreordained for you isn't for your good. It could be that Hashem has prepared a young lady who is going to help you acquire

Gan Eden, because all your sins will be atoned for in this world by the misery she causes you, so you have to get busy and pray to Hashem. That same is true, of course, for girls.

Don't be stingy with your *tefillos*. Put in a lot of words, and if they're accompanied by some tears, all the better. Men and women can weep when they pray for the right one. Better to weep now than later!

Then the Gemara goes on to say that in Eretz Yisrael when a man got married, they would ask him, "*Matzah o motzei?*" There are two kinds of "finding." One is *matzah*, past tense, and the other is *motzei*, present tense, continued action. *Matzah*, past tense, referred to the *passuk*, "*Matzah ishah, matzah tov*—If he found a woman, he found good." It's past tense—he already accomplished a big thing in life. He found the right one. And she found the right one. How? By asking for it. By praying for it. It's past tense. "It's all over, and the rest of his life he's in clover." He's in happiness. Of course, even if you're "in clover," sometimes a bee comes with a sting, too. But it's "clover." There's plenty of honey. Life is more or less smoothed out, and the problem of finding a wife, a spouse, has been settled. The whole matter is in the past tense. That's why it's "*matzah*."

But there's another possibility. "And I find [*motzei*] the woman more bitter than death" (*Koheles* 7:26). *Motzei* means he's "*continuing* to find," not past tense. It's present and continued action. If he didn't pick the right one, there may be a lot of ongoing action. Many times, somebody with the wrong partner cannot find a way out and is embarrassed to divorce, so he hopes that death will release him. It's preferable to that kind of a life.

That's when he didn't get the right one and he's always "*finding*," meaning nothing can solve the dissension. Every day is a new problem. That's *motzei*, the present tense. That's why in Eretz Yisrael, when a man got married, they used to ask: Is it "*matzah*" or "*motzei*"?

This is an important subject and deserves a great deal more talk. We see every day the results of careless marriages. A young lady falls in love with a man not so young, a man who is twenty-eight and doesn't have a steady job. He has no skill, no profession, and he's not a *yeshiva man*, either. He's a drifter. But she is overwhelmed by what she thinks is a real indication that this is the right one. "We communicate so well," she says. Yes, before they marry it's easy to communicate. Afterward, communication is different. So she disregards the advice of her parents and lives the rest of her life with regret.

A careless marriage is a marriage based on no considerations except intuition. What people call love is the weakest of all guides to marriage, the least sensible of all. Anything forbidden is desirable, but after the wedding it loses its romance and then they see each other as they actually are. That's why it turns out to be a great disappointment, a great letdown.

When marriage is based on sensible considerations, true affection between husband and wife begins to develop after the marriage. In the course of time, they will have cemented a bond that's stronger than any other kind of union we find in life. But it's only when it's based on *seichel* and not on emotions.

PRACTICAL ADVICE

Is it necessary to know what one is looking for in a *shidduch*, or should he just wait until the right one comes along?

He must do both. If you don't know what you're looking for, it's like going into a store blind with a pocket full of money. The storekeeper is going to sell you whatever he wants. He'll sell you things you don't need or that are bad for you. Hashem is going to offer you all kinds of merchandise—tall, short, thick, and thin. All kinds—blondes and brunettes. So you must know what you want. That's number one. You must make up your mind. Are you looking for a *frum* girl or do you want a flapper? Do you want a siren? Or do you want an idealist?

So you say that you want everything. She should be a siren *and* an idealist. But you must know that being a siren doesn't happen by itself. She sits in front of the mirror for long hours to make herself look that beautiful. Boys don't know that. They think a siren is born that way. If a girl doesn't work on looking appealing, attractive, she won't be. It takes a lot of time. And to do both things is pretty difficult. So you have to make up your mind.

Now, it could be that Hashem sends somebody who's a big idealist but who looks to *you* like a siren, because He wants you to take that one. This leads to the second point. When Hashem sees that your mind is made up on the right girl, He sends a girl to you. To others she may look ordinary, but in your eyes she's beautiful. It clicks immediately. But you should know that this is a reward for people who are deserving of it. Otherwise, you'll keep on looking and it won't click.

I knew a rabbi who wasn't married. He moved to Brooklyn when he was already in his late fifties. I met him once and asked, "Nu?" and he said "*Es clickst zich nisht.*" Nothing clicked yet. He died a bachelor. So, you have to make up your mind what you want, and then Hashem might make it click for you.

Q **What should one do if he's dating a girl who has money, looks, and personality, but there's no "chemistry"?**

He should marry her—because there is something wrong with his clicker. Every normal man can fall in love with a good-looking girl. If he can't fall—especially if she has *middos* and money, too—then there is something wrong with him.

The truth is that you can love most girls. Hashem made it so that men love women. Unless something is very wrong. But if she's likable and personable, then something is wrong with him. Therefore, he should close his eyes and dive in. He should make up his mind that that's the girl for him.

Now, we have to understand that this "special feeling" is mostly the result of propaganda. The world has been fooled into thinking that there is a certain magic moment when something happens within you and you know that this is the right person.

If you read about the careers of movie actors—today it's this one, next month it's somebody else—these "magic moments" repeat themselves constantly, and they are nothing but deceptions. What's the magic moment in buying a house? When you look at a house, does something click within you and tell you that's the right house? Then beware—because you might discover that there's no wiring in that house. You might discover that the house is rotten through and through with termites! You can't buy a house based on intuition. You need experts. You must pay good money and have an expert examine the house from the roof to the basement.

Marriage should also be based on the expert opinions of others. Then it's not your feelings. Of course, if you feel a repulsion, you can't marry that person. But if you don't have any particular objection to the other party, and all considerations are discovered to be proper—for instance, their families and backgrounds and tastes are similar—then it's an ideal opportunity. If you feel comfortable then, you'll feel comfortable together for the rest of your lives. But if you married by intuition, then the day after the marriage that feeling will disappear, and you'll feel uncomfortable for the rest of your lives.[62]

Q What factors should a boy look for in a girl when deciding who to marry?

First, she has to be a girl who's willing to agree with his opinions of wanting to build a Torah home. Never marry with the intention,

62 Note that in the question above, "Is it necessary to know what one is looking for in a *shidduch* or should he just wait until the right one comes along?" Rav Miller said that sometimes Hashem sends a *shidduch* who looks like a "siren" to him in addition to being an idealist, and Hashem does so to indicate that he should marry her. Here he's not saying that "intuition" is always wrong, but that it needs to be balanced with "the expert opinion of others" and similarly objective factors.

with the hope, that you can change her. Forget about it.

Secondly, she must be healthy—physically and mentally. Now, if *you're* not, you can't be choosy. But if you're physically and mentally healthy, then be selective about who you marry.

Thirdly, she must have good character. Good character is very rare. Very rare! Do your best to ascertain her character. Ask her teachers in the Bais Yaakov schools that she attended. Sometimes they'll tell you part of the truth. If they say very enthusiastic praises about her, deduct 90 percent, and then it might be worth marrying her. If they're not enthusiastic, it could be that you should forget about it.

If possible, she should come from a good family. Family has a big influence. If it's not the right kind of family, who knows what's going to happen to your children! You want to have good grandparents for your children, if possible. Good uncles and aunts, if possible. So if you can find a girl from a good family, that's worthwhile, too.

It's very important to marry a girl who comes from the same environment as you. That's why you should marry a girl from the same country. Don't marry a girl from another country. Sometimes it's successful, but it's always a strain on a marriage. Always. A man and a woman are two different nationalities. The Gemara says that. "Women are a nation unto themselves" (*Shabbos* 62a). And putting even more strain on the marriage is not necessary. So marry someone from the same background. They should have the same interests, eat the same kinds of foods, have the same customs. That makes it easier to remain married successfully.

Now all of this applies before marriage. You should look before you leap. But once you're married, do whatever you have to do to make sure that it's forever.

Q What's the greatest fear a person should have in getting married?

People think that the main problem of marriage is marrying the right party. It's not! Of course, you must try to marry the right one, but the main challenge in marriage is *being* the right one.

That's made up of two parts. One part is preparing for it. You must learn how to be a *mensch* before you're married. Does that mean you'll marry when you're ninety-nine years old?! No, you have to learn how to be a *mensch* as early as possible *and* you'll have to learn on the job, too! When you're married, you must guard your tongue! Of course, you must be patient. Of course, you must adjust yourself to another person. You have to learn these things as early as possible *and* on the job, too!

A *mensch* also means you have to work! You must learn how to work, how to support a family. Or you have to be a learner. If you're not learning, you're earning. To live in this world, you have to do something.

Now, when a man postpones marriage because of fear, he's making a major error! Time is passing by and the older he gets, the less suited he is for marriage because he becomes more fixed in his ways, in his bachelor habits, and it'll be more and more difficult for him to adjust. When you're young and pliable, it's easier for you to change yourself to fit into the pattern of marriage.

Everybody should be afraid of marriage, but that doesn't mean you don't get married. The street is dangerous, but you still go out into the street. Marriage is not as dangerous as the street. Therefore, to be afraid of marriage is natural, but it should never deter somebody from fulfilling his duty.

Q Is it possible for someone to lose his *zivug*? How?

Can a person make a mistake and not marry the right girl? And the answer is that when you marry somebody—*that is* the right one! It's only the *yetzer hara* that tells you otherwise. Hashem knows what He's doing. That's your *zivug*. That's your *bashert*.

Let me explain something to you. According to Hashem's plan, a man can have many wives. A *melech*, a king, can only have eighteen wives, but a regular man could have more. *Al pi din*, it's not *assur*. In certain countries, they still have that *minhag* to have more than one wife. Therefore, a *zivug* is possible with many wives. Of course, after Rabbeinu Gershom said you can't have such a thing in Europe, then you could no longer have more than one wife. But that doesn't mean there's only one woman who's your *zivug*. So this woman you're married to is one of your *zivugim*, and do the best you can with that one *zivug*. That's your success in this world.

Now, when it comes to marrying your *bashert*, it means it's ordained that you should have the *opportunity*. But you could lose the opportunity—in a couple of ways.

One way is if a nice *frum* girl, a decent girl, comes along, but it just so happens that her nose is a fraction of an inch too long, and you decide to say no. So you lose the opportunity. Hashem isn't going to make you get married at the point of a gun. He brought the *kallah* to you. You saw her, and you rejected her—so it's your hard luck. That's one way of losing out on what's *bashert*.

Another way is if you're already married to the nice girl, but you constantly tell her you don't like her. If you're a *meshugener*, you tell her that girls in the street are prettier than she is. Or you're crazy enough to bring up the word *divorce*.

Here's a man who constantly said to his wife, "I'm going to divorce you! I want to divorce you!" Finally, she took the hint and left him. Then he ran around to all the *rabbanim*, asking them to intercede on his behalf and beg her to take him back. But she was so accustomed to the idea after hearing it from him that she finally took it seriously. He lost out on the girl who was *bashert* for him.

So there are two ways. One is to reject the right girl. And the second is when you already have her, but you cause yourself to lose her. If that happens, don't say, "It was *bashert*." Don't say all those things that happened are only a *gezeiras Hashem.* You were too foolish to accept or keep a good wife, so you caused yourself to lose what was ordained for you in heaven. Marriages are made in heaven, but they're destroyed down here on earth.

Torah

"Rabbi Nosson says: 'The time of finding' refers to Torah, as it states, 'He who finds Me finds life'" (*Mishlei* 8:35). (*Brachos* 8a)

Rabbi Nosson offers another explanation. What is the "time for finding" referring to? Torah—that's our real guide in life. The best wife is only a *mashal*, a parable, for the Torah. When it states in *Mishlei*, "*Eishes chayil mi yimtza*—Who can find the wife of valor" (31:10), it means a virtuous wife. But a wife is a human being. When it states further (ibid. 30:12), "She bestowed only good and no evil all the days of her life," which human being can claim such a record? You lived with someone your entire life and never did anything mean? Never once? You did only good? So we understand that it can't be talking about a human wife.

Of course, we should all aspire for such a record as much as possible. The more you invest—the more *tov* you put into your marriage, the more you desire to make the other one happy and exercise *yiras Hashem* in your behavior toward them—there's no question you're going to reap inestimable benefits. But "*Ein tzaddik ba'aretz asher ya'aseh tov v'lo yechta*—There is no righteous person on Earth who does good and never sins" (*Koheles* 7:20). Nobody is perfect. Nobody is an angel. Who, then, is this "wife" who bestows only good and no evil all the days of her life?

Rabbi Nosson says it's the Torah. That's our real guide. We fall in love with the Torah, and all our lives we're going to spend enjoying the company of the Torah. (See *Kiddushin* 30b.)

This career is for every Jew. The Torah belongs to every Jew. It should be his lawful wife, not just a woman he sees far away on the other side of the avenue and thinks it would be nice if he could get to know her. You must get close and "propose" to the Torah. You must make many sacrifices to love the Torah.

Q Why is it forbidden to learn Torah in front of an *am ha'aretz*?

The Gemara (*Pesachim* 49b) tells us that it's forbidden to study Torah in the presence of an *am ha'aretz*, because it causes him excruciating *tza'ar*. It's "as if he took away his bride." It doesn't say "wife." It says "bride." In ancient times, twelve months elapsed between the *kiddushin* and the *chuppah*, between the time a woman becomes a bride and a wife.

Suppose a man put a ring on the finger of an excellent young woman, a young woman with all the virtues. And she's also beautiful. Then, some time before the twelve months elapsed, somebody persuaded her to demand a *get*. Imagine the pain of this poor fellow. Imagine how he feels when, on the day he was supposed to wed her, another man is standing under the *chuppah*. As he passes the wedding hall, he hears the music and knows that his erstwhile bride is now marrying the other man. How his heart would be torn apart!

That's what happens when an *am ha'aretz* sees someone studying Torah. The Torah is *his* bride, only he never had a chance to get close to her. She is always far off. The *am ha'aretz* was always saying, "Someday, when I make my pile of money and finish raising my children, I'll dedicate myself to learning Torah." Someday, when he's past 120 years, he'll sit down and study Torah . . . in the cemetery.

I knew a young man who was in his early forties when I visited him on his deathbed, *nebach*. He was a *yeshiva man*, but instead of learning he went to Wall Street and threw himself into his career. There, on his deathbed, he told me that his hope had been to retire in his forties, go to a *kollel*, and learn to his heart's content all day long. Well, he never made it. In the early forties, he was already in his grave. That's why it states, "Don't say, 'I'll begin learning when I'll have leisure,' for perhaps you won't have any leisure" (*Avos* 2:5), and "If not now, when?" (ibid 1:14). Tomorrow? Who knows what tomorrow will bring?

Therefore, says Rabbi Nosson, for this—for Torah, our bride—we have to pray. For this bride you make a lot of entreaties. For this, it's not excessive to shed tears.

Q Why is Torah called "life"?

"Anyone who finds me finds life" (*Mishlei* 8:35). Torah is life. Therefore, we call Torah a "finding," a "discovery." It's like a man digging on a beach with a stick after the season ends, looking for coins. After a lot of effort, his stick finally hits something hard. He reaches his hand in and takes out a handful of half dollars. At first, he's thrilled. But then he thinks that maybe there's more, so he starts digging down underneath the half dollars. Again his stick hits something hard, but this time it's whole silver dollars. He wants to get them out, so he digs his stick into the sand again—and again it hits something hard. This time he finds golden coins. Each time he digs further down, he finds more and more—until he finds diamonds.

That's how the Torah is. The more we delve into it, the more treasures we're going to dredge up, because there's no end to the wealth of Torah. Torah is such a wealth and happiness. Torah is such a success for a man that it's called "*l'eis m'tzo*—a timely find." The more he digs, the more he finds all the time. His life is one of happiness. He's really living. He's in this world for a purpose and he feels it. The Torah says, "If you find me," you didn't merely find money. What's the big deal about finding money? Rather, "You've found life." Therefore, pray to Hashem for success in learning.

Many people ignore that. They make the mistake of thinking that success in learning is up to them. "I don't need to ask Hashem. The biggest virtue is to do it myself. It's up to me to do virtuous deeds." That's a mistake. Certainly you have to use your free will, but Hashem must be enlisted on your side; otherwise, you're going to hit obstacles.

There are many obstacles that present themselves. Sometimes, for instance, the subject matter is too difficult. It's really not difficult, but sometimes you don't take to it. If you take to it, then automatically it's easier to you. Sometimes you won't find the right *rebbi*. It's difficult to find a good teacher. A *bachur* might go from yeshiva to yeshiva and never connect with the right *rebbi* for him. He must *daven* to find the right *rebbi*. And even if you're not in a yeshiva, it's good to *daven* that you shouldn't have any disturbances. All kinds of things come up in life to prevent a man from learning. There's so much to pray for.

Therefore, put your heart into what Rabbi Nosson says. If necessary, weep and shed many tears, because the Torah is the "wife" a man is going to find true happiness with. If he finds her, he's found life.

PRACTICAL ADVICE

Q **What should one do when his learning gets stuck in a rut?**

He should talk with somebody who is experienced, with a *yeshiva man*. Sometimes it's due to poor preparation. That means he has endured a career of failure. Maybe he never experienced the sweetness of success in learning, and that's sometimes because he started learning late. He didn't know the words properly, so he was frustrated, and he developed an attitude that it doesn't pay to try any longer.

Everyone can succeed in becoming a *lamdan* if you do it in the right way. And you can do it without a *rebbi*. It's remarkable but it's true, only I won't take up the time now to explain that system. But it's possible for a person to get back into learning.

Of course, sometimes it's a temporary cause. Let's say he doesn't go to sleep early enough and he's knocked out. Temporarily, he may be off-kilter. But if it's a more permanent phenomenon, it could be due to this cause, and it's possible for a person to get a new start in life and succeed in learning if he'll consult somebody who is experienced in this field.

Q If a person has two subjects, one he enjoys and one he doesn't, which should he study?

Everybody knows the answer. We have a rule, "A man should always learn Torah in the subject that his heart desires" (*Avodah Zarah* 19a). But suppose he's deciding between learning and not learning. Then he has no choice. It doesn't matter what his heart desires.

But let me tell you something. Suppose a person has a choice between learning Gemara and learning Chumash. Very often that's also not a choice. I'll tell you why. Because it's not that he desires Chumash; it's not that he desires to delve into Chumash and learn what Hashem is trying to tell him. No, it's just that he desires Gemara less. He's looking for an easy way out. He's being lazy. He doesn't want to put in the effort required for learning Gemara, so Chumash is his cop-out.

But if both are of equal difficulty, he should choose the subject that interests him more. That's the rule of, "A man should always learn Torah in the subject that his heart desires." That's because a person will succeed more in the subject that interests him most. And nothing is as important as success in understanding the *d'var Hashem.*

Q Why do yeshivas spend so much time on *iyun* and not as much on covering more ground?

That's a very good question, by the way. The truth is that until recently, the yeshivas used to learn a big part of the *masechta.* They used to cover sometimes an entire *masechta*, sometimes half the *masechta.* Today, however, there's a competition for who can cover *less* ground. That's how it is! A boy says, "In my yeshiva we covered only six *blatt* in *Kesubos* this year." The other boy brags, "That's nothing! My yeshiva only covered four *blatt*!" I don't know if it's such a good thing. But I'm not going to criticize. Maybe in the course of time, they'll see that what they're doing is only for big *ba'alei kishronos*, those with exceptionally good heads. But the majority of the *talmidim* are left out. They're incapable of too much *iyun*. I think it's a good idea to put in a little more time into covering ground.

However, even when you cover ground, it should be done with *chazarah*, not just learning. *Chazarah, chazarah, chazarah!* If you learned even the Gemara alone, not with *Tosfos*, and you know it well—you're a success. You must know it well, however. Learn it until you remember it. Talk it over and understand it. If you have time, look at *mefarshim*, too. But number one—the foundation of learning—is to learn the Gemara alone and know it well. Then later, you can learn a little more in depth if you're capable. It is very important to learn and have a *geshmak* in your learning by being able to know it well yourself.

Q **Should a *yeshiva man* attend a Daf Yomi *shiur*?**

You want to hear my opinion? I say no. I'll tell you why not. A *yeshiva man* has to *shteig*, and Daf Yomi means you're going to forget what you learned. If you learn one *perek*, you must learn it four times *at least*. Don't go away from that *perek*! "If you learn and don't review, it's like a person who plants but never reaps" (*Sanhedrin* 99a). It's a pity. You plant a field with labor, with *yegiah*, and you never bother to reap what grows. When you come back the next time, it's like a new Gemara to you. It's a pity!

But if you review it, not only will you remember it better, but you'll also understand it better. Go over the Gemara again and again, again and again. It's better to know a few *masechta*s well than to go through all of Shas superficially and not remember anything.

Now, many *balebatim* won't bother so much. If they won't bother to learn and review properly, let them at least learn Daf Yomi and they should be blessed. It's a *mitzvah* to learn Torah—very good!

Daf Yomi is Torah. But for a *ben yeshiva* who wants to *shteig*, my advice is that it's not for you. Of course, even a *ben yeshiva* shouldn't waste his time—he should cover ground. He should have a *bekiyus shiur*, too. But even the *bekiyus shiur* means you must review constantly, again and again and again—four times—before you go further. It's important for a *yeshiva man* to learn more deeply, more profoundly than just learning the Daf and then moving on.

Q **How should a *yeshiva man* prepare for a new *z'man*?**

First of all, *tefillah*. You must ask Hashem for help. Say, "Hashem, please give me success this *z'man*... and a little *lishmah*, too." Ask for it! By the way, not only in the beginning of the *z'man*. It's a good idea all the time. Every day, when you're starting a *sugya*, open the Gemara and say: "Ribbono Shel Olam, please help me." It's not a bad idea at all.

Secondly, make up your mind that life is short. You only have 120 years to live. You can't afford to waste time. Make up your mind that in yeshiva, you'll talk only in *divrei Torah*. In the *beis medrash*, don't talk about anything. The *beis medrash* should be only for learning.

Third, make sure to get along with your *chavrusa*. The *mishnah* in *Avos* (1:6) says, "Acquire for yourself a friend, and judge everyone favorably." You can't keep a *chaver* if you're not going to be *dan l'kaf zechus*. Always give your *chavrusa* the benefit of the doubt, and try as much as possible to get along with him. It's very important to get along with your *chavrusa*. Even if he's not such a great help in Torah, it's still a great help in your *middos*. Sometimes it helps you in both. Getting along with people—that means your wife, too—is a very big *shleimus*. It's a great perfection of character, and a very great achievement.

Q What should I do if I have a hard time finding a *chavrusa* in yeshiva?

The first thing is to ask the *mashgiach* to give you a *chavrusa*. He might find someone for you. Another *eitzah* is to learn well by yourself. Some people have succeeded very well without a *chavrusa*. And when your *chaverim* see you learning well, they will come over asking you to be their *chavrusa*.

While you're learning, don't just say the Gemara and keep going. Stop and talk it over in your own words—the *shakla v'tarya*, the back-and-forth in the Gemara. First, it will help you understand that which you didn't understand yet, and secondly, you'll remember it better.

I remember a man I saw in the yeshiva for years and years, just sitting by himself and talking over every little piece of the Gemara, again and again and again and again. At that time, he was an average fellow. Today, he's *maggid shiur* for one of the highest *shiurim* in a *mesivta*. I see him walking in the streets talking *divrei Torah* with his boys, his *talmidim*—because when he was sitting and learning by himself, without a *chavrusa*, he utilized the opportunity to talk it over with himself.

When a person does that, he becomes an *amkan*, he reaches into the depths of the Gemara's words, and he remembers the Gemara well, too. Now, that's in place of a *chavrusa*. But if you do this, eventually you'll get a *chavrusa*, too.

Q Is it wrong to look for financial assistance when looking into a *shidduch*?

It's wrong to *not* look for financial assistance when looking into a *shidduch*! You must have help in a *shidduch*. You don't want to get married when you're fifty-five years old. You want to get married when you're young—twenty, maybe, twenty-one, twenty-two. You can't go out into the world yet. A boy of twenty-two is very raw material. He's not capable of dealing with the world. He must be in the *kollel* for some time. For years and years.

I would say that in most cases you shouldn't go out into the world until you're thirty years old. If you have a good *parnassah* that enables you to continue learning, you can learn even longer. But otherwise, stay as long as you can in the *kollel*, up to age thirty.

But I'm not going to tell you what to do afterward. I'm only telling you the first thing. The first thing is that you must have a certain amount of help to learn Torah. When your parents negotiate with the *shadchan*, they shouldn't be ashamed to speak clearly—how much they're going to give, and for how long they're going to support you. It's very important for the young couple. Every young man must be in the *kollel* for some time! And sometimes his parents should also help out. But if they're not able to help, they must get some help from the girl's parents.

Can a *kollel man* who leaves the yeshiva remain a *yeshiva man* even while he's involved in business?

To some extent he can. But it will require a great deal of cooperation between himself and his wife, as well as a certain amount of heroism and dedication on his part. I'll give you an example. Listen carefully because it means you. And it means me, too.

We have people who come here Friday night. They come here about 7:00, 7:30, and they sit here learning until almost 11:30 at night. They're working people, professionals. They sit here in the shul for four hours on Friday night. Some a little less. That's the program for dedicated men with dedicated wives. The women, of course, have to understand that. They must want it, too, and encourage their husbands. On *motza'ei Shabbos* we have the same thing again. People come here until late, until after 11:00, and learn in groups and as individuals. It's a great phenomenon. But in ancient times that was simply the Jewish way of life.

On Shabbos afternoon, people come to study here, and on the

longer days they study all Shabbos afternoon. And some people study all day Sunday. There are about four *shiurim* on Sunday here, and people attend all of them. Then they sit until late and learn more. Now, that's an example of how a person can continue to be a *yeshiva man* even after he leaves the yeshiva. This man can't afford the luxury of wasting all those odd hours. A *yeshiva man* must get up Shabbos morning early to learn. A *yeshiva man* must spend Shabbos studying. Shabbos night, he can't go out to *melaveh malkah*s with the family. He can't visit relatives; he can't go to weddings. A *yeshiva man* who leaves the *kollel* and begins a life of effort in *gashmiyus* must dedicate himself to Torah learning as well.

That's what the Jewish nation once did, and it's an ideal that many people are beginning to see today. Therefore, if a wife cooperates and doesn't demand her husband's presence at home, that means she understands that it's her partnership, that she is a 100 percent partner. It's in her *zechus* that he's making progress, that he's forging ahead in learning. With such a great partner in life he can forge ahead, as long as he's not lazy and he's willing to commit to a career of study.

I recall a *melaveh malkah* in the old building where I said over from the Rambam, "Anybody who wants to earn the crown of Torah shouldn't waste even one of his nights" (Rambam, *Hilchos Talmud Torah* 3:13). A man who was sitting there heard that, and he changed his way of life. He became great subsequently. He was a working man, but he became great in Torah. Once his wife had to attend a wedding in Riverside Plaza uptown, but that night was a *shiur*, so he drove his wife to Riverside Plaza and then came back to attend the *shiur*. Then he went all the way back to the hall to bring her home. That's dedication!

So, if you won't waste any of your nights, you'll be able to remain a *yeshiva man* forever. Forget about going to weddings. Now you're wedded to the Torah. Some women will say, "What kind of a life is that?" What kind of a life is a *kollel* life? I'll tell you—it's a dedicated life!

Q

Doesn't common sense tell us that one must work to make a living? So is sitting in *kollel* common sense?

You have touched on a very important subject. If a person has funds, or his wife is an idealist and she prefers to work so that her husband can sit and learn, then it will be a *mitzvah* to continue to learn in the *kollel.* But if she doesn't want or isn't able to work, then he is *mechuyav*, he is obligated to support his wife. He made a *kinyan* when he got married. He committed himself in the *kesubah*: "*Ana eflach*—I am going to work." "*Ana eizan*—I am going to support my wife." He's *mechuyav* to go to work.

It's impossible for a man who doesn't have an income to continue learning when he doesn't have any way to support his family. Those people who dodge their responsibility and therefore live in poverty suffer all kinds of troubles just because they're not willing to go out and support their families. Those people are *asidin litein es hadin* (in the afterlife, they'll have to give a reckoning). No question about it. To be in *kollel* when it's possible to be in *kollel* is a beautiful ideal. But when it's not possible, it becomes a *cheit,* a sin.

What's the happy medium between spending time on material things and *avodas Hashem*?

Now, that's a very difficult question to answer. If you can answer that, then you'll become my *rebbi*! Because actually there's no one answer. It depends on the person and on the circumstances.

It's a very complicated question because we know that "A lot of people tried to do as Rabbi Shimon bar Yochai did—to learn only—and it didn't go well for them" (*Brachos* 35b). Rabbi Shimon was against working, but that approach didn't go well for everyone. Now, today a lot of people agree with him—but for other reasons. Rabbi Shimon was against work because he wanted people to devote their lives to studying Torah. When he came out of the cave where he had been hiding for many years and saw people plowing their fields, he was disgusted. To see people who didn't understand their purpose in life, wasting their days on such things! It shocked him.

So, what did Hashem say to him? "Get back into your cave!" And Rabbi Shimon went back into his cave and waited twelve more months. Why twelve months? Listen to what Rabbi Shimon said: "The judgment of the wicked in Gehinnom is twelve months." He considered himself a sinner. He waited twelve months and then came out again. This time he was still dissatisfied, but he kept his mouth closed. As he passed by a field and saw people plowing, he disapproved in his heart, but he had already learned discretion, so he kept his mouth closed. Until finally he saw something that changed his attitude.

It was late on *erev Shabbos*, and he saw an old Jew running with two myrtle twigs, *hadassim*, in his hands. "Why are you running?" Rabbi Shimon asked.

"I'm running," the old Jew said, "because it's late for Shabbos and I'm bringing *hadassim*, fragrant leaves, in honor of the Shabbos."

"Why do you have two, one in each hand?"

He said, "For *shamor* and *zachor*, the two *mitzvos* of Shabbos." One is to not do work on Shabbos—that's *shamor*. The other means to proclaim the Shabbos, to do positive things to honor the Shabbos, like *oneg Shabbos* and things like that. That's *zachor*.

"Oh!" said Rabbi Shimon bar Yochai. "Now I see the greatness of the Jewish people. The greatness is not only in giving up your life for Torah. There's a greatness in living a Torah life, and these people are living it!" And "his mind was appeased."

Therefore, it says that "many people followed his example and didn't succeed." But the *mefarshim* say, "Many couldn't, but *some* did." For some people, that's the right way of living. If you're capable, that's the right way. That's why we support *kollel* people. We support entire families in Yerushalayim who sit and learn Torah. They're acclimated to that lifestyle. They're able to make use of their time, and they're succeeding. If you're able to do it, good! But most people can't devote all their time to Torah learning as Rabbi Shimon bar Yochai did.

Therefore, exactly how to gauge it depends on the person. And it depends on his age, too. Up to a certain age, you should be in places of Torah learning all day long. And after a certain age, you shouldn't work too much, either. You should try to retire and get back to the places of Torah. In between, you also have to gauge it. How much? It's impossible for anybody to give a blanket prescription.

Death

"Rav Nachman bar Yitzchak said: '*L'eis m'tzo*, the time of finding' refers to death, as it states: '*Lamavess totza'os*, issues of death'" (*Tehillim* 68:21). (*Brachos* 8a)

Q **Why does the Gemara say a person should pray extra hard for a proper death?**

Rabbi Nachman bar Yitzchak says that the thing to pray for is a proper death. I'm going to discuss this quickly because I don't like to talk about sad things. People come here to be cheered up, so we'll make it short and snappy. But it's a very important topic.

It's proper for a person to pray to Hashem that he should make a dignified exit from this world, because death is a wasted opportunity for most people. The truth is it's a glorious opportunity.

When Moshe Rabbeinu wanted to criticize his people, to rebuke them most sharply and make the biggest impact on them, he waited until just before his death. Everyone knew these were his last words, and that's why they entered their hearts like nothing he said before.

Our Sages talk about the opportunity for a man to make use of his last hours. He must keep his mind on it, because many people are very discouraged in their last hours. They're thinking, *No more business*. He can't go back to the store, to the beloved place where he spent his life. Never again will he stand in his spot and hear the beautiful tunes of the cash register and the doorbell. No more. It's all over. Never again will he sit behind the wheel of his car. Never will he sit down to a sumptuous repast, to those beloved suppers. It's all over now. He's perturbed and disillusioned. Even though he's a pious man, he's leaving the world ungracefully.

However, if a man lives with a purpose and knows what he wants out of life, then he knows how to make use of his last moments. When our great-grandmothers left this world, they left it lying in bed with a big *Korban Minchah Siddur*, the *siddur* their *chassan* gave them when they got married. It's a huge *siddur*, an encyclopedia of all good things, and in it is a confession to be said on the deathbed. Not like the one we have in our *siddurim*, which is only half a page. In the *Korban Minchah Siddur*, the *Viduy* is pages and pages long. It lists all kinds of sins our great-grandmothers never even dreamed of doing. But it's in there nonetheless. As they said this *Viduy*, they poured out their hearts, shed tears, and purified themselves. When their moment came, they were pure as angels. Even if there was some sin hiding in the back of their head—something they had done fifty or sixty years before—it now came to the surface. Just as we confess all our sins on Yom Kippur—even sins that deserve *skilah* and *chenek*—she confessed as if she did everything, and she left this life purified.

When a man is aware of his last moments and calls together his family, he gives them his last will and testament orally. He adjures them and imposes on them his final wishes. He exacts from them a promise that they're going to be loyal to the Torah all the days of their life, no matter what. They should be loyal to the Torah and fulfill all the *mitzvos* and see to it that their children and grandchildren and great-grandchildren follow in their footsteps. Not one family member should be neglected. Everybody should be watched and guided. A person should see that the entire family remains loyal to the Torah, which they received from their forefathers who stood at Har Sinai.

If that's the way he speaks in his last moments, it enters like arrows of fire into their hearts. Sometimes a person can accomplish more in those last words than all the words he said in his lifetime. That person is dying for a purpose.

There are many other things to accomplish with death, but we're going to stop here for now.

PRACTICAL ADVICE

Q Can one accomplish something with *tefillah* even on his deathbed?

Let's say a man is on his deathbed. He's very old. He's 119. He can't expect to live much longer. But he cries out anyway on his deathbed. He wants to live.

Finally, he passes away. Did he waste his time crying out to Hashem for life? No! In his last minutes he achieved maybe more than he did his entire life. Because he's thinking about Hashem.

Here's an old man who's crying out on his deathbed. He says, "Hashem, please heal me!" "Oh, that's so silly!" you say. Bystanders think it's ridiculous. He wants to be healed! How long do you want to hang around here? Isn't 119 years long enough?

And the answer is—it's not enough. He wants to live a thousand years. Why shouldn't he? He had an ancestor who did. Mesushelach lived almost a thousand years, so why shouldn't he?

So he's crying out. He's allowed to cry out. And don't say that he didn't accomplish what he wanted. He did accomplish! The crying out is the purpose of the deathbed—so that he should cry out to Hashem and become more and more aware of Him. That's the biggest achievement there is.

Therefore, nobody should ever be frustrated in crying out because you are achieving. You're gaining more awareness of Hashem.

Q What's the point of asking for long life?

Life is full of opportunities—*mitzvos*, *zechuyos*, *shleimus*, Torah. Even a businessman, no matter how busy he is, must make Torah part of his life. He must learn Hashem's word and try to remember it. He should tell Hashem, "All my life I'm going to review what I learned. The longer I live, the more I'll review it, and the more I review, the more firmly fixed it's going to be in my mind—so please give me long life." That's what the *passuk* says: "In the right hand [of Torah] is length of days" (*Mishlei* 3:16). Commit yourself to going to Torah *shiurim*, and to learning Torah whenever and wherever you can. Don't let even a minute go lost. It's a good investment. It's life insurance.

All kinds of greatness await you with long life. The longer you live, the more you can accomplish. And it's a good idea to think of all the *mitzvos* you'll accomplish and the Torah you'll learn with a long life. But when you ask Hashem, ask for it *kipshuto*, in its simplest sense—that you just want to live. Don't be in a hurry for Olam Haba. Use this life. Make up your mind and develop a very strong desire to live long, because the longer you live the more you can accomplish, and the more joy you'll get out of life.

You might tell yourself you're not worthy. No, you are worthy. Ask Hashem for long life, and not only on Rosh Hashanah. Always. Don't rely on Shemoneh Esrei alone. As you sit in your car or in your kitchen, as you walk outside, as you go about your daily routine, say, "Hashem, I want to live. '*Techi nafshi*—Let my soul live'" (*Bereishis* 19:20). *Tefillah* is one of the greatest things in the world, the Gemara says (*Brachos* 6b). It's "*devarim ha'omdim berumo shel olam*—something that stands at the height of the world." And that doesn't refer only to the *tefillah* you say in Shemoneh Esrei.

Don't be stingy with words. Don't say, *I won't bother Hashem; I'll take care of it myself; I'll guard my health; I'll guard my safety.* No,

Hashem wants you to "bother" Him. Hashem loves to hear you ask Him for things. It means you're thinking about Him and you believe in Him; you have *emunah* and *bitachon.*

Q How does one deal with growing older?

The *Sha'arei Teshuvah* (*Sha'ar* 2) suggests six motivations for *teshuvah.* The second is when one feels himself growing old. It doesn't mean he doesn't have a lot of years left. He can have a long life ahead of him, a long fruitful life full of opportunities, with good health and *koach.* But he starts feeling age catching up with him. It's not an accident. Growing old is part of Hashem's plan. Its purpose is to motivate us to do *teshuvah.*

Now, David Hamelech says, "*LaHashem ha'aretz umelo'ah teiveil v'yoshvei vah*—To Hashem belong the Earth and all that is in it, the world and all those who dwell in it" (*Tehillim* 24:1). The word *teiveil,* "world," is derived from the word *beis-lamed-hey*—*balah*—which means "to wear out." This is a world that wears out. It's a changeable world. It's not permanent. He calls the world *teiveil* to let us know that we are here only temporarily. We are given only a brief opportunity to accomplish our purpose.

"*Dor holeich v'dor bah*—A generation comes, and a generation goes" (*Koheles* 1:4). A person only has a certain amount of time. Every man has his time, and that's all he's going to get. Therefore, we are warned—"*teiveil.*" This is a temporary existence. We shouldn't become caught up in the business of our lives to such an extent that we forget the grand purpose of our existence. The grand purpose of the whole creation is to spend our brief stay on this Earth, on this "*teiveil,*" achieving an awareness of Hashem, and recognizing His plan and purpose that is evident all around us. And to constantly express our happiness and our gratitude in an outpouring of praise that never comes to an end. That's what we're here for.

Therefore, "*Zechor es Borecha bimei bechurosecha*—Remember

your Creator in the days of your youth" (*Koheles* 12:1). Youth is a glorious time, when the blood courses through your veins and your heart sings within you, when life is full of enthusiasm and *simchah*. That's the time best suited to think of Hashem.

"*L'hagid baboker chasdecha*—To relate in the morning Your kindliness" (*Tehillim* 92:3). It's a *mashal* for the "morning" *of life*. You're not always going to stay young. This is a *teiveil*, a "changing world," so hurry while you're still young and enthusiastic. Achieve what youth is really for. Adolescence is both glorious and disturbing! Those are years when everything is cooking inside of you and confusing your mind, but they are also years of enthusiasm. That's the morning of life.

A little boy sees the world with bright eyes. Everything is glorious. After all, it *is* a glorious world. Therefore, before your eyes grow old and weary and you stop seeing the splendor of Hashem's world—while everything is still new and arouses your youthful enthusiasm—that's the time to praise Hashem. The morning of life is the best time, before the day grows old and weary; when the sun is new, and the dew is still on the garden plants and everything is fresh, when the fragrance of spring is in the air. That's why we *daven* so long in the morning. That's the time of day that's best suited for it.

But the morning is not forever. So hurry, get out of bed before the morning is gone, before it's over, because this is *teiveil*—a world that doesn't endure. The morning passes by and youth passes by. Therefore, hurry up and accomplish while you still have the opportunity.

An old man, of course, also must make use of the opportunity before it's gone forever. He won't come back again. This is the one opportunity in eternity to open his mouth and sing to Hashem, and to thank Him, all day long from early in the morning until late at night. That's our job in this world. Don't be ashamed because of your neighbors. Don't care what the family will say about you. Open your mouth and make *brachos*—whether it's in Hebrew or

English, or Yiddish, or Ladino, or whatever language you know. Speak all day long and thank Hashem. Recognize His wonders. Recognize the miracles of Nature. Recognize the great things He does for you in your private life. Recognize the things He does in history. Speak about all of them at length because this is *teiveil*—it's a temporary world.

Spring is with us now, but spring won't last forever. Soon spring blends into summer. The bright green turns dark green. The cool pleasant days turn into warm days. Of course, warm days are also good. Any days are good. But before spring is over, we must use it to the utmost. That's why David Hamelech tells us that this world is *teiveil*.

As long as you're young, as long as you have a spouse, as long as you have children in the house, as long as you have teeth—think of the glorious gift of teeth that allows you to sink them into an apple and crunch heartily on it—say your *brachos* with gusto and give thanks to Hashem. Do it now because the gifts of the body are not forever. Everything is *teiveil*.

The time will come when you'll have to take off this fleshy cloak. So, while you still have these lips of flesh on you, let that flesh do some talking. "*Hashem s'fasai tiftach*—Hashem, open my lips, *ufi yagid tehilasecha*—and let my mouth relate Your praise." That's what your mouth and lips are for. Hurry up while you still have them, because soon they'll be gone forever.[63]

Health

"Mar Zutra said: '*L'eis m'tzo*, the time of finding' refers to finding a bathroom. In Eretz Yisrael they say: This explanation of Mar Zutra is preferable to all of them" (*Brachos* 8a).

63 For more on this topic, read *Rav Avigdor Miller on Olam Haba*.

Q Why does the Gemara say the best explanation of the *passuk* is to pray for a bathroom?

Mar Zutra says that the best of all the things to pray for—the thing you must really pray to find when you need it—is a *beis hakisei.* Keep in mind that our Sages were men of great intellect, so we must realize this is a deep matter. It's deeper than deep. When the Gemara says anything, it's intended on many levels. But before we study this subject on its deeper level, its proper level, we'll study it at a superficial level.

The Gemara (*Shabbos* 25b) says, "Who is a rich man? He who has a bathroom near his dining room." That's the criterion of a rich man. There's a deeper level here, too, but right now we're hearing what's called rich. Today in America, everybody has a bathroom nearby. But it wasn't long ago that it was rare. So it's hard for us to appreciate the many problems caused by the difficulty of access to a privy. I can't speak about this in too much detail, but you can imagine that people ignored the need for elimination when they had to go out on a frosty night to a place half a block away from the house. The old-time Eastern European houses put the privy at the end of the garden, as far away from the house as possible. They didn't have running water, so they made sure it was some distance away.

Imagine it's nighttime and you're in a cozy bed, undressed, when the urge comes. You lie there thinking about how you have to put on your boots, because the snow is deep and you have to wade through it all the way to the end of the garden. Many times, people changed their minds. They convinced themselves they could wait until the morning. And that compromised their health.

When people are careful with matters of elimination, it's going to show up in their general health. The Gemara (*Nedarim* 49b) relates that a wealthy Roman matron once accused Rabbi Yehudah, who was very poor, of lending money with interest or selling swine. She accused him because his face was rosy; his complexion demonstrated good health. She assumed it was due to professions that made him a lot of easy money. People who lent money with interest or who sold swine made a lot of money. Swine used to be a good business because you didn't have to feed them; they fed themselves and grew fat on almost anything.

He replied that he engaged in neither business. Both were forbidden. "We can't lend money with interest and we can't raise swine."

"Then why," she asked, "is your complexion so rosy?"

He answered, "From my house to the *beis hamedrash*, the synagogue where I go every day, there are twenty-four toilets on the way, and I stop in at every one."

Now, it doesn't mean that literally. It means he never neglected his need for elimination. *Mussar sefarim* talk about the *middah* of *zerizus*, the quality of alacrity, regarding elimination; a man shouldn't be lazy about going to the bathroom. In the olden days, that was a real challenge. Therefore, if Rabbi Yehudah tried the first one and was unsuccessful, he tried the second one. And so forth. By the time he arrived, he had already accomplished his mission. That's why he was in good health.

In a general way, Mar Zutra is telling us that a pious person should pray to Hashem to help him succeed in maintaining good health. Good health is extremely important if you want to be a pious man. If you want to be any kind of a man it's necessary, but to be a servant of Hashem it's essential. It's imperative to have good health.

Of course, sometimes a man, *chalilah*, has poor health and still serves Hashem. But I must disillusion you if you think that maintaining your health is unimportant or doesn't require *hishtadlus*, making an effort. And that includes praying for it. If you see somebody sitting and studying Torah day and night in the yeshiva, he needs exceptional energy. If he maintains his health, it's good because without energy it won't work. Many people don't suspect that the reason for their lack of interest in Torah study is due to low energy. They're physically not up to putting in hours of concentrated study. They don't have the stamina, the pep. You must have in your blood, in your physique, energy sources that enable you to study the Torah.

There's no question that the biggest *masmidim* have considerable physical stamina. It's remarkable. The biggest *tzaddikim* were blessed with good physiques. Now, don't think that's the *reason* they were big *tzaddikim*. It's the opposite. The reason they were blessed with a good physique was because they were big *tzaddikim*. Hashem saw that they wanted to study the Torah, so He gave them the physical ability to do so. "A man is led in the way he wants to go" (*Makkos* 10a). But the *tzaddikim*, we must know, also take care of their health. They *daven* for it. We must pray to Hashem for that.

Who knows how many days a person can lose from work if he suffers from sinus infections? Who knows how many days he might lose from coming to learn Torah? If a man suffers from severe arthritis, *chalilah*, who knows how many days he will be incapacitated? There are so many kinds of illness, *chas v'shalom*, and they all have an effect on our spiritual career. They have an effect on our characters, too. Of course, there are some people who are cheerful, friendly, and charitable despite their suffering, but a person in pain is much more likely to be crabby.

Therefore—"*Al zos yispallel kol chassid*"—you must pray for good health.

Q **Why does going to the bathroom prolong life?**

"Rav Yehudah says: Three things lengthen a person's days and years—spending a long time in prayer, sitting longer at a meal, and spending enough time in the bathroom" (*Brachos* 54b). These are three forms of life insurance. If you take your time and do them slowly, you're going to live longer.

The first is "*hama'arich bitfillaso*"—if you pray longer. Don't be in a hurry when you're davening. The more time you give to *tefillah*, the more time Hashem will give you to live. And not merely proportionately. That doesn't mean He'll give you an extra fifteen minutes to your life for every fifteen minutes you add to your *tefillah*. He's going to give you very much more—months and years! Therefore, it pays not to be in a hurry when you're speaking to Hashem. It's an opportunity to ask for whatever you need, an opportunity to commune with the One you love most. You can pour out all your heart's desires to Him, so take your time. The longer you stand in Shemoneh Esrei or in any other *tefillah*, the more you'll be rewarded with longer years.

And not only will his "years" be longer, but his "days," too. That means he's going to live happier days. He'll have a long and happy life. Of course, it's up to him to make use of it. Sometimes a man can have long years, but he tries his best to be unhappy. If you try to be happy, though, it'll be easier for you and you'll have longer years to do it.

That's the first thing that lengthens life. The second is "*hama'arich al shulchano*"—sitting longer at a meal. That doesn't mean you should dawdle at your meal, that you should read newspapers while you eat and waste a lot of time. But you also shouldn't hurry. Don't gobble your food. Take your time. It's a *mitzvah* to eat properly. Chew your food. And don't talk while you're eating. You can listen, but don't talk because the food might go down the wrong pipe.

While we're on the subject, I wish to criticize a practice some people have of keeping the telephone near the table where they eat. Eating and talking is dangerous, especially when there's nobody in the house to help you, *chas v'shalom*. Even listening on the telephone is dangerous because the other party might say something startling, and just when the food wants to go down one way, the windpipe opens up and the food goes down there instead. It's a wonderful thing that Hashem created in us, that when we're about to swallow, the windpipe closes automatically. But when you talk while you eat, it can force it open and cause food to go down the wrong way. If you came here just to hear that, it's worthwhile. Don't talk while you're eating!

But what does the Gemara mean that if you eat longer, you get longer years? It refers to an ancient practice (*Bava Basra* 93b). In ancient Yerushalayim, when the family sat down to eat a meal, they took a tablecloth and hung it over the doorway outside. This meant that dinner was being served, and anybody who was hungry was welcome to join them. They didn't have refrigerators and ready-made foods, so if an outsider came in and there was nothing to eat, they probably wouldn't cook a meal especially for him. But if he saw that tablecloth—which was really a flag of *chessed*—fluttering in the wind outside the home, it meant, "Come in." When you came in, you shared a meal with the family.

Now, suppose the father of the house rushed his meals. That meant he was a thrifty fellow who would make his meals as short as possible so that if anybody came in, it was before or after the meal. But if you were a kind man, a man of *chessed* who waited for guests, you took your time. Even if the family was finished eating, he would tell them to wait a few more minutes. He would say over some *divrei Torah*, some stories of *tzaddikim*. "Let's spend a little more time here—maybe somebody in need will join us."

In reward for taking in people to eat at your table, you're going to have extra years. That's a big thing to know. Therefore, when a *meshulach* comes to your house to collect funds for some cause, don't forget he's been away from home all day long. He'll probably refuse to eat in your house, but you can try to entice him. Of course, only offer him to come in if your husband is home and he tells him to come in and eat. Sit him at your table and offer him food. Giving a hungry *meshulach*—or a poor Jew, a wanderer—a meal is doing yourself the biggest favor. Someone who sits longer at his table to feed wayfarers is acting like Avraham Avinu.

The third thing that extends a person's life is sitting longer in the bathroom—"*hama'arich b'veis hakisei.*" That's along the same lines as "*hama'arich bitfillaso*" and "*hama'arich al shulchano.*" It means he's being solicitous of his health. If somebody is in the bathroom and you bang on the door because you want to go in to get a magazine, it's wickedness. Leave the poor fellow to do justice to himself. And if the poor fellow happens to be yourself, don't shoo him out, either. Stay there long enough to do what you need. It means longer life. That's what Chazal are telling us. Sometimes, just when you're about to give up, the *yeshuah* suddenly comes, and then for the rest of the day you're walking with vigor. Therefore, don't be in a hurry.

Now, if anybody thinks there are better subjects to discuss, let me tell you an anecdote from the Gemara (*Shabbos* 82a). Rav Huna was a great man, a *rosh yeshiva*. He sent his son Rabbah to Rav Chisda's yeshiva. The son came back immediately, so his father asked, "What's the matter?"

"It's a waste of time," he replied. "I expected a brilliant *pilpul*, but the first lecture the *rebbi* gave was that you shouldn't be in a hurry and force yourself too much when going to the *beis hakisei*. Who needs that?"

Rav Huna—the great *rosh yeshiva*, the *gadol hador*—replied to his son, "He's busy teaching how to be healthy, and you say it's a waste of time?! That's all the more reason to learn in his yeshiva. Go back! That's where I want you to learn."

We shouldn't consider talking about health superfluous. That's why the Gemara says that a *chassid* should pray to Hashem to help Him in health matters. Of course, you must do more than pray. If you pray but then you contradict your prayers with your actions by being negligent with your health, it's not a sincere prayer. You must do whatever's necessary.

While we're on the subject, you shouldn't rush out of the yeshiva without a coat. Some young men think they're heroes. They rush out into the frost—some even without a jacket. You wouldn't send a Jew out on a frosty day without proper clothing. If that Jew happens to be yourself, you have no right to do it, either.

Another Gemara (*Brachos* 62a) teaches—"Ben Azzai said, 'Get up early in the morning and go out to the fields.'" In those days, most people used fields to eliminate. There was no other place. Ben Azzai continued, "In the evening, go out so that you shouldn't have to go far away." Early in the morning nobody is up yet, and in the evening people are already home, so those are ideal times because you don't have to go too far away. But in the middle of the day, you would have to take a very long trip outside the town because people are in the fields nearby. Therefore, get up early in the morning before people are about, and use the evenings when people are already in their homes. Those two times were ideal. Otherwise, it would be very inconvenient.

The subject is so important that I can't do justice to it. A lot of people suffer from constipation. I would counsel those people who have difficulty that they should eat an apple every night and wash it down with a glass of water. This advice is worth diamonds. An apple every night. Wash it down with a glass of water, and in the morning you'll see results. Also, drink a glass of water every morning before davening. It shouldn't be too cold because in the winter it might irritate your throat. If you can drink lukewarm water before prayers in the morning, your health is going to be improved immeasurably.

There are other pieces of simple advice, but the main thing is to treat your health with alacrity. Don't be lazy. Of course, if, *kein ayin hara*, you have a big family, it's a problem to occupy the bathroom too long. That's why it's considered wealth when a family can afford two bathrooms, as the Gemara says.

Now, as regards the deeper meaning, the Vilna Gaon explains that Torah is like rain for a man's soul, for a man's character. When rain falls, it causes things in the soil to grow. If there's nothing in the soil, nothing will grow. But if there are seeds or roots buried in the ground, rain will cause them to sprout. Similarly, Torah is like rain. It causes whatever you have in your character to sprout. It causes your character to develop.

If you have good seeds, good roots, the Torah is going to make them flourish. They'll grow into beautiful flowers, into great fruit trees. Torah will draw out all the latent greatness planted in your soul. But if a person has negative qualities of character, what we call *middos*, the Torah is going to cause those to spring forth. They'll produce a garden of brambles and thorns. If a man doesn't uproot his negative *middos*, the Torah will make him even worse than he was before.

That's a big *chiddush*! If a wicked man studies Torah, he will become even more wicked! Unless he studies it with the intention of getting rid of his wickedness. If he doesn't, if he's satisfied to remain the way he is, the Torah is going to be like rain that waters the hidden seeds of poisonous plants. That's a remarkable statement! But the Vilna Gaon said this is what the Gemara (*Chagigah* 15b) means when it asks how great men like Doeg and Achitofel lost their share in the world to come. Doeg was so great, the Gemara relates, that he was able to say 300 *halachos* on a certain complicated Torah subject (*Sanhedrin* 106b)—300 separate *halachos*! And Achitofel formulated 400 unique questions on a complex topic! So how did they lose their portion in Olam Haba? This was the question that Rav Yehudah asked his teacher, Shmuel.

"Those great men," Rav Yehudah said, "studied so much Torah and yet lost their share in the World to Come. If so, what will happen to us?"

Shmuel replied that there's a big difference: "There was some filth in their hearts." They didn't clean out their hearts. They left the dirt there. Therefore, the Gaon tells us, when they studied Torah, this dirt sprouted forth and became magnified. They couldn't have been as wicked as they were without the added intelligence the Torah gave them. It's like a man with no weapons—he can only do harm within arm's reach. But suppose he had a long lance. Then he could do harm for a few yards. If he could shoot a bow and arrow, then he could do harm from a block away. With a gun, who knows how far his harm could travel?

These men were able to do more harm than the ordinary person. That's what the *navi* said: "The ways of Hashem are righteous—the righteous walk in them, but the wicked stumbles because of them" (*Hoshea* 14:10.) Which ways? The Gaon says "the ways" of the Torah. The righteous walk in those ways and become very good, but wicked people use them to become very bad.

Now, listen to what the Gaon adds. Therefore, every day before studying Torah, practice "elimination." A man should cleanse his heart from the wicked attributes of character that lie there. He should try to think before he begins learning Torah. He should think about fear of Hashem. He should think about fear of sin. That's called "going to the *beis hakisei*." That's what our Sages hinted to when they said, "For this the *chassid* should pray...for a *beis hakisei*.... And in Eretz Yisrael they said that's the best of all prayers."

It's extremely important to pray to Hashem for a good wife, and a woman for a good husband. It's extremely important to pray for success in Torah. It's extremely important to pray that our last moments in life be used properly. But, of all our prayers, the most important is to pray to get rid of wicked character traits, *middos ra'os*, because that's the biggest danger of all. Nothing good can be accomplished when a person has bad things in him and he doesn't address them. All the Torah he's going to study isn't going to help him. To the contrary, it's only going to increase his opportunities for expressing his wickedness.

That's why our Sages say, "*hama'arich b'veis hakisei.*" Spend more time in the *beis hakisei*. Before studying the Torah, don't be in a hurry. Do you think you've cleansed yourself just by thinking for a second or two? Spend more time. The more time you spend on this type of elimination, the better. *Oh, I was angry; I had a malicious intent; I was conceited; I was selfish; I was stingy; I didn't think about other people; I was wasteful with my money; I was too bold; I was too bashful*.... All these are *beis hakisei* things, and they must be eliminated before we begin studying Torah.

That's how the Vilna Gaon explains this Gemara. We shouldn't ignore the plain meaning of the Gemara, but the *nimshal*—that a man must work on his character traits and spend time cleansing himself of bad ones—is even more valuable.

When the Gemara says, "Get up early in the morning and go out in the fields, and at nighttime, too," "the morning" means in your youth. Start working to change your character when you're young. Don't postpone. As soon as you can, start working to change your character.

And when you're old, don't give up, either. Even in the "nighttime" of life, continue to cleanse yourself. Your entire life in between, too. When the Gemara says, "*shelo tisrachek*—so that you shouldn't have to go too far away," it means so that you shouldn't get too far away from Hashem, because that's what bad character does. It estranges people from Hashem. Did you ever hear of people going away from Hashem? It surprises us. We thought they were *frum* Jews. But it happens because of those *middos ra'os* in their nature. Even when they were in the yeshiva and studying Torah, those bad *middos* were there.

The Gaon adds that if somebody is too lazy to go to this *beis hakisei*—he doesn't search out his *middos ra'os*—nothing is going to help, because a wound that's not tended will never heal. Suppose a surgeon is in a hurry to get rid of you and collect his fee. He's a busy man and has no time for you, so he sews you up immediately without draining the wound. You'll have to return to the hospital, sometimes for weeks, until it's finally drained. Otherwise, you'll find even years later that you're not finished healing.

Let's say you're a *ba'al teshuvah*. You've put on a nice beard and a black hat. Now you look like a real authentic Jewish boy. Only it's superficial. It's *on* your head, not *in* your head. You have to know that inside there's work to be done, too. Inside, you're uncouth; you're still a revolutionary. All those bad *middos* from the college campus are still in you. You haven't done a complete job yet. That's a wound that's not healed inside. All you've done is sew it up on the outside. Of course, it's not just *ba'alei teshuvah*. It means anyone who doesn't work on his *middos ra'os*.

The Gaon says that you'd better get busy and attend to this every morning and evening. From the morning of life until the evening of life, spend as much time as you can on it. When you're trying to cleanse yourself of *middos ra'os*, it's never too late and it's never spending too much time—because as important as it is to maintain your physical health, the health of your soul is much more important.

GLOSSARY

Acharon, Acharonim—leading rabbi(s) and Jewish legal decisor(s) living from roughly the 16th century to the present

Adam Harishon—the first man

Aggadeta—sections of the Talmud containing stories, lessons, morals, etc.

Ahavah—love

Ahavas Hashem—love of the Almighty

Aishes chayil—"woman of valor," a good wife

Al Hatzaddikim—prayer in the Shemoneh Esrei for the righteous

Aleinu—prayer that declares the Jewish people's responsibility to praise the Almighty

Aliyah l'regel—traveling to Jerusalem for the Three Festivals

Am ha'aretz—ignoramus

Amein—affirmative response to a blessing

Ana Avda D'Kudsha Brich Hu—"I am a servant of the Holy One, blessed be He," a traditional song

Anav—a humble person

Anavah—humility

Anenei hakavod—the Clouds of Glory with which the Almighty protected the Jews during their forty years in the Wilderness

Anshei Knesses Hagedolah—the Men of the Great Assembly, the supreme Torah law-determining body that functioned at the start of the Second Temple era

Anshei ma'aseh—men of action

Apikores—heretic

Apikorsus—heresy

Arba Minim—the Four Species of fruit and vegetation used to fulfill a Torah commandment on the holiday of Sukkos

Aseih—positive (commandment)

Aseres Hadibros—the Ten Commandments

Aseres Hashevatim—the Ten Tribes

Asher Yatzar—blessing recited after using the bathroom for elimination

Ashkenaz—pertaining to Jews of central or eastern European ancestry

Ashrei—Psalms 145

Askanim—activists

Assur—forbidden

Atah—You

Atah Chonein—prayer in the Shemoneh Esrei for knowledge and understanding

Atzlus—laziness

Atzvus—sadness

Avak lashon hara—gossip-like behavior

Avdus—servitude

Aveirah, aveiros—sin(s)

Avinu—our Father

Avodah—service

Avodah sheb'leiv—service of the heart

Avodah zarah—idolatry

Avodas Hashem—service of the Almighty

Avos—forefathers, the Patriachs

Avoseinu—our forefathers

Az Yashir—song at the Sea of Reeds after the Egyptians were drowned and the Jewish people were saved

B'derech haTorah—in the path of the Torah

B'kedushah—in holiness

B'nei Torah—Torah loyalists

B'shalom—in peace

B'tzelem Elokim—in the image of the Almighty

B'tznius—with modesty

B'derech hakedushah—in the path of holiness

B'nei Yisrael—the Jewish people

Ba'al teshuvah, ba'alei teshuvah—Jew(s) who return(s) to Torah observance

Ba'alei kishronos—capable people

Ba'al chessed—someone who performs acts of kindness

Ba'al ga'avah—a haughty person

Ba'al mussar—a growth-oriented person

Bais Yaakov—Torah school for girls

Bakashah, bakashos—request(s)

Balebusteh—capable homemaker

Bamidbar—the Book of Numbers

Barchu—introductory declaration before the blessings of the Shema

Bareich Aleinu—prayer in the Shemoneh Esrei for livelihood

Baruch Hashem—thank the Almighty

Baruch She'amar—introductory blessing to Pesukei D'zimrah

Batei midrashim—Torah study halls

Bava Basra—Talmudic tractate that deals with a person's responsibilities and rights as the owner of property

Bava Kama—Talmudic tractate that deals with the laws of damages

Bavel—Babylonia

Bechinah—studying the phenomena of the world to acquire the feeling of gratitude to the Creator

Bechirah—free will

Bein adam lachaveiro—between you and your fellow

Beis din—Torah court

Beis hakisei—bathroom

Beis knesses, beis haknesses—synagogue

Beis medrash, beis hamedrash—Torah study hall

Beis Yisrael—the Jewish people

Beitzah—Talmudic tractate that deals with the laws of the holidays

Bekesheh—type of frock

Bekiyus—breadth of Torah knowledge

Bentch—recite Grace After Meals

Bentching—Grace After Meals

Bereishis—the Book of Genesis

Bi'as haMashiach—the coming of the Messiah

Binah—understanding

Birchos Hashachar—morning blessings

Birkas Hamazon—Grace After Meals

Bitachon—trust in the Almighty

Bittul Torah—wasting time from learning Torah

Bli neder—without promising

Boneih Yerushalayim—prayer in the Shemoneh Esrei for the rebuilding of Jerusalem

Borei—the Creator

Borei pri ha'adamah—blessing recited before eating vegetables

Brachah, brachos—blessing(s)

Brachos—Talmudic tractate that deals with the laws of blessings and prayers

Bren—enthusiasm

Brissim—circumcisions

Briyah—the Creation

Briyah yeish mei'ayin—Creation *ex nihilo*, from nothing

Canaanim—the Canaanites

Chacham, Chachamim—Torah scholar(s)

Chachmah—wisdom

Chachmei haTorah—the Torah scholars

Chalilah—Heaven forbid

Chamishah Asar B'Shvat—the fifteenth of Shevat, the New Year for trees

Charatah—regret

Chas v'shalom—Heaven forbid

Chasdei Hashem—thanks to the kindness of the Almighty

Chashmonaim—the Hasmoneans, the priestly family that led the resistance against the Hellenizers and Greeks during the Second Temple era

Chashuv—important

Chassadim—acts of kindness

Chassan—groom

Chassid, chassidim—adherent(s) to a chassidic sect and usually to a chassidic *rebbe* (leader), distinguished by a particular mode of dress and customs that seek to separate them from the surrounding gentile culture; Jew(s) who go(es) beyond the line of duty in service of the Almighty

Chassidishe—characteristic of *chassidim*

Chassidus—extraordinary piety

Chasunah—wedding

Chayvei krisus—sins for which one is liable to the Heavenly punishment of excision

Chayvei misas beis din—sins for which one receives capital punishment

Chazarah—review

Chazerai—junk

Cheit—sin

Chelek—portion

Chenek—the punishment of death by strangulation

Cheshbon—an accounting

Cheshbon Hanefesh—spiritual accounting

Chessed—kindness

Chibburim—writings

Chiddush, chiddushim—novel Torah insight(s)

Chiyuv—obligation

Chol Hamoed—the intermediate days of the holidays of Passover and Sukkos

Cholim—people who are ill

Chovos Halevavos—Duties of the Mind, written by Rabbeinu Bachya ibn Pakuda in 11th century Spain

Chullin—Talmudic tractate that deals with the subject of ritual slaughter and the kosher laws

Churban—destruction

Churban Beis Hamikdash—the destruction of the Holy Temple in Jerusalem

D'Oraysa—of Torah origin

D'rabbanan—of Rabbinic origin

D'var Hashem—the word of the Almighty

D'veikus—clinging, connection (to the Almighty)

Da'as—internalized knowledge

Daf Yomi—daily program of Talmud study, one page per day

Dan l'kaf zechus—judge favorably

David Hamelech—King David

De'ah—internalized knowledge

Derech—path

Derech agav—tangentially

Derech eretz—proper behavior

Derech Hashem—the way of the Almighty

Devarim—the Book of Deuteronomy

Devarim b'teilim—empty or pointless words

Dinei Torah—Torah law

Dinim—laws

Divrei Hayamim—the Book of Chronicles

Divrei mussar—words of chastisement

Divrei Torah—Torah thoughts

Dor Hamidbar—the generation of Jews that left Egypt and lived in the Wilderness for forty years

Doros—generations

Drash—homiletic interpretation

Drashah, drashos—homiletic(s)

Echad—one

Eichah—the Book of Lamentations

Eisav—Esau, brother of Jacob

Eitzah—advice

Elokecha—your G-d

Elokeinu—our G-d

Emes—truth

Emunah—faith

Emunah chushis—tangible faith

Emunah p'shutah—simple faith

Erchin—Talmudic tractate that deals with a type of monetary vow

Eretz hakodesh—the holy land

Eretz Yisrael—the land of Israel

Eruvin—Talmudic tractate that deals with the subject of various types of domains in the laws of the Sabbath

Eved—slave, servant

Frum—religiously observant

Frummeh—religiously observant Jews

Ga'avah—arrogance

Gadol hador—Torah leader of a generation

Galus—exile

Galuyos—exiles

Gashmiyus—materialism

Gedolah—great

Gedolei Acharonim—the greatest of the leading rabbis and Jewish legal decisors from roughly the 16th century to the present

Gedolei Yisrael—the Torah leaders of the Jewish people

Gedolim—Torah leaders

Gedulas Hashem—greatness of the Almighty

Geir tzedek—righteous convert

Geirim—converts

Gemara—Talmud

Gemilas chassadim—acts of kindness

Geshmak—delightful

Geshmakeit—delight

Geulah—redemption; the Redemption

Gevaldigeh—great

Gezeirah—decree

Gezeiras Hashem—Divine decree

Gittin—Talmudic tractate that deals with the subject of divorce

Giyoress—female convert

Go'el—redeeemer

Gomel chassadim—the One Who does kindness

Gra—the Vilna Gaon

Hachna'ah—humility

Hachnasas orchim—welcoming guests

Hakadosh Baruch Hu—the Holy One, blessed be He

Hakaras hatov—gratitude

Hakdamah—introduction

Halachah, halachos—Torah law(s)

Hallel—effusive praise; Psalms 113–118, recited on holidays

Hamapil—prayer before going to sleep at night

Hana'ah—enjoyment

Hanavi—the prophet

Hashem—the Almighty

Hashgachah—Divine providence

Hashivah Shofteinu—prayer in the Shemoneh Esrei for the restoration of our great Torah leaders

Haskel—applied wisdom

Hatzalah—rescue

Hatzlachah—success

Havdalos—separations

Hechsheirim—kosher supervisions

Hespedim—eulogies

Heter—legal permission

Hevel havalim—vanity of vanities

Hislahavus—enthusiasm

Hoda'ah—recognition, gratitude

Ikvesa d'Meshicha—the footsteps of the Messiah, the era preceding the arrival of the Messiah

Imahos—foremothers, the Matriarchs

Ish—man

Ishah—woman

Issur—Torah prohibition

Iyov—Job; the Book of Job

Iyun—in-depth Torah study

Kabbalas haTorah—acceptance of the Torah

Kadosh—holy

Kallah—bride

Kaparah—atonement

Kapoteh—type of frock

Kashya—question, logical difficulty

Kavanah—intent

Kaveyachol—if it were possible to say

Kavod—honor

Kedoshim—holy ones

Kedushah—holiness

Kefirah—heresy

Kefitzas haderech—supernatural hastening of travel

Kehillah, kehillos — congregation(s)

Kesubah — marriage document

Kesubos — Talmudic tractate that deals with the subject of marriage and marriage documents

Kesuvim — the books of the Holy Writings

Keviyus — permanence, constancy

Kevod Hashem — the Almighty's honor

Kevod Shamayim — the honor of Heaven

Kipshuto — according to its plain meaning

Kisvei hakodesh — holy books

Klal Yisrael — the Jewish people

Kloiz — synagogue

Koach, kochos — strength(s)

Kodesh Hakadashim — the Holy of Holies, the innermost sanctum in the Holy Temple in Jerusalem

Koheles — the Book of Ecclesiastes

Kollel, kollelim — institution(s) of advanced Torah study

Korbanos — offerings

Kovesh es yitzro — controls his urges

Kriyas Yam Suf — the Splitting of the Sea of Reeds, where Pharaoh's army was destroyed

Kuzari — Jewish philosophical work authored by Rabbi Yehudah Halevy in the 12th century

L'havdil — in contrast

L'hispallel — to pray

L'ma'aseh — practical

L'shem Shamayim — for the sake of Heaven

L'tovah — for good

Lamdan, lamdanim — learned individual(s)

Lavin — Torah prohibitions

Lechem Hapanim — the holy Showbread in the Holy Temple in Jerusalem

Leitzanus — mockery

Leitzim — mockers

Levi'im — Levites

Lifnim mishuras hadin — beyond the requirements of the law

Limudei chol — secular studies

Lishmah — for the sake of Heaven, without ulterior motives

Litvak — a Lithuanian Jew

Livrachah — for blessing

Lomdishe — in a learned style

M'akeiv — prevents the fulfillment

Ma'amar — statement

Ma'amin, ma'aminim — believer(s)

Ma'amar Chazal, ma'amarei Chazal — statement(s) of the Sages

Ma'asim tovim — good deeds

Maariv — evening prayers

Machlokess — dispute

Machmir — be stringent

Machshavah — thought

Madreigah, madreigos — level(s)

Mah Tovu — prophecy of the non-Jewish prophet Bilam in praise of the Jewish people

Makkos — lashes; the Plagues sent against Egypt as a precursor to the Exodus; Talmudic tractate that deals with punishment for certain sins

Makom Hamikdash—the location of the Holy Temple in Jerusalem

Makom Torah—a place of Torah study

Malach Hamavess—the Angel of Death

Malach, malachim—angel(s)

Malchei Beis David—the kings of the Davidic dynasty

Malkeinu—our King

Mamash—literally

Mamleches kohanim—kingdom of priests

Masechta—tractate

Mashal—parable; example

Masmidim—those who study Torah diligently

Matanah—gift

Matriach—bother

Matzliach—successful

Me'od—very

Me'aras Hamachpeilah—the cave in Hebron in which the Patriarchs and Matriarchs are buried

Mechalel Shabbos—to desecrate the Sabbath; one who desecrates the Sabbath

Mechaper—atones

Mechayeh—a delight

Mechayeih meisim—resurrects the dead

Mechilah—forgiveness

Mechuyav—obligated

Medrash—homiletic work(s) of Torah commentary

Mefarshim—Torah commentators

Meizid—one who acts with willful intent

Mekabeitz—gathers

Mekabel kinyan—acquire

Mekadesh—sanctifies

Mekarev—brings close (to Torah observance)

Mekayem—fulfill

Mekor—source

Melachah—work

Melaveh malkah—meal eaten on Saturday night to escort away the Sabbath Queen

Melech—king

Melech haMashiach—the king Messiah

Menachem avel—comforting a mourner

Menachos—Talmudic tractate that deals with the subject of flour offerings

Menahel—principal of a Torah school

Menahel ruchni—spiritual guide

Meshuga'im—crazy people

Meshugener—crazy person

Meshulach—charity collector

Mesillas Yesharim—classic work of self-improvement by Rabbi Moshe Chaim Luzzatto, 18th century

Mesiras nefesh—self-sacrifice

Mesivta—school for Torah study

Mesudar—organized

Metzuvah v'oseh—one who fulfills Torah commandments that he is obligated to fulfill

Metzuyan—an exceptional person

Mevareich—bless

Mezuzah, mezuzos—scroll(s) containing select Torah passages, affixed to the doorposts of Jewish homes

Michah—the Book of Michah

Midbar—the Wilderness

Middah, middos—character trait(s)

Middos ra'os—negative character traits

Middos tovos—positive character traits

Mikdash—the Holy Temple

Miktzas—partial

Min haShamayim—from Heaven

Minchah—afternoon prayers

Minhagei Torah—Torah customs

Minhagim—customs

Misgaber—overcome

Mishkan—the Tabernacle

Mishlei—the Book of Proverbs

Mishnah—the concise codification of the Oral Torah, assembled by Rabbi Yehudah Hanasi in the 3rd century

Mishnah Berurah—classic work of Torah law authored by Rabbi Yisrael Meir Kagan in the early 20th century

Mishnayos—individual sections of the Mishnah

Mishpechos ha'adamah—"the families of the Earth," the nations

Mitzrayim—Egypt

Mitzvah, mitzvos—Torah commandments

Mizmor—song of praise

Moav—ancient nation that neighbored the Land of Israel

Mocher sefarim—seller of Torah books

Modeh Ani—prayer recited upon arising from bed in the morning

Moser nefesh—demonstrate self-sacrifice

Moshe Rabbeinu—Moses, our teacher

Motza'ei Shabbos—Saturday night, after the Sabbath ends

Mussaf—additional prayer recited on the Sabbath and holidays

Mussar—character improvement

Na'aseh v'nishma—"We will do and we will listen"; declaration of the Jewish people in accepting the Torah

Nachash—snake

Nanu'im—waving motions performed with the Four Species on the holiday of Sukkos

Narishkeiten—foolish things

Navi, nevi'im—prophet(s)

Nebach—tragically

Nedarim—Talmudic tractate that deals with the subject of vows

Nedavos—voluntary offerings

Neder—vow

Neilah—final prayer on the day of Yom Kippur

Neis, nissim—miracle(s); banner

Neshamah, neshamos—soul(s)

Netilas yadayim—ritual hand-washing

Nevuah—prophecy

Nezirim—individuals who take a voluntary vow to abstain from wine

Nifla'os haBorei—wonders of the Creator

Nimshal—meaning of a parable

Nisayon—test

Nosherei—junk food

Nusach, nuscha'os—version(s) of the prayers

Ohr—light

Oisvorf—lowlife

Olam Haba—the World to Come

Olam Haneshamos—the world of souls

Olam Hazeh—the physical world in which we live

Ona'as devarim—saying hurtful words

Oneg—enjoyment

Orach Chaim—first section of Shulchan Aruch, dealing with the laws of daily living

Ovdei Hashem—servants of the Almighty

P'sak—decision in Torah law

P'shat—plain meaning

P'shuto shel Mikra—the plain meaning of the Scriptures

P'sukei D'zimrah—introductory section of praise recited during morning prayers

Parnassah—livelihood

Parshas—weekly Torah portion of

Parush—one who practices self-control with regard to physical enjoyment

Pashtus—simple meaning

Pashut—straightforward

Passuk, pesukim—verse(s)

Passul—invalid

Patur—exempt

Peiros—fruits, results

Peirush hamilos—meaning of the words

Peirush, peirushim—explanation(s)

Perek, perakim—chapter(s)

Perushim—those who practice self-control with regard to physical enjoyment

Pesachim—Talmudic tractate that deals with the laws of Passover and the Passover offering

Pesi—fool

Peyos—sidelocks

Pikuach nefesh—life-threatening danger

Pirkei Avos—Chapters of the Fathers, Talmudic tractate that focuses on moral teachings and ethical behavior

Plishtim—the Philistines, an ancient people that occupied part of the Mediterranean coast of Israel

Poreish—abstain

Poskim—Torah law decisors

Prishus—practicing abstention

Prozdor—corridor, hallway

Pushka—charity box

R'eih V'anyeinu—prayer in the Shemoneh Esrei for assistance with our daily struggles

R'tzeih—prayer in the Shemoneh Esrei for the return of the Divine presence to the Holy Temple in Jerusalem

Rabbanim—rabbis

Rabbanus—rabbinate

Rachamim—mercy

Rachmana litzlan—Heaven forbid

Ramban—Rabbi Moshe ben Nachman, great Torah leader in 13th century Spain

Rasha, resha'im—wicked individual(s)

Rashi—Rabbi Shlomo Yitzchaki, one of the greatest Torah commentators, 11th century France

Rav—rabbi

Rebbe—chassidic Torah leader

Rebbetzin—rabbi's wife

Rebbi, rebbeim—Torah teacher(s)

Refa'einu—prayer in the Shemoneh Esrei for health

Retzon Hashem—the Almighty's will

Ribbono Shel Olam—Master of the World

Rishonim—the leading Rabbis and Jewish legal decisors who lived approximately during the 11th to 15th centuries, in the era before the writing of the Shulchan Aruch

Rosh yeshiva, roshei yeshiva—head(s) of Torah school(s)

Ruach hakodesh—Divine inspiration

Ruach hanevuah—spirit of prophecy

Ruach Hashem—the spirit of the Almighty

Ruchniyus—spirituality

S'char—reward

S'lach Lanu—prayer in the Shemoneh Esrei for forgiveness

S'vara—logic

S'char limud—tuition

Safeik—doubt

Sakanah—danger

Sefer, sefarim—Torah book(s)

Seichel—mind

Selichah—forgiveness

Selichos—prayers for forgiveness

Semichah—rabbinic ordination

Sephard—pertaining to Jews of Spanish/Portugese descent, as well as from the Eastern Jewish communities of West Asia

Sha'ar—gate, chapter

Sha'arei Teshuvah—the Gates of Repentance, classic work of Torah thought authored by Rabbeinu Yonah of Gerona in the 13th century

Sha'ar Habechinah—chapter in the Chovos Halevavos that discusses how to develop gratitude toward the Creator through studying the wonders of Creation

Sha'ar Habitachon—chapter in the Chovos Halevavos that discusses how to develop trust in the Almighty

Shabbos Mevarchim—Sabbath before the start of a new month on the Jewish calendar

Shacharis—morning prayers

Shalom Bayis—marital harmony

Shamayim—Heaven

Shas—the Talmud

Shassen—sets of the Talmud

Shechitah—ritual animal slaughter

Shehakol—blessing recited for foods that are not covered by other, more specific blessings

Sheker—falsehood

Shelo lishmah—for ulterior motives

Shemirah—protection

Shemoneh Esrei—the central prayer of morning, afternoon and evening Jewish prayers

Shemos—the Book of Exodus

Sheva olamos—the seven worlds

Sheva rekiyim—the seven heavens

Shevet, shevatim—tribe(s)

Shidduch, shidduchim—marital match(es)

Shir Hashirim—the Song of Songs, one of the Scriptures

Shivtei Hashem—the tribes of the Almighty, the Jewish people

Shleimus—perfecting oneself

Shliach—agent

Shliach tzibbur—one who leads the public prayers

Shlichus—mission

Shlomo Hamelech—King Solomon

Shmad—religious persecution of Jews

Shmuess—informal Torah discussion

Shofet, shoftim—judge(s)

Shoftim—the Book of Judges

Shor—bull

Shoteh—fool

Shteibel—small, homey synagogue

Shteig—grow spiritually

Shtreimelech—round fur hats worn mainly by *chassidim*

Shuckeling—swaying in prayer

Shulchan Aruch—classic work of Torah law composed by Rabbi Yosef Karo in the 16th century

Sifrei—books of

Siman—sign; section

Simchah—happiness; happy occasion

Simchas Beis Hasho'eivah—celebration of the water drawing ceremony that took place in the Holy Temple in Jerusalem

Sisrei Torah—secrets of the Torah

Siyata d'Shmaya—Divine assistance

Skilah—capital punishment of stoning

Sodos—secrets

Sonei Hashem—enemies of the Almighty

Sotah—Talmudic tractate that deals with the laws of a wife suspected of infidelity

Sugya—topic

Sukkos—holiday that commemorates how the Almighty sheltered the Jewish people in the Wilderness for forty years

Ta'anis—fast day; Talmudic tractate that deals with the subject of fast days

Ta'anis dibbur—voluntary abstention from speaking

Ta'anug, ta'anugim—physical pleasure(s)

Taharas hamishpachah—laws of family purity

Tainah, tainos—complaint(s), argument(s)

Taivos—physical desires

Takanah—enactment

Talmid Chacham, talmidei chachamim—Torah scholar(s)

Talmid, talmidim—student(s)

Tamid—constantly

Tannaim—Sages whose views are quoted in the Mishnah

Targum Onkelos—Aramaic translation of the Torah attributed to the righteous convert Onkelos

Techiyas Hameisim—Resurrection of the Dead

Tefillah b'tzibbur—public prayer

Tefillah, tefillos—prayer(s)

Tefillas Haderech—prayer for safe travel

Tehillim—Psalms

Teka B'shofar—prayer in the Shemoneh Esrei for the ingathering of all the Jewish exiles to the land of Israel

Terutz, terutzim—answer(s)

Teshuvah—repentance

Teva—nature

Tikkun Chatzos—prayer recited in the middle of the night, mourning for the loss of the Holy Temple in Jerusalem

Tikkun hamiddos—fixing one's character traits

Tisha B'Av—fast day of the Ninth of Av, anniversary of the destruction of the two Temples in Jerusalem

To'eivah—abomination

Torah sheb'al peh—the oral Torah

Torah shebiksav—the written Torah

Toraso umnaso—one whose entire life is dedicated to Torah study

Tosfos—Talmudic commentators of 12th century France and Germany

Treifah—non-kosher

Tza'ar—pain

Tzaddeikess—righteous woman

Tzaddik hador—one of the most righteous people of a generation

Tzarah, tzaros—trouble(s)

Tzarchei tzibbur—public needs

Tzedek—righteousness

Tzelem Elokim—made in the image of the Almighty

Tzibbur—the public

Tzidkaniyos—righteous women

Tzidkus—righteousness

Tzion—Zion, usually referring to Jerusalem

Tzipisa liyeshuah—Did you anticipate the arrival of the Messiah?

Tzipiyah liyeshuah—anticipating the arrival of the Messiah

Tzitzis—fringes worn by Jewish males on the four corners of a garment in fulfillment of a Torah commandment

Tziyurim—images

Tzniyus—modesty

Umos ha'olam—the nations of the world

Urim V'tumim—holy scroll in the breastplate of the Kohen Gadol (High Priest) that prophetically communicated the Almighty's will

Uva L'Tzion—prayer recited toward the end of the morning prayers

V'lamalshinim—prayer in the Shemoneh Esrei for the downfall of heretics and slanderers

Vasikin—morning prayers recited precisely at sunrise

Viduy—prayer of confession for sins

Y'hei sh'meih rabbah m'vorach—May [the Almighty's] great name be blessed

Ya'aleh V'yavo—prayer inserted in the Shemoneh Esrei and Grace After Meals on holidays

Yachad—together, united

Yechezkel—the Book of Ezekiel

Yediah chushis—tangible knowledge

Yegiah—effort

Yehudim—Jews

Yemos HaMashiach—the Messianic era

Yerushalayim—Jerusalem

Yerushalmi—the Jerusalem Talmud

Yeshayah—the Book of Isaiah

Yeshivishe—characteristic of strictly Orthodox, non-*chassidic* Jews

Yeshuah—salvation

Yesod—fundamental principle

Yesod hayesodos—most fundamental of principles

Yetzias Mitzrayim—the Exodus from Egypt

Yidden—Jews

Yirah—fear, awe, awareness

Yiras Hakavod—awe of the Almighty's glory

Yiras Hashem—fear, awe, or awareness of the Almighty

Yiras Shamayim—fear, awe, or awareness of Heaven (the Almighty)

Yirmiyah—the Book of Jeremiah

Yissurim—suffering

Yo'atzim—advisors

Yom Hadin—the Day of Judgment

Yom Kippur—the Day of Atonement, the 10th of Tishrei

Yoma—Talmudic tractate that deals with the laws of Yom Kippur

Yotzei—to fulfill

Yotzer Hame'oros—Creator of the heavenly luminaries

Zecher—a remembrance

Zecher tzaddik livrachah—may the memory of the righteous be for a blessing

Zechus, zechuyos—merit(s)

Zeidim—willful transgressors

Zeidy—grandfather

Zekeinim—elders

Zerizus—alacrity

Zichrono livrachah—may his memory be for a blessing

Ziknei hador—elders of the generation

Zivug, zivugim—marital match(es)

Zocheh—to merit

Zt"l—acronym for "*zecher tzaddik livrachah*, may the memory of the righteous be for a blessing"

Zuz — a currency denomination

“The SimchaPod will change your life!”

Treat yourself **today** to a radiant new life of *emunah*, *bitachon* and *deveikus* in *Hashem*. It's a new *Shabbas!* A new *shemoneh esrei!* A glowing new *simchas hachaim!*

- Loaded with 2,000 *shiurim!*
- The entire Thursday night lecture series... at your fingertips!
- Six *mussar sfarim, Rambam, Pirkei Avos* and more
- More than **forty** Rabbi Miller e-books – read right on the screen!

Join the more than **1,300 SimchaPod owners** who made the investment of a lifetime – the complete **Rabbi Avigdor Miller** MP3 library.

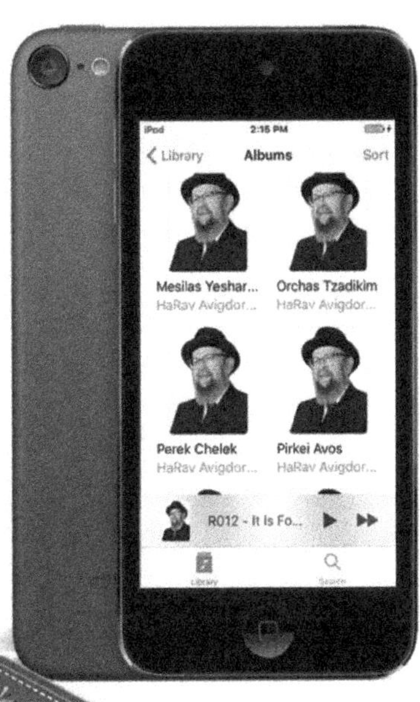

“The Simchapod doesn't just affect the person who's listening, it affects the whole *mishpacha*”

“Tell everybody it's the best investment in the world. It's better than a car, better than a house. It's cheap *olam haba*.”

“I drive a lot and I listen to a lot of *shiurim*. It has literally changed my life.”

180 DAY GUARANTEE
Love it or we buy it back!

NO
Internet
Radio
Video

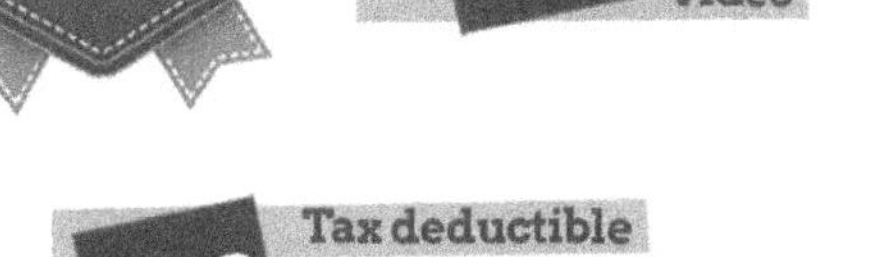

YES
Tax deductible
Pay from maaser*
Low monthly payments

*Ask your rav about using maaser funds for this purpose

CALL NOW: 845.275.3725

845.328.0250

Own the SimchaPod?
Get **the biggest file update** in 10 years!
shpub.me/update or
simchapod@simchapub.com

MP3 Singles
as low as $2 –
shpub.me/judpress